A SHORT HISTORY
OF COMMUNISM

A SHORT HISTORY
OF COMMUNISM

ROBERT HARVEY

THOMAS DUNNE BOOKS ☙ ST. MARTIN'S PRESS NEW YORK

THOMAS DUNNE BOOKS.
An imprint of St. Martin's Press.

www.stmartins.com

ISBN 0-312-32909-1
EAN 978-0312-32909-9

First published in Great Britain by John Murray (Publishers),
a division of Hodder Headline

First U.S. Edition: November 2004

10 9 8 7 6 5 4 3 2 1

For my father

Contents

Part III: The Collapse

Note: With a few exceptions, Chinese names are given in Pinyin throughout. In certain cases, they are followed on their first appearance by the traditional form in brackets for those who may be unfamiliar with the Pinyin rendition.

Illustrations

The author and publishers would like to thank the following for permission to reproduce illustrations: Plates 1, 3, 5, 6, 7, 9, 11, 12, 14, 18, 21 and 32, AKG London; 2, 4, 10 and 35, Novosti (London); 8, 17, 19, 25, 27, 28, 33, and 34, Popperfoto; 13, 15, 16, 20, 23, 26 and 29, Hulton Archive.

Foreword

There have been three great proselytizing religious surges across the world. The first was Christianity, which after initial repression was adopted as the state religion of the Roman Empire and whose human-ist message of virtue in this world leading to redemption in the next had an appeal for millions; the second was Islam, which expanded to subdue the Middle East and two thirds of the Mediterranean littoral, propound-ing a message of respect for the laws in this world leading to paradise in the next. Finally there is Buddhism, which coexisted alongside the Confucian ethic and the power of China, and which was also essentially paternalist.

More than 1,000 years later another religion, born in the nineteenth century, came to dominate some 3.5 billion people, or a little over half the world's population in the third quarter of the twentieth century. At its peak, people were left cowed by the scale of this explosion into believ-ing that it might soon dominate the entire globe. But just as they feared the worst, it collapsed inwards, leaving very little behind. It was the most spectacular rise and fall in global history.

To other faiths, as to communists, calling Marxism-Leninism a reli-gion may seem offensive. Religion, Marx said scornfully, was 'the opium of the people'. Of course it was not in that it opposed religion and the concept of an afterlife. But in every other respect it resembled one. It elevated its greatest figures – Marx, Lenin and Mao – to godlike status, while its lesser personalities – men like Engels, Stalin, Tito, Ho Chi Minh, Fidel Castro – had the status of prophets.

The teachings of Marx, which comprise a vast and impenetrable oeuvre which few read in any depth and even fewer in its entirety, like scripture induced reverence rather than critical appreciation. Lenin and Mao were similarly worshipped (another analogy was that Marx was

Old Testament and Lenin, New Testament). Beneath them a huge hier-archical priesthood of Communism was established to propagate the message and convert the people. The scriptures, although difficult to follow and capable of different interpretations, were sacrosanct; pro-nouncements on any issue had to be made within the proper liturgical framework.

Rituals were created: the huge Central Committee meetings where delegates were required to listen to long speeches, applaud and stand and sit in unison, as at a church service; the Marx and Lenin statues, busts, friezes and murals all borrowed from religious iconography; and even the dingy local Party committee rooms where meetings were held which resembled churches and chapels. As in any church, unqualified obedi-ence and belief were required although terrible schisms ripped the move-ment asunder, usually concerning arcane forms of ideology which appeared to lack importance. Trotsky split from Stalin, Mao from the Soviet model, Pol Pot from the Chinese model, and Guevarism from Castroism in a bewitching display of internecine quarrelling that some-times left hundreds of thousands dead and outside observers scratching their heads.

But the religion's effectiveness, its ability to organize and, at least at the beginning, its huge mass appeal could not be denied. Then, when it was perhaps at the height of its power, it suddenly vaporized, leaving a clutch of supporters and little comprehension as to what it had really been about. This book chronicles that extraordinary phenomenon, the rise and fall of the Church of Man.

Why another book about Communism? When the Berlin Wall fell, it was discovered that there are 14 miles of shelves containing personal files in the archives of the Stasi, the East German secret police. If the litera-ture on Communism was stretched end to end, it would surely exceed this. Why add to it, and by a non-specialist at that?

It seemed to me that specialization was precisely the problem. The great majority of books on the subject are densely written works of analy-sis, many scholarly and discursive, many polemical and most impene-trable to the general reader. There are a minority of superb general books about the communist experience, such as Robert Conquest's *The Great Terror* (which itself became part of the history) and which extend more recently, for example, to Hedrick Smith's *The Russians* or Fox Butterfield's *China: Alive in the Bitter Sea*. Today books such as *The*

Tiananmen Papers and *The Road to Terror* are groundbreakers (although essentially compilations).

But there are no general global narrative studies. Communism was a shattering global human experience, affecting by far the largest number of lives in the last century, opening with a big bang with the first communist seizure of power in Russia in 1917 and imploding almost as abruptly with the 'year of revolutions' in 1989, although pockets linger to this day. No book that I know of tries to make sense of it all by bringing together this epic and defining chapter in human history. I know the pitfalls: in spanning more than seven decades of human global history, I will be guilty of many oversimplifications, errors of judgement and straightforward mistakes.

Nevertheless, I believe the effort to draw up a global balance sheet of world communism has been one worth making; although there were huge differences between national experiences, there were huge similarities and cross currents from which a single narrative can be woven. In the process I have arrived at some general conclusions of my own, which I hope are new. It is for the reader to judge whether I have succeeded. Certainly the attempt to bring together the global experience for a new generation, which can have only a distant idea of how the whole extraordinary phenomenon dominated the political perceptions of my own and previous generations both in the East and the West, seems to me to be justified.

Lastly, I hope to bring to the subject, in addition to such skills as a professional historian as I possess, my own direct experience as a journalist. This has included three revolutions (Portugal's in 1974, Nicaragua's in 1979 and Afghanistan's in 1980), the Eurocommunist phenomenon and being a fly-on-the-wall parliamentary witness of Gorbachev's revolution in the Soviet Union and the reunification of Germany.

I am particularly grateful to the following from whose works I have quoted, or upon whose painstaking research on particular periods I have been able to draw in different sections of the book. I recommend all of these as essential further reading to anyone interested in the subject: J. Arch Getty and Oleg V. Naumov, *The Road to Terror*; Neal Ascherson, *The Polish August*; Robert Conquest, *The Great Terror* and *Reflections on a Ravaged Century*; Norman Cohn, *Warrant for Genocide* and *The Pursuit of the Millennium*; Robert Payne, *Marx*; Francis Wheen, *Karl Marx*; Li Xiaojun, *The Long March to the Fourth of June*; Alexei Myagkov,

Inside the KGB; Edwina Moreton's reports in *The Economist*; Fox Butterfield, *China: Alive in the Bitter Sea*; Gale Stokes, *The Walls Came Tumbling Down*; Gerald Seagal's writings on China; Hedrick Smith, *The Russians*.

Among those who have helped me on this vast, four-year project, I cannot do justice to them all, and it would be invidious to single out a few. But I would like to mention my efficient, patient and painstaking assistant Jenny Thomas and her historian husband Geoffrey, my dedicated editors at John Murray, Grant McIntyre, Andrew Maxwell-Hyslop, Gail Pirkis and Caroline Westmore, the always wise council of my agent Gillon Aitken, Christine, Richard and Emma and Mandy and Brian, the encouragement of my mother and my sister and her family, and the love and support of Jane and Oliver.

Maps

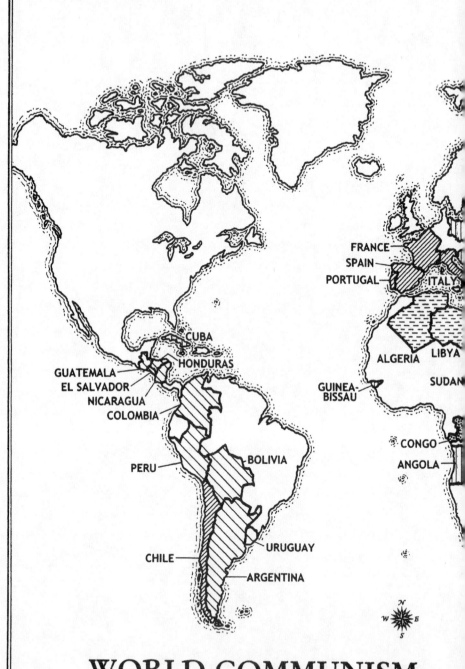

WORLD COMMUNISM
c. 1980

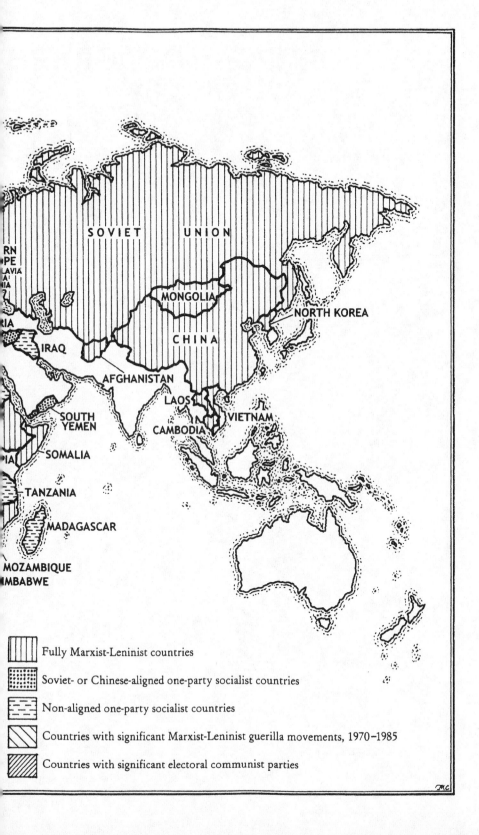

SOVIET   UNION

RN
•PE
LAVIA
IIA
?

MONGOLIA

NORTH KOREA

CHINA

IA

IRAQ

AFGHANISTAN

LAOS

SOUTH
YEMEN

CAMBODIA

VIETNAM

IA

SOMALIA

TANZANIA

MADAGASCAR

MOZAMBIQUE
MBABWE

	Fully Marxist-Leninist countries
	Soviet- or Chinese-aligned one-party socialist countries
	Non-aligned one-party socialist countries
	Countries with significant Marxist-Leninist guerilla movements, 1970–1985
	Countries with significant electoral communist parties

JMC

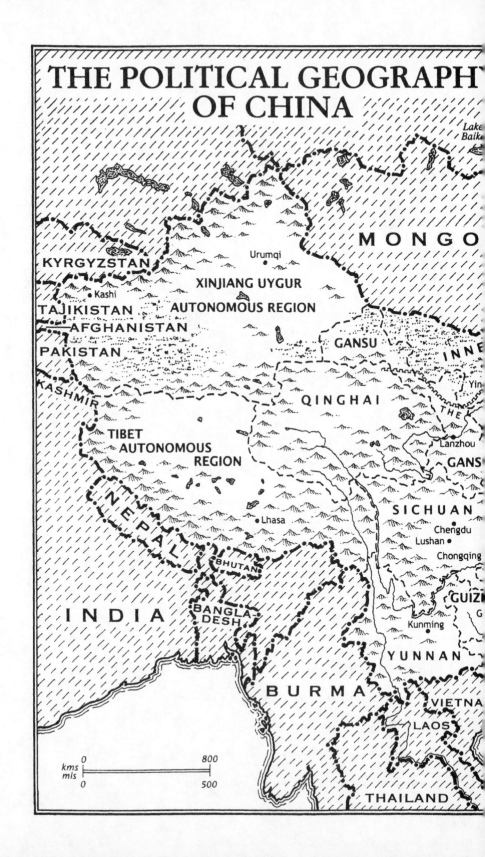

THE POLITICAL GEOGRAPHY OF CHINA

Lake Baikal

KYRGYZSTAN

Urumqi

XINJIANG UYGUR

• Kashi

AUTONOMOUS REGION

TAJIKISTAN

MONGO

AFGHANISTAN

GANSU

PAKISTAN

INNE

Yin

KASHMIR

QINGHAI

THE

TIBET

Lanzhou

AUTONOMOUS

GANS

REGION

NEPAL

SICHUAN

Chengdu

Lushan •

Chongqing

Lhasa

BHUTAN

INDIA

BANGLA-
DESH

GUIZ

G

Kunming

YUNNAN

BURMA

VIETNA

LAOS

kms 0   800
mls ├─────────────┤
     0   500

THAILAND

There are many people in the world who really don't understand, or say they don't, what is the great issue between the free world and the communist world. Let them come to Berlin. There are some who say that Communism is the wave of the future. Let them come to Berlin. And there are some who say in Europe and elsewhere we can work with the communists. Let them come to Berlin. And there are even a few who say that it is true that Communism is an evil system but it permits us to make economic progress. *Lasst sie nach Berlin kommen.* Let them come to Berlin . . . Freedom is indivisible, and when one man is enslaved, all are not free. When all are free, and we look forward to that day when this city will be joined as one, and this country and this great continent of Europe in a peaceful and hopeful globe, when that day finally comes, as it will, the people of West Berlin can take sober satisfaction in the fact that they were in the front lines for almost two decades. All free men, wherever they may live, are citizens of Berlin, and therefore as a free man, I take pride in the words *Ich bin ein Berliner.*

John F. Kennedy, West Berlin 26 June 1963

Introduction

Westminster Hall is the oldest part of Britain's House of Commons, a great open space the size of a football pitch with a magnificent vaulted wooden roof erected by Richard II, where Charles I was condemned to death, Warren Hastings acquitted for excesses in India, the Queen Mother and Winston Churchill lay in state and Nelson Mandela addressed a joint session of both Houses of Parliament.

One winter's day early in 1985, the few parliamentarians scurrying across the giant flagstones would barely have noticed the group of heavily built, thickset men in greatcoats who entered under the great east window and climbed the stone steps to the Jubilee Room, a spacious meeting area, where they sat down opposite their British counterparts at a long table. Some of the men set aside the distinctive flat caps with red trimmings of senior generals in the Russian army; others were top Russian politicians and bureaucrats.

At the centre sat a stocky figure with a bald head disfigured by a red birthmark that was to become one of the most celebrated images of the late twentieth century; at this time he was virtually unknown. His wife, alertly intelligent, slim, good-looking, sat behind him. As I noted: 'She is brown-haired, very elegantly dressed in a chic roll-neck pullover, very composed.' The man himself had a ready smile, a lively and outgoing expression and eyes that lit up with animation as he talked with complete self-confidence, dominating the entire delegation of some of the most powerful men from the world's second superpower.

Although he was no more than the Chairman of the Soviet Parliament's Foreign Affairs Committee – his British counterpart on the opposite side was the amiable but shrewd former Foreign Office Minister, Sir Anthony Kershaw – it seemed clear that this particular Russian was destined for the very highest offices in his country. In fact, within a matter of months, he would be General Secretary of the Soviet Communist Party, the second most powerful man in the world. His name was Mikhail Gorbachev.

What he said on this occasion was unremarkable – a competent but unsatisfying defence of traditional Soviet positions: but the style was worlds apart from the medieval barbarity of Lenin or Stalin, the crude tub-thumping of Khrushchev, or the dreary stonewalling of Brezhnev, Andropov or Chernenko, his immediate predecessors. Having devoted years to writing about the brutalizing and stultifying impact of global Communism, I was agog. It seemed that a light of reason and humanity was burning at the very heart of the 'evil empire' where you would least expect to find it, the window behind the fortified ramparts of the Kremlin that marked the General Secretary's office. It was as though the only good person to be found in hell was the devil himself.

Just a year earlier, I had experienced the vertiginous sense of inferiority of an ordinary visitor to a capital deliberately built to inspire terror into the hearts of the people of the vast continent it dominated. No capital since Ancient Rome was more calculated to project pure power than the square mile of buildings surrounding the Kremlin and Red Square in Moscow.

There are two main ways of approaching it: across the bridge that spans the Moskva River in the south; and from the north, behind the History Museum. The ensemble looks more graceful from the south: the 16-foot-thick fortress walls, designed by Italians, leaven the ever-grey Moscow skyline and allow a tiny glimpse of the stately green palace which houses the Central Committee building of the Communist Party underneath its graceful golden domes. On the east side, the line of the walls gives way to a vast roadway, nearly always empty because so few Russians owned cars, which provides a theatrical setting for the breathtaking absurdity of St Basil's Cathedral, a collapsed Tower of Babel eastern style, where every fantastically coloured tower is crowned by different decorations and styles of dome.

This colourful splash of a building tells the onlooker that the Russians are not a people the West can ever hope to understand. It radiates the splendour and mysticism of an eastern church emulated by its pagan successors because they cannot surpass it. Once past the cathedral, past the spot where Peter the Great himself executed several of his noblemen, the power of the square hits the onlooker like a physical force.

Alternatively Red Square can be approached from the non-mystical side, from Fiftieth Anniversary of the October Revolution Square, where every building seems designed to wring the personality out of man, to say to the individual that he is part of a vast movement of history, an insignificant speck in an eternally toiling mass. The square is vast. The buildings along Marx Prospekt fronting one side of the Kremlin are sullen monuments to pure utility, great slabs, tens of storeys high and, unlike the taller buildings in New York, tens of storeys wide: every man, they suggest, has his own niche in life represented by his office window, exactly the same as any other.

The huddled people, Lowry-like specks scampering across the slurried snow below because of the usually icy wind, are dwarfed by the enormity of the buildings. Most intimidating is the History Museum, which backs onto Revolution Square and fronts onto Red Square, a massive, red-bricked, neo-Gothic monstrosity. Set against more modest, friendlier architecture, this might be merely a picturesque folly; set against the impersonality of the square, it seems to spell the end of hope: severe, cavernous, devoid of human proportion. Up the wide roadway past the building Red Square spreads out, only the blessed, unregulated, multicoloured chaos of St Basil's softening the impact.

The square's power lies in its size and its stark simplicity. St Basil's to the south and the giant History Museum to the north are the two smaller ends of a rectangle: to the east lies the mercifully ornate nineteenth-century Gum department store, to the west the Kremlin wall, its eighteenth-century palaces peering over the top, with red stars placed rather absurdly on the turrets and, in the middle, a large Red Flag fluttering against the dreary sky.

Below the wall squats a monument of spartan simplicity and chilling futurism: Lenin's tomb, black and grey, its steel doors almost always clamped shut, a crowd stamping with cold gazing at the two rigid, frozen soldiers by the entrance. The marble and concrete slab in the white snow, the scurrying black figures, the solid red walls of the Kremlin above and the gaudy red banner create an almost mystical impression: the tomb looks like an altar, the body within it a deity, and the practice of keeping it away from the public gaze for most of the time fully in keeping with the practices of the Russian Orthodox Church.

So too is the secrecy and ritual by which the Soviet Union wields its authority. The Kremlin is not the mysterious, impenetrable citadel the outside world assumes it to be: every day thousands of tourists flock to its magnificent churches, in particular the icon-frescoed Church of the Annunciation, where Ivan the Terrible lies buried. Parties from every corner of the Soviet Union visit the Kremlin, the children to receive Christmas handouts of red boxes full of sweets from red-armbanded Party officials. The grounds are open, spacious, stately, enclosing a park overlooked by the walls.

But across the square from the cluster of historic buildings to which tourists are admitted lies the Central Committee building, where Lenin had an office and visitors are more rarely allowed. Stocky police in grey greatcoats with megaphones and flashing black-and-white batons keep the visitors moving along; no one is allowed to step off the pavement, although occasional black or white limousines slide out of the distant fleet parked across the emptiness of the square. The leaders are remote, all-powerful, spared traffic. This seems to impress, not anger, ordinary people.

Absolute authority appears to impress absolutely, and its cold invisible hand has the city in its thrall. This is not immediately apparent to Westerners, who are pleasantly surprised to see that ordinary Russians look, laugh, and pet their children much as they do. Muscovites, true, are withdrawn and private, their faces locked into inexpression; more so than the inhabitants of most Western capitals. But as people in a group, or with the family on an outing, skating on an ice-rink or slithering down a natural ice-slide, they are relaxed and unaffected, with none of the over-the-shoulder apprehension most Westerners expect. Yet the constant presence of the men in uniform, with their smart thick greatcoats – brown for soldiers in Moscow, black in Leningrad, and grey for the police in both places – reinforces the impression of a country somehow locked into the stiff-necked nationalist authoritarianism of pre-war society.

Authority, reinforcing a power that at its peak is mystical, has much in common with the Russian Orthodox Church, whose services, impressively thronged in many places, shows the awe in which power is held and might appear to be living proof that Communism has failed to root out the traditional values of Soviet society. But witnessing the astonishing hauteur of the service – the wizened, elderly women mouthing chants as they press themselves against stand-up pews mounted along the walls in response to a bearded monk in flowing black cape while the faithful queue to kiss the tomb of a saint or to place legions of tottery, dripping candles – reveals the size of the debt the Communist Party owes to the mysticism, authority and fatalism of the Orthodox Church.

These characteristics are, moreover, inner-Russian ones. It has become an historical cliché to see Russia as torn apart by the conflicting pulls of east and west: yet it is easy to see why the early revolutionaries decided to move the capital of Russia back from western-looking Leningrad to eastern-looking Moscow.

Leningrad, with its astonishing embankment down the frozen River Neva hosting a succession of lavish eighteenth-century palaces and a canal system constructed so purely for ornamental purposes that the bridges are too low for boats to pass beneath; Leningrad, with its sumptuously extravagant Winter Palace, its sumptuously hideous Kazan Cathedral and the foppishly aristocratic barracks of the Paulosky regiment, whose façade, overlooking the Camp of Mars, where the Tsar once reviewed his troops, is a quarter of a mile long. This Mediterranean city in the north, established by Peter the Great who sought to recreate the splendours of a western European capital, only bigger and better, is entirely founded on human caprice, all too human in its visual massage of the senses. It could not possibly be the capital of an austere, mystical, levelling state. Moscow, with its roots in the past, its geographical closeness to the heartland of Russia and its bloody history, is the ideal capital of the new and terrifyingly frugal Soviet Union.

The Kremlin, with its aura of power, is only the hub of a country built to enhance the authority of the Soviet state. Beyond the Kremlin, but still in the centre of the city, soar Stalinist-gothic buildings, like the University of Moscow containing some 30,000 rooms. The grotesque lack of human proportion extends not just upwards but outwards, so that these buildings enclose four sides of a square with identically window-peppered granite. The main shopping street, Gorky Prospekt, is a series of skyscrapers bestriding inhuman department stores along Moscow's most-used road, a four-lane avenue that, by Western standards, is traffic-free.

Beyond the centre lie the apartment blocks that comprise the residential accommodation of the city's 9 million people. Striking for their unyielding rejection of design, they are rectangular, usually about fifteen storeys up and twenty to thirty sets of windows lengthways, with three bare staircases as their pivots. In the residential quarters, no shops or green spaces disturb the monotony. The scale seems unending: in the middle of one such estate, the eye might see nothing but such grey apartment block buildings, stretching into the distance against the grey sky and even greyer snow. The government boasts that every Moscow family has its own apartment. Maybe, but some still consist of no more than a couple of rooms.

This residential uniformity gives the impression of a conveyor-belt society in which people are truly equal, plodding through a universal daily ritual of work and rest. This is enhanced by the astonishing Moscow metro, whose initial wonders are the glittering, chandeliered, cavernous stations straight out of an Eisenstein film set, but whose real claim to glory lies in their efficiency. Because so few Muscovites have cars and the bus system is so irregular, the system funnels millions to work: except at night, the trains are standing-room only.

It is awesome to witness thousands of inanimate, wooden-faced Muscovites clad in furs being whisked – the escalators move at twice the speed of Western ones – to the sullen clanking of machinery, past slab lighting, sometimes 300 to 400 feet under ground. The paying machinery is brutally simple: a 5 kopek piece (about 6 cents) releases the entry barrier. That is that: no tickets, no collectors, no delays. A digital clock times the length between trains – rarely more than two minutes.

Reinforcing the sense of clockwork soullessness is the absence of colour in the barren streets, the walls without advertising except for political posters, whose lack of innovative design or content turns no Russian heads. Shop-window displays are poor and scarce; only a wisp of Christmas bunting provides a little glitter. Most shops, from the outside, do not look like shops at all, and at ground floor level curtains are drawn in office windows.

However, the shops are where the clockwork can be seen to break down: the Gum store, just opposite the Kremlin, is a concourse of commerce, a complex maelstrom of arcades and catwalks usually thronged with people in pursuit of scarce goods. The meat counter, graced by a few remaining lumps of streaked fat, is a favourite objective, with queues stretching around the interior of the shop. The shortages, in a country so endowed with natural resources, and with an enviable population-to-territory ratio, are the most immediate indicators of what is wrong beneath the surface.

The summer of the year I met Mikhail Gorbachev I went to Russia, this time on the inside of the system as his guest, as a member of the House of Commons Foreign Affairs Committee. It was Alice through the Looking Glass. We were now waved past the forbidding passport men into Chekas and Ladas, black limousines that sped their way through the traffic, lights blazing, horns sounding, crossing red lights where they were not changed in advance, racing down the middle of a busy two-lane highway with motorcycles and police cars in relays forcing heavy goods vehicles to mount the kerb, and once in Moscow scattering cars and civilians alike, in much the same way as Cossacks on horseback accompanying important officials must have done a hundred years before.

We were housed in the faded Edwardian grandeur of the National Hotel, with its sprinkler- and microphone-infested rooms and entertained in the glittering elegance of the Bolshoi, seeing a dreary class-war ballet to music by Rachmaninov. The following day we were driven to the elegant Italianate Central Committee building in the Kremlin, where policemen with loudspeakers and flashing batons shooed the crowds away. In successive meetings across Moscow we glimpsed a cross-section of the mighty in the land – the parchment-faced minister of education who told us that education is 'absolutely centralized' and excused himself for addressing us standing up, as he was so tired that if he sat down he would go to sleep; the smooth and brilliant Academician Marcic, head of the Soviet Commission of Science and Technology, with his quasi-religious faith in new technology and nuclear power; and the Robespierre-like public prosecutor with his glamorous, svelte assistant, who boasted that the Russian legal system was 'all-embracing, rigid and centralized' and told us that 'a drive is under way to intensify discipline in all aspects of national life'. We were also told that 'we do not have organized crime, as in Western countries. We are free of violent crime and professional crime.'

Everywhere there was a bust or relief or frieze of Lenin, sometimes small, sometimes huge. When we visited the little waxen corpse behind the glass window in the Lenin mausoleum, we were angrily hushed, as though in the presence of the Almighty. At the Ministry for Religious Affairs the minister assured us that there was no religious persecution in Russia. If a religious leader said something that displeases the authorities, 'we just go along to him and say this is against the law. That usually has the desired effect. If he goes on, we resort to more extreme measures.' We were informed that 'atheism is the scientific view of life. It is inherent in all our teachings. Religion is not a scientific view of life.' Science, thus, was the new religion.

We were told that the press was free and that BBC World Service broadcasts into the USSR were not jammed (our radios showed the opposite). Returning to talks in the chandeliered halls of the Kremlin we were hectored and shouted at by the Soviet propaganda chief, Leonid Zamyatin (shouting being a normal form of Soviet political exchange) while an 82-year-old Politburo member, Boris Ponomarev, an original Bolshevik with a wispy moustache, quick, beady eyes and a soft voice, denounced the Americans for seeking to achieve military superiority. Zamyatin yelled that US-Soviet relations are 'at their lowest possible level for thirty years! Every relation that could have been broken between the two countries has been broken! Sharp words precede sharp conflicts.' This all seemed thoroughly unpromising.

Only as the visit progressed did the tone soften, and one began to sense a sharp undercurrent of change, tied principally to economics. As Gorbachev told us, 'the Soviet Union needs peace to implement its huge development programmes . . . we want to have prosperity through efficiency and growth and this depends on a foreign policy which permits this'. When I asked about economic reform, he said emphatically that it must go ahead. 'We must decentralize and introduce incentives and new technology, just like in your ICI – all within a Marxist-Leninist frame-work, of course,' he added, almost as an afterthought.

When I put the same question of Ponomarev at a reception, he tapped his glass. 'If you give a worker only one glass in reward, he will not work; if you give him a hundred, he will. Of course there must be a change.' Although perhaps a not entirely appropriate analogy for a government trying to crack down sharply on alcoholism, his drift was clear.

The message was reinforced by one of Russia's chief economists: 'Our economy does not reject the limited use of forces of the market through price flexibility and incentives on collective farms. There are quite active market forces at the level of the individual enterprise. Everyone decides to buy according to price and quality. It is wrong to say that socialism does not believe in the market economy and that capitalism does.' Lenin should have been revolving in his glass case. It was clear that a radical rethink was under way.

Within months the concept of *perestroika* (restructuring) was to be unleashed and the whole elaborate myth of Soviet economic might began to crumble. To view the frozen Soviet system begin to thaw, to witness the beginning of a great process, the collapse of the creed which had held more than half of humanity in its grip at its height was a unique, life-defining experience.

The change in attitude was so perceptible, although not yet translated into fact, that we wondered if we had not been the victims of some elab-

orate KGB plot. Back in London I remember being greeted by wary
scepticism from my journalist colleagues, as yet another gullible dupe of
the men in trench coats. Only the *Sunday Times* under the foreign edit-
orship of Stephen Milligan had the courage to publish an article predict-
ing the transformation (reproduced as an appendix), which in retrospect
did not go nearly far enough. It makes for tame reading in the light of
subsequent events, but at this time it was regarded as virtual Soviet propaganda. Equal derision was heaped upon an unpublished essay of mine
that argued:

> Not only has Marxism-Leninism failed to take root in the great majority
> of Third World countries: in most, it is on the retreat as it loses not just
> the battle of ideas, but is being relentlessly driven back by the stubborn
> realities of a world Marx never foresaw. The reality that the better devel-
> oped Third World countries become, the more they need trade and
> credits from the West, rather than the East. The reality that the old
> working classes of the developed countries have been converted by the
> welfare state, higher living standards, and consumer goods into a propri-
> etorial class. The reality that the middle class has grown into a larger and
> larger proportion of the population, reducing the old working class into
> a diminishing rump. The reality that the communist countries themselves
> are changing: as they grow more prosperous, consumer goods appeal to
> the better-off workers and intelligentsia, while Western forms of social
> and economic organization seem more likely to provide the goods.
> Only the welfare element of Communism – education, housing, social
> services – continues to provide the creed with much popular appeal . . .
>
> Even if Marxism-Leninism is on an ebb tide of history, it will still
> collect one or two Third World recruits, just as fundamentalist sects are
> still making converts among the most primitive peoples there. The coun-
> tries most at risk are the ones ruled by feudal relics which have not opened
> up to popular participation . . . Yet most of the Third World has slipped
> past the Marxist-Leninist phase: the military-dominated, fast-growing
> countries of South-East Asia and South America face challenges from
> liberal, even if sometimes irresponsible, democratic urban elites, not
> Marxist-Leninists. Existing one-party systems in the Third World face
> challenges from those who want greater economic freedom, not from
> those who want to rigidify them . . .

I also argued:

> The Russian and Chinese models are taking different roads . . . What
> seems inconceivable [in China] is an overthrow of the system . . . The
> system looks likely to endure, and one day settle into the mould of other

developing countries: a central state which channels funds for development, but which allows a considerable degree of competition. If that
happens, a middle class not dependent on the state is likely to grow up in
a period of, say, twenty years which will eventually demand political rep-
resentation.

Returning to Russia, I concluded:

Reform will have to come, because an economy that continues to wind
gradually down will generate tension. The Soviet system at present is
sharing out a very slowly shrinking share of the national cake a little more
equally. Investment and spending on heavy industry has continued to be
trimmed to meet rising consumer expectations . . . The pressure will
require either the opening of political safety valves or, more likely, greater
repression. By and large the Party, under first Brezhnev and now
Chernenko, holds out the best hope of even modest liberalization. The
reason is that, with the ideologues within it defeated – with the ideology,
indeed, the target of derision – its leaders require something to prop up
the Party's waning authority . . .

No, the Russian system is not about to blow; but in twenty years time
there may be the irresistible pressure of a middle class asserting itself in a
freer economic climate, demanding political rights, and that could push
the Soviet Union at last to Western-style pluralism. Marxism-Leninism
would then be dead; the biggest developing country would be joining the
ranks of the developed.

I was completely wrong about one thing: all this happened much sooner
than I had forecast.

What was Communism, an ideological tidal wave that affected virtually
the entire globe, that left maybe 100 million dead in its wake, as well as
probably twice that number homeless and suffering, and more than 30
million as slave labour of one kind or another, and shaped the lives of
billions? It was certainly the greatest destructive ideology in human
history.

   In one sense the answer is clear: it was the forced imposition of the
levelling, centralizing and hierarchical system of Marxism as interpreted
by Lenin upon subject peoples. But to understand how a method of
political control could be so universal and so successful for so long
requires much deeper analysis. It must be labelled the most successful (if
short-lived) political creed of all time, however disastrous its economic
and human consequences.

In *Reflections on a Ravaged Century* Robert Conquest has eloquently written of the power of 'the idea' in creating Communism. He quotes Pushkin:

> Those in our midst who plan impossible revolutions are either a few young men who do not know our people, or cruel-hearted men who place a low value on their own necks and an even lower value on the necks of others.

Norman Cohn made much the same point in *Warrant for Genocide*:

> There exists a subterranean world, where pathological fantasies disguised as ideas are churned out by crooks and half-educated fanatics for the benefit of the ignorant and superstitious. There are times when that underworld emerges from the depths and suddenly fascinates, captures and dominates multitudes of usually sane and responsible people . . . And it occasionally happens that this subterranean world becomes a political power and changes the course of history.

Conquest argues that these sub-intellectuals fastened upon Marx's convoluted and half-baked theories because of the new turn-of-the-century faith in science as the answer to every problem, including human ones.

> Marx was seen, and saw himself, as 'the Darwin of society': as the originator of a historical science to match Darwin's biological science. He provided his certainties in terms of proven theory. The contrast between his own and Darwin's methods is very striking, and indeed, Marx saw this himself – referring rather patronizingly to Darwin's 'crude English empiricism'. By this he meant no more than the perfectly true circumstance that Darwin accumulated facts before developing his theory, as against the supposedly superior method Marx derived from his German academic background, of inventing the theory first and then finding the facts to support it.

As an early Russian Revolutionary expressed it in Norman Cohn's *The Pursuit of the Millennium*:

> We seized on Marxism because we were attracted by its logical and economic optimism, its strong belief, buttressed by facts and figures, that the development of the economy, the development of capitalism (this was why we were so interested in it), by demoralizing and eroding the foundations of the old society, was creating new social forces (including us) which would certainly sweep away the autocratic regime together with all its abominations. With the optimism of youth we had been searching for a formula that offered hope, and we found it in Marxism. We were also

attracted by its European nature. Marxism came from Europe. It did not smell and taste of home-grown mould and provincialism, but was new, and fresh and exciting.

While this undoubtedly fastens upon a key element of Communism's success – its appeal to intellectuals and to some extent to the masses – it is inadequate as an explanation for this huge and transcendent phenomenon.

This book will argue, with reference to global Communism as a whole in each of its major manifestations, that its success arose from harnessing together four critical ingredients in a lethal brew: a quasi-religious creed (Conquest's 'idea') with its own internal logic, saints and insistence upon unquestioning belief, hierarchy, rules and punishments; the sudden urge of the ruled to overthrow their rulers at a time of unprecedented social mobility and political paralysis (people were not seeking to change the world so much as to vent their anger upon those that had inflicted change upon them – an ironic 'reactionary' feature common to most revolutions); the new systems of organization, control and quasi-wartime mobilization of industrial society, modern technology, Party structures, propaganda and repression; and the chameleon-like ability of the new authoritarians (just like Nazism and to a lesser extent Fascism) to absorb centuries-old feudal nationalist and absolutist traditions into a fearsome new synthesis of the two.

The second and third elements were crucial. For it is no coincidence that Communism and Fascism/National Socialism (and to a lesser extent, militarism) buffeted humanity more or less simultaneously. They were both different kinds of reaction to the colossal changes sweeping across lands – economic modernization and the globalization of capitalism. The more or less stable social relations that had governed countries for centuries were suddenly swept aside by huge impersonal forces that uprooted the downtrodden from the land, employed millions in cramped conditions, hired and fired labour without explanation and crossed borders with impunity, respecting neither nation nor tradition.

Marxism was one response to this bewildering new world of social upheaval and unseen forces: men sought to gain control of their own destiny through overthrowing the ruling classes and levelling society. Extreme nationalism was another response – as ordinary people took refuge in a sense of enhanced national self-identity to assert themselves against the unseen forces transforming the world. To someone who was only one in millions, nationalism gave a sense of belonging, of worth.

At least part of the psychology of anti-Semitism derives precisely from this: the Nazis whipped up anti-Jewish feeling not just for supposed reasons of racial superiority or difference, but because the Jews were supposed to epitomize the forces of plundering cross-border international capitalism – exactly the same villains as in the Marxist textbook, minus the racial dimension (it is interesting too how similar the crude Marxist caricatures of capitalists with their top hats and tails and bulging eyes and stomachs are to the later Nazi caricatures of Jewish financiers – and of course under Stalin, the Russian Revolution was to acquire openly anti-Semitic overtones).

The point is not that Communism and National Socialism were, as is often asserted, similar totalitarian creeds (there were huge similarities, in terms of mass organization and the subordination of the greater good; but there were considerable differences as well). The point is that they sprang from the same root – as reactions to the international phenomenon of impersonal industrialization.

Why did Communism take hold in some countries and nationalism in others? Because countries making the transition from largely agrarian economies to industrial ones lacked propertied classes of sufficient size to block power grabs by communist minorities. In cases like Italy, Germany and Spain the nationalist movements, for all their socialist roots exemplified by the original Fascists, the SA and the Falange respectively, were principally characterized by their decision to compromise with the middle classes; the same thing happened with militarists in Latin America. Nationalism provided a rallying point for the masses while preserving social order. Countries where the communists triumphed (and there was often a venomous struggle with nationalism) tended to be those where the propertied class was so small that one tiny minority could be easily subsumed by another in the social maelstrom of accelerated industrialization.

Of course, communists soon wrapped themselves in the nationalist mantle as well. I will attempt to show that it quickly became difficult to talk meaningfully of Communism except as a crude ideological shop-window. Communist states were soon powered by old fashioned absolutism and nationalism, whatever they proclaimed publicly. If against twentieth-century forces of modernization and change Communism is seen as an essentially reactionary reversion to the hierarchy of national feudalism and rigid social distinction with its accompanying privileges, this has huge implications for the argument of its intellectual defenders – that, although deeply flawed, without its driving force societies like Russia and China would never have escaped their feudal pasts.

As with Nazism, a key element lay in the mass-mobilizing power of the modern state. But there was one crucial distinction. By overtly projecting their nationalism and concepts of racial superiority, Nazis and Fascists could never become universal and indeed excited the fury of peoples in other countries against them. Although by contrast Communism in practice soon subordinated to the nationalism of most of the societies it took over, it projected itself as a global, universal and anti-national creed.

Finally, this book will argue, Communism uniquely made its appeal to societies at a very particular stage in their modern development: not to developed industrial democracies, in which Marx had argued, the imposition of an ever more bloated and diminishing capitalist class upon the masses would revolutionize the latter, but to politically and socially underdeveloped societies, usually very largely agrarian, which were suddenly subjected to the wrenching and disorientating effects of rapid industrialization, creating rootlessness, alienation and intense resentment against the governing class. This was true of virtually every society in which Communism triumphed except those seized by force from outside (such as Eastern Europe), and explains why so many of Communism's exponents hailed from rural or peasant backgrounds.

As suggested, Communism, when it took power, often quickly underwent substantial transformation. The revolutionary urgency, once power had been achieved, could not properly be maintained without both undermining the terror necessary to establish the new regime, and those in charge of the new order (only Trotsky and Mao tried to defy this logic, and then for reasons of pique at losing power struggles rather than from genuine ideological conviction).

Apart from instituting new repression and transforming the ideology of the new rulers into a state religion – something that had happened during seizures of power since time immemorial – the doctrine was transformed immediately into an essentially nationalist ideology, with the advantage that this could command continuing popular support when communist promises of equality and prosperity clearly failed to materialize. This happened in Russia as early as the post-1917 civil war, in China, which soon became quasi-imperialist (Mao's initial success in the civil war owed more to his success in fighting the Japanese than to his communist doctrines) and to virtually every 'communist' liberation movement around the world, which actually owed its main appeal to nationalism.

These nationalist body-snatchers quickly established a need to re-invent the very systems revolution had supplanted – Stalin consciously basing himself on Ivan the Terrible, Mao on the emperors, and so on. Not only did Communism revert to the styles of the ancient feudal systems it replaced, but became just as uniquely prey to the whim of the ruler. Thus the history of Communism became that of giant-sized individuals rather than Marxist-style impersonal forces, to a much greater extent than in more sophisticated societies.

The cult of personality was not some grotesque aberration of Communism, but the very transmutation necessary to its survival. With Communism dependent on individual leaders, nationalist objectives and systems of central state control and mass mobilization, it began, in many respects, to resemble other forms of National Socialism in the way it operated, with the difference that in more developed Nazi Germany rival centres of power – the economic authority of the Junkers, the middle classes and the old Prussian military leaders – were tolerated (although they might not have been so for long).

Communism, as national-feudalism employing modern methods of repression, also contained the seeds of its own destruction: for as national feudalism's expansionist instincts were blocked by stronger countries, in particular the United States, or disintegrated into competing nationalisms (for example with the division between Russia and Yugoslavia, just beyond the former's military reach, or Russia and China), people were less easily convinced of its nationalist successes except in fields like the space race or through stale propaganda invocations that Russians and Chinese were better off than Westerners.

As it became clear that the system was failing to deliver economic equality and prosperity while its nationalist ambitions were also being thwarted, it lost all authority, even among those that ran it: and from their ranks came those that brought about its disintegration (once again individuals), Gorbachev taking the lead.

The communist dream was not quite a fraud: some of its instigators believed in the creed (although probably not Lenin, and certainly not Mao), as did many of its followers and, to begin with at least, probably a large swathe of the workers, peasants and rootless to whom they appealed. But the communist idealism of these revolutionaries, where they existed at all, was replaced almost from the beginning by the cynicism of feudal nationalist dictators who differed only from, for example, their Bonapartist predecessor in the extent of state control and centralization at their disposal – and in this they differed not at all from Nazism. Marxism-Leninism certainly provided a useful means and creed for minorities to seize power violently; but it was almost immediately abandoned except as a state religion, a propaganda tool for external consumption and a foreign policy instrument.

How cynical were the communists? It is impossible to answer this question without straying into areas of pseudo-psychology (what really motivates humans, self-interest or idealism?) that are beyond this book. Lenin, for example, undoubtedly believed fanatically in the revolutionary ideals he espoused in the early part of his political career. But soon his all-consuming pursuit of power by revolutionary means seems to have overshadowed any real concern for those in whose name he sought power. In his view, to stage a successful revolution required dictatorship by a small minority whose interests were identical to those of the proletariat. During the 1920s, as we shall see, Lenin decided that a return to a mixed economy would benefit the proletariat: this ran directly counter to Marxist ideology. No matter: *le prolétariat, c'est moi.* It is extremely unlikely that Lenin consciously believed that he was a cynic: the capacity of the human mind to identify one's own self-interest with a nobler ideal is immense. Doubtless Stalin, for all his famously cynical utterances, believed that his actions were in Russia's best interests. He would probably defend the terrible upheavals he inflicted on his people, which to the outsider seemed motivated by no more than lust for power, in terms of the need for popular revolution to prevent the ossification of society and, later, of national self-defence.

Many early revolutionaries were idealists, but many also were mere fanatics, bore grudges or simply sought power and spoils. Further down Communism's vast hierarchy were hundreds and thousands of, in Stalinist terminology, 'careerists' – men more concerned with their own perks and privileges than the lot of the downtrodden masses. But perhaps the great majority did not see things that way: the secretary of a provincial soviet (a Communist Party committee) probably relished the importance and favours that came with his job, and yet believed he was doing good for the people in whose name he formally held his office.

As ossification, privilege and corruption spread through the latter stages of Communism, many straightforwardly criminal cynics were clearly doing well out of the system. But the large majority of Party and government officials were probably not consciously corrupt and believed they were doing the best they could, while enjoying their authority. After all, had Communism not resulted in great economic strides and increasing living standards over the decades? Only a tiny minority would have much awareness that the West had far outstripped the communist world – and it was that tiny minority that eventually argued for reform of the whole system.

Does this mean it was unfairly blamed for the horrors committed in its name? Hardly. Communist theorists tied themselves in knots to adapt their half-baked analyses to the new realities of power as exerted by these nationalist dictators. The creed, by preaching the destruction of existing historical, social and legal rights and the privileged, lent itself to being hijacked by absolutism. But Communism, however fervently believed in by millions around the world, was hardly ever actually practised anywhere. Indeed it was incapable of so being except for a very short time or through the exercise of levelling terror (the Cultural Revolution, Cambodia).

This leads to the final and most important question of all: could the spectre ever return in other than its last holdouts? The answer, fortunately, is no, because it hardly existed in the first place: the unique circumstances of rapid industrialization of the peasant societies which spawned it now exist only in very remote and backward countries. Those communist parties that have survived – in Russia, parts of Eastern Europe and in Italy – have transformed themselves into democratic parties of the left; some have even participated in coalition governments. Outside the Third World, the 'haves' – mostly reconciled to urban society – frequently outnumber the 'have-nots', whose numbers are steadily diminishing. So, far from the capitalist class shrinking and the proletariat expanding to a point where the latter will inevitably overthrow the former, modern society's main feature has been the growth of the middle class and the wealthy working class, much of which rightly no longer considers itself so.

There is, instead, a more complex danger: that the forces masquerading behind Communism – nationalists and the proponents of overbearing state control – could revive, for example when societies feel themselves at the mercy of remote economic forces, or in the event of a global economic downturn, or with the growth in inequality between and within nations. If all revolutions are to some extent a reaction against progress and change, as already argued, with progress accelerating, the danger certainly remains.

There is a further point. History has experienced a constant 'dialectic' – to borrow an adored Marxist word – between two great forces, centripetal and centrifugal; between the big international idea, encroaching on a large area of different nationalities and ethnic groups, and the reassertion of smaller units of identity.

Thus the Roman Empire eventually disintegrated into smaller national states, which later fell into the embrace of the Church and the Holy Roman Empire. After this in turn fell apart, the Protestant Reformation was another global idea, fragmenting once again into a reassertion of different types of national Protestantism. The Enlightenment (a cross-border intellectual phenomenon) partly inspired the French Revolution and Napoleon's attempts to unite Europe by force in the name of liberalism, which again fell apart.

Meanwhile the new nation states formed in the late nineteenth century (Germany, Italy, Japan) became obsessed with the view that older empires (another big idea) were shutting them out and went to war twice in the last century for their own 'living space', which preceded cathartic defeat and the emergence of the new Russian and Chinese empires. With the collapse of the Soviet Union, nationalist states seem to be reasserting themselves in Europe, but against that the global big idea of American free-market economics has made enormous headway, which in turn may germinate nationalist resentments – as may the encouragingly voluntary attempt to create a more united Europe.

In this 'steady state' theory of global big ideas, followed by withdrawals into nationalism (which need not be taken as a Marxist-style historical law, merely an observation!), Communism occupies its own special place as the most formidable and destructive cross-border idea ever experienced, eventually disintegrating into nationalist reassertion under the weight of its own contradictions. Meanwhile the story of Communism, which is inadequately recounted in the following pages, is intensely exciting, horrific and the story of much of humanity in the last century.

PART I

Explosion

I

The Deity

Far from opposing these so-called excesses, these examples of popular vengeance against hated individuals or public buildings which have acquired actual memories, we must not only condone these examples but lend them a guiding hand.

Karl Marx

Marx and Marxism

Dean Street, Soho, 1852. Vendors ply their wares with hoarse shouts. Prostitutes, coquettishly overdressed in voluminous bustles, wait on street corners. Innumerable restaurants reflect the colourful variety of nationalities that live in the area. Drunkards curse loudly on their way home. The background is one of material poverty, of people just one step ahead of the pawnbroker. Even more difficult to sustain is the endless struggle of those from bourgeois backgrounds in continental Europe to uphold the standards that separate them from the masses.

One man seeking to uphold such standards, because he considers no other his intellectual equal, lives in a squalid two-room flat on the street itself. At the age of 34, he is a man of middle height, robustly built, with a thick, gushing black beard and, in the words of a visitor, 'piercing fiery eyes that have something demonically sinister about them'. His world is one of utter chaos: notoriously unpunctual, he often stays up at night, sleeps during the day, works for days on end and then does nothing for weeks.

The flat is rudimentary in the extreme. His sitting room overlooks the disorderly street, while his bedroom is at the back. The sitting room is covered in half an inch of dust, the chairs mostly broken. In the middle stands a large, solid table covered with an oilcloth, on which lie scattered manuscripts, books and newspapers, cutlery, plates, glasses and an inkpot. The smoke that hangs like a pall makes the visitor's eyes water.

Karl Marx himself is cordial enough when he greets the pilgrims that come to this messy shrine. But intellectual arrogance is never far away. Nor is the sense of injustice, the heady German nationalism, the hatred of most things English, the smouldering temper, the colossal ego. His personal disorganization amounts to a statement of superiority over the established order of things. Yet beneath the surface he craves the bourgeois comforts and respectability he affects to despise.

Marx presides over his household like a traditional German patriarch. He frowns at the mention of anything improper and subjects his wife, two daughters and a son to rambling monologues upon every subject. He takes them for picnics on Hampstead Heath, a large wild sprawl on which thousands of middle-class couples descend for their promenades, frequenting small stalls and donkey rides. Marx rides donkeys too, which amuses his children.

Yet beneath the respectability of that tormented personality lies a further layer: the personal bully, uncaring of the feeling of others. True, he shows a tender side to his family, to whom he rarely speaks sharply. His wife Jenny, an attractive and long-suffering Prussian aristocrat, is so devoted to him that she closes her eyes to the circumstances in which his character compels them to live. But after his infant son's death from tuberculosis, his wife has a nervous breakdown and Marx forces his attentions on his hard-working, long-suffering maid, Lenchen, fathering a bastard son he later refuses to acknowledge.

There is a great humanity about Marx's battery of failings, a humanity that does not often pierce his lumpen prose. He is fond of arguments, singing raucously in the streets, getting drunk. On a pub crawl in London with a friend, Eduard Bauer, they stumble upon a working men's evening out. The German refugees are at first treated hospitably, until the inebriated Marx starts denouncing the British way of life. The Germans have to flee their increasingly enraged audience and, after smashing streetlights with stones, are chased by three policemen until they escape down an alley.

The high jinks are rare. Mainly he broods over his exile, political defeat in his native Germany that he aspired to rule as a revolutionary dictator, his domestic troubles. The hopes aroused by the publication, just four years earlier, of the catechism and bible of his thought, the

Communist Manifesto, lie unfulfilled. This appeared in 1848, when the established order in Europe teetered on the brink of catastrophe and then pulled back. Yet submerged in personal and political failure, he cannot even conceive that his name and thought are to become the labels for one of the greatest upheavals in world history since the Christian Gospels.

For all his defects, for all the sharpness of his tongue wielded mercilessly upon his enemies, Marx was carried forward, ultimately, by a genuine human ideal. When he finished the first volume of *Das Kapital* in April 1867, he told his publisher that he had sacrificed '. . . health, happiness and family to complete it'.

> I laugh at so-called 'practical' men and their wisdom. If one were willing to be an ox, one could naturally turn one's back on human suffering and look after one's own skin. But I would really have considered myself unfulfilled if I caved in before making my book or at least my manuscript quite ready.

For Marx, exploitation explained the brutalized state of the proletariat and the spiritual emptiness of the bourgeoisie. Idealizing a proletariat of which he knew that he would never be considered a member, his innate respect of convention and his rugged assertions of bohemianism were quintessentially middle class – he genuinely, passionately believed in his dream: that of a perfect world, so different from the one he lived in. His goal was a noble one, in spite of the processes he thought necessary for its attainment. Through all the ravages done in his name, Marx would have clung to one thought, now a twentieth-century political cliché: the end justifies the means. The terrible history of Marxism in the twentieth century would, in its creator's view, have been justified if from it had emerged the kind of society he envisaged: one with no classes, no exploiters or exploited, no bureaucracy, and no 'political', as opposed to civil, society.

In this ideal world, there would be pure democracy. Everyone could pursue their own unhindered course of action, so long as this did not impinge on anyone else's independence. Thus, the ultimate Marxist ideal – utopian, if not very original – was that of perfect individual freedom balanced by that of others, sighed over by political theorists throughout the ages.

*

In the beginning was the word; and more than any since the New Testament and the Koran, Marx's word captured the imagination of man. This may astonish anyone dipping, or rather sinking, into the morass of *Das Kapital*'s first nine chapters: how could a complex, convoluted writer with prose anchored in the teachings of the German philosophers possibly find a publisher, let alone a mass audience? Moreover Marx's ideas were largely second hand. As Robert Payne writes in his fine biography, *Marx*:

> 'The workers have no country' was first said by Marat, the French revolutionary, who was also the first to say 'the proletarians have nothing to lose but their chains'. Blanqui had invented the phrase 'the dictatorship of the proletariat'. Though Marx wrote, 'When the people saw the ancient finished coats of arms decorating the backsides of the aristocracy, and incontinently dispersed with wide, loud and irreverent laughter', . . . he was paraphrasing a verse from Heine's *Germany, a Winter's Tale*. Even the most famous phrase of all – 'working men of all countries unite!' – had been borrowed from Karl Schapper and had appeared in print four months earlier. The *Communist Manifesto* was a palimpsest of ideas culled from at least fifteen known sources. Marx had stirred the broth, poured in some colouring matter and then flung the pot at the faces of the bourgeoisie.

Why then did the *Manifesto*, rather than the only partially digestible *Das Kapital*, catch on? Marx claimed for his work an almost unparalleled universality. There had been books of political philosophy of great force like Machiavelli's *The Prince* and Hobbes' *Leviathan* and works of economic theory with similar appeal, like J.S. Mill's *Principles of Political Economy* or Adam Smith's *Wealth of Nations*. But Marx was the first to combine a philosophical background – principally that of Hegel – with the language of the newly fashionable economic theorists and a cascade of statistics (in vogue in the late nineteenth-century) to produce a 'scientific' theory of history claiming to predict the future.

In addition Marx could be as vivid a polemicist as any that had lived. There is genuine compassion and strength of feeling for the victims of the new industrial age in his description of the accumulation of wealth at one pole as 'at the same time accumulation of misery, accumulation of work, slavery, ignorance, brutality and degradation at the opposite pole'.

Yet the main reason the idea caught on was because Marx articulated and knitted together six of the main sentiments of the new mass age.

First, in a society of transparent inequality, he preached equality. Second, in an age of reason, he preached a scientific explanation of the way history worked. Third, in an age when workers could for the first time be organized into a political force, capable of mounting strikes and demonstrations, he preached worker power.

Fourth, he advocated the guiding role of the Communist Party, a party of intellectuals capable of understanding better than the workers themselves where their true interests lay; this was the forerunner of the elitist theories of the twentieth century in countries in which the traditional loyalties that bound society together were breaking down. Implicit in the whole structure was the belief, mentioned earlier, that the end justifies the means, that because history is inevitable anything done in the name of progress is essentially good, no matter what the cost.

Fifth, in an age when nationalism was tearing Europe apart, he preached internationalism. Sixth, he argued that revolutionary violence was acceptable when many social reformers were preaching that change was obtainable only through gradual evolution. The impact of each of these six clarion calls was to be electric: never mind that the framework that connected them was so flimsy.

The Six Commandments

To take each of these commandments in turn: first, Marx's theory of the exploitation of man, so simple that almost anyone could understand it. The vast panorama of human history was telescoped into one brief message:

> The history of all hitherto existing society is the history of class struggles. Freeman and slave, patrician and plebeian, lord and serf, guild-master and journeyman, in a word oppressor and oppressed, stood in constant opposition to one another, continued in an uninterrupted, now hidden, now open fight, a fight that each time ended either in a revolutionary reconstitution of society at large or in the common ruin of the contending classes. This chaotic process had, in nineteenth-century society, essentially been resolved into a direct clash between the workers and the bourgeoisie, which had supplanted the old initially feudal ties that bound man to his natural superiors and has left no other bond between man and man than naked self-interest and callous cash payment.

Marx genuinely admired the bourgeoisie's achievements. It had, he said, 'accomplished wonders far surpassing Egyptian pyramids, Roman aqueducts and Gothic cathedrals; it has conducted expeditions that put to shame all former exoduses of nations and crusades'. He admired the bourgeoisie also for creating the conditions for its own downfall, for bringing into being an industrial working class that would inevitably overthrow it.

Marx was right to play up the inequality of the nineteenth century – especially as it applied to societies he had not envisaged – like Russia, where large numbers of people were migrating from a feudal country-side into industrial cities for the first time. In the countryside they had, as Marx said, been largely cowed by the message of feudal respect for their superiors; furthermore, they could not organize effectively there.

In Russia, country life meant institutionalized inequality. Wealthy landowners, for all their finery, were remote figures, separated from their inferiors by manner and birth; they could ignore the discontent of the farm workers, who lived too close to poverty to have their discontent taken seriously. Peasant smallholders were the most conservative class of all, jealously defending their right to a few acres of subsistence.

But in the city the rural incomers found themselves at the mercy of incomprehensible economic forces. In the countryside the weather, harvest failure or an employer's unpleasantness were to blame for hardship. In the city people could lose their jobs without apparent explanation. Marx made great play too, of the way capitalism required a certain level of unemployment to keep wages down and maximize its profits.

The cramped conditions of the new urban slums destroyed the family and local ties that made rural life so rigid and yet so stable. The urban rich instead lived next door to the poor, had sprung from their ranks, were apparently living off their sweated labour and were unlegitimized by manner or birth. People flung into the cities found themselves rootless and restless – the new creed of worker equality drew them like magnets, giving them an identity within, and explanation of, their terrifying new world.

Thus Russia, where urbanization started late in the nineteenth century, was riper for revolution than England, where enclosures had taken place before the Industrial Revolution, or France, where revolution had preceded the industrial development of the latter half of the nineteenth century. Later in the twentieth century Marxism found its followers almost exclusively among countries in the same state of rushed development.

Marx was to be proved entirely wrong in his prediction of the consequences of urban inequality, in asserting that the bourgeoisie 'produces above all its own gravediggers'. In his view, capital would become concentrated among so few, and productive power among so many, that ultimately the former would be overthrown. In fact revolution succeeded only in countries where power had initially been concentrated in a very few hands – usually those of the old feudal class – when industrial change took place. A representative middle class already holding power when the industrial revolution took place was usually too numerous and too powerful to be dislodged, its base expanding rather than contracting as industrialization proceeded.

Marx's second commandment – that history obeyed scientific laws – was pinched directly from his intellectual mentor, Hegel. The scientific law in question was the dialectic – originally the ancient Greek concept of one point of view being put forward and then opposed, so that a synthesis of opinions, a 'reasonable balance', could be achieved. Marx believed that history worked the same way: he borrowed from Hegel, and many other nineteenth-century thinkers, the certainty that history was a progress. Hegel believed that people in the early stage of history understood only their own individual surroundings; that in a later stage they would understand how the world worked, enabling them to make more balanced decisions about how to react to events; and that in the final stage, through religion and art, people would understand how their own reason worked (he called this 'absolute knowledge of the spirit').

Marx evolved his own theory of scientific political laws. Society started first as feudal; then it became bourgeois; finally, after too much capital had been concentrated in too few hands, the system collapsed and the organized proletariat took over. There were advantages in asserting that history was scientific. It chimed in with the fashionable view of the Age of Reason that everything could be explained. It made historical progress inevitable, and anything that impeded it merely delayed and harmed progress: thus history was just a relentless march forward towards the eventual victory of Communism.

So feudal lords were overthrown by serfs, who later became guild masters in self-governing mediaeval centres; the latter were replaced in turn by factory owners. With the growth of colonialism, the discovery of the new world, and the boom in overseas trade, large amounts of capital flowed in and the bourgeoisie was able to finance still bigger industrial complexes. This, Marx believed, had two consequences: the number of people who actually owned the wealth grew smaller owing to the concentration of capital; and the number employed to create further wealth grew larger. Eventually an explosion was inevitable, as the numerous poor rose up against the elite rich. Proletarian victory was certain because they were 'the self-conscious, independent movement of the immense majority, in the interests of the immense majority. They have nothing of their own to secure and fortify. Their mission is to destroy all previous . . . instances of individual property.'

This, of course, is essential to any understanding of Marxism-Leninism. For Marx, the central progression was from feudalism to bourgeois society to proletarian revolution. Marx's definition of feudalism was, broadly and not inaccurately, a society dominated by a small number of landowners with rigid privileges who held the great majority in serfdom or slavery. The bourgeois revolutionaries, according to Marx, swept this traditional system away, and in this respect he quite admired the bourgeoisie who, by replacing static repression with the conditions for urbanization and industrialization, achieved significant advances.

But because the bourgeois were themselves exploiters, and because of Marx's theory of the concentration of capital in fewer and fewer hands, ultimately they had to be overthrown by the state acting in the name of an idealized proletariat. The big mistake Marx made, in retrospect, was in believing that the state would prove more enlightened than the bourgeoisie. For once the Marxist-Leninists controlled the levers of power, they reverted to the pattern of the feudal state – rulers entrenched in privilege, bound by no legal norms, lording it over a population who, like the serfs, had no rights – because the state, under Marxist-Leninist doctrine, reflected the 'people's' interests. How could the people require rights to protect themselves against themselves?

Once nationalism was added to this brew, it became indistinguishable from feudal tyranny. To a Westerner, Sergei Eisenstein's incredible film, *Ivan the Terrible*, is a repellent, if magnificent, exposition of tyranny and paranoia. To Stalin, who permitted then banned this extraordinary piece of *lèse-majesté*, it gloriously portrayed him as a mediaeval tyrant and nationalist. Similarly, Mao's eventual capricious emulation of the Chinese emperors of old was no accident. He was the new absolute ruler of a vast population stripped of any rights, because as Secretary of the

Communist Party and supreme ruler of the proletariat, he represented their best interests.

The communist creed came to combine the ancient theories of despotism and the divine right of kings, being both nationalistic and feudal with the people stripped of such 'bourgeois' rights as the rule of law, the right to property and the vote. To be fair to Marx, this was not his original formulation, although his espousal of force to achieve his aims pointed in that direction. It was Lenin, with his absolutist invocations to control of the revolution by a select few and the need for ruthlessness and violence in the cause of revolution, who marched the creed forward – one could say backwards – to the feudal idea of an absolute state acting in the name of the people stripped of rights, and Stalin, with his creed of socialism in one country and eventually of heroic resistance to the Nazis, who added the exaltation of nationalism – Alexander Nevsky and Ivan the Terrible fending off the barbarian hordes threatening Mother Russia.

This also explains why Communism was different from other authoritarian systems that accompanied accelerated development in newly industrializing countries. Communists detested the bourgeoisie, even though ironically they would become bourgeois themselves by the third quarter of the twentieth century. The Fascists in Italy, the Nazis in Germany and the militarists in Latin America all cooperated with the bourgeoisie – and (with the exception of a few left-wing Nazis and Fascists) never believed in levelling society as an accompaniment to nationalist dictatorship. Communists were feudal-nationalist autocrats; Fascists, Nazis and militarists were bourgeois-nationalist autocrats.

Because the victory of the proletariat was inevitable, anything that speeded it up, however bloody, was right, and anything that delayed it was wrong. This would profoundly affect Marxist-Leninist attitudes during the later twentieth century, being used to justify all kinds of atrocity. Moreover, it gave Communism its celebrated patience. Communist groups would labour thanklessly for years in apparently lost causes like that of bringing revolution to Britain, Germany and the United States because victory would ultimately be theirs.

Commandment number three was related to the newly discovered organizational power of the proletariat. Marx understood, a little more completely than previous socialist theorists, just how much power industrialization gave to the workforce. Marx was not thinking primarily of union action, such as the power of workers to withdraw their labour, but rather of strength through numbers that would eventually bring down the ruling classes through revolution.

He also insisted that the dictatorship of the proletariat would not merely exchange one ruling class for another, as the bourgeoisie had replaced the feudal class: 'The condition for the emancipation of the working class is the abolition of every class . . . the working class in the course of this development will substitute for the old civil society an assimilation which will exclude classes and their antagonists and there will be no more political power properly so-called, since political power is precisely the official expression of antagonism in civil society.'

This entirely idealistic message was spectacularly wrong, but essential for his argument: the notion that the revolution would create an incorrupt state with no further exploitation of man by man was the one ideal that Marx felt might attract the dim-witted proletariat – for whom he had as much contempt as sympathy, believing them to be incapable of understanding where their own true interests lay.

Marx also spiced up the call to working class solidarity by offering them certain straightforward political goals, over and above the theoretical aims set out in the *Communist Manifesto*: he proposed ten rather arbitrary practical aims for the revolution, when it came to power: the expropriation of land; a heavily graduated income tax; the abolition of all rights to inheritance; the confiscation of the property of all emigrants and rebels; the centralization of credit in state hands; the decentralization of transport and communication; an increase in state ownership of the means of production; a universal obligation to work; the obliteration of differences between town and country (how?); and free education. This of course was a preliminary programme; ultimately the state would become superfluous and wither away, and people would produce exactly the amount society needed.

Commandment number four laid down how the revolution was to be achieved given that the proletariat was probably incapable of doing the job itself. In this, Marx prepared the foundations upon which Lenin built and made a key point:

> Finally, in times when the class struggle nears the decisive hour, the process of dissolution going on within the ruling class, in fact within the whole range of old society, attains such a violent, glaring character that a small section of the ruling class cuts itself aloof and joins the revolutionary class, the class that holds the future in its hands. Just as, therefore, at an earlier period, a section of the nobility went over to the bourgeoisie,

so now a portion of the bourgeoisie goes over to the proletariat, and in particular a portion of the bourgeois ideologues, who have raised themselves to the level of comprehending theoretically the historical movement as a whole.

Marx sought to justify the role of himself and his fellow middle-class idealists in the communist movement as the people who raised the consciousness of the masses to revolution, the backbone of Lenin's theory of the Party as the vanguard of the proletariat. Marx never properly clarified the Party's role; he himself was only intermittently a socialist party member. Nevertheless his line of thinking, seized upon by Lenin, is plain enough: 'The communists are . . . the most advanced and resolute sector of the working-class parties of every country, that section which pushed forward all others . . . They have the advantage over the great mass of the proletariat of clearly understanding the line of march, the conditions and the ultimate good results of the proletarian movement.' The concept of the superiority of the Party's intellectuals over those of proletarian origin was not far off.

Marx's ideas about the role of his own intellectual class led to his notions of what the state should do in a post-revolutionary society. He considered the state a means of class exploitation. In his native Prussia, Marx denounced the domination of the state by a bourgeois bureaucracy that had once favoured equality and meritocracy and now attempted to suppress both through 'the trilogy of mystery, hierarchy and authority'. This reads ironically in the light of the communist experience of the late twentieth century.

After the revolution, he foresaw 'a period of revolutionary transformation during which the state can be nothing less than the revolutionary dictatorship of the proletariat'. This would finally end class division and foreshadow the state's abolition. 'This', Marx wrote, 'has only one meaning for communists as a necessary result of the suppression of classes whose disappearance automatically entails the disappearance of the need for an organizational power of one class for the suppression of another.'

Commandment number five was Marx's appeal to rationalist opposition to contemporary excesses of nationalism and war. Marx himself, hardly immune to nationalist sentiments, possessed an overwhelming sense of German national superiority. But his public view was a historical extension of his belief that the workers' struggle was universal; he ignored, through sublime or deliberate ignorance, those differences between peoples that provoke conflicts. For him, the world, particularly through colonialism and great power competition, was increasingly following the mould of Western society, and therefore all men were affected by similar problems. He was the first globalizer, a century before the 1980s.

Working men, for Marx, had no country: indeed, the revolution could not be achieved within one country. In *The Class Struggles in France*, Marx attacked those of his allies who believed 'they would be able to consummate a proletarian revolution within the national walls of France, side by side with the remaining bourgeois nations'. Marx thus favoured Polish nationalism and the unification of Germany and Italy as this would lead towards the creation of bigger, and in revolutionary terms more promising, entities.

Marx's view of world revolution would have a profound, though unexpected, influence on the Russian Revolution. It was the First World War, above all, which triggered the collapse of the Romanov dynasty and the October Revolution. Lenin's ironclad commitment to peace at any price was to be the most appealing message the Bolsheviks offered millions of ordinary Russians suffering from the privations of war.

Lenin not only cited Marxist chapter and verse in preaching defeatism and pacifism in Russia in 1917; sustained by the belief that revolution was inevitable in all countries, it was only a matter of time before the ruling hierarchy of the ostensible enemy, Germany, was overthrown from within. Thus, for a socialist Russia to continue to fight was futile.

The second impact of the internationalist message was seen in Stalin's struggle with Trotsky. The latter, following on from Lenin, preached the spread of revolution, irrespective of Russian national interests; Stalin preached socialism in one country and, by eventually defeating Trotsky, prevailed over one of Marx's own most passionately held beliefs. Indeed, Marxism's subsequent history would show that socialism had much better prospects when joining forces with, rather than opposing, nationalism. Thus Marx was to be proved wrong once again. Yet in the revolution's birthplace – Russia in November 1917 – Marx's pacifist message had given a major boost to the revolutionary cause by an accident of history: for arguably the main cause of the Russian Revolution was the country's desperate desire for peace.

The sixth commandment of Marxism was the one more usually associated with Lenin: that change must take place through violent revolution. Yet if Lenin forged the message into steel, Marx formulated it, and later claims by socialist parties of fidelity to Marxist thought in advocating non-violent revolution were bunk. The *Communist Manifesto* itself did not carry any invocation to violence, although its language was inflammatory enough. But Marx made his own feelings clear in March, 1850, with the limited circulation of a document entitled *A Plan of Action Against Democracy*, written following the 1848 revolutions, in which the proletariat and the tiny Communist Party were mere spectators.

Marx did not mince words in urging the assassination of government leaders, the burning of public buildings and the slaughter of thousands. 'Revolutionary excesses' were required to fight bourgeois democracy: '. . . the workers will be victorious chiefly through their own courage, devotion and self-sacrifice . . . Far from opposing the so-called excesses, these examples of popular vengeance against hated individuals or public buildings which have acquired hurtful memories, we must not only condone these examples but lend them a guiding hand.'

Marx urged that the bourgeois governments that had seized power in 1848 be given no respite by their former worker allies, who must be organized into revolutionary groups to await the arrival of the central Revolutionary Commune in Germany to take up the reins of revolution. Lenin adopted this precise revolutionary blueprint in 1917. But 1848 was too early; Marx was in advance of his time. That year's upheavals were primarily struggles in which the newly wealthy, but politically excluded, new industrial middle classes, without any great proletariat underpinning, wrestled for power with the old ruling classes. However in Russia, the workers would be those most affected by industrialization and by war.

These were the six commandments to ignite the imagination of the world. There were many others, but at the time they seemed almost irrelevant. Marx's turgid economic theories, barely understood outside a small clique of intellectuals, were quickly repudiated by those who put the theory into practice. When Marx died in 1883, the six commandments seemed destined to wither on an intellectual vine.

Pre-revolutionary Russia: Towards the First World War

The intellectual force, the propaganda effect, the power of the Marxist message were undeniable. It was later to spawn a huge academic discipline in the West, based on Marxist economic determinist analysis.

But during the lifetime of its author and the years thereafter, nothing happened. Proletarian revolutions did not take place in the societies in which they were supposed to. England, where he spent so much time in exile, barely even noticed his existence. In 1849, when he arrived, the Industrial Revolution was at its height and the conditions of the workers had barely started to improve from the kind of wretchedness described in a paper by the Miners' Commission: women and children who were 'chained, bound, harnessed like dogs in a go-cart saturated with wet and are more than half naked, crawling upon their hands and feet and dragging their heavy loads behind them – they present an appearance increasingly disgusting and unnatural'. But there was no revolution: instead, as the social cost of industrialization dawned first upon the old British landed class and then the more enlightened members of the new professional and middle class, steady social reforms, such as Shaftesbury's Ten-Hour Act passed by Parliament in 1847.

Equally, in France and Germany, working class conditions were slowly improving. The bourgeoisie were attempting to improve the workers' lot and, indeed, to extend the franchise. Marx's message – that the workers must seize power as the only way to better themselves – was being dangerously undermined by moderate reformism. The worst blow to befall the communist movement was when the German Social Democratic leader, Engel's close friend, Eduard Bernstein, openly criticized Marx's scientific tenets and his commitment to violent revolution in 1898, advocating instead social reform and democracy.

Even at that stage more enlightened Marxists were realizing that their societies had progressed too far for Marxism to take root. Except for one: Tsarist Russia, uneasily suspended between the embrace of Western European values and their rejection, intellectual obscurantism and enlightenment, and feudalism and industrialization.

Russia would provide the kind of social topsoil in which a communist movement could take root: a society whose existing values and structure had broken down before new institutions could flourish. The despairing liberal reformers of the late nineteenth and early twentieth centuries recognized the danger. 'Give us ten years and we are safe!' exclaimed S.I. Shidlovsky, one of the more enlightened large landowners, as the years ticked away towards revolution. But Russia suffered two almighty strokes of bad luck at the last moment: Tsar Nicholas II, and the First World War.

Pre-revolutionary Russia was a society in tumult. The country was governed by an absolute autocracy, rendered necessary in the sixteenth century by the diversity of its peoples and cultures and its historical susceptibility to external attack. Beneath the autocracy lay a reactionary landowning class, more resistant to change even than the Tsars, with powers of life and death over the peasants that worked the land while the aristocracy amused itself in St Petersburg. Into this frozen social structure were to be implanted Western ideas of republicanism and revolution; rapid industrialization; and a social transformation arising in part both from industrialization and a demographic explosion.

Between 1850 and 1900, Russia's population doubled, and by 1913 it had increased by another third, to around 120 million people. The peasants fled their subsistence existence on the land for the cities. By 1914 there were approximately 3 million factory workers, 1 million miners and 800,000 railway workers. In 1850, Russia had only 660 miles of railway, the arteries of industrial development; some 60 years later there were more than 40,000.

Industry sprang up around the coalmines of the Donets Basin in the south-eastern Ukraine, while pig iron production jumped from 1.5 million tons in 1900 to 3.5 million in 1914. The city of Ekaterinoslav (now Dnipropetrovsk) developed from a middle-sized provincial centre with 47,000 people to an industrial conurbation containing 150,000; around 250 miles eastwards, Rostov-on-Don's population jumped from 80,000 also to 150,000. Black gold to fuel industry gushed out of the Caucasus: in 1840 the Baku wells were producing only 160,000 tons of crude oil annually; by 1905, it was 7 million and by 1913, 9 million.

Russian industrial development, moreover, set the course to be followed by most developing countries in the later twentieth century. The government played the dominant role in stimulating growth from about 1879 onwards, inspired by Count Sergei Witte, who established tariff barriers, invested heavily in the railways and the iron industry and provided export incentives. Foreign companies were encouraged to flock to Russia: by 1900 some 270 had arrived.

The pace of industrialization slowed for a time at the turn of the century: under the prime ministership of Peter Stolypin, however, growth was resumed at a brisk trot for the five years from 1906 to 1911. Stolypin sought to ameliorate the social problems caused by industrialization, for example extending admittedly rudimentary schooling from the third of children that were able to obtain it when he came to office to all children. By 1914 the number of primary schools had increased by half.

The creation, out of nowhere, of a Russian industrial class was to be the key to the Bolshevik uprising: industrial workers, many first-generation migrants from the land, were to be the revolution's storm troopers. Equally significant, although the vast bulk of the Russian population stayed on the land: the cities were surrounded by huge wastes of rural stagnation and poverty. The new urban elite assumed the guiding role previously reserved for the old landowning class; but their numbers, compared to the peasant population, demonstrated that Russia could be controlled by a very small minority indeed – until the peasants struck back.

Even in the first years of the twentieth century, 85 per cent of the population, or around 100 million Russians, still lived on the land. Only in the south was the peasantry relatively prosperous, benefiting from good soil and modern agricultural methods. In the north peasants were indebted to creditors and their government, workers but not owners of their land, prey to famine and overcrowding.

By the mid-nineteenth century, Tsar Nicholas I had freed only state peasants from serfdom. As rural violence grew more common – there were 400 outbreaks between 1855 and 1860 – his enlightened successor, Alexander II, finally emancipated all serfs in 1861. The rural communes (foreshadowers of the Soviet Union's collectives) that now owned the land became as onerous a burden to most peasants as the old landowners. The peasants had to wait to get what they wanted until Stolypin's land reform allowed them to secede from the communes and own their own smallholdings. Between 1905 and 1915 some 2.5 million peasant households applied to secede, and by 1917 around 7 million peasant landowners supported approximately 35 million people.

Alexander II's educational reforms produced a new urban intellectual class, very much in a minority and comprising mainly the children of Russia's legion of impoverished aristocrats, professional men and state employees. From this *paznochintsi* class – educated men who could not fit into the social order of Tsarist Russia – would come the cream of Russia's revolutionaries.

Russia's social revolution was played out against a background of political reforms that were always too little too late. Alexander II, the first of his family to try to nudge Tsarist society into something approaching the political transformation taking place elsewhere in Europe, set up the *Zemstvo*, district or provincial assemblies, which contained members of all classes. Judicial reform gave Russia a modern legal system to enforce an archaic social structure. But just after announcing the establishment of an assembly with real legislative powers, Alexander was assassinated in March 1881 by a terrorist bomb.

His thuggish and reactionary son, Alexander III, presided over a period of unremitting persecution of all opposition, while ushering in the industrial revolution that was to condemn his dynasty to obsolescence. His own son, Nicholas II, a discreet, saintly, weak man with a hard-bitten, wrong-minded German wife, was neither reformist nor repressive, but simply overwhelmed by events.

By the beginning of the twentieth century, as Russia emerged from Alexander III's iron rule, the country was seething. In May 1902, troops had to be called in as uprisings spread through Kharkov and Poltava in the Ukraine. In 1903 the strikes that broke out in Rostov-on-Don eventually paralyzed 500 factories and affected nearly a quarter of a million workers; Cossacks were brought in to disperse the strikers. Meanwhile, Russia's subject nationalities – the Ukrainians, Finns and Poles – were becoming increasingly restive. Nicholas's Minister of the Interior, Vyacheslav Plehve, had only one answer: repress, and repress again. Political arrests rose from 1,580 in 1900 to almost 5,600 in 1903.

By Christmas 1904, a showdown was inevitable. On Sunday 22 January, an Orthodox priest, Father Georgii Gapon, led a peaceful march of workers to petition the Tsar at the Winter Palace. Troops and police opened fire, killing several people and wounding hundreds on what became known as 'bloody Sunday'. The Tsar was transformed from the 'little father' of his people into a hated autocrat overnight. He was given a respite from further mistakes by Plehve's assassination.

After Russia was humiliated by the Japanese in May 1905 at the Battle of Tsushima which ended the Sino-Japanese War, the Tsar half-heartedly considered the demands of the Congress of Provincial Zemstvos for a *Duma*, a legislative assembly. But not until uprisings in St Petersburg and Moscow had left more than 1,000 dead did Nicholas accept the advice of Witte, summoned out of retirement, to grant his people their parliament, elected by all classes.

Even now, Russia might have been rendered safe for democracy. The uprisings of 1905 had been largely spontaneous, with very little political organization by extreme left-wing movements. A new elected parliament might yet save the day: and at the elections of March and April 1906, on a weighted franchise which nevertheless provided for considerable peasant and worker participation, the middle-of-the-road democratic party, the Kadets, won 179 seats, while the no-change Right won only 32. Of the two left-wing parties, the Trudovik group, representing the largely peasant-supported Socialist Revolutionary Party, won 94 while the Social Democrats, who only fought in a handful of areas, won 18; the Bolsheviks were a minority within this second tiny minority in parliament. Thus, the Russian people had voted for moderate reform.

The Tsar promptly undid all the good done by this parliamentary election by firing Witte and dissolving the Duma after a month because it would not do his bidding. Nicholas appointed the able Peter Stolypin as Prime Minister, compelled him to restrict the franchise, and was horrified when the next Duma, which met in 1907, yielded a smaller majority for the moderates: this time the Social Democrats captured 83 seats – still, however, only a quarter of the poll.

But the Left overreached itself; the obstructiveness of its parliamentary members finally led to the election of a parliament dominated by the right-wing Octobrists, with 140 seats. The middle-of the-road Kadets fell back to 54, the Social Democrats won only 20, and the Trudovik group just 13. Many peasants, particularly those benefiting from Stolypin's land reforms, had swung to the right. The enlightened Stolypin governed in cooperation with the new Duma until 1911, while the country continued to expand at speed industrially. But following his assassination at the opera in Kiev in 1911, he was replaced by the reactionary clique favoured by the Tsar. Strikes, which had only affected 46,000 workers in 1910, erupted again. In this worsening but still far from hopeless climate, in August 1914 Russia went to war with Germany.

Russia: Westernizers and Slavophiles

There were two great traditions of Soviet opposition political thought; the struggle between them was not only a feature of the revolutionary movement before October 1917, but also dominated the first three decades of Soviet life.

On one side stood the Westernizers, who looked to St Petersburg as their capital, were inspired by the example of Peter the Great, and passionately embraced all things European, especially French; opposing them were the Slavophiles, who believed that Russia should look to its own Eastern traditions and thereby become an exemplar for the decadent Western world: their capital was Moscow.

Lenin and Trotsky were Westernizers; inspired by Western political ideas, they believed in progress and wanted to carry revolution westwards. In that sense, they were true internationalists. Stalin was to represent the old nationalist Slavophile tradition; he aimed to construct socialism within Russia and overtake the rest of the world through that country's own efforts, relying upon the old, mystical, Russian mores of the cult of personality and barbarism.

In the late nineteenth century, the main socialist party to emerge was the *Narodik* (Populist) Party, principally inspired by the writer Alexander Herzen who, after visiting the West, rejected all its works and proclaimed the supremacy of native Russian virtues. Herzen admired Marx, but argued, not unreasonably, that socialism would be created by the peasants building their institutions through idealized peasant communes. He rather overlooked the fact that most Russian peasants regarded the existing communes as worse slave-drivers than even the old landowners, who were at least absent from the land most of the time.

Another Populist thinker, Peter Lavrov, inspired teachers to preach revolution among the peasantry. There they discovered that Marx was right about one thing: the peasantry, deeply conservative, religious, ill-educated and impossible to organize, was not the stuff of which revolutions are made. Still, the Populists, some inspired by the anarchist teachings of Mikhail Bakunin, who preached the destruction of all government, established the Land and Liberty Party in 1876: its chief contribution to Russia's progress was the assassination in 1881 of Alexander II, the last Russian Tsar to seek political and social reform for his country.

An archetypal Russian intellectual and exiled Westernizer, Georgii Plekhanov, broke away from the Party in Geneva in 1883 to found the Group for the Liberation of Labour, an orthodox Russian Marxist party which argued that revolution required the industrial working class to seize power. Plekhanov had realized the impossibility of arousing the slumbering Russian peasant masses to do anything; he borrowed most of his ideas from Marx, but wielded little influence among Russian exiles in Germany. They were soon riddled with faction fights: many agreed with Bernstein that democratic reform was the preferred way to improve the lot of the working class. While the Geneva group squabbled, small Marxist cells sprang up inside Russia. They appeared to be no more than tiny, uncoordinated, insignificant minorities. However, few could have guessed at the time the scale of the whirlwind that would follow.

2

The Prophet

'We stand for organized terror . . . terrorism is an absolute necessity in time of revolution.'

Felix Dzerzhinsky

Lenin

Onto this unpromising soil stepped a 21-year-old student. Expelled from law school at Kazan University for taking part in a student demonstration, he then successfully crammed a four-year law course into eight months. If there were features of Lenin that stood out at the age of 21, as they would through the rest of his life, they were his unwavering dedication to hard work and his unremitting commitment to the pursuit of personal power, wrapped in the mantle of revolutionary zeal.

Short and stocky, very little about him seemed exceptional, his slightly obtuse red face offset only by the visionary, intolerant, deep-set Mongol eyes common among Russians of mixed racial origin. The impressive domed forehead, the determined thrust of the jaw, the cruelty of the lips hidden by the beard, has been deified so much in Soviet revolutionary iconology that the quality of irresistible leadership seems to be chiselled into his features. True, his achievements and power were to give them authority in later years; but he made an unimpressive young man on first acquaintance, his invariably untidy and ill-fitting clothes a mark of every impoverished small-town Russian intellectual.

Maxim Gorky commented doubtfully on first meeting him: 'He was somehow too ordinary and did not give the impression of a leader.' In Russia, leadership was still conveyed by larger-than-life personalities like the Prime Minister, Stolypin, a great warm bear of a man. The age of the tireless bureaucrat was to come. To Pavel Axelrod, a colleague of Plekhanov's, Lenin 'smelt of the land'. Although no son of the soil, his somewhat wooden expression, his coarse features and build did suggest a peasant origin.

In fact, he came from a family of comfortably middle-class high achievers – within, that is, what was possible at the time in Russian society. His father, Ilya Nikolaevich Ulyanov (Lenin's own surname until he took on his famous pseudonym), was a schoolmaster who passed his penchant for hard work to his son, rising to become an inspector of schools. On his father's side, Lenin inherited a trace of Asiatic blood. His mother, a strong and energetic woman from a better background than her husband (she was the daughter of a military surgeon), was probably of German origin.

Into this humourless, ambitious, austere, hard-working and respected hearth in Simbirsk (later renamed Ulyanovsk), a town on the Volga about 425 miles east of Moscow, Lenin was born on 22 April 1870, the second son of six children. From an early age he showed a tendency to compete with his equally intelligent elder brother, Alexander, cut short when Alexander was hanged in May 1887 for taking part in a plot to assassinate the reactionary Tsar Alexander III. There is no doubt that this tragedy helped to embitter and steel the young Lenin. Lenin's mother, Maria Alexandrovna, who had lost her husband the year before, bore it with steely fortitude. Lenin himself was not to be deflected by grief: showing the near-inhuman coolness he would display throughout his life, he passed his high-school exams with flying colours the same year.

At about that time, Lenin discovered in Marxism the perfect fusion of a believable social creed with his own impatience for revolutionary conflict, together with a justification for any action that would bring him closer to power. In 1893, aged 23, he published his first significant political pamphlet, which attacked not the ancien régime but his fellow revolutionaries, the Populists. A couple of years later, Lenin, by now a struggling lawyer in St Petersburg increasingly preoccupied with revolutionary writing and study, visited Plekhanov in Geneva and for a while even believed he had met his intellectual match.

Lenin, in the cliché, was a man for his time. Allied to his zest for work were his gift for vigorous, polemical writing (which often, however, reads tediously in retrospect), his instinctive understanding of other people and never accepting no for an answer where his ends were concerned. In another age, these talents would not have got him far; his intellectual arrogance and absolute contempt for the opinions of others would have denied him office in any but a tightly disciplined authoritarian movement.

Lenin was not without his human qualities: he adored his mother, as much for her strength of personality as out of family affection, and was devoted to his wife, Krupskaya, who nevertheless was in many ways an extension of his work. They married in 1898: they had no children. An earnest, severe schoolmistress who admired him as a leader, she had asked to be sent into exile with him in 1897 after he had been jailed for fifteen months for actively spreading the Marxist gospel in St Petersburg. Devoted to him and to Communism, she was content to take a supportive role. She spent the mornings on her honeymoon helping him to translate Sidney and Beatrice Webb's *Industrial Democracy* and the afternoons assisting him with his first important book, *The Development of Capitalism in Russia.*

Lenin, nevertheless, was happier in exile with her in Shushenskoye in Siberia than his concern not to appear vulnerable to bourgeois pleasures led him to admit. He went shooting, swam in the summer and skated in winter. Typically, however, he suggested that he enjoyed his earlier imprisonment in St Petersburg better, because there he was spurred to work harder.

Yet in Lenin the pursuit of personal power and of communist revolution merged indistinguishably. Moreover, he bulldozed his opponents and ignored advice. He alone was right; his opponents, a dangerous nuisance, were to be, if necessary, physically eliminated. In the end, his ruthlessness and single-mindedness lifted the Bolsheviks to power in Russia. Without his actions, the supposedly inevitable socialist revolution would have remained a footnote on the second page of an entirely different chapter of Russian history.

In 1900, aged 30, Lenin was released from exile and established a rival newspaper, *Iskra*, (The Spark), to bypass the Marxist Party's official newspaper and establish his own claim to revolutionary leadership, which he pursued with a venomous intolerance equal to that he would display towards his class enemies in 1917. His second task was to organize the revolution. The Marxist Party had been born in March 1898 with the holding of the First Congress of the All-Russian Social Democratic (Labour) Party in Minsk. It was an inauspicious start. Riven by disputes and some delegates' support of 'economism' – placing the immediate interests of workers, such as higher wages, above political objectives – the congress earned the scorn of Plekhanov and Lenin.

But in 1902 Lenin revealed himself to be not just a high-calibre Marxist theoretician but, unlike most of his intellectual peers, a man with a shrewd grasp of reality and of the concrete steps needed to attain power. In his most famous work, *What is to be Done?*, he developed Marx's rather vague notion of an elite helping to guide the working class into a central theory of revolution: a professional, small, centralized, disciplined and highly qualified Communist Party that alone would lead the masses to salvation. This ran counter not just to mainstream nineteenth-century political thinking, which advocated ever-widening emancipation and the extension of education to the working class, but also to Lenin's comrades' vision of a party broadly based upon the proletariat.

As a theory of socialism Lenin's concept was elitist, if not downright authoritarian. As a theory of how to seize power and install a revolutionary dictatorship, it was beautifully crafted for early twentieth-century Russia and for other countries in a similar stage of development. Lenin reconciled the two by arguing that the imposition of revolutionary dictatorship was a necessary condition for the subsequent emancipation of the working class. Yet in Russia in 1917, such a prospect seemed utterly implausible.

Perhaps the foremost historical influence in Leninist theory was the fate of the revolutionary Paris Commune in 1871, which had seized Paris after the French defeat in the Franco-Prussian War. Marx himself had wholeheartedly supported the Communards, while doubting their ability to prevail. In his immensely powerful *The Civil War in France* he argued that 'there can be neither peace not truce possible between the working men of France and the appropriators of their produce . . . The battle must break out again and again in ever growing dimensions . . .' For his espousal of violent revolution, Marx was vilified as a 'red Terrorist'; and the split between his followers, the British Labour Party and the German Social Democrats, can be traced to this event.

But the Commune had a still more potent effect on Lenin's imagination. As he wrote in 1908, it had failed, he believed, for two reasons:

The proletariat stopped half way; instead of proceeding with the expropriation of the expropriators, it was carried away by dreams of establishing supreme justice in the country . . . institutions such as the Bank [of

France] were not seized . . . The second error was the unnecessary mag-
nanimity of the proletariat; instead of annihilating its enemies, it endeav-
oured to exercise moral influence on them; it did not attach the right
value to the importance of purely military activity in civil war, and instead
of crowning its victory in Paris by a determined advance on Versailles, it
hesitated and gave time for the Versailles government to gather its dark
forces . . .

Later Lenin wrote that 'the Commune was lost because it compromised and reconciled'. For every day of the Russian Revolution that lasted
longer than the Commune, Lenin declared 'Commune plus one,' or
'Commune plus two . . .' and after his death, his body would be wrapped
in a Communard flag. From the lessons of this dry run in France nearly
half a century earlier were borne the chilling inhumanity and ruthlessness that, having carried Lenin to the top, would savagely be imposed
upon the Russian and other revolutions across the world. For if Marx
had been the pen, Lenin was to be the sword.

Lenin's concepts ran into trouble immediately: at a congress intended
to be held in 1903 in Brussels but subsequently transferred to London
after police pressure, the Party split into pro- and anti-Lenin factions.
Lenin wanted Party membership only for those who gave it their 'regular
personal cooperation under the direction of the Party organization'. A
former supporter of his, Julius Martov, a Jewish intellectual, proposed a
wider definition. Martov won the initial vote, but Lenin astutely manip-
ulated the Party votes to secure a majority of his supporters on the Party's
Central Committee and the editorial board of *Iskra*. From then on
Lenin's supporters became known as Bolsheviks (Majorityites) and
Martov's as Mensheviks (Minorityites).

Lenin's victory was short-lived: the *Iskra* board, which became the model
for the Politburo – the tiny committee which dispensed real power in
Soviet Russia – was wrested from his control shortly after the congress,
and Martov and his supporters rounded on the would-be dictator. In
particular a former ally of Lenin, Lev Davidovitch Bronstein, launched
a vicious and perceptive attack on Lenin as a 'despot and terrorist who
sought to turn the Central Committee of the Party into a committee of
public safety – in order to be able to play the role of Robespierre'.
Bronstein was better known to his comrades by his pseudonym of
Trotsky.

The son of a wealthy Jewish landowner in the Ukraine, Trotsky was everything Lenin was not. With his flamboyant personal appearance and overbearing personality, his gifts of wit, quick thinking, repartee and the felicitous phrase made him every inch a leader of men – although better suited to mass politics than a disciplined revolutionary movement from which Lenin, the less brilliant but more gifted conspirator, would emerge as leader.

This was hardly apparent in 1905, when a spontaneous uprising swept the country: the Mensheviks set up the St Petersburg Soviet of Workers Deputies, dominated by Trotsky at the age of only twenty-six. Lenin, at the time bidding to regain the upper hand at another unofficial Party Congress in London, was openly critical of the Soviet. After the uprising collapsed, both sides sought to heal the divide and a further Congress was held in 1906, at which Lenin headed the minority. But Martov accepted Lenin's original proposal to limit Party membership. In the following year, Lenin was forced to leave Russia, finally settling in Switzerland in 1914.

Lenin's conciliatory behaviour was just a front: ignoring the decisions of the congress, he worked to re-establish personal control over the Party. By the following year, the Bolsheviks were in a majority again. Lenin's disregard for the formal organs of decision-making became so blatant that in 1909 the Central Committee of the Party considered expelling him. In the event, three years later, it was he who expelled his opponents, allowing only Bolsheviks to remain and denouncing as renegades all who refused to accept his leadership.

The ruthless focus on his own dominance that characterized Lenin's seizure of power over the Social Democratic Party was to characterize the Russian Revolution itself. Few people outside bothered with this murky group of withered and rabid intellectuals lacking contact with the workers they claimed to stand for, without a popular following and wholly irrelevant to the struggles between the Tsar, the liberals and the social revolutionaries. Three years before the Russian Revolution, the prospect of a Bolshevik victory in Russia was laughable. That was how things appeared in August 1914, as Europe went to war.

From War to Revolution

Russia in 1914 was, in a sense, the first developing country as it sought to catch advanced industrial Europe and America within the space of a few decades, absorbing the impact of industrialization and modernization from a very low base. Yet the installation of a new working parliament with a moderate majority seemed to show the danger had been passed. If it could gain a wider legitimacy through an expanded franchise among the country's worker and peasant masses, it would gradually turn Tsar Nicholas II into an impotent constitutional monarch.

The First World War shattered the hopes of the constitutionalists. Once the imperial court regained quasi-dictatorial powers, which it then wielded with such ineptitude, democratic reform was stripped of the support it had acquired over the previous nine years. The war also destroyed the morale of the one institution the regime required to ensure continuity and constitutional order: the armed forces. Without armed force, the Romanov dynasty was naked and unprotected. Because Nicholas had prevented a more representative group from wielding power during the final fatal years, there was a constitutional vacuum that could be filled by any small group that was sufficiently ruthless and determined. Thus the Russian Revolution was not to be a mass revolution, but the substitution of one elite for another.

When war broke out, the nation appeared to unite behind the Tsar. The day after the declaration of war on 2 August, a rapturous crowd sang 'God save the Tsar' on their knees before their emperor. Six days later the Tsar greeted the president of the Duma with the promise, 'I am your friend until death. I will do anything for the Duma. Tell me what you want.' The Duma voted him a huge war budget. The Kadets (centrist Democrats) voted for the appropriation; the Trudovik group (Socialists), led by a dashing, eloquent revolutionary, Alexander Kerensky, and the Social Democrats could not bring themselves to vote against the 'imperialist war': instead, they abstained.

Only Lenin, from exile, raised a furious voice in favour of the defeat of Russia, insisting the imperialist war be converted into a civil war. Nicholas, meanwhile, drew precisely the wrong conclusion from the nationalist fervour that swept Russia, assuming the adulation for his office represented a surge of personal loyalty to him in the nation's hour of need.

Then the slaughter began. Nicholas ordered three Russian armies into Prussia. After their defeat at Tannenberg at the end of August they were forced to withdraw, having suffered some 300,000 casualties. Meanwhile the Austro-Hungarians invaded Russian Poland but were repulsed, losing 250,000 men in the process. In May 1915 the Germans advanced on Poland and Lithuania, forcing the Russians back. One of the German commanders, General Ludendorff, spoke with the awe of 'the supreme contempt for death' displayed by the Russians. In the first ten months of the war the Russians lost 3.8 million men. The Russian economy was also reeling from the burden of supporting the war. The logistics behind the war effort had become a major scandal.

The outcry was such that the Duma reassembled in August, only to be adjourned by Nicholas. The Tsar's response to the crisis was that his ministers had failed him and, advised by the Empress and a sinister necromancer, Gregory Rasputin, assumed supreme command of the army. Grand Duke Nicholas, his uncle, who had led the Russian armies ably – except when the Tsar interfered – was fired. The Tsar departed for the front, leaving the Empress and Rasputin in charge in St Petersburg.

In June 1916, the Russians attacked along a 300-mile front from Lutsk in north-western Ukraine to the Carpathians; 1.2 million men were killed, but the offensive made slow headway. Back in Moscow, as inflation ran wild in the cities and food shortages became acute, Rasputin's crony, the Prime Minister Boris Sturmer, administered the country ineptly and corruptly. Constitutionalist politicians were seething. When the Duma met in November, the government was denounced for 'stupidity and treason', Sturmer was forced out of office and, in January 1917, Rasputin was murdered by a patriotic, aristocratic clique. But it was too late.

The uprising began on 8 March, as demonstrations and strikes against food shortages broke out spontaneously in a number of cities and factories. Unlike previous protests, the army and the Cossacks did not intervene. With the best troops at the front, officers could not rely on raw recruits to fight strikers demanding relief from the hunger from which most of the soldiers' families were suffering.

On 11 March, troops fired on demonstrators in Znamenskaya Square on the orders of General Kharkov, who commanded the military district of Petrograd (as St Petersburg was now called). But elsewhere soldiers began openly fraternizing with the workers. Nicholas, away at the front, did nothing except formally dissolve the Duma that, as the only centre of legitimate power, continued to sit as authority crumbled all around it.

But on 12 March, in the palace where the Duma had met, another self-appointed parliament had convened: the Soviet of Workers' and Soldiers' Deputies. All over the country, soviets were set up, unopposed by the army. For the moment the Petrograd Soviet accepted the authority of the 'governing committee' which had been set up by the Duma: the ragbag of workers, intellectuals and soldiers and a few peasants that comprised the 3,000-strong Petrograd Soviet agreed on a bourgeois revolution before a socialist one. The Duma takeover was the former.

On the morning of 15 March, Russia's high command and Grand Duke Nicholas advised the Tsar at his northern front headquarters to abdicate to prevent civil war. That same evening the Menshevik leader of the Petrograd Soviet, Alexander Kerensky and the Kadet leader of the Duma, Paul Milyukov, agreed to set up a provisional government. When a single-carriage train bearing the Duma's representatives arrived after a day's trudge through the frozen flats of north-western Russia to demand the Tsar step down, the little, weak man whose errors had contributed so much to Russia's present pass, abdicated with dignity. Bolshevik thugs murdered him and his family in confinement on 16 July 1918.

The provisional government, the Duma and the Soviet failed to realize that the ancien régime had collapsed because of the war; only ending it would satisfy most Russians. The main leader of the chaotic Petrograd Soviet at the time, Heracles Tseretelli, argued that the war must continue until other countries followed Russia's lead in overthrowing their governments. Tseretelli's policy ruled the day at the first All-Russian Congress of Soviets, to which thirty-seven soviets and seven armies sent their representatives. Only a tenth of the delegates attending were Bolsheviks. But that was before Lenin arrived at the Finland station in Petrograd on the fateful evening of 16 April.

Lenin and his group of thirty-one people had been provided with a carriage by the German government, delighted by his thundering denunciations of the war from exile. They were allowed to cross Germany from Switzerland without customs inspection or passport examination, although no one was allowed to step off the carriage (which therefore had its own cook) onto German soil. Lenin's apprehensions about being arrested as a collaborator with the enemy upon arrival in Russia turned out to be unfounded. A delegation of the Petrograd Soviet was sent to greet him in the imperial waiting room. Lenin popped out into the churned-up snow covering the long platform, ignored the delegation and marched out of the station to be greeted by a large crowd, curious to see the famous exile. He addressed them from the bonnet of a car, and carried on haranguing all and sundry from the armoured car that took him to the Bolsheviks' temporary headquarters in the

Kshesinskaya Palace. From its balcony he made a speech advocating the ending of the war, which did not go down well among many of the soldiers listening to him.

Soon he was agitating that the Bolsheviks should seize the opportunity and stage an immediate revolution. His comrades, having welcomed the fall of the Tsar as an historic achievement and disposed to support the provisional government, were astounded: they believed the bourgeois revolution was now beginning, and that the socialist revolution Lenin urged was years away.

But unlike Lenin, they had missed the essential point: there was now a power vacuum at the centre of Russian politics that would not reoccur. Whatever Marxist ideology preached, Lenin was a man of action. Like the leader of a military coup, he understood that for a small minority movement like his to fill the void ahead of the larger, less organized groups, they had to move quickly to seize power from the hands of an even smaller, less popular clique.

The provisional government's authority was tenuous. On 3 May, 30,000 demonstrators demanded – and then got – the resignation of the foreign minister for supporting continuation of the war. Around the country, according to one prominent witness, 'lynch-law, the destruction of housing and shops, jeering at and attacks on offices, on provincial authorities, or private persons, unauthorized arrests, seizures and beatings up were recorded every day by tens and hundreds. In the country, burnings, and destruction of country houses became more frequent . . . More than anything else it was the unbridled rioting soldiers who were destroying law and order.' The law's upholders had become brigands.

Throughout Russia, a yearning for authority, firmness and discipline set in. The rule of the soviets, of Kerensky, of the provisional government began to seem a shambles to ordinary people. In July, large numbers of soldiers went wild in Petrograd, invading the Tauride Palace and demanding that the soviets grab power from the provisional government. Lenin and the Bolsheviks initiated the disturbances, in which dozens were killed. Kerensky rushed to Petrograd from the front to demand Lenin's arrest; but the latter had slipped away to Finland.

Now Kerensky decided to take decisive action. He supplanted the Liberal government and became Prime Minister on behalf of the Social Democratic majority in the Petrograd Soviet. The Duma's power had evaporated. But Kerensky's policy of continuing the war with Germany while seeking a negotiated end to it proved politically disastrous; as shortages spread, ordinary Russians saw Lenin's 'peace now' campaign as the only way out. Furthermore, the only disciplined army units remained at the front, leaving Kerensky with few reliable troops to enforce order.

Events moved quickly that summer. As Kerensky sought to enforce his authority, his newly appointed Commander-in-Chief, General Kornilov, reckoned that only a military coup could restore order. Kornilov's main bêtes noires were the Bolsheviks, whom he regarded as German spies. 'It's time to hang the German supporters and spies with Lenin at their head,' he thundered. Kornilov proposed to seize power at the head of his well-organized Cossack and Muslim troops, installing himself as Prime Minister and demoting Kerensky to the post of Justice Minister. In August he sent a Cossack cavalry corps and a Muslim division to a point midway between Moscow and Petrograd.

The coup attempt backfired disastrously. Kerensky, siding with the Left, announced he would resist the coup; Kornilov's soldiers were stopped by sabotaged railway lines and left-wing propagandists. The Bolsheviks organized an armed workers' militia and a Red Guards corps of 25,000 men to defend the Revolution. Kornilov, deserted by his men, was arrested; the disciplined strength of the Bolsheviks, whose support Kerensky was compelled to seek, had powerfully asserted itself for the first time.

Lenin knew that the moment of truth was near. His pamphlets – *The Bolsheviks Must Take Power* and *The Crisis is Ripe* – urged immediate insurrection. On 23 October Lenin slipped into Petrograd and persuaded his fellow Bolshevik leaders that it was now or never. Two days later a military revolutionary committee of the Petrograd Soviet was set up under Trotsky to seize power in Petrograd. Kerensky acted too late. On 5 November he ordered the Bolshevik newspapers closed down and reinforced the Tauride Palace.

But two days later the Bolsheviks seized Petrograd's two main railway stations and the telegraph exchanges. A frigate, the *Aurora*, anchored in the vast, half-frozen expanse of the Neva River, landed Bolshevik sailors to seize the Nikolai Bridge. Kerensky found no forces willing to risk their lives for his government: the three Cossack regiments in the city refused to fight. The Prime Minister, who sought unsuccessfully to straddle both sides of post-Tsarist Russia, escaped in an American Embassy car to try and raise support at the war front. Bolshevik control of the capital was

consolidated the same afternoon. The huge, magnificent baroque
Winter Palace, gazing across the ice floes at the needle spire of the Peter
and Paul Cathedral, fell in the evening with the loss of just six lives.

The Russian Revolution was no more than the seizure of power by one
armed faction from another in a political void; the great majority of the
Russian people had had no say in this at all. The Mensheviks were dismissed the same evening by Trotsky with the memorable phrase, 'miserable bankrupts, your role is played out; go where you ought to be – in the
dustbin of history'. A force of 700 men assembled by Kerensky to fight
the Bolsheviks was defeated at Pulkovo Heights near Petrograd. Around
the country, the Bolshevik insurrection was followed by similar uprisings.

In Moscow, however, some 10,000 soldiers loyal to Kerensky captured
the Kremlin and its arsenal. But on 15 November, 50,000 Red Guards
and armed workers took the sprawling fortress after bloody fighting.
The acquiescence of the Russian units at the front was secured when
Kornilov's successor as Commander-in-Chief, General Pukhonin,
resigned his command to a Bolshevik ensign, Nicholas Krillenko, and
was subsequently beaten to death.

The Bolshevik slogan of 'Peace, Bread and Land' had secured passive
acceptance of the new regime if not the loyalty of a sceptical workforce,
soldiery and peasantry. This seizure of power, like the March uprising,
occasioned wary hope among the suffering masses, although few people
knew what the Bolsheviks really stood for.

One last obstacle remained: the provisional government's plans for
elections to a constituent assembly. The proposal to consult ordinary
Russians was too widely supported for the Bolsheviks to ignore. The
elections took place on 25 November: the Bolsheviks, in whom high
hopes had been invested, won 25 per cent of the vote, mainly in the cities
and among soldiers desperate for peace. Some 15 per cent of the vote
went to the Right, and some 50 per cent to moderate socialist parties.
On 18 January the assembly rejected the measures taken by the Bolshevik
government. The next day the assembly members found their way into
the Winter Palace barred by Red Guards. Democracy in post-Tsarist
Russia had lasted one day. The People had hijacked the people.

The early revolutionary days were frantic. The Second All-Russian
Congress of Soviets, now Bolshevik-packed, set up a Lenin-selected
cabinet with fifteen members. A Central Executive Committee of 101
members formed the main legislative body when the congress was not

sitting. Appearing before the congress, Lenin advocated public ownership of land: a week later the nationalities of Russia were given the right to self-determination. A month later 'inequality' was abolished in the army and soldiers were given the right to elect their officers. Legislation formalized equality between men and women and divorce was made available on demand (in many areas of Russia, free love enjoyed a brief flowering).

A Supreme Council of National Economy was established to confiscate private firms; workers' committees gained the right to manage enterprises. Large houses were expropriated by the soviets. Ordinary criminal courts and revolutionary tribunals to deal with counter-revolutionaries replaced the Tsarist legal system. The Orthodox Church was disestablished and religious education abolished. A constitution promulgated in January 1918 confirmed the soviets as the main source of power, to be elected democratically by universal suffrage.

But even in these heady early days, behind the flood of ideas – some idealistic, some hopelessly impractical, some even disciplinarian – lay the overwhelming objective of the Revolution: the consolidation of dictatorial power by Lenin and his supporters. According to Lenin's *The State and Revolution*, the dictatorship of the proletariat – in reality the dictatorship of the Bolshevik Party acting in the name of the proletariat – must govern until an economic system to meet everyone's needs could be established; then the state could wither away. But Lenin was quite prepared to tack backwards and forwards from his revolutionary goals while pursuing power.

With the formation of the Communist International (Comintern) in 1919, Lenin set out in unyielding terms the dictatorial, autocratic, nature of communist organization, binding upon the Russian Party as well as all the other members of the Comintern:

> The Communist Party must be built on the basis of democratic central-ism. The basic principles of democratic centralism are that the higher Party bodies shall be elected by the lower, that all instructions of the higher bodies are categorical and necessarily binding on the lower; and that there shall be a strong Party centre whose authority is universally and unquestioningly recognized for all leading Party comrades in the period between congresses.

In practice, no elections ever took place except as rubber stamps of approval: the higher bodies elected and promoted the lower. This was the cornerstone of communist discipline for the next seven decades.

The revolution's three mainsprings were an iron chain of command from the top, cloaked by an elaborate democratic camouflage involving the elimination of all opposition; deals with power groups to ensure survival; and revolutionary terror. As regards the war, Lenin urged the proletariats of all nations to unite to overthrow their masters and make peace, while in reality seeking to extract Russia, as had been promised. By February 1918, Trotsky had negotiated a humiliating Russian surrender to Germany at the Treaty of Brest-Litovsk.

So poor were the settlement terms that Lenin added to the circle of the Revolution's enemies not just the Western powers, appalled by Bolshevism as such and by their separate peace, but also the left-wing communists and the peasant-based socialist revolutionaries. The counter-revolutionary forces gathered strength. The pillage of Sevastopol by pro-Bolshevik sailors after the withdrawal from the Crimea of a 'White' (anti-communist) army sparked off civil war in February 1918, which provoked massive, if ineffectual external intervention on behalf of the Whites.

The conflict raged throughout Russia until 1922. The government went onto a combat footing, nationalizing steel, textiles, pig iron and coal and, eventually, all mechanized industries. Rationing was introduced, making some 35 million people directly dependent on the state. Workers and soldiers received four times as much as others, marking the beginning of Communism's institutionalized inequality.

Thousands perished in the famine-struck winter of 1917–18, a foretaste of terrible ones to come. By the summer of 1918 the bread shortage was desperate. Committees of the village poor, set up to organize food distribution, engaged in savage conflicts with the richer peasants: horrific tales abounded of people being hacked to death with scythes, beaten to death, or burnt alive. Over a hundred serious uprisings broke out in the countryside between January and September 1918.

The crushing of the only remaining organized opposition party, the left-wing Socialist Revolutionaries representing the peasants, followed the frenzy of violence in the countryside behind the Bolshevik lines in the civil war. The Communist Party at the time numbered some 270,000 members and was tightly disciplined by comparison with the peasant party. Following an assassination attempt on Lenin on 30 April, revolutionary terror began in earnest. Five hundred people were shot in Petrograd in reprisal. The 30,000-strong *Cheka*, literally the 'Extraordinary Commission', headed by Felix Dzerzhinsky ('We stand

for organized terror . . . Terror is an absolute necessity in time of revolution,' he insisted) declared war on the middle classes. Some 50,000
people died in the campaign unleashed in the summer of 1918, victims
of the most brutal torture and murder ordered by Lenin well before
Stalin. The anti-revolutionary 'Whites' also committed appalling
atrocities.

The civil war finally ended with a Bolshevik victory – largely because
of the organization and ferocity with which they fought, the passiveness
and terror into which the great majority of the people who did not sym-
pathize with them had been cowed and the disunity of the White forces.
Some 27 million people are reckoned to have perished in the eight years
Russia had been at war.

The communist victory over the Whites did not, however, signify the
end of the Russian people's agonies. Entirely misreading the mood of
their supporters, Trotsky and Lenin decided that 'war Communism' – a
central command economy established to support the war machine –
could also solve the country's acute shortages; soldiers could be mobilized against economic problems, as they had been against the enemy.
The Third Army, for example, was renamed the First Revolutionary
Army of Labour and worked on industrial projects in the Urals.

But the soldiers who had fought against reaction and for revolution
were not prepared to do menial work. Desertions and revolts spread. In
1921, a one-third cut in the bread ration almost sparked off revolts in
Moscow and Petrograd; in the western province of Tambov, the authorities had to quell, as murderously as usual, a rebellion by 20,000
workers; and in the spring, the 15,000-strong naval force on the
Kronstadt Island base off Petrograd mutinied, denouncing the regime as
another enemy of the workers. This revolt by the most fervent of revolutionaries was suppressed only when Soviet forces camouflaged in white
sheets stormed across the frozen river and inflicted an orgy of killing.

Once again, Lenin tacked. Expediency triumphed over revolutionary
ideology. The dull, inevitable tramp of history as sketched out by Marx
precluded the possibility of a retreat. But Lenin went into ideological
reverse without batting an eyelid. The 'New Economic Policy' unrav-
elled Communism. Private enterprise was to be encouraged. Companies
employing fewer than twenty people were denationalized. By 1923, no
less than 88.5 per cent of industrial management was in private hands.
Small industries producing consumer goods sprung up, while the few

heavy industries still under state control continued to suffer from poor productivity.

In agriculture, private enterprise was vigorously encouraged: peasants could trade their surplus production on the market and were given incentives to increase production. The *kulaks* – the richer and more productive peasants – flourished. The United States provided food relief to some 10 million of the 22 million Russians facing starvation in 1921. Indeed, Lenin had encouraged capitalist countries to trade with Russia by retreating from his support of world revolution at the Third Comintern Congress in January 1921.

By the following year, normality was returning, and yet as Lenin championed free enterprise, he knew he must strengthen his authority to retain control of his perplexed Bolshevik following. At the Party Congress that met in March 1921, Lenin insisted that it was essential 'to put an end to opposition, to put a lid on it'. A resolution forbade all forms of opposition and denied the Russian trade unions any say in industrial management. The congress ended with the first great purge of the Party. 'Careerists' would be weeded out by 'checking commissars'. Out of 730,000 Party members, 136,000 were removed – although nothing worse happened. The show trials and killings would come later, although Lenin, not Stalin, began the evil.

Lenin's appointment of Joseph Dzugashvili – commonly known as Stalin to the outside world and 'Koba' to those within his inner circle – as People's Commissar for Nationalist Affairs in 1917 demonstrated that the Soviet Union's recognition of the rights of the nationalities within Russia to self-determination was a sham. Stalin crushed opposition ruthlessly throughout the provinces. After Georgia, Stalin's birthplace, proclaimed its independence, its Menshevik government was given de facto recognition by the Allied powers in January 1921. Four months later, the Soviet and Georgian governments signed a treaty, but in February 1921 Stalin used the pretext provided by a rebellion within the country to send in the Red Guards; a Soviet regime was established on 25 February to bring Georgia back into the Soviet fold – with horrific loss of life.

What Lenin now intended to do remains a matter of conjecture. He had consolidated his power ruthlessly, abandoned most of his revolutionary goals at home and abroad and was master of a Russia now moving full speed back towards capitalism. His power, and the prospect of Russian resurgence after the last four dark years, seemed to rest upon

the continuance of capitalist methods. Perhaps, under the circumstances, he might have allowed his sense of self-preservation to smother
his unrealistic socialist goals and grown mellow in office, an autocrat
prepared to postpone his revolutionary dreams indefinitely.

But on 16 December 1922, a stroke paralyzed his right side. The illness
brought on a fit of remorse: his power machine might, in another man's
hands, become the instrument of tyranny – forgetting that he had
wielded tyrannical power himself. He realized, too, that the other man
might be Stalin: in January 1923, he wrote a withering criticism of him:
'Stalin is too rude and this fault . . . becomes insupportable in the office
of the General Secretary [of the Soviet Communist Party, as Stalin had
now become]. Therefore I propose to the comrades to find a way to
remove Stalin from this position and to appoint to it another man . . .
more patient, more loyal, more polite, more attentive to comrades, less
capricious.' Lenin feared that the rivalry between Trotsky, his old rival
but favoured successor, who had brilliantly, loyally, performed alongside
him during the Revolution, and Stalin would split the Party. In March
Lenin had another, worse stroke. His condition improved mildly in the
summer, permitting a visit to his old office in Moscow in October. But
in January 1924 a final stroke killed him.

The Revolution: International Repercussions

With the triumph of the Russian Revolution, Western 'bourgeois' countries had been deeply apprehensive. Could Communism spread? There
were two insurmountable obstacles in the West: the first was the comparatively sophisticated state of development, with a large middle class
and even the more prosperous part of the working class opposing revolution; the second the fact that Russia's revolutionary triumph had been
the seizure of power by one tiny minority from another in unique conditions imposed by wartime defeat. Tiny minorities were in no position
to seize power further west: in democracies such as France, Britain and
the United States the will of the majority prevailed; in other countries
there was a substantial conservative class. Unlike in Russia, with the
exception of Germany at the end of the war, in most countries the army
and the conservative machinery were intact to prevent revolution.

The country closest to Russian revolutionary conditions at the end of
the First World War was, of course, Germany. The January 1919 revolu-

tion did indeed break out with a general strike paralyzing the country and Berlin effectively being taken over by workers in the Spartacist uprising. This was the very reverse, however, of the conspiratorial seizure of power favoured by Lenin; it was undisciplined, spontaneous and horrified true Leninists like Rosa Luxembourg, who shortly before had argued that 'it would be a criminal error to seize power now. The German working class is not ready for such an act.' Nevertheless, she immediately urged, 'Act! Act courageously, decisively and consistently. Disarm the counter-revolution, arm the masses, occupying all positions of power. Act quickly!'

But unlike in Russia, the German army was still intact and not demoralized by defeat. By 13 January the German *freikorps* (unofficial private armies) under Gustav Noske, the Minister of Defence, had reoccupied Berlin and dispersed the revolutionaries after a brutal armed attack to recapture police headquarters and the despatch of armoured cars to threaten any group gathering on the streets. Later the same month, Germany held its first democratic election: some 30 million voted, the moderate majority Socialist Party winning 39 per cent of the vote and conservative parties much of the rest, with the mildly radical Independent Socialist Party winning just 7 per cent. The Revolution was clearly not for export to Western Europe.

Over the next couple of decades, Communism secured a toehold in two Western European governments: Léon Blum's Popular Front in France, where they were heavily outnumbered by bourgeois socialists; and during the civil war in Spain, where they played a vicious and disproportionate, if at times heroic, role in the Republican government holding Madrid, enabling the enemy, Francisco Franco, to tarnish it as a communist one. Nowhere – not even in elections in revolutionary Russia – did communists have the support of a substantial minority: the People's Party was simply not popular, which sharply limited its appeal to countries with universal suffrage.

Marx himself had proclaimed some seventy years earlier that 'the English revolution began yesterday in Hyde Park' after witnessing a violent Chartist demonstration in June 1855. But a week later he was forced to conclude that the 'slavish and sheepish' British workers were not the stuff of which revolutions are made:

Last Sunday the masses were confronted by the ruling class as individuals. This time it appeared as the state power, the law, the truncheon. This time resistance meant insurrection, and an Englishman must be provoked for a long time before he breaks out in insurrection. Hence the counter-demonstration was confined, in the main, to hissing, jeering and whistling at the police wagons, to isolated and feeble attempts at liberating the arrested, but above all to passive resistance in phlegmatically standing their ground.

In Britain, of course, the nineteenth century had seen the gradual evolution of universal male suffrage, with the Conservative and Liberal parties competing for working class support through the enactment of social reforms. In addition, the Labour Party had evolved out of a long tradition of trade union struggle, in alliance with Fabian intellectual socialism and the more moderate non-revolutionary elements of Marxist thought long separated from the continental mainstream (which itself had evolved into the non-violent socialist parties of Germany and France, with the violent, insurrectionary and revolutionary elements peeling off).

The Labour Party espoused the achievement of power through the ballot box, rejected all forms of violent and minority revolutionary rule, was intensely patriotic and after the First World War steadily grew in electoral size until it had overtaken the Liberals as one of the two pillars of the British political system. There was no incentive for a violent revolutionary seizure of power when the representatives of the working class could achieve it through legitimate democratic means. The small British Communist Party languished as a tiny minority, occasionally securing the return of an MP to Parliament, for the most part powerless and ostracized.

In the United States, the reaction to the Russian Revolution was to stage the first of the country's great anti-'Red' witch-hunts. A Socialist rally in Madison Square Garden was broken up after the Armistice, and 'sympathizers' with the Russian Revolution were beaten up. The Attorney General, A. Mitchell Palmer, launched raids on newspaper offices and private houses suspected of harbouring communist sympathizers. America's generous immigration laws were revised to screen out foreign carriers of this dangerous disease. In the United States the Socialist Party was only a tiny minority, and the Communist Party merely a just-tolerated splinter: organized labour – the bulwark of the socialist and communist parties elsewhere – was riddled with racketeers and professed its allegiance chiefly to the Democratic Party. To be a communist in America was equated with being unpatriotic – 'un-

American' – a virtual spy in the service of foreign powers. Of course there were significant communist cells in America, blown out of all proportion by their persecutors, particularly in the labour movement. What was entirely missing was popular appeal.

There were fears that this might be supplied by the Depression. But the closest America ever came to a popular uprising was during the 1932 'Bonus March' on Washington, when malnourished war veterans camped in Washington and were dispersed by the army, which tore down their 'city' of jerry-built huts outside the capital. There is no evidence that communists played a significant role in this, and little that this essentially peaceful demonstration was in any way a threat although the Chief of Staff, General Douglas MacArthur, justified his repressive tactics by claiming it was.

Again, the spectre of Communism raised its head in the United States during the early 1950s, with the investigations of the House Committee on Un-American Activities and the populist rantings of Senator Joe McCarthy. Again the threat, if there was one, was minimal: a few alleged spies in the State Department and some real ones outside. But it justified an anti-liberal witch-hunt in the press and entertainment industries that is still remembered today. McCarthyism said more about the American psyche than it did about the strength of Communism in America.

3

The Butcher

Wait for me and I'll return,
   only wait very hard.
Wait when you are filled with sorrow
   as you watch the yellow rain.
Wait when the winds sweep the snowdrifts.
   Wait in the sweltering heat.
Wait when others have stopped waiting
   forgetting their yesterdays.
Wait even when from afar no letters come to you.
   Wait even when others are tired of waiting.
Wait even when my mother and son think
   I am no more and when friends sit around the fire
drinking to my memory.
   Wait and do not hurry to drink to my memory too.
Wait for I'll return, defying every death,
   and let those who do not wait
say that I was lucky.
   They never will understand that in the midst of death
you, with your waiting, saved me.
   Only you and I will know how I survived.
It's because you waited as no one else did.

                        Konstantin Simonov

The Rise of Stalin

Even while the leader was alive but incapable, the leadership struggle had commenced. Initially there were four protagonists. Three of them, Leon Trotsky, Lev Kamenev and Gregory Zinoviev, were of Jewish descent. The outstanding figure was Trotsky – orator, man of action, and a towering intellect. He had also been a civil war leader – a defining moment in the hardening of the revolutionaries. His arrogance made him see himself as Lenin's natural heir; this alone ensured that the other contenders would gang up against him. In point of fact, Trotsky, having been defeated by Lenin in the first Soviet power struggle, was regarded as fatally flawed and on the way down by the new group of power contenders.

The bearded, studious Kamenev, a railway engineer's son who had bettered himself at law school, was a typical Russian intellectual; Lenin's hatchet man, Zinoviev, by contrast, was a loud-mouth braggart, a showy dresser and intellectual poseur, and the least impressive of the three. 'Whenever there was an underhand manoeuvre to be carried out, a revolutionary reputation to be tarnished, Lenin would charge Zinoviev with the task,' wrote a jaundiced Bolshevik observer.

The fourth man, Stalin, was the quietest and least visible; taciturn and hard working, he was an enigma, 'a grey blur floating dimly across the scene and leaving no trace' according to one observer. His modesty in person-to-person arguments made Trotsky dismiss him as the 'outstanding mediocrity of our party'.

Although earlier in his life, he had shown bravery and ruthlessness, he appeared to have a serious inferiority complex with regard both to Lenin and Trotsky, who outshone him in eminence and public identification. This resentment of Trotsky burst out during the civil war, when Stalin insisted to Lenin that Trotsky, as the Commissar of War, should not impose his orders upon the forces Stalin commanded in Tsaritsy. Stalin cabled Lenin to this effect, in particular resenting Trotsky's attempts to centralize control of the war effort and impose former Tsarist officers upon the men he commanded. Lenin's response was to get Trotsky's agreement to humour Stalin.

Lenin noticed too late that Stalin had amassed enormous power, first as commissar responsible for the nationalities from 1917, where he lorded it over 65 million people, then in his post overseeing the Party during the civil war. In 1922 he was appointed General Secretary of the Central Committee, while retaining his portfolio as, in effect, head of senior Party personnel, quietly infiltrating his men into key positions and gradually building up a Party machine that depended entirely upon his command. Only Lenin understood that in this new Russian regime, the man who controlled the organization might be king.

As Lenin lay dying, Stalin, to avoid a further broadside from the stricken leader, supported Kamenev and Zinoviev who had combined against Trotsky. At the Party Conference in April 1923, he modestly accepted Lenin's criticism of his handling of Russia's minorities and promised to do better. By October, as Trotsky began to find his succession blocked, the leadership contest flared into the open. Trotsky denounced 'secretarial bureaucracy, the principal trait of which is that the Secretary is capable of deciding everything'. He demanded 'Party democracy – at any rate enough of it to prevent the Party being threatened with ossification and degeneracy'.

In December Stalin and Zinoviev decided to publicly oppose Trotsky, and at the Party Conference the following month Stalin bitterly attacked him. The conference authorized a sudden expansion of Party membership to include some 240,000 new members of 'proletarian' origin, mostly loyal Stalin supporters. Kamenev's and Zinoviev's main weapon was to build up Lenin's cult of personality, downplaying Trotsky's achievements by implication.

At the Thirteenth Party Congress in May 1924, Trotsky, trying to defend himself, was angrily barracked. Zinoviev insisted he accept that he had 'made a mistake and the Party was right'. The congress concluded by denouncing 'petty bourgeois deviations'. Trotsky retired hurt, to fire off one further angry attack the following September. The ruling group dredged up Trotsky's youthful attacks on Lenin as evidence of his treachery so vehemently that Trotsky's health broke. Finally, he at last accepted defeat, resigning from the Central Committee but still refusing to admit he was in the wrong.

With the main threat removed, Stalin turned on his comrades. His final rise to power demonstrated how a man can unscrupulously manoeuvre from one end of the political spectrum to the other, irrespective of principle or revolutionary zeal. Stalin first tacked sharply to the right, towards a group under Nikolai Bukharin, perhaps the most popular of the Bolshevik leaders, although a political amateur. Whereas Stalin's previous position was that the peasants must serve the workers, Bukharin and his allies, Prime Minister Alexei Rykov and trade union leader Mikhail Tomsky, proposed making concessions to the peasantry to defuse their discontent – a peasant uprising had taken place in 1924 – so they would produce more food. He urged the richer peasants to work harder for larger profits, thus contributing to the well-being of the whole economy.

Kamenev and Zinoviev recoiled from Stalin's new view: they urged that the richer peasants be absorbed into large-scale collectives. Kamenev was soon ousted from his power base, control of the Moscow Party machine, by an appeal for loyalty to the General Secretary. But Zinoviev still had a firm grip on the Leningrad machine. He had reversed his stance as a peasants' champion to oppose Stalin. In December 1925, Kamenev publicly denounced Stalin for being unable to 'perform the function of uniting the Bolshevik general staff'. Stalin's carefully crafted resolution calling on the General Committee to 'unite around him' won the day, however, by an overwhelming 559 votes to 65. Within months, Zinoviev had been stripped of control of the Leningrad machine by Stalin's henchman, Sergei Kirov, who went to the city to appeal for Party discipline.

In spring 1926, Zinoviev and Kamenev, rubbing sore chins, proposed to Trotsky an alliance against Stalin, even staging demonstrations against the new leader. It was no use; they were stripped of their authority in the Party. By 1927 the three men had been expelled. Zinoviev and Kamenev were humiliated into apologizing to the Party. Trotsky would not stoop so low and went into exile, later to be murdered in Mexico.

Stalin extended his tentacles as Party Secretary. He controlled the Politburo, the guiding hand of the Secretariat, the central Party machine controlling the provincial parties that mushroomed from around 750 in 1922 to 20,000. Within it he established a secret apparatus connected with the OGPU (the United State Political Administration which had succeeded the Cheka as the secret police force). He also dominated the Orgburo, a shadowy organization that acted as his personnel office, seeking out talent and making senior appointments. The only major force outside his control was the army.

The Red Army had acquired immense power and status throughout the civil war; but while it lasted the army did not threaten Party control, being too busy fighting. However, in 1924 a regular army of 522,000 men was finally established and conscription introduced. Trotsky's old role as military commissar caused Stalin to doubt the army's loyalty. Trotsky had appointed men to senior positions not because of personal loyalty but because of their ability to prosecute the war.

Stalin made the army directly answerable to the Central Committee and shrewdly reduced the status of Lenin's political commissars who kept an eye on former Tsarist officers. This made Stalin popular among the officers, while altering nothing: the commissars continued to report back. Meanwhile, the Communist Party members in the army had increased by over a third to 200,000 men, many of them officers. The OGPU provided a further buttress to Stalin's rule; its chairman, the former Cheka chief Felix Dzerzhinsky, had become Stalin's loyal servant after Lenin's death.

The Secretary then turned, with exceptional ferocity, upon his erstwhile right-wing allies, led by Bukharin, Rykov and Tomsky. By December, 1927, Stalin had decided that he could both defeat them and entrench his policy of national socialism by reversing the policy of returning Russia to private enterprise: to proceed, in fact, with revolution.

His vehicle for this, the 'socialism in one country' doctrine first unleashed against Trotsky, proved a more popular rallying cry against his rivals than Stalin had initially expected. The token Marxist justification for socialism in one country – a repudiation of internationalism – was that, as Communism was clearly unable to make headway in other Western countries, Russia would have to advance towards socialist goals alone.

Thus anything that served the revolution in Russia, whatever its impact elsewhere, was justified; Communism and Russia's national self-interest had become identical. The crude attraction of the theory was, of course nationalist: Stalin was appealing to the gut instincts not just of the Russian worker but also the peasant, going back into history in seeking a different path for Russia than the rest of the world, a reversion to Moscow's Slavophile approach to the West.

The importance of the socialism in one country debate far transcended what most historians regard as its primary role: the excuse for Stalin to act decisively against Trotsky. This final great leap of the Russian Revolution from idealistic Communism to national Communism was the culminating moment in the process of Communism 'losing its innocence'. Liberties had long been taken with Marxism, notably by Lenin: in seeking an alliance between the urban proletariat and, to Marxists, the decidedly unrevolutionary peasantry, Lenin had already violated a sacred Marxist canon, justifying this as a necessary temporary alliance. Later, of course, the peasantry was to spearhead many communist revolutions across the world, for example in China and Cambodia; indeed 'Maoism' became the label for this particular heresy, one appropriated by peasant guerrillas right up to modern times, from Peru's *Sendero Luminoso* (Shining Path) to Nepal's Maoists.

But if Lenin had led the way, Stalin's heresy was worse. Marx had despised nationalism as a relic of feudalism. If Communism meant anything, it was internationalism. The *Communist Manifesto* decreed that 'the workingmen have no country'. Trotsky had merely stated communist orthodoxy when he insisted 'the real creation of a socialist economy in Russia will be possible only after the victory of the proletariat in the most important countries of Europe'. To Trotsky, it seemed that unless the Russian Revolution spread into other countries, it was doomed. Otherwise the bourgeois countries would isolate and overwhelm it, or – Trotsky argued – its culturally and economically primitive environment might corrode it.

But Stalin realized something Trotsky had not: Marx had been wrong – there would be no revolution in the developing societies of the West. In Britain and America there was barely a hint of revolutionary zeal. After the failure of the Paris Commune in 1871, the French bourgeoisie had ensured that there would be no recurrence of the conditions that might spark any further attempts at revolution, and in Germany, the fiasco of the Spartacist revolt of 1919 was followed by the even less promising uprising of 1923. Moreover, Stalin was merely being grimly realistic in tossing the torch of world revolution onto the pyre, as it gave him the excuse – the building of socialism in Russia – for the massive dislocations he would inflict on his country over the next few years.

Most significantly, he had harnessed nationalism to his rule. If the Russian revolution's purpose was no longer to ignite world revolution, then the only way a communist could be true to his revolutionary ideal was to defend the revolution inside Russia. Henceforth, the interests of revolutionary Communism were identical with, and subordinate to, the interests of Russia. By presenting himself first and foremost as a Russian nationalist in a country where homeland patriotism was one of the most powerful of all political emotions, Stalin had immensely strengthened his position.

But this had also hugely weakened the cause of Communism: not only did Russia time and again abandon its revolutionary allies abroad because of national self-interest, forcing foreign communist parties into embarrassing about-turns in support of Russian foreign policy – for example, most famously with the signing of the Nazi-Soviet pact in 1939, when communist parties were compelled to abandon their violent hostility to Nazi Germany overnight – it also became extraordinarily difficult to advance the cause of global revolution when its only practitioner was pursuing determinedly nationalist, rather than idealism-inspired, policies. The doctrine of socialism in one country was not so much a nail in the coffin of utopian Communism as the slamming shut of the coffin lid itself.

The irony was that although Stalin was right in the short term, in the long term Trotsky was; his prophecy proved to be uncannily accurate. For not only did Russian Communism become horribly corroded and disfigured – the state, far from withering away, grew to be all-powerful and murderously repressive – but Russia was indeed eventually surrounded and overwhelmed by its bourgeois enemies and their transparently more successful economies. True, this process took a full sixty years, but Trotsky had correctly forecast that Marxism would fatally lose its idealistic international appeal as a result of the doctrine of socialism in one country. Subsequent communist revolutions – often, as in the case of China, with only half-hearted support from Stalin – also followed determinedly nationalist paths, not least in rivalry with the unashamed nationalism of the Soviet Union.

This theory also allowed Stalin to justify his claim that Russia must build an industrial power-base equivalent to that in the West as quickly as possible. Thus, back to 'war Communism', instant socialism, the imposition of collectivism on the people – the very policies Lenin discarded in 1922. This ran counter to everything that Stalin had urged over the previous three years. But his was not a communist platform, but a nationalist one. He did not envisage a society of equals but rather a Russia which would overtake the rest of the world: only centralized planning, he believed, could achieve that. Apolitical, amoral, and respecting neither the Left nor the Right, Stalin's sudden ratting, meanwhile, on his old conservative allies ensured he could take supreme power.

This about-turn caught Bukharin, Stalin's other 'Himalaya' (his word) and virtual co-ruler, entirely by surprise. In July 1928, Stalin proposed expropriating the rich peasants in order to provide the capital necessary to build up industries: he cited the food shortages of late 1927 as demonstrating the inefficiency of the new capitalism he had just finished promoting. Bukharin won the argument after a furious exchange with Stalin. Lenin's new economic programme was endorsed.

Bukharin, rattled, went to see Kamenev, exclaiming that 'Stalin is an unprincipled intriguer who subordinates everything to his appetite for power. At any given moment he will change his theme in order to get rid of someone.' Bukharin denounced Stalin as the 'Genghis Khan of the Secretariat'. But by December 1928 Stalin felt secure enough to resubmit his proposals for full-scale socialism in Russia to the Central Committee. In February, after Bukharin had attacked the Party Secretary publicly in *Pravda* (literally 'Truth', it was originally founded as a workers' daily paper in 1912 in St Petersburg and became the official Communist Party newspaper in 1918), he and his allies were summoned before the Central Committee. At the following committee meeting in April Stalin denounced him. Obliged to accept the new policy or risk his life, Bukharin was gradually stripped of his posts. By the end of 1929, aged 50, Stalin was undisputed master of Russia: his personality cult, glorifying him as 'the Lenin of today', had begun.

Bukharin, in 1930, was dragged before the Central Committee once more, where although still partly defiant, he was a shadow of his former self. He frankly admitted to the 'fundamental mistakes committed by a group of comrades to whom I myself once belonged, mistakes which I have long ago repudiated and which I now completely disavow'. It had been necessary, he said, to engage in 'the crushing of a class enemy, of the kulak capitalist stratum . . . the Party's relentless and determined pursuit of the general line that gave us victory. At the same time – and it was absolutely right to do so – the Party leadership had to crush the most dangerous rightist deviation within our party.' Stalin's military henchman, K. Voroshilov, interrupted brusquely: 'And those infected with it.' Bukharin still had the force of character and independence to turn the remark back on him: 'If you are talking about their physical destruction, leave it to those comrades who are to one degree or another given to bloodthirstiness.' Laughter broke out in the room.

Bukharin then teased his persecutors, asking to be allowed 'to conduct a vicious struggle not only against myself but also against all of my former allies who are now getting away with the frivolous flight of the butterfly and with smirks'. He recited a ditty: 'They may beat me senseless, they may beat me to a pulp, but nobody is going to kill this boy, not with a stick or a bat or a stone.' Laughter broke out throughout the Central Committee. One of his opponents asked who the boy and the stone were. 'Oh how witty you are,' replied Bukharin. 'Obviously it was I who was struck and beaten with a stone. And now not a single member of the plenum, I dare say, thinks that I am concealing some sort of "stone" of resentment, not even the stone-faced Kamenev [*kamen* meaning "stone"].' Molotov, another Stalinist, icily interrupted soon afterwards: 'A little more modesty, a little more modesty, and less confusion.'

The pretext for Stalin's attack on his old right-wing allies was to become the real Russian Revolution. This had not taken place in 1918, or during the 1920s; Russians had no inkling of the terrifying disruption ahead. Stalin's goal was nothing less than 'the catching up and over-throwing' of the capitalist countries, a nationalist not a socialist aim, even if socialist rhetoric was conscripted to justify the mass national effort required. The Party Secretary, as his record showed, had no time for egalitarian creeds, or the spread of revolution; he wanted to be remembered as the ruler of a Russia that was a model for the world.

Stalin understood only too well that disruption in itself was a source of his power. If the Soviet Union were allowed to muddle along as a society dominated primarily by small private capitalists, the Party's hold on power would sooner or later be challenged; within the Party, if conditions remained static, more appealing leaders would emerge to oppose him. Much has been made of the dictator's personal insecurity. In fact, it was justified; and for this man with his quickness of wit but all-too-obvious personal failings as a leader – his intellectual shallowness, his less than commanding presence and his poor oratory – the fear of rivals was entirely understandable. He was forced to wrap himself in a cult of personality to obscure his own apparent lack of personality.

Stalin's seizure of power involved bureaucratic manipulation, promoting mediocrity and cutting down rivals more obviously talented than himself – all features of his merciless rule. This would blight the Soviet leadership for decades to come. Stalin was to become a tyrant and mass murderer presiding over a totalitarian regime – that is, one that sought to control every aspect of its citizens' lives. But his powers were not godlike or all-encompassing. He was the leader, rather than creator, of a Soviet ruling class, the *nomenklatura*, whose origins are explained by the historians J. Arch Getty and Oleg V. Naumov in *The Road to Terror.*

Since the early 1920s, full-time professional Party leaders had become the administrators of the country. They became accustomed to giving commands, enjoying privileges, and living well. The process of the formation of an official social stratum had begun. This had been the gist of Leon Trotsky's critique of the Stalin regime and one of the reasons the ruling elite had been so fierce in its destruction of Trotsky's group. This ruling segment of the Party, its elite, became more and more conscious of itself as a group separate from the Party rank and file and from the population in general. Self-selected and replenished by a system of hierarchical personnel appointments, or nomenklatura, the Party elite enjoyed increasing power, prestige, and privilege as time went on.

Technically, the word 'nomenklatura' refers to the list of positions, appointment to which requires confirmation by a superior Party body. Thus, the nomenklatura of the Central Committee was the list of high positions reserved for CC confirmation. With time, however, the word became a collective noun referring to the ruling stratum of the Party itself.

This nomenklatura in turn comprised several strata with different interests. It included members and staffs of the Politburo and Central Committee, first secretaries of regional Party committees, and full-time paid officials and organizers at many levels down to urban and rural districts. These various subgroups had differing parochial interests that sometimes conflicted with those of other nomenklatura groups, but they shared a group identity as insiders. They were the ones with power, great or small, whose membership in the ruling caste distinguished them from the multitudinous outsiders.

The nomenklatura's motives were varied. On one level, they jealously protected their position as the elite. If the regime fell, their various privileges and immunities would disappear. The more exclusive and authoritative they could be, the more secure were their personal fortunes. On another level, though, there is no reason to believe that they were not also true believers in Communism. In fact, there was little contradiction between the two. In the world-view they had constructed, the future of humanity depended on socialism. Socialism in turn depended on the survival of the Soviet revolutionary experiment, which depended on keeping the Bolshevik regime united, tightly disciplined, and in control of a society that frequently exhibited hostility to that regime. The long-standing Bolshevik self-image as 'midwives of the revolution' was alive and well throughout the 1930s. Even without crass self-interest as a conscious motive, this tradition made it easy to equate nomenklatura power with the good of the country.

Stalin was simultaneously creator, product, and symbol of the nomenklatura. As chief of Central Committee personnel, he controlled the most important appointments. But he was also a product and representative of the new official stratum; its members supported him as much as he supported them. As several scholars have noted, Stalin had 'won over a majority cohort of high and middle-ranking Party leaders' rather than creating that cohort. Trotsky agreed, and always maintained that Stalin was simply the representative of the new official stratum.

His growing cult was more than ego gratification. It was the symbol of the unity, common purpose, and unerring political guidance that the nomenklatura wished to project to the public. Stalin's cult helped to cloak their privileges, conflicts, and mistakes behind a banner of wise leadership and teaching.

Moreover, the central government was by no means wholly in control of the vast Soviet heartland, even during the 1930s:

> Transportation and communication were poor, and the regime's representatives were few in number, especially outside the cities. There was not even a telephone line to the Soviet Far East until the 1930s. In the relatively developed European part of Russia, most communications with Party committees were by telegraph or letters delivered by couriers on motorcycles. Weather, mud, and snow isolated numerous villages from any contact with the regime for months out of the year. Local Party officials frequently interpreted and misinterpreted Moscow's directives in ways that suited their local purposes. The Central Committee complained constantly throughout the decade about the lack of 'fulfilment of decisions' and spent a great deal of time creating mechanisms to check up on miscreant and disobedient local leaders.

Even as late as 1935 open dissent was voiced, for example by a member of the Komsomol (young communists):

> To execute sixty people for one Kirov [who had been assassinated] means that [Soviet] power is showing weakness by relying on terror to put down the growing discontent. I am absolutely sure that among the executed were many people who were completely innocent. Where is that glorious freedom here which the Bolsheviks ranted and raved about so much and which is in fact practiced in Germany and other countries, where every citizen can join any party he wishes without the risk of being executed for it? I hate [Soviet] power, which oppresses our people. I have really begun believing in the truth of Holy Scripture, where what is written is now being fulfilled.

Finally, it seemed that Stalin's personal supremacy at the centre was not completely established until his conservative rival Bukharin was put on trial in 1936, and until the military purges of 1937.

The Real Russian Revolution

So the real Russian Revolution began. The cost, unlike that of the Bolshevik coup d'état in 1917, was stupendous. Targeted at Russia's 100

million peasants, the aim was to destroy the power of the richer peasants, the kulaks, to drive a large number of the Russian people off the
land, and to collectivize agriculture, supposedly to increase its efficiency.
The traditional Russian peasant's death knell sounded on 27 December
1929, when Stalin announced that 'we have recently passed from a policy
of confining the exploitative tendencies of the kulaks to a policy of the
liquidation of the kulaks as a class'.

This uncontrolled wave of official disruption swept all before it. Some
5 million kulaks were deported to Siberia; more than 1 million died. At
least 1.5 million were killed as Stalin first despatched an army of 25,000
workers to drive the rich peasants off the land, then contingents of
poorer peasants to inflict murder against those better off and, finally, the
OGPU as agents of persecution. The peasants fought furiously, destroying rather than surrendering their livestock: of Russia's national stock of
34 million horses, some 18 million were killed. Nearly half the cattle herd
and nearly two-thirds of the national flock of sheep were butchered. This
appalling slaughter achieved its object: while in October, 1929, only 4
per cent of peasants had been persuaded to join collective farms, by July,
1934, more than 70 per cent of the peasantry had been forcibly collectivized. Bitter peasant rhymes expressed the anger. Two ran:

> Stalin stands on a coffin
> Gnawing meat from a cat's bones.
> Well, Soviet cows
> Are such disgusting creatures.

And:

> We fulfilled the Five-Year Plan
> And are eating well.
> We ate all the horses
> And are now chasing the dogs.

Stalin applied the brakes in 1930, claiming mendaciously that his
over-enthusiastic followers had been responsible for the excesses and
giving the peasants the right to withdraw from the collectives. Most
peasants, to his dismay, promptly did so. The proportion of peasant
households belonging to collectives fell to 24 per cent. Stalin hastily
reversed his policy reversal.

Meanwhile, to replace the slaughtered horses and to improve agricultural efficiency, the government began a programme to establish
Machine Tractor Stations, which only took off after a slow start. This

hurricane through the Russian countryside had, not surprisingly, the reverse effects of those intended. Production had actually fallen by 1933. Following a drought, the death toll in the winter famine of 1932–3 may have reached 2 million, which stemmed directly from the policies adopted by Stalin in 1929.

The holocaust in the countryside was designed to provide a massive labour force for industry. The industrial revolution, for Stalin, was just beginning. New blast furnaces disfigured the land, increasing steel output by two-thirds. Machine tractor power doubled. Coal production jumped by a quarter. Oil production jumped by a similar proportion and electrical capacity doubled. Heavy industrial production as a whole rose by 133 per cent.

This staggering achievement fired Communist Party members and many young people with an undeniable enthusiasm; many were genuinely proud to be participating in this economic transformation. Propaganda told workers' brigades to compete with each other – not for greater reward, but for honour in the eyes of the socialist state. To meet the desperate shortage of skilled workers Stalin launched a major training programme, setting up technical colleges that took in some 200,000 students by 1933.

However, the key to persuading workers to labour harder was coercion. Strict discipline was introduced into the factories. As peasants flooded into the cities, workers had to fight to keep their jobs. A day's absenteeism was enough to ensure dismissal. The advent of internal passports prevented peasants flooding the cities and urban workers seeking employment in another industrial centre. Piece rates, that classic form of capitalist exploitation, replaced timework in many factories.

Although this frantic industrialization under state duress could be justified in Marxist terms, Stalin was more intent in justifying it on his own terms: those of Russian nationalism. 'To retard the tempo [of industrialization],' he argued in 1949, 'this means to drop behind. All those who are backwards are beaten. We do not want to be beaten . . . The history of old Russia was, among other things, that she was beaten because of her backwardness. The Mongol khans beat her. The Turkish beys beat her. The Swedish feudal lords beat her. The Polish-Lithuanian nobles beat her. All beat her – for her backwardness. For military backwardness, cultural backwardness, governmental backwardness, industrial backwardness, agricultural backwardness . . . We are fifty to a hundred years behind the advanced countries. We will make up this gap in ten years. Either we do this or they crush us.'

The Party itself was next to experience Stalin's ruthlessness. M.N. Ryutin, a former Moscow Party chief, openly criticized him in 1932 as 'an unscrupulous political intriguer . . . to place the name of Lenin alongside the name of Stalin is like placing Mount Elbrus alongside a heap of dung'. Stalin ordered his arrest and demanded his execution – the first time so drastic a punishment had been suggested for a prominent Party member. Already, after show-trials in which Party members who had been tortured confessed to plotting against the regime, sentences of long-term imprisonment had been issued. Investigations, purges and uncertainty were becoming the norm. Between 1931 and 1933, the Party Control Commission investigated 50,000 members, purging 15,000. Vigorous purges also took place in the Ukraine, Byelorussia, Caucasus and in the Central Asian provinces.

By the Seventeenth Party Congress in January 1934, at which his old rivals Bukharin, Rykov and Tomsky were forced to admit their mistakes, Stalin's ascendancy appeared absolute. His only possible challenger was his protégé, the good-looking Secretary of the Leningrad Party, Sergei Kirov, who had urged a gentler pace in the gallop towards collectivization and industrialization and was said to be the choice of senior officials to replace Stalin. In December he was shot dead in a corridor outside his office by an assassin, Nikolaev, who was possibly put up to it by the security forces – although the real reason may have been Nikolaev's unjust dismissal.

The killing inaugurated the first really murderous purge to sweep the Party. Stalin's targets were veterans from the original revolution, whom he suspected of lingering sympathies for Trotsky, exiled in 1929 and now issuing his *Opposition Bulletin* from abroad. A close scrutiny of Party membership reduced the numbers from 3.5 million in 1933 to 2.3 million by the end of 1934 and below 2 million by January 1937.

At first senior Party members were lulled into a false sense of security when the OGPU, which Stalin feared was getting too powerful and independent, was dissolved. In its place came a People's Commissariat for Internal Affairs, the NKVD, under one Genrikh Yagoda, which existed entirely to do Stalin's bidding. By January 1936 Stalin was confident enough to release a secret document to all organs of the Party entitled 'On the Terrorist Activity of the Trotskyite-Zinovievite

Counter-Revolutionary Block.' The men in grey coats, later to become notorious around the world, rounded up thousands at dead of night.

In August the trial of the Six was sprung upon an astounded Russia; top Party members, it was assumed, were immune from capital punishment. Many idealists outside Russia who believed that it was constructing a perfect society were equally astonished. Others, although puzzled by the trial, refused to accept anything was amiss: since the accused promptly confessed, Stalin had been right to order their arrest.

The real sensation was the seniority of those involved, accused, ludicrously, of being 'white guards in disguise'. They included Zinoviev and Kamenev, falsely accused of Kirov's murder at Trotsky's instigation, found guilty and shot. Stalin's motive for a public trial stemmed partly from necessity: famous revolutionaries like Kamenev and Zinoviev could not disappear without explanation. But the trials also demonstrated Stalin's power to the world: he would not have moved against such eminent figures without complete self-confidence in his authority.

The trials were also 'pour encourager les autres'. Bukharin, Tomsky and Rykov were now placed under investigation. Tomsky, the leading, veteran Bolshevik trade unionist, promptly committed suicide. Rykov and Bukharin were denounced but, astonishingly, in December 1936, Bukharin defended himself, instead of recanting, against charges of issuing directives in 1932 to kill Stalin. Even more strangely, Stalin did not press the charges and the two 'Rightists' – those who thought Stalin had gone too far, too fast and too murderously, which may have included huge sections of the Party, particularly in the provinces, and the army – were not even arrested or expelled from the Party. The existence of such a debate on the Central Committee has remained a complete secret until recently and suggests that Stalin feared the backlash from the Right, particularly in the far-flung regions and, perhaps, from the army. Even at this moment of supposedly supreme personal power, Bukharin was still a potentially dangerous rival.

So Stalin moved quickly. His old Georgian crony, G.I. Ordzonikidze, who had opposed the execution of all his old comrades, suddenly was said to have died from a heart attack. Yagoda, the secret police chief, was despatched to run the post and telegraph service and replaced by a Stalin favourite, N.I. Yezhov. Terror swept the land, as virtually anyone who had been denounced by anyone else was arrested. As rumours of the secret purge spread, people accused their neighbours to curry favour with the authorities for fear of being denounced themselves. Tens of thousands were rounded up.

By January 1937, the trial of the Seven had been staged; directed at second-ranking figures it was designed to terrify the front-rankers who had escaped the last purge. After the horrors of their interrogation, the accused were only too relieved to incriminate themselves. Stalin's opponents did too little, too feebly, too late. By 1937 it was clear that his old comrades were seeking the help of their colleagues in the Red Army to halt the excesses and, maybe, to unseat Stalin himself.

With the purges in the provinces, Stalin at last felt confident to move on his old former co-ruler of Russia, Bukharin. The latter refused to plead for clemency by immediately accepting guilt and confessing, but brazenly contested the charges and went on hunger strike. In 1937 Yezhov accused Bukharin of instigating an anti-Stalinist manifesto (known as the 'Competing Discourse') in 1932 and that he and Rykov had at least known of the preparations for the Kirov assassination and were planning a 'palace revolution'. At the Central Committee session Stalin himself became chief prosecutor against the hunger-weakened Bukharin:

Khlopliankin: But why did you write that you won't end your hunger strike until charges against you have been dropped?

Bukharin: Comrades, I implore you not to interrupt me because it is difficult for me, it is simply physically hard for me to speak. I'll answer any question posed to me, but please do not interrupt me just now. In my letters, I described my personal psychological state.

A voice: Why did you write that [you won't end your hunger strike] until the charges are dropped? . . .

Bukharin: I won't shoot myself because then people will say that I killed myself so as to harm the Party. But if I die, as it were, from an illness, then what will you have lost by it? (Laughter).

Voices: Blackmailer!

Voroshilov: You scoundrel! Keep your trap shut! How vile! How dare you speak like that!

Bukharin: But you must understand – it's very hard for me to go on living.

Stalin: And it's easy for us?

Voroshilov: Did you hear that? 'I won't shoot myself, but I will die!'

Bukharin: It's easy for you to talk about me. What will you lose, after all? Look, if I am a saboteur, a son of a bitch, then why spare me? I make no claims to anything. I am just describing what's on my mind, what I am going through. If this in any way entails any political damage, however minute, then, no question about it, I'll do whatever you say. (Laughter). Why are you laughing? There is absolutely nothing funny about any of this . . .

Stalin: Why should Astrov [who had implicated Bukharin] be lying?

Bukharin: Why should Astrov be lying? Well, I think –

Stalin: Why should Slepkov [an obscure official who also implicated Bukharin] be lying? After all, that won't do them any good.

Bukharin: I don't know.

Stalin: No good whatsoever.

Bukharin: After Astrov testified, you yourself said that he could be released.

Stalin: You wouldn't say he is a swindler, would you?

Bukharin: I don't know. (Laughter). Try to understand now the psychology of people. You have just declared me a terrorist, a wrecker, along with Radek and so on –

Stalin: No, no, no! I'm sorry, but may I re-establish the facts? You were at the face-to-face confrontation on the premises of the Orgburo, and so were we, members of the Politburo. Astrov was there and some of the others who were arrested. Piatakov was there, so were Radek and Sosnovsky and Kulikov and others. When I or someone else asked each of these: 'Tell me honestly, have you given your testimony freely or was it squeezed out of you?' Radek even burst out in tears when asked this question: 'Squeezed out of me? Are you kidding! Freely, completely freely.' Astrov gave us all an impression of an honest man, so we took pity on him. Astrov is an honest man, who does not want to lie. He was indignant. He turned to you several times and said: 'You organized us, in your hostility you turned us against the Party, and now you want to wriggle your way out of an answer. You should be ashamed of yourself!'

Bukharin: I believe that all of these young folks are lying about me for a simple reason.

Yezhov: Why are they doing you in?

Bukharin: First of all, everyone who has been arrested thinks that I am the cause of their arrest.

Shkiriatov: But they are all testifying against themselves.

Bukharin: It's not that I informed on them, but rather that they were arraigned because I am under investigation.

Voroshilov: They were arrested before you were.

Stalin: On the contrary, at the first face-to-face confrontation, we included not only Bukharin but also Pugachev, the well-known military official, whose testimony we wanted to check. After all, a face-to-face confrontation is notable for the fact that the accused – when they show up at the confrontation – feel as follows: how wonderful, the members of the Politburo have arrived, now I can tell them everything in my defence. That's the psychological state which arises during a confrontation in the minds of those under arrest. I admit that the Chekists [secret police] do exaggerate here and there – it's in the nature of their work to allow for certain exaggerations – but I do not in any way doubt the sincerity of their work. Still, they could get carried away. But at the last confrontation, where the old minutes fully coincided with the testimony taken in our presence, I became convinced that the Chekists were working properly and honestly.

Petrovsky: Honestly?

Stalin: Honestly. After all, Radek and the others had the opportunity to tell the truth. We pleaded with them: in all honesty, tell the truth. I'm telling you the truth, even his eyes, the tone of his story. I am an old man, I know people, I have come to know many of them. I may be wrong, but my impression here is that he is a sincere man.

Bukharin: If you think that he told the truth, that I issued terroristic instructions while out hunting, then I won't be able to change your mind. I consider this a monstrous lie, which I can't take seriously.

Stalin: You and he babbled on, and then you forgot.

Bukharin: I didn't say a word. Really!

Stalin: You really babble a lot.

Bukharin: I agree, I babble a lot, but I do not agree that I babbled about terrorism. That's absolute nonsense. Just think, comrades, how could you ascribe to me a plan for a palace coup? Tomsky was to become Secretary of the Central Committee and the entire CC *apparat* [administrative structure] was to be manned by Slepkovists! Bukharin was allegedly always opposed to Lenin, he is an opportunist and so on, but is it conceivable that the entire CC apparat was to be taken over by Slepkovists? . . . There is nothing funny about the notion that Tomsky was being prepared for the post of Secretary of the CC, but there is something funny about the idea that the entire apparat was to be occupied by Slepkovists. It was a question of a palace coup in 1929–30 . . .

In Rykov's humiliation on the same charges, Stalin comes over as an implacable bully and persecutor:

Rykov: First, comrades, I must apologize if I cannot give a detailed answer to everything that has been said, because I did not have the strength to listen to everything and was absent part of the time from the room during the discussion of this question. The plenum is making what is for me, strictly speaking, the last decision. This meeting will be the last, the very last Party meeting of my life. From what I have heard here, this is absolutely and completely clear. But since I have been a Party member for over thirty-six years, this has meaning for my entire life. Accusations of the widest scope have been brought against me – i.e. criminal accusations which dwarf anything possible. And all of these accusations are considered proven facts. Many speakers have cited testimonies against me. In my first speech I tried to characterize these eyewitness testimonies. Not one testimony alone but five or six have been brought against me, and I wanted to prove that among these people some – for instance, Radin [a leading physician] – slandered me maliciously; certain others, perhaps, slandered me without malice, but, just the same, here I'm dealing with slander . . .

I cannot say what I said. But I assure you that if everything that people say is recorded with precision, if minutes have been kept over the course of the past five to six years, then I must tell you that they are lying. We ought not to believe that they can remember all this. There is no doubt in my mind that if they had retained anything in their memory, if anything had been stamped on their memory eight years ago, if, in the ensuing eight years, new layers had accumulated in their minds concerning this question, then everything would be forgotten and shrouded in confusion. I am not a jurist or a lawyer, but you will probably find a zillion examples in our legal proceedings of cases where a crime comes to light after several years and where innumerable major discrepancies, crucial discrepancies, appear in the testimonies relative to them.

Postyshev: There are no particular discrepancies.

Rykov: On the other hand, any discrepancy as to whether I was or was not a Trotskyist-murderer is no trifle for me.

Postyshev: There is no discrepancy here.

Shkiriatov: He was only talking about rabbits.

Stalin: There are those who give truthful, though horrifying, testimony but with the aim of shaking off completely the filth that sticks to them. And there are also those who don't give truthful testimony because they have come to love the filth which sticks to them and don't want to part with it.

Rykov: In moments such as these, under the conditions that I find myself now, you find yourself saying something that never was – just to get out of the dead end you are in.

Stalin: You have lost your head. What profit is there in it?

Rykov: What, what?

Voroshilov: Where is the advantage?

Stalin: What have we to gain?

Rykov: I am saying that here, in spite of oneself, one says something that never was.

Stalin: Mrachkovsky, Shestov, Piatakov [who had all been arrested] – they wanted to pull themselves out of the filth they landed in, at whatever cost. Such people ought not to be chastised as harshly as those who give untruthful testimony because they have become accustomed to the filth that sticks to them.

Rykov: That's true. It is now absolutely clear to me that I will be better treated if I confess. This is absolutely clear to me and many of my torments will also come to an end, at whatever price, just so long as it comes to some end.

Postyshev: What's clear? What torments? He is painting himself as a martyr.

It is significant that Stalin himself acted as the chief inquisitor against Bukharin and Rykov. This reflects the importance he attached to intimidating their natural constituency, even though the two may have long been detached from it and virtually powerless. Whether or not there was an organized conspiracy against Stalin (and it would be surprising if, in the Jacobin-like atmosphere of the Party, there was not) he certainly believed there was, and that it was linked to the army. Stalin said privately in 1937:

We knew something even last year and were getting ready to deal with them, but we waited in order to gather more clues. They were getting ready at the beginning of this year to take action. But they couldn't decide. They prepared in June to seize the Politburo in the Kremlin. But they were afraid – they said 'Stalin is beginning executions and this will cause a scandal.' I said to our people: 'They can't make up their minds to act,' and we laughed at their plans.

In retirement Stalin's loyal aide Molotov said of Tukhachevsky, the senior Soviet commander and a Soviet Marshal:

Beginning in the second half of 1936 or maybe from the end of 1936 he was hurrying with a coup . . . And it is understandable. He was afraid that he would be arrested . . . We even knew the date of the coup . . . 1937 was necessary . . . We were obligated in 1937 [to ensure] that in time of war there would be no fifth column. Really among Bolsheviks there were and are those who are good and faithful when everything is good, when the country and the Party are not in danger. But if anything happens, they shiver and desert. I don't think that the rehabilitation [by Khrushchev] of many military men, repressed in 1937, was correct. The documents are hidden now, but with time there will be clarity. It is doubtful that these people were spies, but they were connected with spies, and the main thing is that in the decisive moment there was no relying on them . . . If Tukhachevsky and Yakir [a general] and Rykov and Zinoviev in time of war went into opposition, it would cause such a sharp struggle, there would be a colossal number of victims. Colossal. And on the other hand, it would mean doom. It would be impossible to surrender, it [the internal struggle] would go to the end. We would begin to destroy everyone mercilessly. Somebody would, of course, win in the end, but on both sides there would be huge casualties.

Stalin moved implacably upon his generals. Commissars were reappointed as joint commanders alongside them. In June 1937 Marshal Tukhachevsky and seven other top generals were tried and then shot. Three marshals, twelve out of the fifteen army commanders, and 220 out of the 406 brigade commanders were purged, as were 35,000 officers, most holding senior posts, with many arrested and executed. Around half of the officer corps was affected – as it turned out, on the eve of war. Altogether, in 1937, more than 936,000 people were arrested, followed by 638,000 in 1938. Some 328,000 were executed that year, mostly for 'counter-revolutionary' crimes, bringing the total to around 750,000 in two years.

Stalin made clear himself that the Terror applied as much to families as to the accused themselves. 'We will destroy any such enemy, be he Old Bolshevik or not, we will destroy his kin, his family. Anyone who by his actions and thoughts – yes, his thoughts – encroaches on the unity of the socialist state we will destroy. To the destruction of all enemies to the very enemy, them and their kin,' he declared in a toast on the anniversary of the October Revolution in 1935.

The wife of one executed minor bureaucrat, Alexander Tivel, for example, was fired from her job, prevented from finding work and evicted from her apartment. She found refuge with her mother but, together with her mother and her young son, was subsequently exiled to Omsk in western Siberia. There, as 'a member of the family of a traitor to the Motherland', she spent nearly nine years in prison or labour camp, and then a further eight in exile in Siberia, her son having been taken away to an orphanage. Only in 1957 was the conviction overturned so that her son could escape being labelled 'a child of an enemy of the people'.

Having neutralized the army the security forces could move against Stalin's old enemies, Bukharin and Rykov. In March, 1938, along with Yagoda, the former secret police chief who had started the purges, they were put on trial on a succession of blood-curdling charges – conspiracy to murder Stalin, sabotage, conspiracy to assassinate Kirov, spying for Japan and Germany, plotting with Trotsky. Bukharin was even charged with plotting to kill Lenin.

This was the greatest purge of all: tens of thousands were arrested. The Gulag Archipelago dates from the period, the *Gulag* being the central organization that ran the labour camps. Largely concentrated in Russia's frozen, inhospitable (and hence under-inhabited) northern and Siberian territories, they were once thought to have held up to 14 million people. Hundreds of thousands died: those failing to meet their production targets were given only 300 grams of bread a day; those that met them received double and a hot meal. It was the largest reintroduction of slavery since Wilberforce inspired its abolition in the British Empire in 1833. Altogether around 3.5 million were arrested and 2 million died for political reasons during the 1930s, according to the latest evidence.

The view of Stalin held by many is that he was a mindless tyrant, a paranoid murderer for whom the slaughter of huge numbers of people when not an end in itself was evidence of paranoid brutality on a vast scale. A more considered view that emerges from highly significant recently released Russian documents compiled by Getty and Naumov suggests that there was method in his monstrousness. Specifically, after using Kamenev and Zinoviev to shoot down the fading star of Trotsky, then dumping them, he ruled in alliance with the moderate Bukharin before embarking on a radical nationalist course. Stalin was fearful of acting against Bukharin, who had a huge natural constituency, until 1935, when it became clear that a major anti-Stalinist reaction, also involving the army, was under way, the objective being the possible replacement of Stalin by Bukharin, the last credible 'old Bolshevik' leader. When he had assembled his forces, Stalin crushed this with over-whelming brutality. Throughout the decade following his deposition of Bukharin, it was not simply that Stalin perceived his position to be under threat, it probably *was* under threat – which explains, but does not in any way excuse, the savagery of the purges.

The postscript to this terrible era of power struggle and mass murder is the recently published letter Bukharin wrote to Stalin ('Koba') from his prison cell, at once undignified, pathetic and pleading, yet exhibiting a

humanity that suggests Russian history would have been very different if
he had taken the reins of revolution in the late 1920s instead of Stalin:

> I've come to the last page of my drama and perhaps of my very life. I agon-
> ized over whether I should pick up pen and paper – as I write this, I am
> shuddering all over from disquiet and from a thousand emotions stirring
> within me, and I can hardly control myself. But precisely because I have
> so little time left, I want to take my leave of you in advance, before it's too
> late, before my hand ceases to write, before my eyes close, while my brain
> somehow still functions . . .
>
> I bear not one iota of malice towards anyone, nor am I bitter. I am not
> a Christian. But I do have my quirks. I believe that I am suffering retri-
> bution for those years when I really waged a campaign. And if you really
> want to know, more than anything else I am oppressed by one fact, which
> you have perhaps forgotten: once, most likely during the summer of 1928,
> I was at your place, and you said to me: 'Do you know why I consider you
> my friend? After all, you are not capable of intrigues, are you?' And I said:
> 'No, I am not.' At that time, I was hanging around with Kamenev . . .
> Believe it or not, but it is this fact that stands out in my mind as original
> sin does for a Jew. Oh, God, what a child I was! What a fool! And now
> I'm paying for this with my honour and with my life. For this forgive me,
> Koba. I weep as I write. I no longer need anything, and you yourself know
> that I am probably making my situation worse by allowing myself to write
> all this. But I just can't, I simply can't keep silent. I must give you my final
> 'farewell'. It is for this reason that I bear no malice toward anyone, not
> toward the [Party-state] leadership nor the investigators nor anyone in
> between. I ask you for forgiveness, though I have already been punished
> to such an extent that everything has grown dim around me, and dark-
> ness has descended upon me.
>
> If I'm to receive the death sentence, then I implore you beforehand, I
> entreat you, by all that you hold dear, not to have me shot. Let me drink
> poison in my cell instead. (Let me have morphine so that I can fall asleep
> and never wake up.) For me, this point is extremely important. I don't
> know what words I should summon up in order to entreat you to grant
> me this as an act of charity. After all, politically, it won't really matter, and,
> besides, no one will know a thing about it. But let me spend my last
> moments as I wish. Have pity on me! Surely you'll understand – knowing
> me as well as you do. Sometimes I look death openly in the face, just as I
> know very well that I am capable of brave deeds. At other times, I, ever
> the same person, find myself in such disarray that I am drained of all
> strength. So if the verdict is death, let me have a cup of morphine. I
> implore you . . .

Iosif Vissarionovich! In me you have lost one of your most capable generals, one who is genuinely devoted to you. But that is all past. I remember that Marx wrote that [Tsar] Alexander I lost a great helper to no purpose in Barclay de Tolly [a leading Russian general – later a Field Marshal – in Russia's war against Napoleon] after the latter was charged with treason. It is bitter to reflect on all this. But I am preparing myself mentally to depart from this vale of tears, and there is nothing in me toward all of you, toward the Party and the cause, but a great and boundless love.

Bukharin's desperate pleas to Stalin on the method of his death were ignored; he was shot on 14 March 1938.

By the summer of 1938, Stalin judged he could call a halt to the purge; he would project himself as the man to save Russia from his own terror. In December, 1938, Yagoda's successor, Ezhov, became Commissar for Inland Water Transport; shortly afterwards he disappeared. The purgers were purged: 'Communist-careerists' prepared to extract 'false confessions through torture' were jailed, executed or sentenced to labour camps. Torturers sharing cells with their old victims found that their common, desperate plight made comrades of them. The harsh regime of the labour camps was somewhat eased, and some prisoners were released. Stalin had rescued his people from the terror of the 'fascists' who had mysteriously infiltrated his security services. And the people had to believe in him and his new image of the kindly uncle, because they had no choice.

Just as the exercise of power in the Soviet Union reached a peak of absolutism and oppression, Stalin had introduced a shamelessly democratic-sounding constitutional façade for the Russian system, much of it inspired less by Marxism than by those liberal Western ideals the Soviet Union decried. Another aspect of Stalin's insecurity, as well as of his cynicism, it marked the beginning of an attempt to improve Russia's image abroad. The constitution approved in December 1936 departed from the assumption that after collectivization and industrialization, the classes of Russia would no longer exist. Workers, peasants and intelligentsia, it asserted, lived happily side by side. However, the state could not be allowed to wither away, according to Marxist theory, because Russia was encircled by hostile powers. Here again Stalin used nationalism as a justification for his rule.

Because there was such class harmony, the Russian system could afford to be different from a 'bourgeois constitution'. The governance of the USSR, said Stalin, 'is the only thoroughly democratic constitution in the world', because it provided for democratic rule by the workers' representatives, the members of the Communist Party. The constitution gave the Soviet Union's eleven republics the right 'freely to secede'. In reality, they could not.

The Supreme Soviet, the new Russian parliament, had two chambers: one consisted of members representing constituencies of 300,000 votes, the other, the Soviet of the Nationalities, was biased towards the regions. Suffrage was by one-man-one-vote secret ballot. In practice, in Russia's first election in December 1937, only Communist Party candidates were permitted in most places. Turnout was 96.8 per cent and the Communist Party vote 98.66 per cent – some 90 million people. Every communist who stood was elected.

Formally parliament appointed the ministers. In practice Stalin did, and his lieutenants chose the parliamentary candidates. The constitution also contained a complex series of constitutional rights, provided they were exercised 'in conformity with the interests of the working class and in order to strengthen the Soviet system'. There was freedom of conscience and of the judiciary – subject always to the interests of the working class.

Apart from strengthening Stalin's already tight control, the main result of his purges was to create a new class of unromantic, managerial types a generation younger than himself; uninterested in ideology and loyal to a fault, they shared his vision of a more powerful Russia. Yet even they might not have survived Stalin's thirst to renew the men beneath him had not the war years intervened, causing minds to be concentrated at the expense of political rivalry, and giving Stalin a mantle of national leadership that visibly endowed him with the self-confidence he would display among the West's leaders at Yalta and Potsdam.

A British diplomat, Oliver Harvey, gives a vivid description of this terrifying man at the height of his powers:

> Stalin came padding in, very like a kindly bear. He is not very tall, hair slightly grey; he wore a grey uniform suit and walked quietly round among us all shaking hands without any sort of ceremony. There is nothing striking about him except his extreme simplicity and quietness . . . The old boy was most genial . . . He told [Anthony Eden] he always went to bed at 5 a.m. and got up at 11.30 a.m. We drank and drank – pepper vodka – which is like fire – wines red and white – champagne and

brandy. All Russian wine from the Crimea or Caucasus and we had 36 toasts in all. The two Soviet marshals (Timoshenko and Voroshilov) were obsequious to a shaming degree to Stalin. Timoshenko soon got very drunk and kept getting up and making speeches out of turn and going round to clink glasses with Stalin. Stalin said to (Eden), 'The better my generals are, the more drunk they get!'

The bedrock of Stalin's authority was absolute power and terror, reinforced by both the chaotic disruption and achievements he could identify as a result of industrialization. Stalin was not the initiator of Russian industrialization: starting under the Tsars, it had been interrupted by the First World War. But under Stalin, Russia took the giant step of becoming a significant industrial economy faster than any society had done before. Before the First Five-Year Plan (1928–32), some 75 per cent of Russians worked on the land and 15 per cent in industry. By 1939, after the Second Five-Year Plan, industry's share had jumped to 25 per cent and agriculture had fallen to 55 per cent. In that same year, the urban population was twice what it had been in 1926; twenty million had been forced from the land into the cities, so that Leningrad's and Moscow's populations had doubled, to 3.2 and 4 million respectively.

Collectivization, which had made such strides under the First Five-Year Plan, was pushed through to the bitter end. By 1940 97 per cent of all farms were organized into 250,000 collective farms. If the official figures are to be believed at all, collectivization was initially successful at raising production. The harvests during the first half of the 1930s sharply improved, marred only by the drought years of 1932 and later, 1937. Food consumption, which had halved between 1928 and 1932, returned to its old level by 1934. By 1937 it had climbed a further 9 per cent – hardly spectacular, but impressive enough in the circumstances.

This success had a number of explanations. After the disruption of the 1920s, things had settled down. The climate of fear in the countryside followed by a climate of political terror in the 1930s also ensured a certain degree of compliance. Centrally appointed Party hacks ran the collective farms, determined to ensure that workers served the needs of the state as decided by the central bureaucracy. Many of the new managers were not too bad and were strongly motivated to show results. A quota system forced the peasants to channel some of their food to the cities, allowing rationing to be abolished.

Russian grain lands were ideal testing grounds for modern planting and mechanization, barely tried previously. By 1938 there were 5,800

Machine Tractor Stations with 1.5 million people ploughing nearly three-quarters of the arable land and producing almost all the grain. Tractors usually transformed the yield, and their availability to all collectives ensured economies of scale. In addition, food production was boosted by the elimination of millions of inefficient peasant smallholdings and the transplantation of Russia's enormous surplus rural population.

Finally, for all the ruthlessness of the anti-peasant campaign, Stalin cleverly allowed a significant degree of incentives and private ownership to continue. The collectives were paid very little for the produce required for the cities but could sell any surplus on the open market. Farmers also were paid on the basis of time worked; productive ones got further bonuses and every farmer had the right to a small plot in addition to his collective holding. Most peasants, with little interest in the common weal, did as little as possible on the collectives; by 1939, an official survey found that some peasant plots had illegally absorbed 3.5 million acres of land.

For the workers, uprooted from the land, it was very different. The Second Five-Year Plan set up more realistic goals than the first, but was still ambitious. Industrial production was set to increase by around 16 per cent, compared to more than 20 per cent under the first plan, with investment in steel production more than doubled and machine tool production tripled. The clothing and food-processing industries had to expand their existing production fourfold. However, consumer goods production was also to be raised, despite the danger of denying investment to heavy industry.

Housing, which was appalling as workers thronged into the cities, was to be increased by a third and hospital capacity by 50 per cent. The second plan poured money into communications; railways and waterways were improved, new roads were built linking Moscow and Leningrad and air services, appropriate to the huge distances within Russia, were extended from 22,000 to 100,000 miles.

The work ethic was pushed hard, and workers were also given incentives. A Ukrainian miner, Alexei Stakhanov, was made a national hero for introducing a system – which would have made him a successful entrepreneur in any capitalist country – to keep the mine machinery working round the clock. Under his team allocation, he earned a month's wages in a single day. Workers could make money and be honoured – ultimately with titles like Hero of Soviet Labour and Diligent

Scientific Worker, giving them access to goods and perquisites not available to ordinary people.

Proletarian privileges were abolished. Privilege and class returned to Soviet life as part of Stalin's promotion of a nationalist, not a communist, ethos. Cosmetics production was permitted. Divorce became hard to come by. Abortion was banned, free love frowned upon and the family exalted. Children were taught to be obedient. Discipline in the schools was emphasized and competitive exams allowed. In higher education, a meritocracy that favoured the brightest – so long as they were also disciplined and loyal to the system – ruled the day. The Soviet Union's finest educational achievement dates from this period. In 1900 76 per cent of Russians were illiterate; by 1926 it was 50 per cent and by 1939, under 20 per cent.

Conformity now ruled in other areas as well. It was a long way from 1920, when the author and politician Anatoly Lunacharsky, appointed People's Commissar for Education in 1917, wrote: 'Revolution brings with it ideas of a wonderful depth and inner appeal. It lights up feelings of heroism and self-sacrifice. If revolution can give art a sword, then art must give revolution its service.'

Following a number of important cultural developments in the first decade and a half of the century, including the early Stravinsky ballets for Diaghilev, the rising reputations of the writers Maxim Gorky and Alexander Bely and the poets Anna Akhmatova, Alexander Blok and Sergey Esenin, the movement by the painters Natalia Goncharova and Mikhail Larionov towards primitivism and symbolism and the discovery of abstraction by Kandinsky and Malevich, the Revolution saw artists engage enthusiastically with what they saw as a new era of cultural freedom, and the opportunity to bring revolutionary culture to the Russian people. An outstanding feature of this mass propaganda exercise (in the words of the poet Vladimir Mayakovsky, 'Let us make the streets our brushes, the squares our palettes') were the posters, hugely popular and published in thirty-four towns, which utilized the creative and visual skills of, among others, El Lissitzky, Alexander Rodchenko, Vladimir Tatlin – the founder of Constructivism – and Mayakovsky himself. Officials and creative artists also travelled the country on 'agit-trains' and 'agit-ships'; the painters decorated the trains with appropriate messages, with one 'Literary Instruction Train' named 'October Revolution'.

Many of the leading cultural figure in the visual arts gathered under the umbrella of Constructivism, whose vocabulary of abstract, geometric forms and the use of industrial materials like plastic and glass proved an ideal vehicle for painters, sculptors, theatrical designers, architects, town planners and furniture designers. The twenties also saw the emergence of a constellation of gifted young authors including the short-story writer, Isaak Babel, and Mikhail Bulgakov. But perhaps one art form above all others sums up the excitement of those heady years after the revolution – the cinema (of whose propaganda possibilities Lenin was well aware) and particularly the work of Eisenstein. Technically outstanding – for example, in their editing – films like *Battleship Potemkin* and *October* (or *Ten Days that Shook the World)* have defined many people's image of the events of the Revolution.

Yet from around 1930 the ideological restrictions on cultural activity in Stalin's Russia grew increasingly sharp; officialdom decreed that artists should become virtual propagandists for the Communist Party and the state, and 80,000 censors ensured adherence to the Party line – every one of them fearful for their lives in case they missed some heresy not yet invented. In the visual arts the 'complexities' of abstraction gave way to the narrative simplicity and 'accessibility' of Socialist Realism, deemed to be more appropriate for the masses. While Gorky became a public supporter of Stalin (for whom writers were 'engineers of human souls'), the relationship of major figures like Shostakovich and the great poet Anna Akhmatova with the authorities was troubled, to say the least. Both, together with Prokofiev and a number of other writers and composers, would suffer virtual cultural exile after 1946 when Andrey Zhdanov, the cultural commissar and the Party's chief theologian, instituted a policy of even tighter ideological control with a strong anti-Western bias.

Shostakovich, Akhmatova and Prokofiev survived; but others did not, although Akhmatova had to write poems in praise of Stalin to facilitate her son's release from detention. The destructive pressure exerted by the communist regime may be measured by the fate of some of the century's finest Russian poets; in the sixteen years leading up to Hitler's invasion of Russia, Esenin, Mayakovsky and Marina Tsvetayeva committed suicide, while Osip Mandelshtam and the short-story writer Isaak Babel both died in prison camps.

The Second World War and After

The Second World War was sprung upon a Russia that had barely known peace in the twentieth century. The collapsing political system in the first decade, the hideous losses of the First World War, the upheaval of the 1917 Revolution, the horrors of the civil war had all preceded the Stalinist revolution. Russians were shell-shocked, accustomed to keeping their heads down and doing what they were told simply to survive. After that, they might have hoped for some respite and an improvement in their standard of living following modernization; instead, they got four years of war.

It was not Stalin's fault. He did everything he reasonably could to avoid being dragged into the war, making the awful mistake, in August 1939, of signing a non-aggression pact with Hitler to deflect the Nazi dictator's ambitions westwards, only to be attacked by the German armies two years later.

In one respect, Stalin had prepared his country poorly: the purge of the army had left it demoralized and ill trained, run by men with little experience of conflict. In another respect, though, Stalin had equipped his nation well. Russia's industrialization and mass mobilization had helped build an economy that could handle the demands of war. Discipline and strong nationalist sentiment also helped to see the Russians through.

Unlike Tsarist Russia, given the coup de grâce by the First World War, Stalin's Russia was unified in conflict around a strong, fearsome nationalist leader whose personal aura was only a shade less awesome than those of Ivan the Terrible or Peter the Great. Following the German surrender at Stalingrad (now Volgograd) in 1943, Stalin identified with the success of the army: military heroes became the stars of Russia. The Party was downgraded and communist goals virtually forgotten. Stalin now stood unmistakably for Russia, not revolution.

After Hitler's defeat in 1945, Russia staggered out of its war effort battered beyond belief. The Germans – and the Russians through their scorched earth policy – had destroyed some 3,000 medium-sized towns and 70,000 villages. Some 49 million people, according to recent authoritative estimates, had died, some 25 million were homeless and around 30,000 collective farms and 85,000 schools had been destroyed. Agriculture was devastated and the quantity of livestock drastically diminished – the number of horses by as much as half – from the desperately low figure during the collectivization period. The national stock of machinery was greatly reduced and the labour force scattered. Russia's industrial base, constructed at great cost, had been devastated: coal and electrical output were around three-quarters of the 1941 level; oil, pig iron, and steel around half; machine tools two-thirds, and trucks well under half.

Soon after the end of the war, Stalin's hopes of benefiting from post-war American aid through the Marshall Plan diminished as the super-power climate grew frostier. In the Fourth Five-Year Plan of March 1944 the masses had been exhorted to achieve the impossible: an increase in industrial production by half as much as before the war by 1949. Some 3,000 steel plants were to be rebuilt and 2,700 new ones to be constructed. Stalin's fifteen-year goal for Russia was to leapfrog the United States by tripling annual steel output to 60 million tons and coal production to 500 million tons.

In farming, the aim was more realistic: grain production, for example, was supposed to rise by 7 per cent above that of previous years. By 1952, the industrial effort had partly paid off. Output rose to two and a half times that of the pre-war period. Stalin had proved that the great resources of his country could be hammered into a modern economy, except as regards agricultural production, where improvements took much longer to show through.

Stalin became mellower, more relaxed and self-confident in his mantle as national leader during the immediate post-war period. He disregarded the formal organs of government – the all-union Party Congress, the Central Committee and the Politburo. The only political disturbance in Russia under his stern gaze, at the age of 66, was the jousting over the succession. The favourite was Georgi Malenkov, from 1941 until 1945 a member of the State Committee of Defence and subsequently placed in charge of the Party machine.

This efficient Party bureaucrat in the Stalin mould, a man overwhelmed by his master (otherwise he would not have survived), enjoyed Stalin's confidence. His principal rival during the 1940s was Andrey Zhdanov. This hard, ambitious man had pushed Malenkov into second place in 1946, but he died two years later and Malenkov returned as the front-runner, ahead of two rivals. One, Lavrenti Beria, was Minister of the Interior and head of the security service; but the latter, although a good training ground for those who aspired to the top, was not a power base in its own right. And Beria himself had too many enemies in the country and the Party.

The second was Nikita Sergeyevich Khrushchev, the Party whiz-kid. In 1929 he had arrived in Moscow from his native Ukraine; by 1935 he was the First Secretary of the Moscow Communist Party. Khrushchev had absolutely no interest in, or commitment to, ideology. An alert, dynamic, tireless man, he was a manager who wanted to get jobs done as speedily and effectively as possible. Of humble origin, his training had been that of apprentice fitter; by far the most human and attractive of the men in the Soviet leadership, he was the temperamental opposite of Stalin, the sinister behind-the-scenes manipulator. Khrushchev loved people, showing off, arguing, and putting his associates down. Occasionally in the heat of the moment prone to impetuous ruthlessness, he was more often disposed to be kind. He believed in winning his opponents over rather than killing them, and in practical solutions and new ideas, not old dogmas.

Khrushchev's period as proconsul of agriculture in the Ukraine came under fire from Malenkov in 1946, but he survived. In 1949, Stalin put him in charge of the Moscow Communist Party, to offset Malenkov. Over the next couple of years Khrushchev persuaded Stalin to enlarge the Politburo into a wider Party presidium, thereby bringing in new blood. It was already clear, as Stalin's terrifying reign drew to a close, that although Malenkov was next in the pecking order, Khrushchev was close behind. The communist system was not yet so stratified that power automatically passed to the natural heir. A man of authority near the top could yet make it.

Khrushchev, when he eventually climbed over Malenkov, completed a pattern of three entirely different types of Soviet leadership: Lenin, the power-hungry, organizational and conspiratorial genius, ideologically driven but prepared to change direction drastically once in power; Stalin, the outright power broker, uninterested in ideology, bent merely on personal power, who ruled with a previously unseen ruthlessness and authority, wielding far greater control than any Tsar. And Khrushchev, an altogether more twentieth-century figure who, in a Western country, might have been a successful democratic politician, content to govern rather than control.

Before then, there was a sting in the old dictator's tail. Khrushchev would later describe Stalin during this period as 'even more capricious, irritable and brutal; in particular, his suspicions grew. His persecution mania reached unbelievable dimensions.' More purges began. The 'Doctors' Plot' was uncovered, suggesting that American spies had infiltrated the medical profession and had helped to kill Zhdanov. The stodgy old Marshal Voroshilov, an ally of Stalin who represented the armed forces, Molotov, his tireless Foreign Minister, and Anastas Mikoyan, another crony, all came under suspicion. Another terror was on the way: this may have contributed to Stalin's genial mood one Saturday night, when he invited his top lieutenants to his lavish country dacha for dinner. By Monday he had suffered a stroke and was unconscious; by 5 March 1953, he was dead.

Stalin's Legacy: Russia and Eastern Europe

The Russia Stalin left was a country that could, possibly, be on the brink of something new. But the Russians themselves had not lived long enough in a peaceful, as opposed to a warlike, environment for anyone to say, conclusively, that Communism had failed. Stalin's successors might yet be able to make something of the original ideal. Yet, in most essential respects, the system Stalin bequeathed was barely Marxist at all. Politically, the state had not withered away, as prescribed by Marx: it had become more powerful than ever before, headed by a new autocracy with an overarching authority that had never existed under the Tsars. Moreover, Stalin considered the Party merely an adjunct to his own personal authority, with no decision-making power. He was literally all-powerful, like any Fascist dictator or absolute monarch.

Agriculture and industry were in the hands of the state. Theoretically they were in the hands of the people, through the Communist Party; in practice they were controlled by a machine dictating to the people from above. In terms of hierarchy, the reintroduction under Stalin of status symbols and ranks and decorations in the army marked the increasing dominance of bourgeois values among the ruling classes. All these things, it could be argued, were necessary in the turbulence of post-revolutionary Russia.

Now the country was to enjoy an unbroken half-century of peace. The climate existed for the construction of a new society. Moreover, now there was a difference: Russia was no longer alone in the world.

It had been 'joined' by the liberated countries of Eastern Europe. In reality, Russia had merely annexed them. When visiting Moscow in

1944, Churchill remembered how the first draft of the division of Europe was drawn up.

'So far as Britain and Russia are concerned, how would it do for you [Stalin] to have 90% predominance in Romania, for us to have 90% of the say in Greece, and we go 50-50 on Yugoslavia?' While this was being translated, I wrote out on the half-sheet of paper: 'Romania – Russia 90%, the others 10%; Greece – Great Britain, 90%, Russia 10%; Yugoslavia – 50-50%; Hungary – 50-50%; Bulgaria – Russia 75%, the others 25%.'

I put this across to Stalin, who by then had heard the translation. There was a slight pause. Then he took his blue pencil and made a large tick upon it and passed it back to us . . . At length I said, 'Might it not be thought rather cynical if it seemed we had disposed of these issues, so fateful to millions of people, in such an offhand manner? Let us burn the paper.'

'No, you keep it,' said Stalin.

Stalin broke his side of the bargain: but both men knew that the extension of Soviet influence would amount to the communist colonization of Eastern Europe: the countries involved would have no opportunity to choose their system of government. Since Communism was to be spread by armed force from outside, Russia could not claim in any real sense to be exporting revolution from below. The domination of Eastern Europe was dictated not by any revolutionary ideal, but by Stalin's obsession with secure boundaries for Russia, and with castrating Germany once and for all.

The absorption of Poland followed a similar pattern. With the cruelty of a tartar warlord, Stalin had paused in 1944 to allow 20,000 Poles in Warsaw to be slaughtered by Hitler to decimate the free Polish movement and allow his communist stooges to take power. After 1956, however, Polish nationalism bubbled up so vigorously that the Russians had to meet the Poles halfway, allowing the nationalist Wladyslaw Gomulka to take office provided that he kept the country in the Warsaw Pact, set up by the Russians to tighten their hold on communist Eastern Europe in 1955.

In Hungary, it quickly became apparent that the Communist Party, with little domestic support, was kept in power only by force of outside arms. The communists' economic policy brought about a large drop in living standards, as agricultural production fell catastrophically and industrial production stagnated. By 1956 the country was approaching an explosion. Khrushchev's liberalization followed by the overthrow of the Party boss, Matyas Rakosi in July, gave Hungarians hope that change was at hand. However, the ruling group became seriously alarmed, and tried to screw the lid down again, banning meetings and demonstrations in October.

When police fired on crowds in Budapest, hundreds of thousands of workers went on strike, setting up revolutionary committees and demonstrating to reinstate the liberal communist Imry Nagy, briefly Prime Minister in 1954. Nagy was swept to power and formed a coalition with other political groups: the system seemed to be becoming democratic. When large parts of the army decided to support the Nagy government, the Russians decided to invade. On 4 November the Soviet tanks went in. Janos Kadar, a liberal communist who had suddenly betrayed Nagy, was installed. He began by ruling through terror: the death toll in the hopeless cause of resisting Russian tanks had been high enough. Thousands of strike leaders and intellectuals were arrested and Nagy and other politicians were secretly executed.

The uprising in Hungary could, in Marxist-Leninist terms, be explained away: after only a decade of Stalinist rule, the Hungarian people still retained their class loyalties. Yet such resistance to socialism was dismaying. Some Hungarian communists, trying to explain the phenomenon, observed that the 1956 uprising was due to purely anti-Russian nationalist feeling. None dared suggest that the country was too advanced for Communism to survive other than by coercion.

Although the communist seizure of power in Czechoslovakia was slower, democracy was blatantly violated. In relatively free elections in 1946, the Czech Communist Party had emerged on top, yet the non-communist parties were allowed to continue. The communists had a coalition with the Social Democrats, some of whose ministers – for example, the minister of justice – refused to endorse the bullyboy tactics of the police. The coalition collapsed. When the Social Democrats ousted a temporary pro-communist leader and installed a more independent man, the Russians had had enough: the Party, with Soviet tanks standing by on the country's border poised to invade, organized mass demonstrations and seized effective power. The non-communist parties were dissolved. Jan Masaryk, the Foreign Minister, fell to his death from his office. The ailing democratic President Benes was succeeded in June 1948 by Klement Gottwald. Antonin Novotny, the pro-Russian Party chief, became the country's effective ruler.

Bulgarian Communism got off to a relaxed start, only to become the tightest in Eastern Europe, with 95 per cent of its farms collectivized by the mid-1950s. General Kimon Georgiev was allowed to remain Prime Minister of Bulgaria for two years after the war, even though he was a visceral anti-communist; the 9-year-old King Simeon II was not exiled until the autumn of 1946.

Yet from the beginning the Party took control of the security police, the media, the army and the Ministry of the Interior. They also infiltrated the Peasant Party, the main left-of-centre grouping in Bulgaria, and forced it into an alliance. In 1945 the Social Democratic Party was suppressed and its newspaper seized. By 1947 the communists had announced that they would no longer tolerate opposition, and the Party started putting some of its opponents to death. From then on a rigid Stalinist clampdown was imposed, and Bulgaria's system of government was carbon-copied from Russia's.

Romania followed a slightly different path, after starting in much the same direction. The Russians in Romania had behaved like occupying proconsuls: the Russian representative, Marshal Vyzinsky, insisted in March 1945 that the Prime Minister, General Radescu, be replaced by Petru Groza, a communist strongman from an aristocratic background. The Peasant Party, with a larger following than the communists, was dissolved and its leaders arrested in 1947.

After that, grim Stalinism prevailed, while the Romanian economy continued to perform at a bare minimum. Khrushchev eased the grip. After the Stalinist leaders, Anna Pauker and Vaske Luca, were purged, the more pragmatic Gheorgiu Dej was allowed to take control. In 1958 the occupying Russian army withdrew. Dej pushed hard to lessen Romania's dependence on Russia: reparations paid to Russia ceased, and the Russian-Romanian companies, which channelled the country's wealth, such as it was, into the Soviet Union, were dissolved. However, Dej continued centralized economic planning, and the government's repressive machinery remained as vicious as ever.

Dej put Romania on the road to virtual independence. In April 1964, the Romanian Communist Party declared that all socialist states were equal, independent and sovereign. Dej's successor, Nicolae Ceausescu, carried this further, and even criticized the Russian invasion of Czechoslovakia, although he carefully refrained from over-provoking the Russians. Ceausescu got away with it because the Russians approved of the harshness of his regime. The spartan Romanian model was unlikely to appeal to anyone, whereas the more liberal Czech and Polish models were potentially infectious.

Two countries that escaped the Soviet embrace were Austria and Greece, neither claimed by Stalin as within his sphere of influence at Yalta. But the Russians continued to occupy part of the former right up to 1955, with Vienna becoming a byword for espionage and contraband. In that year the four occupying powers signed a treaty guaranteeing Austrian neutrality and withdrawing their forces from the country. The treaty was an early boost for Nikita Khrushchev, who claimed he had traded 'boy's pants for adult's trousers' during the negotiations. Although Austria's porous borders with Eastern Europe – often used as an escape route for Easterners heading west – remained an irritant to the Russians, they scrupulously respected the neutrality agreement.

In Greece, the communist National Popular Liberation Army controlled much of Greece after the Nazi withdrawal had left the country bruised and bleeding. The British sent forces to support the monarchy against what seemed an imminent communist takeover, and civil war broke out. The Russians at Yalta had agreed to leave Greece to the West and refused to support their communist allies, but backing was forthcoming from Tito's Yugoslavia. The Greek communists refused to participate in the 1946 election and the civil war dragged on bitterly for three years. At last Tito realized that it was unwinnable and ended his support for the guerrillas, who came to the negotiating table.

Albania's 2.5 million people were of little concern to any of the great powers. In 1946, communist guerrillas seized power and declared the country independent. While practising vigorous Stalinist repression, they bitterly opposed the Serb-led Yugoslav federation to the north whose sheer size protected them from Russian interference. Gradually they evolved links with the Chinese communists after the latter came to power, thereby asserting their independence of all European blocs. The obscurantist regime of Enver Hoxha effectively cut off the little mountain state from the outside, turning it into an isolated redoubt of primitive Communism. Desperate refugees seeking to escape to Corfu or Italy told of grinding poverty and harsh repression; not until the 1990s was this hermit state free at last.

Yugoslavia

Yugoslavia proved to be the exception. By 1945 in a sense both Yugoslavia and tiny Albania represented the only authentic expansions of world Communism – the others had been imposed by Soviet military might – since the 1917 revolution. The anti-German resistance in Yugoslavia had been led by Tito's partisans, who seized effective control as soon as the Germans left. Tito had not been installed by the Russians and refused to kowtow to them. In particular, Tito felt that if the Russians moved into his country, he could wage just as effective a guerrilla war against them as he had against the Germans. Stalin was well aware of the resistance that would ensue if he tried to occupy Yugoslavia.

Tito was a tough hardline Marxist-Leninist: he urged the spread of revolution, and could not understand Stalin's agreement to limit this at Yalta. In March 1948 the disagreement between Tito and the Soviet Military Mission in Yugoslavia resulted in the latter being withdrawn. Stalin denounced Tito as a 'Trotskyist' and a 'nationalist' – accusations with more than a grain of truth. The Russians also accurately – if ironically – chided him for suppressing democracy within the Communist Party. By June, the Party had been expelled from Cominform (the Russian-inspired propaganda agency for international Communism established in 1947 by Andrey Zhdanov that had effectively succeeded the Comintern, dissolved three years earlier), and economic agreements between Yugoslavia, Russia and its Eastern European satellites had been torn up.

As the quarrel with Russia became increasingly bitter, Tito decided to emphasize his independence and capitalize on his popular support by creating a more representative form of Communism: firms were given greater freedom from central state control and workers' councils established to run factories. Tito even tried cracking down on the abuse of power by senior Communist Party officials.

The Yugoslav economic and political experiment resulted from the need, after the break with Russia, to define an entirely new course, partly because the Cominform imposed an economic blockade, forcing Yugoslavia to trade with the West. Furthermore, changes in the Yugoslav economy, initially modelled on the Soviet one, were clearly required. Largely, though, Tito realized that he needed an alternative theory to justify the break with Stalinism to his own party and other communists as well. When the Russians accused the Yugoslav Communist Party of focusing on 'conspiratorial' resistance rather than democracy, Tito was determined to show that his party was a great deal less conspiratorial than the Soviet one.

He decided to go for economic reform only later: not until 1949, for example, did he resolve to press ahead with collectivization, the number of collective farms jumping fourfold from 1,700 to some 7,000, with 2 million peasants and 930,000 acres – one-fifth of agricultural land in Yugoslavia – affected. Inevitably, production fell sharply and livestock was slaughtered. Total agricultural production fell to 73 per cent of the pre-war level, grain production to just 41 per cent. Nationalization of industry also proceeded rapidly: there were 2 million working in state-owned industries in 1949, compared with under 500,000 in 1945. The Yugoslavs used forced labour – 'class enemies' – for major projects like the Belgrade to Zagreb highway. However, after the initial success in post-war industrial reconstruction, bureaucratic hardening of the arteries set in.

Western aid prompted the Yugoslavs to consider reform. In 1950 President Truman issued the Yugoslav Emergency Relief Act, to help what he considered to be 'the sole independent communist country'. The same year, Tito summoned his colleagues to find a different path to socialism from the Soviet Union's. Tito's eight Politburo colleagues put their heads together. Milovan Djilas, an intellectual and the propaganda chief, says he read Marx carefully and proposed a 'free association of producers' – independent facilities subordinate to the state only in that they paid taxes, but otherwise representative of the workers.

Djilas recounts: 'Tito paced up and down, as though completely wrapped in his own thoughts. Suddenly he stopped and exclaimed: "Factories belonging to the workers – something that has never yet been achieved!" With these words the theories worked out by Kardelj and myself seemed to shed their complications and seemed to find better prospects of being workable. A few months later, Tito explained the Workers' Self Regulation Bill to the National Assembly.' Suddenly it had become the rage to proclaim 'decentralization, debureaucratization and workers' self-management'.

This new thinking quickly affected the system. By 1950 the collectivization of agriculture had stopped and the Party was returning to the old-style cooperatives, with joint marketing and machinery based on peasant plots, with which the peasants could do whatever they wanted. Three years later, Yugoslav agriculture had virtually returned to private hands. By the end of 1953 only 1100 collectives were left, as peasants rushed to lease them. In industry, consultations between the state and workers' representatives led to the formation of workers' councils, and the decentralized federal government shed 100,000 jobs.

In June 1950, the state economic enterprises formally became the property of the workers: the workers' councils acted as a kind of shareholders' meeting, approving the balance sheets and appointing managers to run the business. In practice senior managers were nominated by central government, but retained considerable autonomy. The five-year plan concept was replaced by annual plans, in which the state could suggest – but not direct – industrial priorities and investment.

Quotas were abolished. Companies now competed for customers, were loaned capital by the government and had to repay the interest. Industrial grants were ended, to encourage efficiency. Foreign investment was promoted, and grew strongly. By 1953 the economy was flourishing, while national income was growing by 19 per cent; the boom would last a decade.

Milovan Djilas, one of the reforms' organizers, looked further ahead: if economic decentralization was possible, if pluralism could be allowed in farming and to a lesser extent in industry, why not in politics? 'The class structure of society has changed,' he argued, 'but the theory remains more or less unchanged . . . Continuing the struggle against the bourgeois reaction . . . must not deviate into bureaucratism, into conflict with plain people because they hold differing opinions . . . Stories about raising the class struggle above the law and in spite of the law could undermine legality and democracy.' Djilas favoured 'socialist democracy', with plenty of discussion.

He had misjudged his man. Tito was prepared to quarrel with Stalin and to chart his own independent socialist course, but would not brook any challenges to his political grip. Djilas, in Tito's view, ignored the danger posed by the class enemy. 'The class enemy exists . . . in the very breast of the league of communists, and assumes the most varied forms' – including that of Djilas himself, who was purged and imprisoned.

The fall of the king's favourite froze political development for years. Yet Tito successfully proved that a government could relax its economic grip, while retaining an authoritarian political system, a lesson that would be lost on most of Yugoslavia's Eastern European partners.

The mixture worked so long as the economy boomed. Employment shot up from 1.8 million in industry in 1950 to 2.4 million in 1951. Iron, steel and machine tool production tripled. Only consumer goods lagged behind. The boom gathered momentum towards the end of the decade: state sector production rose by 62 per cent, private consumption by nearly 50 per cent. Economic growth was the second highest in the world. The outcome of the experiment prompted Tito to go for greater freedom still. By 1957 the catchwords were 'freer income distribution' and 'the strengthening of enterprise independence'.

By 1958 worker profit sharing had become 'income sharing', which in practice meant straightforward differential pay. Companies were free to determine wage and profit levels and to invest as they saw fit, becoming, to all intents and purposes, operationally independent.

A further set of reforms was enacted in 1965, by which price differentials were further increased – with the result that many goods became available only to the rich in Yugoslav society. The state ceased to be the sole provider of investment and stopped subsidizing industry, which reduced the state's tax 'take' of the national income from around 49 per cent to 29 per cent. Private peasants were given access to credit and equipment. Vested state interests campaigned furiously against the reforms, however, and only after a bitter struggle were they made to stick. Their results were decidedly mixed, and largely reversed by 1968. Yugoslavia seemed to have reached a level of equilibrium as a mixed economy, yet by the 1970s it was growing again at a reasonable rate.

When Tito died in 1980, the main problem he left was the succession. He set up a complicated collective leadership apparatus in 1978, in which office-holders were rotated regularly: the Prime Minister, Mrs Milko Planic, was given a four-year term of office. But the presidency was collective and changed hands every twelve months. Some daring reformers advocated, after Tito's death, that there should be direct elections for the various parliaments instead of the indirect structure of votes to federal, republican and local assemblies. Others even suggested that a second political party be set up. The temptation seemed likely to be resisted. Democracy would not just challenge the vested interests of the communist institutional hierarchy, but would arouse the ire of the Russians – although even they would think twice about invading mountainous Yugoslavia.

But the race to keep living standards growing meant Yugoslavia had accumulated huge foreign debts of around $18 billion. When the economy staggered to a stop in the early 1980s, inflation shot up to 30 per cent, unemployment to 13 per cent and shortages materialized, although not as acute as in other Eastern European countries. This gallop downhill convinced many Yugoslavs that there was a need for further economic liberalism, to reduce in particular the government's massive spending: yet the goals of reducing unemployment and containing inflation were probably incompatible. Many reformers suggested that the country had to learn from peasant farming; the country's 4.3 million private farmers cultivated 85 per cent of agricultural land and raised 90 per cent of all livestock. Few could envisage the terrible nationalist hatreds that would unravel Tito's inheritance.

Berlin

The limits to Communism's western expansion were finally to be drawn in Germany. The country had been placed under four-power control in distinct zones. Berlin, the former German capital, was well within the Russian zone, but was split between the occupying powers, although the Americans soon resolved to avoid the mistakes of the post-First World War era and rebuild Germany. As the American Secretary of State, James F. Byrne, expressed it: 'The American people want to return the government of Germany to the people of Germany. The American people want to help the German people to win their way back to an honourable place among the free and peace-loving nations of the world.' The British largely agreed, although the French, still fearful of Germany, did so with much less enthusiasm.

To Stalin, however, crippling Germany by permanent division was eminently desirable, with the American stance merely an attempt to enlist Germany's support against Russia. By early 1948 the Western allies had concluded that a unified Germany was impossible and decided to create a West German state with its own currency to end the terrible privations of its people and to 'hold Europe against Communism'. On 7 June 1948 they authorized its establishment and secretly prepared to circulate a new currency.

But on 24 June the Russian commander in Berlin, General Vassily Sokolovsky, blockaded the city, cutting off all road, rail and canal links to West Germany. At first it seemed the Russians had called the West's bluff: the city needed some 12,000 tons of supplies a day to survive. Two days later the Berlin Airlift began, initially providing no more than a twelfth of the city's needs. Often buzzed by Soviet planes, old, rickety aircraft flew in through all kinds of weather, landed at two overcrowded airfields, unloaded and took off in minutes.

A new airfield was built: by October the tonnage had expanded to some 4,500 a day. With electricity limited to four hours a day, enough coal was brought in to keep the population from freezing, although luckily the winter was mild. By the spring of 1949, some 8,000 tons a day were being landed. In May, just after a year, the blockade was lifted. The West had signalled its determination to make a stand against Stalin. But he had frozen East Germany into part of the Soviet satellite system, and the country was to remain divided for another four decades.

4

The Dreamer

There was an old man in north China in ancient times, by the name of Yu Kung [foolish old man] of the north mountain. His house faced south and its doorway was obstructed by two big mountains. With great determination he led his sons to dig up the mountains with pickaxes. Another old man, Chih Sou [wise old man] witnessed their attempts and laughed, saying 'What fools you are to attempt beyond your capacity.' Yu Kung replied, 'When I die, there are my sons, and so on to infinity. As to these two mountains, high as they are, they cannot become higher but, on the contrary, with every bit dug away, they will become lower and lower. Why can't we dig them away?' Mr Yu Kung refuted Mr Chih Sou's erroneous view and went on digging at the mountains day after day without interruption. God's heart was touched by such perseverance and he sent two celestial beings down to earth to carry away the mountains on their backs.

Now there are also two big mountains lying, like dead weights on the Chinese people: imperialism and feudalism. The Communist Party long ago made up its mind to remove them. We must work persistently, work ceaselessly, and we may be able to touch God's heart. This God is none other than the masses of the people throughout China. And if they rise and dig together with us, why can't we dig these two mountains up?

The Young Mao

To Mao Zedong (Mao Tse-tung), who told this parable, politics was the art of the impossible. When he came to power in 1949, he had achieved it. He had, for a start, led an army through one of the most awesome ordeals of history to escape annihilation, dwarfing Hannibal's crossing of the Alps and presenting this communist milestone as a great victory; in reality, the Long March (1934–35) salvaged a great failure.

The march was undeniably epic. Mao described traversing passes some 15,000 feet up through deep snow: 'we kept reaching down to pull men to their feet only to find they were already dead'; they waded across swamps where men had to sleep standing in pairs or groups of four, back-to-back so as not to drown in mud. And they crossed, altogether, eighteen mountain ranges and twenty-four rivers. And as if nature's opposition was not enough, 'For twelve months we were under daily reconnaissance and bombing from the air by scores of planes. We were encircled, pursued, obstructed and intercepted on the ground by a big force of several hundred thousand men; we encountered untold difficulties and great obstacles on the way, but by keeping our two feet going, we swept across a distance of more than 6,600 miles through the length and breadth of eleven provinces.' Some 70,000 soldiers and 15,000 camp followers, plus 7,000 political activists, were laden with weapons and equipment. Mao, often sleeping by day and walking by night, carried two blankets, an overcoat, a sheet, an umbrella and the books from which he could never be parted. Only 40,000 or so survived.

Mao's feat exceeded Lenin's. True, the Party's victory would have much in common with the Russian Revolution: for one, the Party emerged triumphant from the ashes of an old and decaying feudal system. Mao also took a revolutionary road to power before China could build up an effective bourgeoisie. As in Russia, the Chinese industrial revolution, the raw material of class conflict, had begun before the communists took over. War, too, was the catalyst for the seizure of power. But the Chinese revolution, unlike the Russian one, would require that most difficult of qualities: patience.

Mao's own long march began with his birth on 26 December 1893 in a village called Shaoshan in Hunan province in Central China. While his mother was a gentle Buddhist, his father was a prosperous peasant by Chinese standards, a hard, conservative man who employed farm workers and was able to educate his son while also providing him with a comfortable family home.

Like Lenin's father, Mao's father was ambitious for his children. Mao went to the village school, to imbibe classical learning; his florid literary style and poetic bent date from this period. Next came teachers' training college, where he began to formulate his political ideas; and politics touched everyone in the China of Mao's youth. As a schoolboy he lived through the Boxer Uprising in 1900, the death of the Dowager Empress

Zi Xi (who instigated it) in 1908 and the 1911 revolution that ended the rule of China's Qing (Ch'ing) imperial dynasty, established by the Manchu in 1644.

It was an unremarkable early life. He worked as a librarian at Beijing University, where the scholars snubbed him, a possible cause of his repeated attacks on 'intellectuals' – or more probably he simply saw them as a threat. He did his obligatory six months military service in the army. On his own admission, by the age of 24 his political ideals were still muddled. 'I had somewhat vague passions,' he said later, 'about nineteenth-century democracy, utopianism and old-fashioned liberalism, and I was deeply anti-militaristic and anti-imperialist.' Here was a man with an open, searching mind, not a closed fanatic in the Lenin mould.

The very few accounts of him as a young man that survive agree on the general description. A tall, gangling, dreamy impractical youth with a faraway look in his eyes, he enjoyed poetry and devoured the romantic Chinese classic, the *Story of the Marsh*, about rebels fighting an oppressive government. Although he enjoyed exercise, in particular swimming and walking, his deliberate, deeply serious and softly spoken manner, although intermittently leavened with a sparkle of ironic humour, made him appear somewhat languid and effeminate. His detachment concealed an inner will to get things done. 'Knowledge without action is not true knowledge,' he insisted. In his youth, this distant, detached intellectual could hardly have been less like the self-confident, single-minded Lenin.

After leaving the training school, he started writing for the small-circulation university press while teaching small children. From the start, his ideas were vigorous and extremist, although they showed a degree of open-mindedness and genuine inquiry. By 1920 he was trying to set up a Marxist Study Society in Hunan and had been chosen to attend the First Communist Party Congress. There was no sign that the Party had a future or that he would become anything in it.

Peasant Power

The China in which the Communist Party sprung to life seemed, at first glance, to be rather less promising ground for the kind of take-over of power at the centre that had occurred in Russia. A series of rebellions, like the Taiping Rebellion of 1851–64, which had devastated large areas of China, caused the old order to collapse. The large 'gentry' class, the grass roots support of the old imperial dynasty, showed little interest in the modern commerce and industry that were beginning to affect the country. The main sources of capital at the time were overseas companies, and as they penetrated traditional Chinese markets, so a small working- and middle-class grew up with a grudge against foreigners, compounded by the Chinese defeat at the hands of the Japanese in 1895.

The Qing dynasty finally fell in 1912, but the men who replaced the emperor had no inkling where China was headed. China's first President, Yuan Shikai, was a military dictator who tried to set up a new dynasty for his family. His successor, the former Vice-President and soldier, Li Yuanhong, governed ineffectually and was forced to resign after a nearly successful military rebellion.

This huge, populous, decaying empire was in effect splitting apart. The real power was held by feuding warlords; one group was based in Manchuria, one in Hunan, another in Beijing. China's outlying regions were run by their own military governors, in association with one or other foreign powers.

Most rural Chinese barely noticed central government: village life, controlled by the family clans of the gentry and heads of villages, continued to trudge tranquilly and miserably along governed by the Confucian 'Five Cardinal Relationships': sovereign and subject, father and son, older and younger brother, husband and wife, and friend and friend.

It was an ordered but extremely poor existence, partly due to the population explosion that began in the eighteenth and nineteenth centuries. In the mid-seventeenth century China had fewer than 100 million people. Within 100 years it had half as many again and by 1841, 413 million. By 1928 it had levelled out at 465 million. The area of cultivated land, however, had only increased by about a seventh and the vast majority of Chinese lived on the borderline between survival and starvation. By the mid-1930s, average income was reckoned at $12 a year per person. By 1921 some 80 per cent of the population was still based on the land. By twentieth century standards, industrial production was pitiful: China produced approximately 4,800 tons of steel, 85,000 tons of oil, 1.3 million tones of iron ore and 20 million tons of coal.

At the beginning of the twentieth century, the tiny new intellectual class was inspired by a ferment of ideas – almost wholly borrowed from the West – which broke over this unbelievably poor, static, headless society. The earliest intellectuals opposed the rigid order of the Five Cardinal Relationships. One of them, Kang Youwei, seized upon the idea of a dialectic in three stages: an age of disorder; an age of nationalism; and an age of peace. In his perfect world, there would be no family or private property, and governments would be directly elected.

Another of the early revolutionaries, Tan Sitong, was executed at the age of 34 in 1898 after urging a revolt against the 'enmeshing net of the pursuit of self-interest and of official enrichment'. Yet self-interest, to some extent, had a genuine intellectual pedigree in China: anarchism found numerous adherents in China, as early Chinese Taoist theorists had long advanced views such as 'the people have no sovereign, there are no laws unless they follow nature'. By 1915–6, however, the anarchist fad was dying as the country itself began to undergo the reality of social disintegration into anarchy.

Socialism, when it first sprouted in China, was of a humanist kind that reflected the country's traditions. Jiang Kanghu, one of its fathers, preached nationalization of industry, free education, the redistribution of land, and the end of war, the army, the death penalty and inheritance. However, his brand of socialism was soon tempered by practical considerations: he came to accept nationalism and dictatorial rule, and in 1939 even collaborated with the Japanese. The other father of moderate Chinese socialism was Sun Yat-sen, whose concepts were woolly and adopted late in life in response to intellectual trends.

It was the Russian Revolution that drove serious thinking about more extreme forms of Marxism in China. China had a grudge against the Western powers over their refusal at the Treaty of Versailles to insist on the withdrawal by Japan of the 'Twenty-One Demands' made against China during the First World War. These were designed to turn the country into a Japanese protectorate. When, on 4 May 1919, 4,000 students staged a protest outside the Gate of Heavenly Peace in Beijing, nationalist sentiment mushroomed into a generalized anti-government revolt that lasted until mid-June; one thousand students were arrested. The 'May Movement' was in no sense communist, although like the 1905 uprising in Russia it became idealized as a milestone in Chinese communist history.

Mao later claimed blithely that 'the May 4th movement was [that of] the revolutionary petty bourgeois intellectuals and bourgeois intellectuals . . . as soon as it developed into the June 3rd Movement it became a nation-wide revolutionary movement'. As the Communist Party did not even exist at the time, the Party could claim no credit for the uprising; but certainly, the successful revolution in Russia had had its impact. When the Chinese Communist Party was formed two years later, it had the princely total of 57 members and by 1925, still fewer than 1,000.

The Communist Party's insignificance can partly be explained by the fact that China's urban working class was so small that predictions of working-class revolution looked a little far-fetched. In 1913, out of the 400 million or so Chinese, there were around 650,000 industrial workers. By 1919 this had increased to 2 million, of whom over 300,000 worked for foreign companies. By contrast, China's large rural artisan class numbered 12 million. The tiny urban working class went on strike occasionally: the communists reckoned that only 78 strikes took place between 1895 and 1913.

The Chinese Communist Party was founded by two university professors, Chen Duxiu and Li Dazhao. The former, an elderly academic bachelor, was to become the Party's first Secretary. He began preaching Marxist philosophy in his magazine – *Hsin ch'ing nien* (New Youth), initially published as *Ch'ing-nien* (Youth) in 1915 – appealing to his intended youthful readers with only very slight Marxist overtones. There were vague invocations to 'be independent, not servile; be men of progress, not bound by nature; be brave, not fearful, be internationalist, not isolationist'.

It was not until 1919 that he published a first analysis of Marxism, while not whole-heartedly endorsing Marx. For example, Chen insisted that 'we acknowledge the function of political parties in politics, but we will not want just any party that supports the interests of the minority of one class and does not work for the happiness of society as a whole'. His colleague Li formed a Society for the Study of Marxist Theory in December 1920. The same year, a Russian emissary from the Comintern came to China to promote the new creed. The start was hardly auspicious: just twelve people, six of whom would soon leave the Party, attended the inaugural Congress in Shanghai in 1921. Mao, then aged 28, hardly contributed to the proceedings. The Party had little clue where to begin: some wanted to work towards socialism through democracy; the more adventurous preferred a revolutionary seizure of power.

The hopes of this miniscule, desultory band seeking to stir the tiny industrial working class to revolution in a country with a deeply conservative peasantry and large and reactionary armed forces seemed negligible. The Western powers ignored them. The Bolsheviks, considering the cause equally hopeless, sent an envoy, Adolf Joffe, to Sun Yat-sen. Sun had failed to receive backing from the Western powers, who preferred to divide and rule China.

Following the overthrow of the Qing dynasty in 1911, Sun Yat-sen, leader of the Kuomintang (the Nationalist Party), had been elected President of the Republic of Southern China. Sun believed in setting up a strong parliamentary democracy based on a huge mass of small, peasant proprietors owning their own land. He was also vehemently anti-colonialist. Sun's main crusade was against the regional warlords that dominated the rest of the country and, rather surprisingly, he became impressed with Bolshevik forms of organization, setting up his own army with Soviet advice.

The tiny Chinese Communist Party, which as set up in 1921, took its cue from Moscow and joined the Kuomintang in 1923 to form a United Front. In 1925, however, Sun died unexpectedly, and his successor the following year, Chiang Kai-shek, immediately moved to purge the communists, whom he suspected of infiltrating the Kuomintang and urging peasants to revolution. Mao was undoubtedly inspired by Sun's strongly anti-imperialist and anti-warlord doctrine, but considered him 'bourgeois' albeit progressive.

Joffe, on the other hand, in 1922 offered him money as well as the neutralization of the Communist Party. In exchange for Russian support, Sun in 1924 agreed to allow communist participation in his nationalist Kuomintang government based at Guangzhou (Canton). Mao was one of the first to join, and was based in Shanghai. The aims were to develop a joint fighting force capable of defeating the warlords, and provide a central administration that could shake off China's foreign exploiters. Socialist revolution was no part of the programme. The countryside was to stay as it was, with both parties agreeing it could only accept gradual change.

Yet Marxism had an insidious attraction. As Li Xiaojun (a pseudonym for a prominent but disillusioned modern Chinese communist leader) writes:

> With the exception of Chen Duxiu, who was a profound scholar, the Party's leaders – knowing no German, and possessed of little senior or higher education – could not grapple with Marx's writings at first hand. Accordingly they read Marx in translation, or learned his views through lectures and discussion. And indeed some of the great texts of Marx,

Lenin and Stalin were not available in China for a long time. The Communist Party was founded in 1921, but Marx's *Das Kapital* did not appear in Chinese translation until the mid-1930s. There is indeed no evidence that Mao ever read it . . .

A reading of Mao's works shows that, unlike other Marxist theoreticians, he very seldom quotes Marx's writings. The author from whom he chiefly quotes (but even then only occasionally) is Stalin. We also find that some of Marx's more important theses find no place in Mao's thought. For example Marx wrote that 'a society will not collapse when there is room in it for the development of productive forces'. Mao either ignored or was ignorant of this central view. There is a well-known passage in Mao's writings: 'There are so many arguments in Marxism. We can summarize them all, in the final analysis, in one sentence: to rebel is justified.'

The new alliance began its campaign in 1925, when the 'May 3rd Movement' broke out in foreign-dominated Shanghai, China's only modern industrial city with its docks, railways and industry. The French and other international concession holders ruled three-quarters of it. The Chinese ruled the old centre, which became something of a sanctuary for political agitators who resented foreign influences. On 30 May, British-controlled policemen killed eleven demonstrators in the city. As strikes spread, the British in Guangzhou killed some fifty Chinese. A general strike ensued: some 100,000 workers tramped out of factories, from Hong Kong to Guangzhou, setting up strike committees. The unrest also spread to the countryside, where small groups of Marxist and nationalist propagandists had been stirring up poorer peasants in an attempt to undercut the support of the warlords. By 1925 it was reckoned that some half million peasants belonged to such groups around Guangzhou, where Mao was now head of the Kuomintang's Propaganda Department.

Sun Yat-sen did not live to see his dream fulfilled: after his death in March 1925, the ablest and toughest of the nationalist leaders, Chiang Kai-shek, set out to subdue the northern warlords. In August 1926, Chiang launched the 'Northern Expedition' from the Kuomintang heartland of Guangzhou across Mao's native Hunan. As ordinary peasants rose against their old feudal rulers, Chiang found the way open before him, reaching Wuhan on the Yangtze. After a one-month siege, this vital river port and communications centre fell. The Nationalist army now moved on to other parts of southern and central China.

But the growing numbers of his previously insignificant communist allies profoundly disturbed Chiang. Their message found widespread support among the poorest peasants with the worst land: it is estimated that landlords representing 3% of households possessed more than a quarter of the land in China, and rich peasants representing some 7% had a further quarter. Middle peasants representing 22% of households had 25% and poor farmers representing 70% only some 22%.

This poorest 70% warmed to the communist message of land redistribution. Just as in Russia, the absolute lack of rights of the poorest class meant that, once the old landlords lost their political power, the peasant was radicalized – unless he was offered the possibility of private ownership of his land. In China the demise of the power of the warlords and gentry brought about a surge in communist support. By the end of 1925 there were 20,000 Party members and by 1927, 58,000.

Following the departure of the Northern Expedition, Mao returned to Hunan in November 1926. As the communists' base clearly lay in the poorer peasantry, Mao jettisoned the Marxist ideological message that suggested the peasantry was unfitted for revolution; Mao reckoned that China's peasantry *was* the revolutionary class. This not just defied a cherished Marxist tenet but created a precedent. The Russian Revolution had begun in the cities because of the peculiar circumstances created by the disintegration of military authority there. A minority had thus seized power in the urban centres. In China, Mao decided that the desperately poor peasants once mobilized, could bring revolution to the cities, showing how Mao stretched the Marxist original to fit local conditions. Peasant uprisings had a long and celebrated history in China, and had been crucial in most of the changes of dynasty in the imperial past. Mao's greatest work on the subject was his *Report of an Inspection of the Peasant Movement in Hunan*. Mao wrote:

> Revolution is not a dinner party; it is not like writing an essay, or doing embroidery; it cannot be so refined, so leisurely and gentle, so temperate, kind, courteous, restrained and magnanimous. To right a wrong we must exceed the 'proper' limits, otherwise the wrong will never be righted.

Mao also carried out substantial land reform to benefit the poorer peasants – something Chiang promised but never delivered, except at the end of his life in Taiwan. Mao declared:

> In a very short time, in China's central, southern and northern provinces, several hundred million peasants will rise like an ugly storm, a hurricane,

a force so swift and violent that no power, however great, will be able to hold it back. There are three alternatives. To march at their head and lead them. To trail behind, gesticulating and criticizing. Or to stand in their way and oppose them. Every Chinese is free to choose, but events will force you to make the choice quickly.

Mao then formulated his second maxim: that political power 'grows out of the barrel of a gun'. (This was anathema to true Marxists, for whom the masses were the main sources of political power; guns were used in a revolutionary seizure of power.) Mao's idea was to set up an entirely peasant-staffed army to counteract that other army now consolidating its hold on China – that of the Kuomintang. Mao's means to power would thus not be revolutionary mass support but traditional Chinese warlordism.

When in 1927 Chiang Kai-shek rounded upon his communist allies and expelled them from the Kuomintang, Mao fell out with the Party leader, Chen Duxiu, in urging that the Party give up its wan hopes of cooperation with the Nationalists. At the Party's Fifth Congress at the end of April, Mao's views were defeated. He was ill at the time, and appeared to be a fading force.

But in October 1927, following a brutal and bloody uprising in Hunan which had been opposed by orthodox Marxists, Mao, by now a middle-ranking communist leader, led a motley group of survivors to a remote mountain fastness called Jingangshan, narrowly evading capture. A hilly, remote, scrub-covered and wooded area, interrupted by mountains 5,000 to 7,000 feet high, it offered perfect protection for Mao's forces. With narrow valleys and no roads, it was classic border territory, straddling the provinces of Hunan and Jiangxi so that neither provincial governor would pursue Mao's forces into the hills. Here he was joined by what remained of the communist forces after a revolt in Jiangxi under Zhu De, a legendary military commander and former Kuomintang officer. Yet this posed no threat at all to the Nationalists, who now switched their attention to defeating the warlord of Manchuria, Zhang Xueliang, only to see him gobbled up in 1931 by the Japanese, against whom Chiang knew he could not prevail.

But in his native province of Hunan, Mao's appeal to the peasantry was the Party's only possible way forward. Mao, who alongside Zhu De now emerged as the leader of the communist rump, had learnt from the appalling reversal of the unsuccessful Hunan rebellion. During the years he spent in Hunan, the willowy, 35-year-old intellectual crafted an ingenious theory of guerrilla warfare, centred on the maxim 'The people are the sea, we are the fish.' In fact Mao's guerrilla tactics were mostly unoriginal: for centuries, warring armies fighting in mountainous territory had been using them. They included dispersing guerrillas to proselytize the countryside and living off the land without causing too much disruption to local life, thereby reducing hostility. Mao believed his men should be disciplined and respect ordinary people, a sharp contrast with the Nationalist forces. 'Do not take a single needle or piece of thread from the masses' was one iron rule.

His 'eight points' by which guerrillas were supposed to abide included, 'speak politely; pay firmly for what you buy; return everything you borrow; pay for anything you damage; do not hit or swear at people; do not damage crops; do not take liberties with women; do not ill-treat captives'. Mao's other main guerrilla tactics were to assemble men from different areas for a fight, to surprise the enemy through ambushes, and to retreat whenever attacked, thus minimizing losses. 'The enemy advances, we retreat. The enemy stops, we harass. The enemy tires, we attack. The enemy retreats, we pursue.'

Mao also sought peasant support by abandoning his earlier ideas about wholesale land reform in favour of 'voluntary' cooperatives. The reform was not, in fact, as modest as many people subsequently made out: maybe 600,000 people were killed as poorer peasants rose up against richer ones in the course of the redistribution of some 250,000 acres. The main purpose of this was to provide plots for Mao's soldiers that would be worked in their absence. Land owned by the revolution's opponents would be confiscated.

But Mao demanded, at least on paper, that land committees must explain all aspects involved to the peasants and not use brute force. He also insisted there could be no land reform until the mass of the peasants at the bottom and middle levels gave it their direct support. The middle level peasants were too important to his army for him to contemplate grabbing their land. In this he showed the same tactical good sense as Lenin, who cast aside abstract revolutionary ideas when they hindered the prosaic necessity of winning support.

It was not the only thing he had in common with Lenin. Mao's three years in the mountains were marked by fierce faction struggles, in which the leader ruthlessly assumed total control over his movement. The first power struggle, when Mao already had near total ascendancy over the Party, began when the leadership betrayed twenty-three leading communists to the British police in Shanghai, who shot them. The event was the subject of one of the most haunting poems of modern Chinese literature, directed as much against Mao's ruthlessness as against the Nationalists and the British:

> It is spring
> At Lung-Hua the peach-trees are in flower
> They flower through these nights
> These nights flecked with blood
> These starless nights
> these windy nights
> These nights filled with widows' sobs
> But this old earth!
> It seems a wild beast athirst and ravenous
> Which laps the blood of the young
> The blood of the unyielding young
> After the long winter days
> After the ice and snow
> After the endless exhausting wait;
> These traces of blood, these flecks of blood
> In a legendary night
> In a black eastern night
> Burst into bud
> And adorn all the south of the River with their spring
> You ask: 'Where has the spring come from?'
> And I reply 'from graves outside the town.'

During the last weeks of 1930, some 4,400 members of the Party were imprisoned and accused by Mao of belonging to the 'anti-Bolshevik league'; this provoked a rebellion by part of the Red Army, which spread rapidly. Mao put down the rebellion and up to 10,000 Party members were executed. The following year a violent purge in the southern port of Huangpo resulted in the execution of some 3,000 people, including two divisional commanders accused of plotting against Mao.

Since reaching their mountain sanctuary, the communists steadily increased the area under their control, and in November 1931, Mao's Chinese Soviet Republic, with its capital in Juichin in Jiangxi province was founded. Lasting three years, it embraced some 3 million people in an area of 15,000 square miles. And Mao and Zhu De had transformed the original motley collection of men into the Fourth Red Army, which grew to some 100,000 men.

Chiang Kai-shek's first response was to send relatively small units to deal with the communist stronghold. The Nationalists made all the standard errors of regular forces engaging guerrilla armies. The communists easily spotted their ponderous full-scale sweeps, taking evasive action and picking off isolated units. This 'extermination' campaign, involving some 50,000 men, got nowhere.

Following advice from the Germans on the conduct of an anti-guerrilla war, Chiang surrounded the communist-held territory with a network of outposts that blocked the inward and outward movement of supplies and were gradually pushed further forwards, increasing the pressure on the communists even though Chiang's forces could not penetrate deep into their territory. After four futile campaigns, Chiang appeared to have found the right strategy. Between October 1933 and October 1934, the communists steadily lost ground. By the latter date they had decided that they were trapped and had to break out.

The Long March

The Long March is not as unique an event in Chinese history as the Party would have people believe. China is a big country, and generals had staged similar marches before, like that of General Shih Dakai a century earlier. Even some Kuomintang armies had covered as much ground as the communists. The tradition of long marches – and Mao understood this well – was for rebel armies to move along the border areas from one province to another: provincial governors tended to leave such itinerants alone.

The route of the Long March twisted and turned, largely to confuse the harassing Nationalist forces. Mao, whose poetry was only occasionally inspired, encapsulated its achievement:

The Red Army fears not the trials of a distant march
To them a thousand mountains, ten thousand rivers are nothing.
To them the Five Ridges ripple like little waves
And the mountain peaks of Wumeng roll by like mud balls
Warm are the cloud-topped cliffs washed by the River of Golden Sand
Cold are the iron chains that span the Tatu River
The myriad snows of Minshan only make them happier
And when the army has crossed, each face is smiling.

In fact, three armies were involved: the First Field Army, the main force that had to fight hardest, commanded by Zhu De and accompanied by Mao, had around 90,000 men and 30,000 camp followers. Marching in a series of columns they broke through the lightly defended enemy lines in October 1934. The Second Field Army, led by He Long, trekked circuitously from south to western China and the Tibetan border. The third, Zhang Guotao's Fourth Field Army, based in Sichuan province, had a shorter journey. The ragged remnants of all three met after a year in Yan'an (Yenan) in Shaanxi province.

Having marched through Guizhou, one of China's most backward provinces, a remote hilly area in which people lived in a centuries-old sink of rural squalor, the First Field Army headed north to Sichuan province, a huge plateau of uninhabited grasslands swept by winds from Tibet. The main obstacle, a deep marsh, slowed the communists down to a crawl. After the grasslands came the nearly insuperable barrier of the wide, raging Tatu River, with enemy troops on the opposite bank, which was secured by a group of Red Soldiers swinging themselves across by the chains of the suspension bridge that had been blown up by the Nationalists.

Finally the marchers reached North Shaanxi, on the edge of the barren Mongolian steppe, an impoverished and remote area whose principal town was Yan'an. On the march the communists had lost over 40 per cent of their soldiers; only 30,000 survived. But now, far enough away from Chiang Kai-shek's forces, they could regroup in safety.

On the way, at Zunyi, a meeting of the executive committee in January 1935 formally elected the 43-year-old Mao Zedong, who had correctly insisted that the revolution depended on the peasantry, as Chairman of the Chinese Communist Party. But Mao cannot have been confident that his exhausted forces in Shaanxi could hold out much longer. The terrain around Yan'an was a mixture of bogs and high plateaux, broken by cliffs rising to 3,000 feet. The region was drought-plagued, with no modern roads. To the south lay the Great Wall: to the east, the Yellow River. The communists, literally and symbolically, had been sidelined.

Yet the poverty in Shaanxi enabled the communists to find recruits among the peasantry, doubtless attracted by Mao's simple egalitarianism. Merely being able to join an army was some respite for the poor people in this provincial backwater, although ultimately these raw recruits would probably have buckled under a concerted attack by Nationalist forces – when one could have been mounted. Mao was to be saved, however, by an extraordinary combination of good luck and an external enemy: the Japanese.

The Japanese, at the time, were ready to invade mainland China. They already controlled Manchuria and Inner Mongolia; they occupied most of the province around Beijing and had attacked Shanghai. The communists, now close to Mongolia, threatened any further Japanese advance in the north. The Japanese hoped to profit from the divisions among the Chinese; but Mao envisaged two benefits from a Japanese attack. He could claim to be a patriot, fighting for his country; and he could wage the type of guerrilla campaign the communists were so skilled at against the Japanese, extending his control over the countryside in anticipation of the day the Japanese left.

Chiang, well aware of the danger, decided to destroy the communists before taking on the Japanese; 'internal pacification before resistance to aggression' became his slogan. But real control over the country was in the hands of local warlords, and in 1929 he was humiliated by two of them, Feng Yuxiang and Yan Xishan, in a battle on the Central Plains involving over 1 million men. To defeat the communists Chiang required the support of the Manchurian army, led by the Young Marshal, Zhang Xueliang, the son of the former local warlord, Zhang Zuolin, the Old Marshal. At the end of 1936, Chiang flew to Xi'an, the Young Marshal's headquarters, to plan the eradication of Communism from the face of China.

Chiang's arrival was an awkward one. To his astonishment, he found that the Young Marshal's forces had been fraternizing with Red Army troops. Mao's policy had long been to sue for peace in the civil war and fight the external aggressor. 'Chinese do not fight Chinese', and 'Unite to resist foreign imperialism' were the Party slogans. The Young Marshal detested the Japanese, and considered a united front with the communists essential.

Chiang, entirely right to worry about the possible extension of communist influence on such a front, was furious. He ordered the Young Marshal to attack the communists immediately and then left to spend Christmas at a hot spring resort near Xi'an that had been patronized by the Tang dynasty in the seventh century. There the Young Marshal's men suddenly arrested him. His captor made it clear that his release depended on his reaching agreement with the communists. Otherwise he would be executed.

Chiang angrily and bluntly refused. The news of his kidnapping reached his headquarters in Nanjing. His wife flew out to try to persuade the kidnappers to release him, but failed. The Nationalist commanders in Nanjing made plans to bomb Xi'an and to send a force in the depths of winter to rescue him. A civil war looked likely between the Nationalist forces (in addition to the one with the communists) while the whole country faced a Japanese invasion. The extraordinary situation in which the commander of the Nationalist forces was a prisoner of his own troops grew more extraordinary still: offering themselves as mediators came his sworn enemies, the communists, in the person of Zhou Enlai (Chou En-lai), Mao's right-hand man.

Zhou was a cultivated upper-middle-class Chinese with considerable diplomatic finesse. He offered Chiang every conceivable inducement to form a government of national unity: Chiang would be its undisputed leader; the Red Army would be placed under his command. Yan'an would accept autonomy, but become part of Nationalist China. At length, Chiang accepted these terms, and was spared execution. A National Government was formed, and the communists escaped anni-hilation. Chiang insisted, however, that the Young Marshal return with him to Nanjing for an official reprieve before resuming his command. Revenge was sweet. The luckless Chang, who probably did more than any single non-communist to ensure the success of the creed in China, still languished in jail twenty years later, having been dragged to Taiwan after Chiang's final defeat to spin out his sentence.

The Red Army became the Eighth Route Army. Following the 'China incident' of 7 July 1937, when the Japanese claimed, probably falsely, that they had been fired upon by Chinese troops, the invasion of China began. The Chinese were quickly swept out of Hebei province, south of Beijing. Chiang rallied his armies in Nanjing, but the better equipped and more disciplined Japanese forces pushed him a thousand miles up the Yangtze, where his soldiers found a safe refuge in the river's impreg-nable gorges. By now controlling all the ports and coastal towns, the Japanese stopped and waited for a surrender that never came because Chiang (as later events were to prove) never gave up.

In North China, the communists fought a different war, mounting the sporadic guerrilla campaign to which they were accustomed. The Japanese played straight into their hands. Aiming to turn northern China into a grain and mineral store for the Japanese empire, the

Japanese seized stores, forced farmers and workers to labour for a pittance, and ruthlessly oppressed the local people. The communists, subtly blending their own message of resistance to exploitation with that of opposition to foreign invaders, found overwhelming sympathy among occupied northern China's 90 million people. As the guerrilla war – a model for subsequent conflicts – spread, the Japanese found that they controlled only the cities and small areas outside them which returned to Chinese hands the moment they withdrew. As the Japanese became increasingly defensive, they initiated the savage 'Three All' policy – Kill all, Burn all, Loot all. This merely added new recruits to the communist army, which by the war's end had swollen to half a million men.

While the war against Japan raged, the hatred between Mao's and Chiang's forces bubbled along. In 1942, Mao set up a peasant army south of the Yangtze to carry out guerrilla operations. Chiang was furious that Mao should seek to expand his influence, which already covered a third of the Chinese population, into what he regarded as his southern territory. As Commander-in-Chief, he ordered Mao's forces to withdraw. Mao reluctantly agreed, only for Chiang's forces to open fire as his men were retreating across to the north shore. Chiang blamed the incident, implausibly, on a 'mistake by the local commander'.

Mao's main concern, as he waged guerrilla war against the Japanese, was to consolidate his hold on the peasantry and, more importantly, to train up a large army capable one day of defeating the Nationalist forces. The Communist Party was expanded, to allow in new recruits. At one point, Mao grew worried that the Party was becoming diluted with non-communists. In 1942 he purged it thoroughly.

The two Chinas continued their uneasy alliance against the outside aggressor until 1945; both sides expected that the war would end with a conventional American intervention, allowing – so Chiang Kai-shek hoped – his forces to retake the areas occupied by the Japanese. Instead, the United States dropped atom bombs on Hiroshima and Nagasaki and the Japanese surrendered in situ. Mao was caught napping, unprepared to move into the cities his forces surrounded north of the Yangtze.

Chiang moved quickly, asking the United States Air Force to airlift his men into the cities, invoking his right as Commander-in-Chief to do so. Mao reacted with his usual cool imperturbability: the communists ripped up the roads, railway lines and bridges between the Yangtze and the northern cities. Now let Chiang rescue his men! Just like the

Japanese, the Nationalist forces were in effect cut off in the cities. Furthermore, Chiang did not improve matters by absorbing into his own ranks the tame, unreliable and despised Chinese army set up by the Japanese.

The outbreak of civil war was delayed only by token negotiations started by the Americans; both sides, preparing for conflict, knew they were meaningless. Chiang proposed, unacceptably, that the communists disband their army and take part in a democratic election. Mao despised elections and no communist believed Chiang would hold them. Without his army, Mao knew he was powerless. Chiang turned down the communists' wild demand for full participation in the government as an equal and for fusion of the two armies, knowing this would merely allow Mao to extend his influence southwards.

The civil war began with a curious episode that revealed that Stalin, for one, was no friend of Mao. After the dropping of the atom bombs, the Russian leader, persuaded by the Americans to join the war against Japan only to find that Japanese resistance had crumpled overnight, moved his armies swiftly into Manchuria as far as the Great Wall, and into North Korea. By March 1946, the Russians had decided to pull out, having looted the region of minerals, machinery and livestock. This was too soon for Mao to get his communist forces organized on the ground.

It seemed that Stalin preferred a weak and divided China, rather than a unified colossus. The Russians in fact handed over power to the Nationalist forces that had been flown in, once again, by the Americans. Chiang, not for the first time, had overreached himself. Because the Japanese had developed Manchuria into a major industrial area, he feared that if the communists gained control and created a military force, they would transform it into a powerhouse capable eventually of crushing the south. Therefore, he further dispersed his forces throughout the northern cities. The communists promptly disrupted communications again, so that Nationalist outposts became besieged garrisons. In April 1946, Mao's forces also briefly took the city of Changchun, before the Nationalists expelled them.

At the start of the civil war, few outside observers gave the communists a chance. They had around 1 million men under arms, but a third were ill-trained militiamen. The Nationalists had some 4 million men, with many trained by the Americans, and an air force. The communists had no air force, but were able, in the north, to pose as a patriotic army fighting the external oppressor; they also stood vaguely for land reform, which peasants hoped would usher in a new dawn of prosperity. By contrast, the Nationalist force, as alien to the northern Chinese as the Japanese, stood for the old system, both politically and in the countryside.

South of the Yangtze, the communists could not expect widespread support. This was not the case for the Nationalists, because their army represented the main anti-Japanese force and because ordinary people for the most part accepted a social system in which Chiang presided rather loosely over a group of traditional warlords – generals who stood at the apex of the landed gentry. The latter principally officered the army, and were not especially popular among the conscript peasants they commanded; the officers were corrupt and incompetent and the men rarely paid on time. Chiang, although not personally corrupt, tolerated corruption because he lacked the power to stamp it out. The communist People's Liberation Army, by contrast, built up from the bottom by Mao and fired by his simple revolutionary goals, was usually better behaved towards civilians.

Subsequent propaganda campaigns and histories have etched the idea of a happy, high-morale Maoist army versus a seething, discontented Nationalist army; in fact, the former was less well disciplined than is made out, and the latter not as poorly officered. What turned the tide was Chiang's idiotic military strategy of seeking control of all China in one bound, rather than consolidating his hold in the south and gradually wearing the communists down.

Instead of following American advice to concentrate on opening a line of communication to the cut-off armies in Shenyang (Mukden), Chiang launched three separate offensives. First he attacked Yan'an, Mao's original headquarters, lightly defended as it no longer mattered much to the communists. Unsurprisingly, the Nationalist forces did well in this sideshow. Chiang also launched a campaign from the cities of Manchuria to regain control of the ammunition dumps and railways in the countryside. This failed.

He listened to the Americans to the extent that he sent a force – much smaller than required – to open up a line of communications to Manchuria. However communist guerrillas slowed the Kuomintang advance up the Beijing to Manchuria railway line to a crawl. When Chiang sent small forces forward, larger contingents of guerrillas blocked their way. Whenever the main force advanced, the communists moved to cut it off at the rear.

With Chiang hopelessly overextended and getting nowhere, Mao decided on a decisive push forward. Like Lenin in 1917, he knew he must move quickly, or not at all. Eventually the tide could turn in Chiang's favour, since he would eventually realize that he must regroup and consolidate, thus barring Mao from southern China. Above all, Mao feared that America might be tempted in on Chiang's side. Mao quashed the opposition to his plan, led by the cautious Liu Shaoqi (Liu Shao-chi), a senior Party member who apparently reflected Stalin's views on the matter. Boldness, for the moment, had replaced Mao's traditional caution.

Both the two prongs of the communist thrust were directed south towards the regions of Shandong and Henan. In April 1948, they seized Jinan, the capital of Shandong (and soon ended Chiang's hopes of supporting Shenyang through the railway south to the Yellow Sea), and threatened the Nationalist heartland of Wuhan and Nanjing, having cut off the Nationalist forces defending Beijing from their main armies in the south.

The plight of the stranded Nationalist armies in Manchuria as winter approached was becoming desperate. After an airlift proved inadequate, the only way to get supplies and reinforcements to them was to capture some of the Manchurian coastline. So in October 1948 Chiang despatched some of his best American-trained troops to open yet another front. But this force was repulsed by Lin Biao (Lin Piao), one of the ablest Chinese commanders, who subsequently defeated the huge Nationalist army that had come out of Shenyang to link up with the relief forces in one of the most tactically brilliant military operations of the twentieth century. The battle, in the region of Suzhou, consisted of a huge strategic ambush of the Kuomintang's mechanized formations. Following the seventy-two-hour engagement, Shenyang and Changchun surrendered. Within a few months Manchuria was communist, and Mao released the defeated Nationalist forces to impress the evidence of his victory on the south.

The end was near. One of Mao's armies marched to destroy the remaining resistance around Beijing in the east and to advance on Chiang's main southern forces, while a smaller army moved against Tianjin until it surrendered. In the north, only Beijing remained. The city was besieged in December 1948; in January, it surrendered.

After their opponents' success in the north, the Nationalists were extremely apprehensive. That same December Mao's main force

advanced on Chiang's armies amassed on the north shore of the Huai
He River in one of the biggest battles since the beginning of the Second
World War; the communists had around 300,000 men, compared to
Chiang's 550,000, but the latter were demoralized and, to the last, the
victims of his bad generalship. Fearful of being routed, Chiang ordered
his soldiers to give no ground on the largely flat battle site. Mao's more
numerous mobile forces simply surrounded one division after another
and forced them to surrender. Within days, Chiang withdrew across the
river and moved to Nanjing. The historic battle of Huai-Hai had
been won.

Mao triumphantly offered humiliating terms to the Nationalists,
whose leader, temporarily supplanting Chiang Kai-shek, was General Li
Zongren. The Nationalist army would be swallowed into the People's
Liberation Army; the Kuomintang could serve in a government dominated by the communists. But Chiang, who had retreated to the island
fastness of Taiwan, insisted that the Nationalists reject the terms Li was
disposed to accept.

Li was forced out. The war was resumed. But the outcome was a fore-
gone conclusion. Mao's forces crossed the Huai river and took Nanjing.
The warlords in the west sued for a separate peace with Mao. Shanghai
fell without a fight. By 1 October 1949, all mainland China was in communist hands, and the People's Republic of China had been set up in
the country's historic capital of Beijing. Only Taiwan remained, a lonely
offshore enclave of anti-Communism.

So the Long March of the Chinese Communist Party to power was
over: around 700 million people in the earth's most populous nation had
fallen to the Marxist-Leninist revolution, multiplying by nearly four
times the number of people under communist rule. Now some two-
fifths of mankind was under the hammer and sickle. The march of
history, which appeared to have halted after the 1917 revolution and certainly excluded the forcible 'liberation' of Eastern Europe had, through
a genuinely home-grown revolution, won the biggest, if one of the
poorest, prizes the world had to offer.

The course of the revolution in no way resembled the Marxist blueprint.
Both Russia and China were principally primitive peasant societies
when the communist fight for power began. But unlike Russia, where
industrialization had started under the Tsars, Chinese industrialization,
largely financed and owned by foreigners, took place in the developed

fringes of the country. This created a tiny educated class who, dissatisfied with the status quo, overthrew a dynastic empire that depended not on repression but largely on a frozen social structure where no one raised their sights above their level in life – in which, indeed, ignorance bred consent.

With the collapse of the old order, three tiny minorities competed for power among the educated intelligentsia. First were Sun Yat-sen's liberal followers, whose prospects were not bright in a country where even the liberals recognized that some sort of repressive authority was required to hold the social fabric together. Next came the hardliners, commanding an authoritarian army, whose power base had been the old gentry that had lost its national cohesion with the fall of the dynasty. To win, they needed to establish, throughout China, a monopoly of armed force; a military dictatorship might then have ensued, based on the old social structure in the countryside, with the warlords and the gentry complementing each other in providing stability. The third course had been that of revolution, supported by the smallest minority of all, the intellectuals.

Mao had forged that minority into a winning combination by loosely adopting only the two pieces of Marxist-Leninist theory that suited China: the need for violent revolutionary change, and the creed of equality, the ending of exploitation of one class by another. He argued that in China revolution must come first from the peasantry, not the industrial proletariat. The concept of equality in fact won far greater support among a peasantry living on the very margins of existence than among an urban workforce that, although disorientated, felt its lot had improved through migration to the cities. It was the peasantry who carried Mao to power.

But Mao's revision of Marx went even further: instead of liberating the peasantry through some great revolutionary upheaval, he organized it into a traditional Chinese army like that of almost any powerful regional commander in Chinese history, thus taking a classic path to power. His approach had sometimes been novel: for example, urging that the soldiers treat the peasantry respectfully, although his concept of guerrilla warfare was pinched from previous Chinese examples.

So Mao's revolution was ultimately victory in a civil war: victory over a force almost as new as his, but weakened by the misjudged strategies of a stubborn but tactically inept leader. The revolutionary element in the victory was simply that Chiang's army was hierarchical and based upon the social structure, whereas Mao's was a hierarchy of merit and ability. Otherwise Mao was merely the latest in a long succession of Chinese warlords.

The third of the three ingredients of Mao's victory – in addition to the appeal to equality and the use of military force to gain power – was nationalism. Here again he broke with Marx just as Stalin had in Russia. Mao could have failed, but for Japanese aggression. This diverted Chiang's forces from comprehensively defeating the communists, who brilliantly exploited Japanese brutality, presenting themselves as China's foremost nationalist force and the natural ally of those oppressed by Japanese rule.

Was China the second milestone in an inevitable march of history? Hardly: it was the diffusion of power in China that allowed the communists to take control. A small group of well-led armed men had filled the vacuum after a traditional feudal ruler had fallen, had fought other groups importing other creeds from the developed West and had, by good judgement and luck, won in the field.

No overwhelming concentration of capital brought about the inevitable collapse of the system and a proletarian uprising. Capitalism, and the middle classes that might have sustained it, had never existed in China. Unlike Russia, Mao's victory was not even a Communist Party victory, but rather a triumph of his leadership and his army. The next thirty years were to show, indeed, the extent to which Mao very largely despised the Communist Party, challenging its authority to promote his own revolutionary goals.

For if his achievement of power was traditionalist Chinese to a fault, Mao himself was a genuine revolutionary and determined to reshape China in his own mould. In this he differed sharply from Lenin, a man without imagination in pursuit of power. Lenin would discard every principle and even reverse the revolution to ensure his political survival. Mao was prepared to forfeit power – as he later did for eight years – to further his revolutionary goals, although these were also based upon his ambitions.

This made him more dangerous than Lenin, because he was prepared to unleash continual upheavals upon his people in the pursuit of his objective. Lenin's pragmatism made him call an early halt to his revolution. Stalin sought absolute control and Russia's modernization in order to overtake the West, neither of which were remotely revolutionary aims; the instigator of Russia's biggest upheavals had an all-too-cynical understanding of how little human nature was susceptible to change. Mao, by contrast, refused to give in. Thus, at the end of the 1940s, the world witnessed two awesome spectacles: a durable communist regime in Russia that had presided over impressive industrial growth and proved itself in times of trouble, upheaval and hardship. And China, which lay at the feet of a communist dreamer.

Perpetual Renewal

Mao had two big advantages over Lenin in 1917. China's civil war had already been won: not until just before his death in 1923 could Lenin claim to have pacified the country. Secondly, middle-class opposition to Mao's rule was negligible, unlike Russia where an existing – and substantial – entrepreneurial class vigorously opposed change until butchered by Stalin. Mao's only comparable challenge came from the gentry and the rich peasantry – China's kulaks. However, Mao had one large disadvantage: although the revolution's inspiration, he fully controlled neither the army nor the Communist Party.

As so often after war, a people's energy can be channelled astonishingly quickly towards reconstruction. Central planning contributed, as it usually does in countries emerging from war, in a great national effort. The Chinese economy was in chaos; inflation had soared and communications had collapsed. China could not trade abroad since most of its merchant fleet had fled to Taiwan, and the wholesale destruction of industry and the prospect of famine had even endangered Shanghai.

The new government acted quickly. Its first priority was to restore communications. The People's Liberation Army, willing to remain under arms in a country where demobilization might have meant starvation, rebuilt the railway lines, in particular the north-south railway link, mobilizing large numbers of people who were paid and fed. Thus coal could be brought from the north to Shanghai. Rice was sent to the cities, which the army were also rebuilding, from Sichuan province along the Yangtze. As the slack in the economy was taken up, so the wind went out of inflation. China was on the road to recovery, but Mao insisted it must be of a unique kind.

Mao started with the peasants, who had put him where he was. They were China's greatest problem, their mushrooming population pressurizing resources, their food consumption threatening, even at the best of times, supplies for the urban masses. The problem had three interlinked components: overpopulation, poor food distribution and antique agricultural practices.

Mao saw it in terms of a fourth: the unequal system of landholdings. His first reform, blatantly populist, was directed against his old opponents and supporters of Chiang Kai-shek – the gentry. He swept away the whole Chinese landlord class by instigating a series of show trials, in which landlords were brought before their tenants and either 're-educated' or executed. The normally accepted estimate of the numbers killed in this early, vengeful phase of the peasant revolution is around 2 million – considerably less than in the Russian campaigns against the kulaks and a much smaller proportion of China's population. Re-education, in the literal Chinese phrase, meant brainwashing, so that forced confessions could be obtained. However long it took, the interrogators sought to erase any lingering nostalgia a person might have had for his earlier life. The victim then had to imbibe the works and thoughts of Mao – an equally long and painstaking process.

Only the strongest of wills could survive this psychological battering (at this stage unaided by drugs). Almost all the old governing class succumbed to the process, simply to save their own skins. Largely shunning physical torture, the Chinese were ahead of the Russians, whose use of mental torture only began to develop in the late 1950s. Up to 10 million people may have been funnelled through re-education camps, many for only a short time. Mao at this stage wanted to eliminate opponents among the hostile classes, rather than indoctrinate ordinary people.

Ordinary peasants were bought with the promise they most wanted: ownership of their own small patches of land. But this made an inefficient form of land tenure worse. Yields increased as peasants cultivated more for themselves and worked areas that had lain fallow under the old owners. But in many places, any existing economies of scale within the larger units were lost. To counter the threat of famine in large parts of China, Party cadres in the countryside preached neighbourly cooperation: peasants should grow their crops in adjoining fields and harvest them together. 'Mutual aid' teams were set up, often forcibly, to plan production and harvesting.

This created, in effect, a new landlord class of central Party functionaries. In some ways they were better than their predecessors, being willing to experiment and cultivate previously untouched land. But in other ways, they were worse, possessing little understanding of the practicalities of farming. China was at the time fortunately spared drought; but food production for the cities, except around Beijing where modern machinery began to be used, did not significantly increase. That rural families grew more for themselves than before was a noticeable improvement; the old system, under which the landlord reaped the benefits of selling surplus products while workers lingered at starvation level, had been abolished.

Parcelling out the land, rather than introducing large-scale collectives, as Mao wanted at the end of the civil war, represented his first significant defeat. The army leaders and the Communist Party pragmatists, led by Liu Shaoqi, insisted that the revolution must not proceed full-speed ahead. Mao's second defeat lay in his grandiose plans for industry. The pragmatists insisted on reconstruction first, with China's small group of middle-class managers being conscripted for the task.

Chinese firms stayed in private hands, although the rules governing their operation were changed: firing workers was prohibited, the government defined production targets and the manufacture of 'luxuries' was forbidden. Foreign firms were nationalized. But with most of China's merchant fleet in Taiwan, what remained in China was in foreign capitalist hands, because the Chinese lacked the resources to build ships.

Mao was not yet at his weakest. Faced by static food production and flagging industrialization, Mao rallied opinion in the Politburo, unleashing a first purge against the conservatives in the army and the Party. The 'Three Antis' campaign of 1951 was an attack against corruption, waste and bureaucracy in private industry and among the Party pragmatists. As many as 2 to 3 million may have been fired, imprisoned and re-educated, although no executions were reported. By the following year the purge encompassed those convicted of the 'Five Antis' – bribery, tax evasion, fraud, supplying industrial information to foreigners and theft of state property. Mao was determined that one set of masters would not replace another in China.

The purges raised the curtain on the real Chinese revolution, rammed through by Mao over the protests of his comrades. All companies were now nationalized, under a system labelled 'state private management of business'. This allowed the old private owners only a 5 per cent return on their investment, and left all management decisions to the state. The First Five-Year Plan (1953–57), based on Stalin's model, set ambitious targets for capital goods production. The new industrial workforce required for this could be found more easily in dirt-poor China than it had been in Russia, and so primitive were the factories that skilled workers, of which China had virtually none, were not in great demand during the early period. Capital was scarce, and largely supplied through the nationalized companies.

China looked set to repeat, although rather more haphazardly, Stalin's crash nationalization from a low base. The stakes were high: Mao intended China to be primarily an industrial economy, drawing the surplus peasant population off the land and easing chronic rural over-population. During those early years, many people migrating to the cities suffered appalling privations due to shortages in housing and basic services. To some extent the government could control this by refusing permission for rural people to leave the land. A crash education pro-gramme was also launched, to teach basic skills to an overwhelmingly illiterate population.

In the countryside, Mao gave the green light to collectivization, nor-mally at first in village-based 'voluntary' cooperatives, and later in larger units as big as provinces. Centrally administered, with labour moved from one part to the other as required, they would become the new organs of local government, meting out such rudimentary welfare and justice as existed. The cooperatives were in charge of new schools and promoted dormitories, kibbutzim-style, for children to be reared away from their parents. Private property was outlawed.

In practice, apart from a few model cooperatives close to Beijing, the programme started slowly and was highly unpopular among the peas-ants. It led to outright clashes between the peasants and the government, and to government retreats. Where the communes were imposed willy-nilly, the farms were more inefficient than ever. As both collectivization and industrial production faltered, Mao had to try ever harder to main-tain the revolutionary momentum.

In 1956, at about the same time as the collectivization campaign began, Mao launched the 'Hundred Flowers' movement to release the frustrated revolutionary sentiments of Chinese intellectuals whom he considered were stifled by his comrades' conservatism, and to attack the conservative bureaucratic forces and their rigid centralized thinking that he believed were hijacking his revolution. 'Let a hundred flowers bloom, let a hundred schools of thought contend,' he declared, following this up with a pamphlet, 'How to handle contradictions among the people', which suggested that 'conflicts of interests and opinion are the driving forces for society and are healthy' – a radical break not just with Stalinism but with Marxism.

Restrictions governing freedom of expression and art and literature were relaxed. As most Chinese intellectuals could recall seven years before when, despite Chiang's inefficient tyranny, they could express themselves relatively freely, they immediately attacked the Communist Party, demanded that opposition parties be set up and attacked the Party leaders and even Mao himself. Not even Mao could permit such liberties, and he appears to have been persuaded to join forces with his bureaucratic enemies to suppress the freedom of speech he had himself set in motion, which seemed to threaten the monopoly of the Party. The critics who had so rashly stepped forward were treated harshly, being dismissed or sent into internal exile. Mao hastily replaced the lid and to unleash the creative tensions within society turned to his latest bright idea: the 'Great Leap Forward', the craziest of all his far-fetched schemes during this period of experimentation, and part of the Second Five-Year Plan (1958–62).

The Great Leap Forward and the Commune Movement of 1958 held that if insufficient numbers of rural people were available to work in city-based industries, then industry must be brought into the countryside, thereby elevating the village commune as the main unit of social organization and once more bypassing Mao's enemies in the central Party and bureaucracy.

Under the Great Leap Forward, China – theoretically – could overtake Britain, particularly in steel production (a not inappropriate choice of industry or country) if in every village peasants collected scrap iron, set up home-made smelters, and turned out pig iron. This 'small-is-beautiful' concept was in many ways an attractive one and the scheme was modelled on Hebei province around Beijing, where coal and iron ore existed in reasonable quantities. But the quality of the iron produced elsewhere was very low, and the fuel was often unobtainable.

And there were other significant problems: agricultural labourers could not be turned into local industrial workers overnight; the scheme – whether by design of Mao or his enemies – had to be enforced throughout the country by central cadres, who elevated commune chiefs as the new petty local tyrants with a frenzied rigidity that crippled traditional village structures and ways of doing things; and the major industrial centres were temporarily depleted of capital and raw materials while agricultural production ground to a stop.

The programme had to be almost totally abandoned, but not before agriculture had been so disrupted that some 20 million died in the subsequent famine. Li Xiaojun gives an appalling summary of the consequences:

> The most serious consequences of the 'Great Leap Forward' – the mass starvations – occurred in the early 1960s, when the destructive policies had had a few years to take their worst effect. City dwellers were rationed to thirteen kilos of grain, a quarter of a kilo of meat, and a quarter of a kilo of sweets or cakes per month. Vegetable supplies were more variable, but on average each person could get a quarter of a kilo per day. All who lived through that time remember these figures well, as if burned into the memory . . . hardly anyone could think of anything but eating. Physical education classes at school were discontinued because pupils did not have enough energy for them . . . Like everyone else I often ate food mixed with grass and leaves to increase its bulk. In rural areas many peasants had to eat *guanyintu*, a kind of white clay. Malnutrition resulted in large numbers of people suffering from swollen hands and legs.

Moreover, China had broken with Russia. How this happened will be left to a later chapter, but it profoundly affected the development of the Chinese Revolution. Mao's relations with Russia were always problematic: Stalin had offered little help in the civil war, and China's historic territorial disputes with Russia still rankled. Still, for Russia, China represented the next stage in a continuing world revolution and the Chinese government, which America and much of the world refused to recognize, needed international support. In 1949, Mao visited Moscow to seek Russian support, declaring 'we lean to one side' in the Cold War, and securing a substantial loan for reconstruction. In return, the Russians were given access to Manchurian ports.

The mutual distrust from the start of the relationship made nonsense of the prospect, already ingrained in American minds, of a monolithic communist block expanding its influence across Asia.

The Korean War further soured the relationship between the two countries. North Korea had become a communist state after the Russian occupation of the northern part of Korea following the Second World War. When the North Koreans, encouraged by the Russians, sought reunification by attacking American-supported South Korea, the Chinese were taken almost completely by surprise. Then American forces, armed with United Nations Security Council legitimization after a vote the Russians inexplicably failed to attend, landed in Korea. Russia, now taking a back seat, appeared to have embroiled China in a conflict that would directly affect its security.

As the war turned in South Korea's favour, and the Americans approached the Chinese border, the Chinese reckoned they had to send in their armies – loosely described as 'volunteers'. Although the Americans had little intention of advancing beyond North Korea's northern border, the Chinese considered the North Korean buffer essential. The communist armies forced the South Koreans back, until an armistice was concluded in 1952.

The Korean War not only soured relations between Russia and China; it boosted Chinese morale, and encouraged those in the Chinese army who advocated conventional military strategies rather than Mao's 'outdated' guerrilla methods. Following the armistice, the army's power increased until a gruff military pragmatist, Peng Dehuai, challenged the regime, angry at what he thought were Mao's unnecessary disruptions and social experimentation. China, he felt, needed order. Furthermore, it seemed that Stalin was dipping his hand into Chinese politics: to him, Mao, with his constant calls to revolution, uncannily resembled Trotsky. The Russians forged links with the Chinese army, which insisted that cooperation with Russia would enable China to acquire the equipment it needed to defend itself.

In 1953, however, Stalin died, and not until 1956 did Khrushchev emerge as the clear successor. Obviously the new generation of Russian leaders distrusted Mao as a primitive and radical idealist even more than Stalin had, and they thought his days of power in China were numbered. The Russians gave the Chinese no advance warning that Khrushchev would denounce Stalin in 1956. Mao, though holding no brief for Stalin, was furious; for example, he publicly forbore to thank the Russians for building a bridge, designed by their experts, over the Yangtze at Wuhan. In 1957 he visited Russia, proclaiming delphically that the 'east wind prevails over the west wind' – meaning that Chinese Communism would prevail over Russian Communism. The Russians angrily retorted that the phrase was 'wholly without Marxist-Leninist content'.

Khrushchev, when he visited Beijing shortly afterwards, took an intense personal dislike to Mao; the feeling was mutual. The dreamy poet of revolution was the polar opposite of the nuts-and-bolts, non-ideological man of action. Mao considered Khrushchev to be a boor and a fool – an opinion he did little to conceal. Injury was added to insult when the Chinese decided to retake the islands of Jinmen Dao (Quemoy) and Mazu Dao (Matsu) from Nationalist forces in 1958 and opened an artillery bombardment from the mainland – but could stage no attack while the Taiwanese possessed overwhelming American-supplied air superiority. Russia refused to supply China with aircraft or missiles. The following year Khrushchev met President Eisenhower at Camp David in the first mild thaw of the Cold War.

The Fall and Rise of Mao

Now Mao's internal enemies, the army in particular, seized their moment. In 1958 the former Defence Minister, Peng Dehuai, had scathingly attacked Mao's policies and demanded a return to pragmatism and cooperation with the Soviet Union. Mao was outvoted in the Politburo and being unable to make his voice heard on substantive issues, saved face by resigning as head of state in December; he retained, though, his guiding ideological role within the Party.

Liu Shaoqi, Mao's old adversary, stepped into the presidency. Liu had shrewdly not joined in the military's attack on Mao, but mediated between the two factions. In the civil war, he had organised the underground resistance in Kuomintang territory and had the support of the urban-based communists in Shanghai. Conspiratorial and secretive, with a firm grasp of the Party bureaucracy, he was China's nearest equivalent to Stalin. He maintained close contacts with the Russians, but while benefiting from their backing, in practice kept his distance once in power. The growing frost between the two countries thawed slightly after 1958, but no more than that.

Domestically, Liu believed that elite Communist Party rule along hierarchical lines would bring order and economic growth to China. This put him at odds with Mao. However, by meeting Mao half way on the Russian question Liu prevented the revolution's historic leader going into outright opposition. Having neutralized Mao, Liu decided that the main threat to his leadership and to the guiding role of the Communist Party came from the army, formerly his main ally. So China was astounded when Liu mustered a majority on the Politburo, including Mao, and dismissed Peng in August, 1959.

Under Liu's strong guidance, supported at a distance by Zhou Enlai, the regime's most subtle political strategist, and a tough young Party boss, Deng Xiaoping, China saw economic growth at home and uneasy relations abroad, the latter underlined by the border dispute with India. After the Chinese had invaded Tibet in 1950 (then independent, though the Chinese traditionally regarded it as part of China) they had unsuccessfully requested India to open negotiations about their common borders in the eastern and western Himalayas. The atmosphere worsened when the Indians gave asylum to the Dalai Lama, who had fled Tibet in 1959. Both sides moved troops to the disputed territories, and after hostilities finally broke out in October 1962 the subsequent Indian defeat was a political humiliation that haunted Nehru, who had wanted good relations with China, for the rest of his life.

China at that time was mistrusted by both superpowers. The Russians in particular had hoped for better things from Liu and were displeased that Chinese foreign policy, as they saw it, was being dictated by traditional Sino-Soviet rivalries. Thus in the Indo-Chinese border conflict, they supported India, with whom they had developed a close relationship within the context of Nehru's policy of non-alignment. The Chinese were furious, and began to vie with the Russians for influence among the revolutionary movements both of Indo-China and in Africa, with mixed results in the latter case as the next chapter makes clear. They also found a thoroughly insignificant ally in President Enver Hoxha of the impoverished republic of Albania, which decided to adopt Maoist ideology to demonstrate to the world its independence from both Tito and Russia.

China by the early 1960s seemed to have settled down much more quickly than Russia as a second-generation communist state: that is, a country in which the revolutionary ideal had largely died, whose foreign policy was governed by pragmatic nationalism and which sought not equality but economic growth through central planning. Liu wanted to be judged on whether China's way of producing wealth in fact produced more, faster, than a capitalist economy. Yet he ignored Mao's inexhaustible desire for power, which involved challenging anything that resembled the status quo.

Mao in opposition painstakingly started rebuilding a power base. One presented itself immediately: the army, smarting after it had been used, and then tossed aside, by Liu. The Defence Minister, Peng Dehuai, had rashly written a poem criticizing the Great Leap Forward: 'Grain scattered on the ground / potato leaves withered / strong young people have

left for steel-making / only children and old women reaped the crops.'
The new Defence Minister, Lin Biao, was an old comrade of Mao's and
a civil war hero. Once in contact with Mao, he set about winkling out
conservative officers.

The Vietnam War came to his help. By 1965 the extent of United
States involvement in South Vietnam caused the Chinese army high
command to consider how best to resist an American attack. While the
army commander, Luo Ruiqing, advocated conventional warfare, as in
Korea, Mao and Lin Biao urged old-style guerrilla fighting. As the
effectiveness of the Vietcong guerrilla campaign became more apparent,
Lin Biao won the argument.

At the same time he was busily spreading egalitarian ideas in the army.
Uniforms were standardized, irrespective of rank, and the officer hierarchy abolished. In practice, officers still existed as 'comrades commanding' specific forces, but the gesture won widespread support. *The
Thoughts of Chairman Mao*, the famous 'little Red Book', was first issued
in around 1965 to indoctrinate soldiers with Mao's theories of guerrilla
war and perpetual revolution. For all the derision heaped upon it at the
time, the book was a highly readable set of pithy, down-to-earth maxims
that almost any ordinary soldier could understand.

Mao was busy elsewhere. In 1962, as the revolution's ideologue, he
launched a 'socialist education' campaign, to revive the spirit of socialism and of resistance to exploitation among the younger, post-civil war
generation. This was aimed specifically at Mao's old rural strongholds,
which were not controlled by Liu's urban-based Party machine. Most
Party leaders ignored this, considering that the children involved –
mostly aged between 12 and 17 – had no political clout. Liu's authority
seemed to have been confirmed in 1965, when Mao was convincingly
overruled on a number of major issues at a meeting of the Party's Central
Committee.

Mao and Lin Biao struck with military precision. The ruling group
only realized that something was up when Mao, whom the regime was
depicting as a mere figurehead, if not senile and in poor health, went for
a televised dip in the Yangtze swimming, it was claimed, for nine miles.
Although he probably covered nothing like this distance, the message
was clear: Mao was back. Liu and his allies tried to pre-empt the
expected assault. In 1966 the Deputy Mayor of Beijing and Liu's close
associate, Wu Han, produced a play that clearly attacked General Peng's
dismissal. The Party appeared to be mobilizing conservative army

support, so Mao's followers responded with a vigorous poster attack on Wu Han.

A few months later, in 1966, the coup took place: in an unprecedented show of force, the army bussed some 1 million young people from the socialist education programme into Beijing where they were exhorted at the first of a series of mass rallies by Mao and Lin Biao. Fanatical, disciplined and convinced of their rightness as only young, unquestioning minds can be, these 14- to 19-year-old sons and daughters of uneducated peasants, not university students, represented virtually a new ideological army. The regular army moved in behind this children's army of occupation.

'To rebel is right' proclaimed Mao in a new revolutionary slogan. Behind the smokescreen of the children's revolt, the army had taken control of all key installations, communications and Party buildings in the capital. Liu, the Communist Party and government bureaucracy could do nothing once the army had sided with the radicals: it was a fait accompli. Liu was put under house arrest, while for a time still retaining his post of head of state. During a march past his residence, young guards shouted slogans against the 'bourgeois leader', the 'Chinese Khrushchev' and the 'revisionist taking the capitalist road'. The General Secretary of the Chinese Communist Party, Deng Xiaoping, was fired, as were the army commander, Lo Ruiqing, and the Mayor of Beijing, Peng Zhen.

China's revolution had, it seemed, not spent itself. Mao, now back in charge, would demonstrate that ossification was not inevitable in a still young communist state. Where Liu wanted to show Communism could work even at the expense of ideology, Mao wanted to prove that ideology could live, even at the expense of workability. The Cultural Revolution was under way.

5

Global Conflagration

'If ever the tiger pauses, the elephant will impale him with his mighty tusks. But the tiger will not pause and the elephant will die of exhaustion and loss of blood.'

Ho Chi Minh

Ho Chi Minh

As the colonial world disappeared, the two superpowers and the systems they represented vied for the allegiance of the large majority of the world's population.

The largest that escaped from Marxism-Leninism, and also the earliest, was India, whose multiplicity of peoples, traditions and customs were better suited to Western-style democracy than collectivist ideals. Marxism-Leninism, while providing a cutting edge to the Indian anti-colonial struggle, was also defeated by the British government's own response to the movement: the British gave way, under the impact of Gandhi's campaign of non-violence, preventing more extreme methods gaining currency. Similarly, it was British government policy in Africa to yield before moderate nationalist movements to prevent extremists gaining support – a policy failure only in Southern Rhodesia. Other colonial powers yielded only slightly less quickly. The various one-party governments and military cliques which came into being hardly provided an ideal or lasting form of government for developing countries, but at least kept them from Marxism-Leninism.

Indo-China was different. Inspired by Mao's example in the 1940s, the struggle inaugurated by Ho Chi Minh on 2 September 1945 when he proclaimed Vietnam's independence commenced with a ferocity that astonished his opponents. Ho cheekily quoted Thomas Jefferson: 'We hold these truths to be self-evident, that all men are created equal!'

It was typical of the man who largely created the Vietnamese revolution. He came, like so many prominent revolutionaries, from an upper middle-class civil service background. Born in 1890 in Vietnam, he was a restless youngster and in 1912 boarded a merchant steamer as a cabin boy and eventually reached France. Then he got caught up with the nationalist movement and in 1919 petitioned the Versailles peace conference for Vietnamese independence. The French were unmoved. Joining the Communist Party, he became a tireless organizer. In 1930 he presided over the founding of the Indo-Chinese Communist Party, but fled after being condemned to death as a revolutionary. After visiting Hong Kong, Moscow and China, in 1940 he returned to Vietnam; the German occupation of France suggested to him that the colonial master was merely a paper tiger and he set up the Vietminh in the hills of Pac Bo in the north-east of the country.

Much more than Mao, Ho was a genuine internationalist, a communist dedicated to Marxism-Leninism in its original form, a revolutionary first and a nationalist second: he named the mountain near his hideout Marx and the river, Lenin. Yet it was nationalism, as in China, that drew support to his movement. A slight man, with gentle eyes, a wispy beard and a thoughtful, reflective look, this deceptive appearance masked the ruthlessness and shrewdness of Lenin.

As with the communists in China, the war with Japan played into Ho's hands. In 1940, the Japanese occupied northern Vietnam. They bullied the local population, while allowing the French, who were considered hopeless militarily, to administer the region under their supervision. As hatred of indolent French colonial and brutal Japanese rule merged, by 1945 Ho had assembled an army of 5,000 men under the generalship of Vo Nguyen Giap. An American intelligence unit also supported him in the early years of his anti-Japanese struggle. The basis of his movement was threefold: founded on North Vietnam's militaristic traditions, it was strictly disciplined; its ideology was unadulterated Marxism-Leninism, although with some borrowings from the Chinese concept of peasant organization; and finally, it was rooted in the urban working class in Vietnam's industrial north and founded on Mao's principles of guerrilla warfare.

Following Mao's example however, Ho primarily recruited his soldiers from the impoverished mountain peoples of the north. The Marxist-

Leninist message of equality appealed, the prospect of joining an army was enticing. After the Japanese surrender in 1945, Ho's men tossed aside the flimsy French colonial façade and proclaimed Vietnam's independence in Hanoi.

The reality would not be so easy. Northern Vietnam was different from the South, a fertile, gentle land whose people were less willing to be organized. With help from the British, who moved in after the Japanese withdrew north of the Seventeenth Parallel, the arbitrary line that divided the country, the French expelled the communists from Saigon in desultory fighting and regained control of the South. A year of negotiation between the French and the Vietminh got nowhere. War was triggered in November 1946, when the French shelled Haiphong from the sea, taking 6,000 lives.

President Roosevelt had advocated trusteeship leading to independence for Vietnam as part of his wider anti-European colonialist ambitions. But Franco-British opposition forced him to abandon this, and under Truman the United States moved closer to its European allies. As communist insurgencies broke out in both Malaysia and Indonesia, the Americans identified their world role as containing communist expansion and securing South-East Asian raw material supplies, while having regard for the Pacific Ocean's overall strategic importance. The State Department, increasingly concerned that France could not hold Southern Vietnam against attacks from the North, really wanted a moderate nationalist alternative to succeed French colonial rule. Early on, in the very bosom of the Cold War, Truman had made his own assessment of the threat posed by Ho.

The State Department has been roundly criticized for its assessment at the time that America could not afford to assume that 'Ho is anything but Moscow-directed'. Yet the conclusion was well rooted in Ho's past record. Despite the apparent lack of formal contacts between Ho and the Soviet Union in 1947, it seems clear that he was close to Russia at least partly to offset Chinese influence as much as out of ideological common cause. In fact, Ho was playing a triple game: in addition to receiving help from the Russians and the Chinese, he sought American assistance in the struggle against France, even suggesting that Indo-China would be 'a fertile field for American capital and enterprise'. He had learnt a trick or two from his ideological mentor, Lenin.

By 1949 all China was communist, and the United States decided to halt Marxism-Leninism's Asian expansion. The French, although holding the main Vietnamese cities, were under increasing pressure outside them. Guerrillas attacked French forces in the countryside, reoccupied it when the French returned to base and attacked French units in the cities as well. Ho's strategy was simple: 'If ever the tiger pauses, the elephant will impale him with his mighty tusks. But the tiger will not pause and the elephant will die of exhaustion and loss of blood.'

The United States finally persuaded the French to install a puppet Vietnamese government nominally headed by Bao Dai, the former Emperor of Vietnam. A weak man, he failed to win support. Meanwhile the Vietminh controlled some two-thirds of the countryside, were inflicting some 1,000 casualties a month, and had confined the French to protected enclaves. In 1950 General Giap triumphed over the French at Cao Bang north of Hanoi, inflicting some 6,000 casualties. The Americans reacted by pouring in some $133 million in aid to the French. In 1950 Marshal de Lattre de Tassigny became the commander of French forces in Indo-China. Following a spectacular victory against the Vietminh in the Red River Delta, he overreached himself and was badly defeated when he attacked their positions south of Hanoi. His death in 1952 left the French position more precarious than ever.

By now the French were quarrelling with the Americans, who were financing one-third of the war's cost. The French reluctantly agreed to raise a local army of 38,000 men, fearing this would end their dominance in Vietnam. But they refused the Americans any role in directing the war effort.

The Truman administration protested, produced the money, and watched it wasted. By 1952 the French controlled only small areas around Hanoi, Haiphong and Saigon and along the Cambodian border. Fighting had spread to Laos and Thailand. Three thousand tons a month of Chinese aid poured into Vietnam, while the Russians provided somewhat less. When Eisenhower took office, his Secretary of State, John Foster Dulles, increasingly convinced that Communism had to be stopped, insisted that the French take the offensive, instead of keeping to 'safe' cities. The French commander, Navarre, drew up just such a plan and Dulles grandly promised a French triumph by the end of the 1955 fighting season.

Giap, in response, marched away from the main concentration of French forces into Laos. Navarre raced after him, bringing some 12,000 troops to the village of Dien Bien Phu, near the Laotian border. Giap, moving out of Laos, surrounded the French position in a well-defended valley. The Vietnamese brought up artillery onto the surrounding 1,000-foot-high hills simply by taking apart and then reassembling the guns. The airfield was shelled, cutting off the garrison's supply route.

The French appealed desperately to the Americans to rescue them. The Americans would only join the war as part of an international force that included the British. The British refused. Dien Bien Phu was battered into submission. The French went to bargain at Geneva with, according to their Prime Minister, Georges Bidault, 'a two of clubs and a three of diamonds'.

Eisenhower, meanwhile, laid the foundations of American intervention in Vietnam at a press conference in April, identifying Indo-China as an essential source of tin, tungsten and rubber. He used a later celebrated expression: 'If Indo-China falls, South Asia will go out very quickly, like a row of dominoes.' Yet America, still reluctant to get involved, pressed the French to keep fighting. When it became clear that the French wanted out, American threats of intervention prompted the Russians and the Chinese to press the North Vietnamese to accept partition along the Seventeenth Parallel. The division would only be temporary, while elections watched by Canada, Poland and India were held.

Elections were a dead letter: the Vietminh would not install democracy in the North. The population of both Vietnams behaved as though partition were permanent. Thousands of Vietminh guerrillas moved north while some 100,000 civilians from the north moved south. The Americans accepted their new responsibility to support the South. In October 1954 Eisenhower pledged to their favoured candidate to head the government, Ngo Dinh Diem, that America would hold South Vietnam 'in its present hour of risk'. Diem, a staunch, stubborn anti-communist, had resigned as Interior Minister in the French colonial government, and therefore they thoroughly disliked him.

The tension between the French and the Americans over Diem boiled over in May 1955 when Edgar Faure, the Prime Minister, said that he was 'not only incapable but mad'. But after the Americans refused to depose him, the French began to sidle out of Vietnam. With American backing, Diem denied the South its promised election, winning instead a 'referendum' with 98.2 per cent of the vote.

Thereafter the Americans poured money into South Vietnam to make it viable: between 1955 and 1961, the allotted sum exceeded $1 billion dollars and 1,500 American advisers arrived in the country. The aid largely supported booming consumption by the Vietnamese, but provided little in terms of an industrial base. Diem meanwhile resembled an archetypal despot; by abolishing local elections, and by appointing his own men to run villages he united the whole countryside against him. Criticism was ruthlessly suppressed and some 20,000 people were jailed in 1956.

In 1961 John Kennedy took office determined to stand up to international Communism. In 1956, as a senator he had stated that 'the fundamental tenets of this nation's foreign policy ... depend in considerable measure upon a strong and free Vietnamese nation'. Furthermore, he proclaimed, unashamedly mixing his clichés, that 'Vietnam represents the cornerstone of the free world in South-East Asia, the keystone in the arch, the finger in the dyke', and that 'It is our offspring, we cannot abandon it, we cannot ignore its needs.'

By 1961 Diem considered South Vietnam's plight to be desperate and sought American aid to expand his army by 100,000 men. The main cause for concern had been the opening of the 600-mile Ho Chi Minh Trail from the North through Laos and Cambodia into the South, bypassing the Demilitarized Zone between the two countries. By 1959, some 1,800 Vietcong had infiltrated down it, and around 2,000 followed the year after. Kennedy, rejecting large-scale intervention, reiterated his support for Diem with 'Project Beef-up'. The advisers increased from 3,000 in December 1961 to 7,000 in 1962. Diem initiated a programme that borrowed from the war against the communist guerrillas in the Philippines in the 1950s and the British experience in Malaya, securing villages with moats and bamboo fences to keep out the Vietcong. This merely antagonized the peasants; the Vietcong infiltrated the hamlets just as easily as before.

A fact-finding mission sent by Kennedy to Vietnam in early 1963 returned with an ambivalent conclusion, namely that the United States and South Vietnam were 'probably winning', but that the war would 'probably take longer than we would like'. Many American officials blamed Diem for his brutality and inefficiency. American officials encouraged a group of South Vietnamese generals when they plotted his overthrow, and Kennedy dithered. On 1 November the generals seized power and murdered Diem. Kennedy, on hearing of the murder 'leaped to his feet and rushed from the room with a look of shock and dismay on his face which I had never seen before', one eyewitness recalled. Three weeks later Kennedy was assassinated.

By the time of Kennedy's death, the Vietcong, from their heavily defended base in Tay Ninh province bordering Cambodia, controlled a third of South Vietnam, including much of the region around Saigon. They had their own government structure, their own flag, levied their own taxes and administered their own economy. Their soldiers were well-trained – for example standing in water up to their noses for hours and cooking with smokeless charcoal to avoid detection by enemy planes – and ruthless: they beheaded government officials and stuck their heads on stakes as an example.

In mid-1964 the Americans decided to expand their commitment to the war. The Gulf of Tonkin crisis in August provided the pretext: three Soviet-supplied North Vietnamese ships fired on the American destroyer, USS *Maddox*, from the 125-ship Sixth Fleet. American aircraft retaliated instantly by raiding the naval bases at Hon Gay, Loc Chao, Phuc Lo and Quang Khe, destroying twenty-five ships. By February 1965, the war had escalated sharply, as American and South Vietnamese made bombing sorties against North Vietnam. In March the first American combat forces arrived and 3,500 marines were landed in Da Nang.

The American forces initially protected Saigon and a series of ports that could be reinforced or evacuated by sea. They left field operations to their South Vietnamese allies, supporting them with massive bombing raids. By the year's end, the American army numbered around 185,000 men and the US Defence Secretary, Robert McNamara, recommended a further increase to 300,000 to match total Vietcong numbers, of which some 67,000 were regular troops. To date, the war had cost the Vietcong 36,000 killed and 8,000 captured and the South Vietnamese 11,000 killed and 8,000 captured. American losses were some 1,300 dead.

By October 1965, the war was spreading to Cambodia, whose self-important neutralist leader, Prince Norodom Sihanouk, accused South Vietnam and the Americans of bombing his country. Eventually in April 1966 Sihanouk admitted that the North Vietnamese and Vietcong had long found refuge in his territory. Meanwhile in Laos, the government's 70,000 soldiers faced two armies in a civil war: the 35,000-strong Marxist-Leninist Pathet Lao and the 10,000-strong 'neutralist' army. Cloaked by the fighting, the North Vietnamese continued pouring down the Ho Chi Minh Trail.

At this stage the Americans still considered the war winnable.

President Johnson offered to stop bombing North Vietnam in February 1966, if the North ceased attacking the South. The offer was rejected. The strategic position changed slowly once the Americans joined the South Vietnamese on field missions while attempting to secure the province around Saigon – an increasingly difficult objective as the Vietcong infiltrated the city and struck at targets there. The Americans also tried policing the nine tributaries – 'nine dragons' – of the Mekong Delta with light 'water-jet' patrol boats, but suffered heavy casualties. Ten helicopters were lost in one action on 15 February 1966.

The war slowly became more vicious: while the Americans were denounced for using napalm and saturation bombing, the Vietcong were using terror to consolidate their hold on the countryside. For example, in December 1966, 114 hill-dwelling Montagnard Vietnamese were slaughtered for cooperating with the government. The Vietcong killed some 4,000 civilians in 1967 – probably more than died that year from American bombing.

In January 1968, the Vietcong launched the Tet Offensive. It began in the towns in the northern and coastal provinces of South Vietnam and was directed against thirty of the forty-four provincial capitals. In Saigon, up to 5,000 men were infiltrated into the city, equipping themselves with arms that had frequently been smuggled in inside coffins at fake funerals. Suicide squads attacked the presidential palace, the Saigon radio station, the US naval headquarters and the American Embassy, where they broke into the outer compound, but were held off by an American helicopter. The Vietcong captured and held almost all the suburb of Cholon. American reinforcements rushed to Saigon, and the radio station was recaptured. Only towards the end of the month were the guerrillas finally driven out of the city.

During the offensive the Vietcong also captured the coastal city of Hue, the former imperial capital, where it took three weeks of fighting to dislodge them. In the process, 119 Americans were killed and 961 wounded: 363 South Vietnamese died, as did some 4,000 Vietcong. Overall, the Vietcong extended their stranglehold over the countryside, while failing to gain control of the cities. The American commander, General William Westmoreland, accepted that the 'enemy had obtained a certain psychological advantage'. The Americans had 'underestimated the enemy's capacity to employ the tactic of infiltration into inhabited centres'.

*

The war, meanwhile, was being lost in the United States. The anti-war movement kicked off strongly when a generation of American youth suddenly realized it might have to fight a full-scale war, with which they had little sympathy, in a faraway country of only questionable strategic importance to the United States. As early as April 1966, 5,000 students had demonstrated in front of the White House. By November two people had burnt themselves to death, one in front of the Pentagon, the other in front of the UN building. The basis of the anti-war argument at that stage was largely that Americans were dying, although soon the principle of American interventionism was questioned, as was the morality of the South Vietnamese regime it was supporting, with its 'tiger cages', corruption and human rights infringements.

The main problem, as 1968 dawned, was the substantial American casualties, with no end to the war in sight. By the end of 1967 estimated Vietcong losses were 88,000 dead, 30,000 disabled, 35,000 killed through disease, 18,000 deserters and 6,000 prisoners. But still they came on, with greater and greater desperation. The worse their military plight, the harder they fought and the more they sapped American military resolve.

The anti-war protests were starting to affect President Johnson, a larger-than-life free-spending post-Roosevelt idealist who announced in March 1968 that he would not seek re-election: he offered peace talks to the North Vietnamese. In April the North Vietnamese agreed, and American bombing of the North was greatly reduced, although they insisted the Vietcong be represented in exchange for withdrawing some of their own troops from the South.

General Westmoreland, a superb logistical organizer but poor military tactician, grumbled publicly about his hands being tied by the politicians. He wanted to attack the Vietcong in set-piece battles using his immense army, now some 400,000 strong. But the American commitment to South Vietnam was already waning, and the administration aimed to keep casualties down.

Westmoreland, contemptuous of his South Vietnamese allies, never gave them whole-hearted support. Thus the American role had been largely defensive, confined to limited sorties in full strength, while the South Vietnamese did most of the countryside fighting. The Americans relied on air strikes and bombing raids – insufficient by themselves – which anyway, after March, were confined to South Vietnam. The scale of the communist effort probably made the war unwinnable: it was not, as many Americans suggested, merely a question of political will, but the overall political climate that made this outcome virtually inevitable.

Ho Chi Minh, the father of the revolution, died in September 1969. He had stamped his personal authority, his utter ruthlessness upon his people in a way unmatched since Lenin. His eleven-man Politburo never changed, between 1945 and 1967, when one member died. Absolute discipline and ruthlessness in the pursuit of revolutionary goals combined with nationalism and egalitarianism: these were the source of his, and North Vietnamese, strength.

Nevertheless, as the North Vietnamese were uncertain about keeping up the pressure on the Americans, a split developed between those like General Giap and Truong Chinh, Chairman of the National Assembly, who favoured continued guerrilla warfare, and those like Le Duan and Pham van Dong, the Prime Minister, who had initiated the Tet Offensive and believed in more conventional military attack. The latter group reasoned that they could win politically by sapping the American will to resist, although this might involve heavy North Vietnamese losses. The politicians proved more far-sighted than the military men.

The war after Tet became even more unpopular in the United States. Protests spread until a 'mobilization against the war' was staged on 15 November. America's new President, Richard Nixon, had some breathing space, because he was not perceived as the man who had brought America into the war. Nixon's hope was to 'Vietnamize' the war, shifting the burden of fighting onto the South Vietnamese. As American resolve weakened further, the North Vietnamese began to look towards ruling, not fighting; a provisional revolutionary government was set up in June 1969.

In 1969 a series of small-scale Vietcong offensives were designed to inflict casualties and pressure the Americans to pull out. One such was the celebrated battle for Hamburger Hill, Hill 937, finally captured by the Americans after nine unsuccessful assaults. By the end of 1969 the casualty figures were awesome: some 9,000 Americans killed, 69,000 wounded and 152,000 Vietcong killed. It was only a matter of time before the Americans left. In June the Senate voted to repeal the Gulf of Tonkin Resolution. Nixon withdrew some 150,000 men, but combined this with raids on North Vietnam that, although militarily effective, stirred up further opposition within the United States.

Meanwhile, the war spread. The Vietcong had long operated out of sanctuaries along the Cambodian border: the Fish Hook, the Parrots

Beak and the Bulge. The Cambodians, reluctant to be drawn into the war, had left them alone, but the Americans tired of this and looked benignly on a coup engineered by the Cambodian army chief, General Lon Nol in March 1970. This helped ensure Cambodia would be the next domino to fall after Vietnam. Only a figure like Sihanouk, content to suck up to his powerful neighbour, could have kept the country at least notionally independent. Now it suffered a bitter civil war between not two, but five, competing forces. Lon Nol ordered the Vietcong out of Cambodia and cut off another supply trail that ran through the port of Sihanoukville to Vietnam.

The Vietcong promptly advanced against his puny 38,000-strong army. A South Vietnam-based American-trained group, the Khmer Serai, rallied to Lon Nol's side. A second army of local insurgents, the Khmer Rouge, took advantage of the Cambodian army's distraction with the Vietcong to stage new offensives. Soon much of southern Cambodia was in insurgent hands, and there were indescribable blood-baths elsewhere; the Mekong river flowed with mutilated bodies.

The Americans decided to go in. Around 43,000 South Vietnamese and 31,000 Americans poured into Cambodia: many bases were destroyed, and approximately 1,200 Vietcong killed. However, the Vietcong, as usual, withdrew before the advancing forces, so the incursion's results were hardly definitive. On the debit side, the Vietcong joined with the Khmer Rouge and controlled nearly all of Cambodia except the main cities and the Mekong valley. They were now only a few miles from Phnom Penh.

The war also spread into Laos, which the Vietcong had long viewed as a supply route and a refuge. The civil war there had been worsening: the Marxist-Leninist Pathet Lao seized the Plain of Jars in north central Laos in May 1979; the government would retake it in September. The Thais had despatched a force of some 5,000 men to bolster the Laotian army. In March some 25,000 South Vietnamese soldiers punched over the border at Khe Sanh to cut the Ho Chi Minh Trail. Ambushed by a tank force, they fled with the loss of some 500 men, a disturbing augury for the South Vietnamese army when it took over the fighting. During the same year, the number of American soldiers in the South had fallen from 338,000 to 139,000 men.

In April and May 1972, the Vietcong went for the kill. Around 15,000 North Vietnamese, supported by heavy artillery, crossed the Demilitarized Zone either side of the Seventeenth Parallel, winning a series of firefights. Another major assault was staged on the town of Quang Tri, between Hue and the Demilitarized Zone. The local South Vietnamese garrison panicked, and refugees fled to Hue; some 25,000 South Vietnamese soldiers were killed or wounded in the retreat. The North Vietnamese also advanced in Binh Long province, next to the Cambodian border, and mounted a further offensive in the central highlands, surrounding the town of Kontun.

The Americans responded with heavy bombing of North Vietnam, using laser precision targeting for the first time: some 1,000 sorties were launched during three days in August. In May President Nixon had also ordered North Vietnamese ports to be mined. This contributed to a Vietcong pause and reinvigorated the South Vietnamese army, which fought with unexpected ferocity. A force of 8,000 South Vietnamese repulsed Vietcong irregulars surrounding Saigon. The South Vietnamese also broke through to Kontun and relieved the besieged city of An Loc, north of Saigon. This respite allowed President Nixon to continue American disengagement. Meanwhile in Cambodia and Laos, the communists were gaining the edge. By August of 1972, the Khmer Rouge and the Vietcong controlled some four-fifths of the countryside and half the population. In Laos the communists retook the Plain of Jars.

On 23 July, largely through the efforts of President Nixon's National Security Adviser, Henry Kissinger, a peace agreement between the Americans and the North Vietnamese, the South Vietnamese and the Vietcong was initialled in Paris. This provided for the withdrawal of all American forces, the release of American prisoners, a ceasefire, and a general election. Both President Thieu of South Vietnam and Le Duc Tho, the Prime Minister of North Vietnam, welcomed the agreement as a victory for their respective countries.

In reality, the agreement was merely a fig leaf to cover American withdrawal. The ceasefire quickly broke down and the final offensive began, ending in South Vietnam's total defeat and a humiliating helicopter escape by the American Embassy staff.

This was a victory for Vietnamese nationalism, as well as for Communism, but the North Vietnamese achievement should not be overplayed. The means had been war, and to suggest that ordinary Vietnamese supported one side or the other is mistaken. As in any war, the local population was terrorized by both sides, and the South Vietnamese had as little time for the corrupt government of President

Thieu as for the puritanical harshness of the Vietcong, who had the requisite determination, manpower, equipment and, in relation to South Vietnam, overwhelming military superiority. The Americans lacked the political will to die in the numbers needed to keep Vietnam free.

Ho Chi Minh summed up the system that had defeated the United States in his political testament, written in May 1969:

> In its close unity and total dedication to the working class, the people and the fatherland, our party has been able, since its founding, to unite, organize and lead our people in an outside struggle to carry them from victory to victory. Unity is an extremely precious tradition of our party and people. All comrades from the Central Committee down to the cell, must preserve unanimity and unity of mind in the Party as the apples of their eyes . . .
>
> Each Party member, each cadre, must be deeply imbued with revolutionary morality and show industry, thrift, integrity, uprightness, total dedication to the public cause [and] exemplary selflessness.

Unity, under the ideas of one man; discipline in carrying them out. The North Vietnamese Party was the apotheosis of a Communist Party as an instrument of one man's vision, or dictatorship: the exact reverse of neighbouring China, with its constant convulsions within the ruling group.

The American withdrawal from Vietnam marked a sensational victory for world Communism. In Indo-China both Russia and China had supported fellow revolutionaries to the point where they had humiliated the world's most powerful nation. Their support had helped to make it impossible for the Americans to rescue an ally whom Congress and public opinion were not convinced was worth rescuing.

Vietnam represented the first clash between the two systems since the Korean War had ended indecisively. This clash had ended decisively – with an American defeat that Kissinger's peacemaking could not camouflage. The world had received a clear signal: that Marxist-Leninist revolution, not just in Indo-China but throughout the developing world, was on its way. Marxism-Leninism was the wave of the future, and capitalism the system of the past. Yet no one foresaw, in the wake of that astonishing American defeat, that the system would fall over its own two feet.

Year Zero: Cambodia

On 17 April 1975, black-garbed young peasant boys wearing Chinese caps, their faces bewildered at seeing a city for the first time, marched into the outskirts of Phnom Penh. The war for Cambodia had ended. A mood of intense relief fell on the capital after nearly a decade of bloody civil war in which a small country of 8 million people had been sucked into the wider Indo-China war, into the last stand of a superpower, the United States of America, defending its brand of democracy in a far-flung corner of the globe. Even those who had fought the Khmer Rouge were relieved that finally the suffering was over, even if they feared that some form of enslavement was about to begin.

One week later Phnom Penh was empty. Some 3 million people, expelled from the city at gunpoint by the Khmer Rouge, were prodded into the farthest reaches of the Cambodian countryside at the height of a burning dry-season summer. Hundreds of thousands of the sick, evacuated from their hospital beds, the old and small children died along the way. The peasant soldiers' casual and often sadistic brutality put paid to many more. 'It was a stupefying sight,' said one victim, 'a human flood pouring out of the city, some people pushing their cars, others their overladen motorcycles or bicycles overflowing with bundles and others behind little home-made carts. Most were on foot, like us, and heavily laden. The sun was fierce, but we were so dazed we hardly minded it. Children were crying, some were lost and searching vainly for their parents.'

'The worst part of the whole march was the stopping and starting. There was such a crowd that we could never go forward more than a few yards at a time before we had to stop again. Sometimes the Khmer Rouge fired into the air to scare us and make us go faster.' A former electrical technician remembered how on 19 April '. . . I saw the Khmer Rouge arrest about twenty young men with long hair. They shot them before our eyes. Everybody was terrified and had their hair cut at once, even in the middle of the night.' All the refugees spoke of piles of corpses on the roadsides, of mothers in childbirth left to die or groups of people shot along the route, of bodies driven over several times by trucks so that their forms were barely recognizable.

Announcements along the way suggested that all offenders and officials could return to Phnom Penh to work for the Anghor – the People. Those that stepped forward were well fed; most were shot the same night, some on the spot and others in Phnom Penh. The same story was repeated in provincial cities: in Battambong, according to one refugee, 'on 24 April around six o'clock loudspeaker cars advised the civilian population to leave Battambong within three hours. Anyone caught in the city after that would be killed . . . there were hundreds of bodies lying by the roadside with their hands tied behind their backs. I learned later they were the non-commissioned officers from Battambong who were supposedly going for retraining . . .

'Near Phnom Thom at the place called Mecohbar I saw more bodies . . . according to a large number of witnesses this farm was the scene of atrocious happenings: hundreds if not thousands of soldiers were executed there. In particular an entire company was massacred, with their wives. The children were standing crying as their parents were shot before their eyes. "Why are you crying over enemies?" they were told; "If you don't stop we'll kill you too!"'

Some survivors of the exodus had to undertake hard, relentless, backbreaking work in the villages to which, as urban dwellers, they were wholly unused. Woken at 5 a.m., they would usually go on until as late as 11 p.m., sometimes by the light of the moon or by torchlight. They pulled ploughs, because of the shortage of oxen. Other survivors went to slow deaths in special camps, or were shot. Several hundred thousand were relocated between September and December 1975 to other villages hundreds of miles away, in conditions that again caused thousands to lose their lives.

It is reckoned that about 600,000 people lost their lives in the Cambodian war, with as many injured. During the ensuing 'peace' at least 1.4 million people were killed; the real figure may approach 2.5 million. 'One or two million young people are enough to make the new Kampuchea [as Cambodia's new masters renamed the country until their overthrow],' proclaimed Khmer Rouge slogans baldly. Neither peasant soldiers' brutality nor dire economic necessity caused the holocaust. True, the Khmer Rouge Foreign Minister, Ieng Sary, cited security as one reason for Phnom Penh's evacuation: 'Many of Lon Nol's troops who had surrendered were actually hiding weapons and had plans to overturn us after our victory in Phnom Penh.' But evacuating a whole city was a wholly disproportionate reaction to the threat from a defeated and demoralized enemy.

Feeding the city had been another problem: the Americans had daily airlifted 30,000 to 40,000 tons of food into the city. But according to a

Khmer Rouge representative, 'We had no means of transporting such quantities of supplies to the capital. So the people had to go where the food was.' Another insufficient explanation: feeding hundreds of thousands of people on the land was immeasurably harder than feeding a city.

The real explanation was ideology, pure and simple: to hardline ideologues like the revolutionary leader, Pol Pot, city life epitomized the corruption of man, work in the countryside liberation and revolutionary purification. The French journalist, François Ponchard, reported a Khmer Rouge official's thinking: 'The city is bad, for there is money in the city. People can be reformed, but not cities. By sweating to clear the land, sow and harvest crops, men will learn the real value of things. Man has to know that he is born from a grain of rice.'

Marx's thought had been turned on its head. From representing the ideal of a new industrial society, emancipating people from the drudgery and slavery of the land, it had been warped to that of an idealized peasant existence to free man from the city's corruption. The Cambodian revolution was intended to reverse the tide of progress as it had affected that country in the twentieth century, returning it to its brutalized peasant past. In the process, Cambodia, the region's most fertile country, the breadbasket of South-East Asia, would suffer endemic poverty and starvation and beg for international relief aid.

The Khmer Rouge insistence on instant results gave this extraordinary ideology of regression its cutting edge. As one official put it: 'The Khmer's methods do not require a large personnel, there are no heavy charges to bear, because everyone is simply thrown out of town. If we may take the liberty of a making a comparison, the Khmers have designed this method which consists in overturning the basket with all the fruit inside; then choosing only the articles that satisfy them completely, they put them back in the basket. The Vietnamese did not tip out the basket, they picked out the rotten fruit. The latter method involves a much greater loss of time than that employed by the Khmers.' In such banal farmyard images was expressed the horror of Cambodia.

It did not last long. Cambodia's traditional enemy, Vietnam, used the pretext provided by a refugee exodus into its territory and by border clashes to invade the country, occupying Phnom Penh in 1979 and installing a puppet government. The Vietnamese were unable to clear the countryside however, of Khmer Rouge fighters based in the north and west, various far-right bandit groups and the handful of those still loyal to the country's old ruler, Prince Norodom Sihanouk. The war continued sporadically; the sufferings of Cambodians were not over, although the new regime represented a vast improvement in the life of most who had survived.

The Cambodians thus had to thank another socialist country's traditional nationalist ambitions for freedom from the most terrifying application of scientific socialism since Stalin. The revolution underlined just how far could be taken the creed of impersonal historical forces, of the subordination of man's will to the people's will (in the case of Cambodia, defined as the will of the Anghor, so mysterious a deity that the country's collective leadership and its leader, Pol Pot, were named as uncertain reincarnations of earlier revolutionary figures to prevent their identification as individuals). The end justified the means; in the Cambodian case this meant the end of some two million people, a quarter of the country's population, in order to turn back the clock of modern industrial progress.

Africa

The Vietnam War marked the final chapter in Asia's decolonization. The struggle had begun with Mahatma Gandhi's fasting in *satyagraha* (the philosophy of non-violence, literally 'truth force') that marked the first victory of the movement for passive resistance in 1919; it continued with Ceylon winning self-government from Britain in 1931 and dominion status in 1947. It had affected the Philippines, where there had been a revolt as early as 1898 against Spain and a guerrilla war from 1916, resulting in the country gaining full independence from the USA in 1946. Indonesia had similarly been affected by nationalist sentiment in 1908; Sukarno founded his National Party there in 1927 and after prolonged agitation, the Dutch granted Indonesia independence in 1949.

Much of Africa, however, had been colonized in the twentieth century. The speed of the colonial withdrawal, partly to forestall communist revolutions sweeping the continent, left the nationalist movements that took over power gasping for breath and ideas.

Initially, this African rush to independence proved surprisingly easy. The first nationalist seeds were sown with the education of African students in the United States and around the world, where they began to discuss racial solidarity and independence. During the Second World War, thousands of Africans were combatants in Europe, where they learnt they were fighting for democracy against tyranny and Hitler's racist doctrines. By October 1946, the first African party had been founded – the Rassemblement Démocratique Africain – in French West Africa. In 1947 there was a revolt in Madagascar, followed by the Mau Mau rebellion in Kenya.

The revolution was largely inspired by democratic ideals and the Christian beliefs that had accompanied colonization and which, in most cases, had not been rejected. Nationalists favoured Christianity, because it replaced the passive fatalism of local religions. Moreover, it preached equality, which found favour among Africans working for white colonialists. The African nationalists were not able, though, to rediscover native political traditions, as they had hardly existed before the colonists arrived.

Some claimed, with more than a little licence, that Africa had been a peaceful pre-colonialist nirvana, into which foreign companies had introduced competition and tension. Furthermore, an observer of the early movements noted that many African nationalists 'rejected a democratic system that is simply transplanted from Europe to Africa. In their opinion liberal democracy is no use in Africa because the general personal education of the people is not sufficiently advanced to allow them to give the voting process its proper significance.' The opening for Marxist-Leninist ideas is clear.

The communists did not waste time. As early as 1918, a League for Emancipation for the East was set up as a Soviet front organization for Africa and Asia; Africa and Asia should progress 'over the heads of both feudalism and capitalism and advance from their pre-capitalist system to socialism without first going through the painful stage of capitalism'. This was a nod and a wink to what had happened in Russia – the skipping of an entire chapter of Marxist historical inevitability. In telescoping the early stages of revolution, the Russians were tacitly acknowledging that the developing rather than the developed world offered better prospects for revolution. The Party at that stage accepted that communist parties, which were small, should co-operate with 'bourgeois' nationalist movements.

This approach did not survive the Second World War, from which the Soviet Union emerged as a competitor for power with the United States. At the inaugural meeting of the Cominform in 1947, its founder, Andrey Zhdanov, declared that there were only two camps: imperialist and anti-imperialist. The bourgeois leaders had to be shelved. This proved ludicrously over-optimistic: local communists in a number of countries had little regard for leaders who were popularly identified with the struggle for freedom. Gandhi, of course, had been anathema to the Indian communists, who called him 'a traitor and a degenerate'. In Iran, in the early 1950s the communists turned on the Prime Minister, Mohammed Mossadeq, who had nationalized Western oil interests, because he stood for the bourgeoisie, not the proletariat. Even Gamal Abdul Nasser and his colleagues in Egypt were scorned as 'a reactionary group of officers in alliance with the United States'. Most of the African nationalist movements received the same treatment. Kwame Nkrumah's first government in Ghana was described as 'a shield behind which the reality of British colonial dominance conceals itself'.

By 1957, as middle-class nationalist movements started to score striking successes in spite of non-cooperation from local communists, the latter began to praise the bourgeoisie as being 'objectively interested – in so far as it's not connected with imperialist circles – in carrying out the chief tasks of the anti-imperialist, anti-feudalist revolution'. The Russians decided to support such struggles regardless of their degree of socialist commitment. They only required that a nationalist 'be filled with an abiding hatred of the imperialist exploiters and carry on a relentless struggle'. The Russians pressed modestly for agrarian reform and the masses' right to participate in the formation of public policy; full-scale socialism was off the agenda.

This made the process of decolonization in two countries run in Russia's favour. In Guinea, Ahmed Sékou Touré, the county's future president, successfully persuaded his fellow countrymen in September 1958 to reject de Gaulle's offer to stay within the French community; he then established a political system along primitive, orthodox Soviet lines. The system won 'legitimacy' in a referendum in which Sékou Touré won 1,571,580 out of 1,576,747 votes cast – or 99.999 per cent.

The similarities were no coincidence. A young man from a good but impoverished family, he had studied Marx and Lenin and had joined the Confédération Général du Travail, the main French communist trade union. Sékou Touré put this training to good use. After being elected Mayor of Conakry, Guinea's capital, in 1955, he travelled extensively around the countryside, holding meetings, building up his party organization and seeking to break the hold of the old tribal chiefs. The Russians reckoned that Sékou Touré was their man: a new Ambassador, D.S. Solod, was despatched to the country.

Solod had been the Russians' chief Middle East troubleshooter, during which the Syrians in particular had moved closer to Russia. His good friend, the Syrian Economy Minister, Maaruf al-Davalid, claimed that he would rather see 'Arab republics become Soviet republics than victims of Zionism'. Solod later became Ambassador in Cairo and deputy chief of the Middle East desk of the Russian Foreign Office.

By the time Solod had arrived in Guinea, the Russian press was applauding the country as a 'people's democracy'. However, a curious pattern emerged in Guinea that would recur elsewhere in the developing world: while the cash grew ever scarcer, the Russians became more confident that they were pushing Guinea in a genuinely socialist direction. Such aid as came was characterized by delays and poor quality. Snowploughs were even sent by mistake to this tropical African country. By 1961, the government was beginning to reconsider the Russian connection. When a series of big demonstrations broke out, Sékou Touré accused their instigators of being communists and Solod was kicked out.

The Guinean experience was an object lesson to the Soviet Union. It showed that the Russians could provide revolutionary legitimacy and financial help but then be discarded. It demonstrated that even a Leninist one-party system was not necessarily pro-Russian. And it became the pretext for other similar revolutionary about-turns that the Russians sponsored. The Soviet problem in Africa, unlike that in Eastern Europe, was that it could not use force of arms to dictate events; it had to rely on local forces and when, like Sékou Touré's party, these developed nationalist aspirations, the Russians came a cropper.

Another possibility for Soviet penetration was Ghana, under Kwame Nkrumah, the father of Pan-Africanism. Nkrumah, once a reassuringly moderate nationalist, soon developed a surreal folie de grandeur and imposed a one-party state: he called himself *Osagyefo* – the Redeemer, *Kukurundi*, Brave Hero, *Kasapreko,* He who has the Last Word, and *Nufeno*, the Immortal Ruler over Life and Death. The party's doctrine, modelled on Marxist-Leninist lines, featured bizarre adaptations, including the 'Lord's Prayer': 'I believe in Kwame Nkrumah, The Creator of Ghana, the founder and benefactor of Ghana's schools and villages. I believe in the Revolutionary Convention People's Party, its imperishable organization and our salvation, granted to us by the inspiration of history, liberator of the masses, persecuted and repressed with harsh laws until they arose from the despair in the third month.'

In 1960, a 'referendum' rejected the British monarchy and substituted Nkrumah as President. Repression sharply increased. The opposition leadership was seized. By the end of 1966 there were over a hundred political prisoners in jail. Nkrumah's opponents within the Convention People's Party were purged. A decree allowed people to be imprisoned for up to twenty years without trial.

Links between Ghana and the Soviet Union grew apace: the staff of the Russian Embassy swelled, and no longer was Nkrumah dubbed a 'mouthpiece of white colonialism'. Pan-Africanist thought evolved from suggesting that there should be equidistance between the superpowers to advocating a privileged relationship with the Soviet Union.

Nkrumah also announced that around 3,000 Ghanaian students would study in Russia – a large number by any standards – with even suggestions that Ghanaian officers would be trained there. The Ghanaian leader visited Russia, and declared that socialism was his party's aim. Shortly afterwards, the United States announced that it would finance the Volta Dam – indicating that it would compete with the Russians for influence.

In practice Pan-Africanism was a dead duck, based on the unrealizable goal of a United States of Africa. National rivalry, and the dislike of most African leaders for Nkrumah, ensured that he was one of the first nationalist leaders to play the Soviet Union for what he could get and thereby encourage the West to outbid the East. But his dictatorial pretensions and repression brought about his overthrow by a military coup in 1966. Ghana's new rulers followed a more pro-Western course, making clear that for them Russia held few attractions.

Mali looked like another suitable case for Soviet treatment. The country's ruler, Modibo Keita, came from a traditional clan that hailed back to the Middle Ages. Impatient and arrogant, in 1960 he broke away from the federation in which Mali and Sudan had been joined to Senegal – long the pioneer of French-style democracy in Africa under Léopold Senghor.

Keita was influenced by the Sudanese one-party system, closely modelled on Marxism-Leninism, which its leaders had studied during the 1940s and 1950s. The Sudanese attempted to seize control of the federation when it had been formed, seeking to prevent Senghor's election as its President. In July 1960 they even attempted a coup in Senegal's capital, Dakar, taking over the ministries of Defence and the Interior. However, Senghor loyalists managed to hang onto the radio station and beat back the attack.

Mali went its own way, linking up with Ghana and Guinea in the Russian-advised Union of West Africa. A further alliance bound Mali to two conservative Arab states, Morocco and the United Arab Republic (the joint Egyptian/Syrian state from 1958 to 1961), and one radically anti-Western one, Algeria, which supported Patrice Lumumba's pro-communist group in the Congolese civil war. Morocco had joined as insurance against the spread of revolution from Algeria; the UAR had joined in order to moderate the extremism of the group – and to buy off radical nationalists at home. Mali also established diplomatic relations with China and voted to allow it into the United Nations. Yet Mali's allegiance remained primarily with the Russians. As a delegate from Mali told the Twenty-Third Congress of the Russian Communist Party: 'Marxism-Leninism's correctness is being confirmed every day by the success of the Soviet Union in the scientific and technological sphere. Imperialism is digging its own grave . . . Communism has become synonymous with freedom.'

The West worried about the immediate post-colonial period in Africa. The Soviet Union appeared able to take advantage of the anti-Western sentiments of the nationalist movements, and in some cases export their own revolutionary models. The departing colonial powers could point to the independent territories still in moderate nationalists' hands then, and later – Kenya, Uganda, Tanzania, Botswana, Malawi, Cameroon, Senegal. But one country, Guinea, had been seduced by Russia and had imposed a Soviet-identikit one-party apparatus, as opposed to the rather loose largely one-man structures that dominated countries like Kenya. Another big one, Ghana, was veering the same way. Mali appeared to be in Soviet hands. Russia had considerable sway in Sudan and, by patting Emperor Haile Selassie on the head, was winning over strategic Ethiopia, as well as nearby Somalia.

A breakdown of Soviet aid to Africa at the time gives an idea of the degree of penetration: Ethiopia, between 1958 and 1962, got $114m from Russia and its allies, compared with $188m from America; Ghana, $196m from Russia, $157m from America; Guinea, $125m from Russia, $14m from America; Mali $98m from Russia, $5m from America; Somalia, $63m from Russia, $26m from America; Sudan, $123m from Russia, $65m from America. By the mid-1960s it seemed the colonial powers' gamble in hurrying through independence to pre-empt Marxist-Leninist revolution might not be paying off.

Moreover, Marxism-Leninism was advancing on two fronts. For the African states which distrusted both sides in the Cold War, there was newly independent China, as primitive in many of its provinces as the African continent itself, and highly flexible in its approach. While violently criticizing the Russians for backing bourgeois nationalists, the Chinese did exactly the same whenever it suited them. The Chinese even traded with Rhodesia and South Africa. Noting that Russia's star was waning in Guinea, the Chinese competed for influence there, inviting Sékou Touré to Peking in September 1960.

The Chinese also built a relationship with feudal Morocco, largely to gain influence in Algeria's struggle with France, viewing this as another Vietnamese-style liberation epic. China was the first country to recognize the Algerian provisional government set up in 1958, and repeatedly pressed its favours on the Algerians who, however, were chary of becoming too involved with China. The revolution was conducted along nationalist and Marxist-Leninist lines organizationally; but from the first it tried to carve its own independent 'non-aligned' path as an example to the developing world. Nonetheless, the Algerians pointed out to the French that they might be pushed into Chinese arms unless France proved more amenable.

The Russians, on the other hand, tried hard to bring about a peaceful settlement. They provided the Algerians with only a decent minimum of military support, since friendship with France as a counterpart to Germany's influence in Europe had been an overriding priority of Russian foreign policy since Tsarist days. Moreover, de Gaulle, who had long pursued détente with the Russians, was currently taking a more independent French line within NATO, which suited the Soviet Union.

Chinese revolutionary propaganda did however help forge Algerian nationalism. As one prominent jailed Algerian claimed, 'All my fellow inmates read Mao's words in prison . . . I read all of Mao Tse-tung's writings, which steeled my will to fight and strengthened my confidence.' Yet in the Algerian revolution the local Communist Party had a surprisingly small impact upon events: during the mid-1960s in municipal elections, for example, it polled no more than 4 to 5 per cent. It was clear from the outset, moreover, that the Algerian government was prepared to use communist support against its old colonial masters, but not to put itself in hock to the Chinese.

In 1965, shortly after independence, communist relations with Algeria became strained after the Algerian Communist Party was suddenly banned; China, for one, angrily protested. The Chinese also got on less well with Colonel Houari Boumedienne, considered too pro-Soviet, who had thrown out the revolution's most colourful and idealistic figure, Ahmed Ben Bella, in the same year. Because they disapproved of the new regime, the Chinese boycotted the Bandung Conference of non-aligned countries, which subsequently had to be cancelled.

Another country that looked promising to the Chinese was Cameroon. A post-colonial rebellion had persuaded the President, Ahmadou Ahidjou, to seek French assistance. The main challenge was posed by Ruben Um Nyobe, a guerrilla leader, and later by Felix-Roland Moumie, responsible for a particularly bloodthirsty series of attacks on isolated government posts. Moumie openly acknowledged his communist antecedents: he claimed to be the 'first professional communist revolutionary' in Africa. After becoming Vice-President of the Students' Union in Dakar and visiting Eastern Europe, he travelled to British Cameroon, Congo, Nigeria and finally France, where he set up a Cameroon exile organization.

Moumie was well supported financially, and even met Khrushchev on a visit to Russia. Slowly, however, the anarchy in Cameroon was brought under control. Intriguingly, Moumie switched to the Chinese after the Russians decided he was a loser. In 1960 Moumie visited China. One of Moumie's henchmen claimed that 'the Chinese people have never hesitated to support our struggle', and referred to the 'great Chinese contribution' to the Cameroon revolution. But by 1962 it was becoming apparent that the government was going to succeed in quelling the revolution.

A high point of the rush by the major powers to influence the situation in post-colonial Africa was the Congo. In January 1959, near the end of Belgian colonial rule, rebels from the province of Katanga headed by Patrice Lumumba staged an insurrection in Léopoldville, backed by the Russians. However the rebels also happily accepted Chinese assistance: ample funds to 'support the Congolese people in their struggle against colonialism' were promised. In September 1960, with the Congo now independent and Lumumba its first Prime Minister, his deputy bluntly asked the Russians and the Chinese to urgently provide, 'personnel (volunteers), arms (various weapons with ammunition, fighter planes, helicopters, artillery tanks, armoured reconnaissance cars); finance (the sums necessary for certain urgent expenditures); and foodstuffs (rice, flour and tinned flour). This . . . would make it possible for the government of the Congo to ensure the independence of its country, which is at present dangerously threatened.'

In the event, the Russians gave nothing, and the Chinese too little. In December 1960 Lumumba was arrested. Congo's new leader, General Mobutu quickly rounded up his followers, and UN troops went in to restore order amidst the savagery. The Chinese went to town after Lumumba's murder shortly afterwards: millions demonstrated in Peking and 400,000 in Shanghai. The chairman of the Peking Afro-Asian Solidarity Committee denounced the Americans as 'a group of cannibalistic monsters who will never voluntarily give their colonial people the boost of independence'. In practice the Chinese display was less concerned with solidarity for Lumumba than with blaming the Russians for failing to put their money where their mouth was, thus winning the Chinese support from other African revolutionary movements. The Chinese, too late, started to assist the lingering pockets of post-Lumumba resistance in that heart of African darkness; but Mobutu's forces mopped them up inexorably.

The Chinese also made a significant effort to win friends in eastern Africa, with Zanzibar and Tanzania the two main targets. In January 1964 the Sultan of Zanzibar was overthrown, and a People's Republic was set up under Sheik Abeid Karume, a genuinely non-aligned moderate. But his Vice-President, Abu Rahman Mohammed, had long enjoyed close connections with the Russians. So the Chinese muscled in; among the first to recognize the new regime, they offered it economic aid.

A seizure of power by Rahman, widely known as Babu, seemed imminent until in 1964 President Nyerere of Tanzania announced that the two countries would merge. He intended to bolster Karume and the moderates with Tanzanian military muscle, and neutralize the danger of the country drifting into Russia's or China's orbit. The struggle proved harder than anticipated; but Nyerere succeeded by skilfully exploiting the superpower rivalry. For him it was the Russians, with their insistence on substantial trade concessions, the presence of military advisers and loyal support for their views in international forums, who posed the greater threat to African independence.

Nyerere, while publicly slating Western countries, had no wish to antagonize them as they were Tanzania's main trading partners. So he leaned towards China, importing Chinese advisers and engineers to construct the railway from Zambia to Dar es Salaam, bypassing Rhodesia, an engineering feat that finally made a number of African nations take China seriously. Although Nyerere became a close friend of China – and even adapted the Mao-style uniform for his own use – in practice the Chinese exerted little control over his government.

The Chinese were attracted to Africa for a number of reasons. Chinese policy at the time was genuinely ideological: many Chinese who went out to help African revolutionaries were still dazzled by the early revolutionary experiences of their own country, and not cynics like so many Soviet military trainers. The Chinese were less inclined to throw their weight around: the attitude of poorly-educated Russians towards those they considered racially inferior should not be underestimated as a source of tension between the Africans and the Russians.

The latter also exacted payment in kind for their aid. Young Africans sent for ideological training in the Soviet Union were horrified to discover that from their 900 rouble 'scholarships' they had to spend some 600 on lodging, food and books. Some Africans also disliked the courses, although the great majority returned home ready to spread a fine set of simplistic beliefs.

One African student gave a vivid description of life at a Soviet training centre.

> Worst of all perhaps was the interference we had to suffer from our fellow Russian students and roommates. No one doubted that they were only there to spy on us . . .

He went on to describe the indoctrination.

> [In] the first two or three months . . . there were four full lessons a day with, in addition, homework . . . Our first exercises were all to do with Russian popular heroes and people's leaders. Comparisons were made and parallels drawn with our own countries. Finally we were asked whether we would not want such heroes and revolutionary leaders in our own countries, and it was made quite clear what reply was expected.
>
> This method of indoctrination was intended not only to indoctrinate and mould us, but also to discover our own ideas and tendencies. If we started to discuss things or to ask awkward questions, we were told we were wasting valuable time and ought to apply for a transfer . . . The teachers deliberately dragged on their lessons and never lost an opportunity to slip in little political homilies, at the same time sounding out our views in order to be able to sift and classify us. Once I realized this, I pretended to be naïve.

Many of them, though, were genuinely naïve, and, so the Russians hoped, would tilt their countries in a pro-Soviet direction once back home.

In February 1960, the Patrice Lumumba Friendship University was set up with places for 4,000 students; no fewer than 43,000 people applied for the first 750 places, such was the African urge for education, and the nationalists' friendly perception of the Soviet Union. Even though the first results of Soviet and Chinese penetration of Africa had been mixed, clearly the Russians felt that, given time, the continent would be susceptible to the appeal of revolution.

The importance of Africa to the Russians was both strategic and ideological. A revolutionary victory in Africa would demonstrate that revolution was striding forward and that capitalism was on the run. Africa also offered access to raw materials hitherto enjoyed by the European powers and to the main oil route westwards from the Middle East.

Although the Russians encouraged revolutionary movements and governments that looked to them for help throughout the continent, their main hopes rested with those countries closer to the Red Sea and the Suez Canal that were part of the string encircling the oil-rich Middle East. Ethiopia, Zanzibar, Sudan and Somalia were prime targets, as were countries that still had colonial regimes – in particular the Portuguese dependencies of Guinea-Bissau, Angola and Mozambique. Beyond them lay white Rhodesia and the most glittering, but unattainable, prize of all, South Africa.

Portugal: The End of Empire

The West's worst fears about the future of post-colonial Africa appeared to be realized with the Portuguese revolution of 1974. For a country as small as Portugal to hold on to so large an empire well into the 1970s in the teeth of world hostility was remarkable. The Portuguese had done this partly from the sheer determination of their dictatorship. Unlike the other colonial powers – the British and the French in particular – they did not leave the continent when armed opposition made itself felt because potential domestic protests about any casualties inflicted were stifled.

The Portuguese were also successful colonial administrators: they intermarried and mixed easily, appointed Africans to senior positions and usually responded to guerrilla fighting with conciliation and aid to pacify the countryside. Moreover the government was absolutely convinced of its moral rectitude in fighting for empire: Portugal, a tiny country largely irrelevant to mainstream Europe with almost an African-style economy, desperately needed a role: as a master of empire it had one.

Yet African wars could not indefinitely draw on the resources of such a small country. As the casualty figures mounted, the Portuguese were compelled to field an army of 200,000 men, who mostly had to spend some four years in uniform. Although their empire provided ample trade for Portugal, in particular an outlet for its exports, the war was draining away, by some reckonings, as much as $600m a year. Given Portuguese and colonial economic expansion, the war was affordable. But the oil price shock of 1973 dealt these economies a hammer blow.

By then, many Portuguese government officials considered the policy unsustainable, but while Antonio Salazar, the country's veteran dictator, was alive, change was impossible. Following his incapacitation by a stroke, the slightly more open-minded Marcello Caetano came to power. He believed he could set up a 'Portuguese community', similar to the failed French experiment in Africa, in which Portugal's African colonies would gradually assume an equal role in government. This satisfied no one. It angered many conservatives and was too limited for the radicals; above all, it provoked a virtual mutiny within the army, whose conscripts were restless and whose professional officers were furious at possibly having to slog on in Africa with ever longer terms of service and poor pay. Eventually a group of young officers plotted Caetano's overthrow.

They were led by three men: Major Otelo Saraiva de Carvalho, a stocky, good-looking, bombastic character with an eye for high living and women, also naïvely romantic enough to have imbibed many of the doctrines of the African liberation movements he had fought in Angola; Colonel Vasco Goncalves, an inflexible Marxist-Leninist who had probably always been a pro-Russian infiltrator in the armed services; and the naval Captain, Rosa Coutinho, an outwardly friendly, hardline Marxist who also leaned towards Russia. Around this nucleus a group of some 200 middle-ranking officers coalesced. As the coup's figurehead, they appointed a leading general recently fired for publishing a book criticizing Portuguese colonial policy, General Antonio de Spinola. On 25 April 1974, the 'Revolution of Flowers' took place, which would have far more impact on Africa than on Portugal.

From the first, the captains and majors who actually ran the revolution stated that their main objective was granting independence to the African territories. Cease-fires were negotiated in all of them, and Rosa Coutinho, the 'Red Admiral', was appointed Governor of Angola to supervise the independence negotiations. Installing Communism in Portugal, although important, was less urgent. The captains quickly suppressed the domestic freedoms so briefly attained: any political party that described itself as right-of-centre was banned, leaving only one, the Centre Democrats, struggling to survive, although denied access to radio and television. Communist mobs stormed its headquarters and those of other middle-of-the-road parties.

General Spinola was ousted in September, when he tried to prevent a massive left-wing rally in Lisbon. After an abortive plot in March 1975, Spinola fled into exile and the revolution gathered momentum. The promised general election was held in April 1975, and Mario Soares's Socialist Party did surprisingly well. The communists won the disappointing share of 18 per cent, although insisting they would continue to back the leaders of the armed forces movement, and that the elections were irrelevant.

However, during the summer of 1975, angry crowds, protesting that the election result had been ignored, sacked the Communist Party's headquarters and tried to blockade Lisbon. Goncalves, the doctrinaire communist Prime Minister, was forced to stand down; Otelo, the romantic left-wing revolutionary, was pushed out by a well-organized military coup under General Antonio Ramalho Eanes who installed democracy and was elected President in 1976.

Thus popular protest largely frustrated the communists' single attempt to seize power in a Western European country since the Second World War. Their efforts had been made not with organized mass support, based on the pro-communist trade union movement, Intersindical, but by armed force. Yet even impoverished Portugal's electorate was sufficiently sophisticated, westernized and pluralistic to oppose the Left's imposition of a military dictatorship.

Not so, however, Portugal's colonies. Against Spinola's furious objections, independence agreements had been negotiated with unseemly speed: Guinea-Bissau won its 'freedom' in 1976, two years after the coup, and was promptly swallowed up by a rigid Marxist-Leninist regime. Mozambique gained independence in November 1977. The beneficiary was the Marxist Samora Machel's FRELIMO – the Mozambique

Liberation Front – whose history is a case study of a Marxist-Leninist takeover of a genuinely non-aligned national independence movement when a colonial war had dragged on.

Machel's hard line won over moderate FRELIMO leaders like Domingos Arouca as the war was clearly becoming one of attrition. Arouca, a roly-poly politician and potentially a splendid figurehead for a non-aligned Mozambique, went off to found FUMO, the United Mozambique Front, and for long controlled pockets of the countryside; but he made little headway, owing to a shortage of arms and cash, against FRELIMO's better-equipped forces. Machel, a rabid and slightly eccentric revolutionary, was unwilling to choose between the Soviet Union and China in his early days of power: he enjoyed playing one off against the other. But of major African leaders he was the most orthodox Marxist-Leninist, although he softened later.

In Angola the imposition of Marxism-Leninism proved more difficult. As Portugal withdrew three liberation movements rushed to fill the gap. In the north, supported by Mobutu's arbitrary but violent anti-communist regime in Zaire, the sinister Holden Roberto headed the FNLA (National Front for the Liberation of Angola); in the centre of the country there was the MPLA (Popular Movement for the Liberation of Angola), under an orthodox Marxist-Leninist, Agostinho Neto; and in the south and west, the charismatic, larger-than-life Jonas Savimbi's UNITA (National Union for the Total Independence of Angola), the smallest of the three, occupied large tracts of bush but little else. As a departing colonial power, Portugal should have convoked a national conference to agree some kind of power-sharing arrangement and, possibly, elections. Instead, Rosa Coutinho recognized the MPLA as the constitutional government with almost indecent haste, and prodded other countries to do the same. The MPLA, armed with international recognition, could now seek external support.

Neto's problems persisted: as Holden Roberto's and Jonas Savimbi's forces advanced on the capital, he had to seek assistance from the Cubans, who initially sent in some 2,000 military advisers. They helped to turn the tide against the FNLA's forces in the north. But UNITA threatened to break through in the bush country to the south and advance on the capital, Luanda, assisted – as soon became obvious – by a substantial South African contingent. This provided Neto with the pretext for a massive infusion of Cuban troops; some 18,000 men were airlifted in Soviet planes to Luanda, which dangerously escalated tension. The American Secretary of State, Henry Kissinger, pleaded with Congress for authority to send military aid to Savimbi's forces. Congress refused. The South Africans, bereft of international support, decided to withdraw, fearful of getting bogged down in a war with the Cubans. Savimbi's forces retreated, using the vast Angolan bush to avoid the superior Cuban forces that also decisively defeated Holden Roberto. Thus Neto won control of the country, although UNITA continued to be a nuisance.

The Portuguese empire's collapse could hardly have worked out worse for Western interests. With Marxist-Leninist regimes in Guinea-Bissau, Angola and Mozambique, something similar threatened in Portuguese East Timor, where a Marxist-Leninist independence movement began to resist the territory's absorption into Indonesia. The Indonesian army's answer to guerrilla war was genocide. After hundreds of thousands had been killed, East Timor became part of Indonesia. In Macao, the Portuguese government even tried appointing a left-wing military governor; but the Chinese, appalled that this trading window on the outside world might fall into irresponsible hands, insisted a solid Portuguese colonial appointee replace him.

Soon after, Communism staged another leap forward in strategically vital East Africa. The feudal regime of Emperor Haile Selassie was overthrown in a coup in 1974 and a hardline Marxist-Leninist faction under Colonel Mengistu Haile Mariam rose to the top, inflicting a reign of terror of Stalinist proportions upon the country's peaceful people.

Further south, the Marxist-Leninist triumph in Mozambique and Angola left white-ruled Rhodesia encircled. It could no longer continue to defy the world. Whereas formerly the Zambian frontier to the north represented the only one that needed patrolling, now four-fifths of its borders overlooked hostile territory, and the Rhodesian army lacked the manpower to prevent infiltration. Thus began the Rhodesian guerrilla war, involving some 20,000 fighters in two armies.

As the conflict spread, the whites were pushed into holding a provisional election, won by a moderate, Bishop Abel Muzorewa, in the absence of the men who commanded the armed forces. These were Joshua Nkomo, who ran ZANU, the Zimbabwe African National Union, backed by the Russians, and Robert Mugabe, who ran ZAPU, .the Zimbabwe African People's Union, supported primarily by the Chinese. While the war continued under Muzorewa, Britain intervened to broker a settlement at Lancaster House in 1979. Mugabe, whose men had been in the front line of the fighting, won the subsequent election overwhelmingly, winning 63% of the vote. Nkomo gained 24% and Muzorewa 8%.

The Russians had backed the wrong horse, Nkomo. Mugabe slowly shuffled his country towards a one-party state. In 1983 the United States reduced aid – largely because the Zimbabweans appeared to be shifting towards a pro-Soviet alignment. But South Africa's policy of encouraging guerrilla movements in both Mozambique and Angola seemed to be holding back these potential revolutionary springboards. Within South Africa, despite the regime's brutality, the Marxist section of the opposition appeared to be making little headway. Although South Africa's fall seemed inevitable, the rise of a Marxist-Leninist 'southern cone' of Africa appeared less likely. In the 1980s the fate of southern Africa was balanced between Marxist-Leninist and ordinary, nationalist liberation movements.

The only sub-Saharan country with a substantial population of workers and significant urbanization was, of course, South Africa. While the Communist Party of South Africa had been a tiny splinter at the beginning of the Second World War, numbering only some 300 supporters, the Russian entry into the war suddenly made it respectable, with prominent public figures such as the Minister of Justice, Colin Steyn, even becoming patrons of communist front organizations like the Friends of the Soviet Union. The South African Broadcasting Organization permitted the Jewish Workers' Club to sing the Internationale over the radio and to broadcast the May Day speech by the communist leader, Bill Andrews.

In the 1943 general election the Party won a respectable 7,000 votes and soon afterwards secured four municipal seats in Cape Town. To begin with it had uneasy relations with the major black movements; the communists were cautious and Stalinist, preferring to use their influence in the unions to discourage strikes that would damage the South African war effort. But by 1948 the Party's relations with the African National Congress, the South African Indian Congress and the major black union organizations had grown warm.

The communists were an immediate target of the National Party government under Daniel Malan that assumed power in the 1948 election. A committee set up to investigate Communism in the unions concluded in 1949 that the communists 'posed a danger to our national life, our democratic institutions and our Western philosophy'. In June 1950, the Suppression of Communism Act outlawed the Party. The Justice Minister, Charles Swart, defined Communism as any organization that sought to bring about the dictatorship of the proletariat or that sought to bring about 'political, industrial, social or economic change in South Africa through the promotion of disorder or through actions that could be deemed by the authorities as having the possible consequence of disorder . . .' or 'encouraging hostility between black and white in order to further communist objectives'. The sole communist MP was ejected from parliament and the Party went underground. Not until 1990 was the Party to be legalized again under its veteran leader, Joe Slovo.

The Party played a significant, although hardly central, part in the struggle against apartheid. Its true significance was as a bogeyman for the government, which increasingly labelled all anti-apartheid opposition 'communist' and which, with the establishment of Marxist regimes in nearby Mozambique and Angola, sought to raise the spectre of a communist South Africa as a real danger. The purpose was twofold: to alarm the white population of South Africa and to secure geopolitical support from the United States and its allies in the global struggle against Communism in which South Africa was of potentially key strategic significance.

By the 1980s the apartheid government had become convinced by its own propaganda: visitors were astonished at how senior officials were convinced that organizations like the ANC had been infiltrated and become merely communist front organizations. Yet although many ANC activists were trained in the Eastern block and its leader Oliver Tambo gratefully acknowledged Soviet money, arms and training and the ANC espoused broadly collectivist goals of nationalization and state direction of the economy, it was not a communist party.

However, the Soviet Union's backing certainly secured it considerable influence over the ANC; many ANC leaders privately admitted that Mikhail Gorbachev's rise to power in the Soviet Union was crucial to the reconciliation process with the Afrikaners that began in the 1980s. Specifically, a new leader espousing free-market policies, Thabo Mbeki, was eased in as right-hand man to the ailing Tambo (Nelson Mandela was still in prison) and to make clear to the whites that economic revolution was not on the agenda. Gorbachev threatened to withdraw support unless the new line was followed in the late 1980s; this helped to steer the ANC to the negotiating table.

Fidel Castro and Latin America

In January 1959, Fidel Castro walked triumphantly from one end of Cuba to another, the rapturously received hero of the Cuban people. A middle-class, bearded, cigar-puffing former law student, he presented himself as a romantic revolutionary who had won the respect of his people and could therefore be taken seriously by the world.

Castro had tried to seize power for a long time: his first attempt was in January 1953, aged only 26, when he and his brother Raul launched an easily repulsed assault on Havana's Moncada Barracks. Cuba's dictator, Fulgencio Batista, pardoned the young extremist. Then in December 1954, a boat, the *Granma*, landed a band of armed Castroists in eastern Cuba. Although easily suppressed, the expedition aroused some sympathy around the island. Batista tightened security, closing the University of Havana – which encouraged the students to join Castro's movement.

Castro took his men to the Sierra Maestra mountains, an unpoliceable area where Batista's men found it difficult to pursue him. In a masterly public relations coup, he implied his guerrillas controlled a far larger area than they actually did, arousing sympathy in the West and suggesting that a mass movement stood ready to liberate Cuba from the ravages of the Batista regime. The dictator, a demagogue in the best Peron tradition when he ran Cuba from 1933 to 1940, had been widely detested. A former soldier, he had a peasant's shrewdness and had to some extent modernized society: he had given Cuba its first public education system, allowed the unions to organize and had extended the franchise to women.

When Batista returned to power in 1952 after a dismal period of military rule, he aroused great expectations that were quickly disappointed. He institutionalized himself as a dictator, amassed a huge personal fortune, shelved social reform and adopted a pro-business policy towards the economy and foreign investment. The results were impressive: light industry and tourism boomed, health care became widely based, literacy increased and American ownership of the Cuban sugar industry fell to a quarter by 1958.

This was the old story: a country whose rapid economic transformation was creating a new bourgeoisie to supplant the old families, but not quite large enough to grow proper roots. Moreover as Batista, too old and jaded to command continuing respect, neutralized the visible opposition, Castro became the obvious alternative. Although shrewdly not yet portraying himself as a communist, Castro's two closest associates, his brother Raul and his military commander, Che Guevara, were Marxists – although Guevara of a rather loosely aligned kind. Castro by contrast was vague about the kind of society he wanted and promised, in any event, free elections.

Batista's government disintegrated. After a rigged election in December 1958, his own political movement, the army and the police were clearly unwilling to support him. Castro's guerrillas came down from the mountains to engage the government openly, but after some small skirmishes, the army made it clear it would not intervene in open conflict. On 1 January 1959, Batista fled without a struggle.

Castro was a wholly new Latin American phenomenon: no country in the continent had actually fallen to a guerrilla-led revolution other than Mexico, which had settled down to good relations with the United States. Castro commanded considerable sympathy within the United States and among most Cubans; even middle-class Cubans considered he had the potential for constructive change. Castro first consolidated his revolution: to reassure the middle class Manuel Urrutia was appointed President and Miro Cardona Prime Minister, both moderates. Within months, however, revolutionary tribunals were trying, and shooting, 'enemies of the Cuban people' in their hundreds. Castro turned to the United States in April 1959, proposing to support the West in its struggle against Communism and was offered considerable American aid.

Underneath, however, Castro's revolution was moving steadily away from the United States. By July Urrutia had walked out, being replaced by Osvaldo Dorticos, who was close to the Communist Party chief, Carlos Rafael Rodriguez, a veteran campaigner and archetype of his profession, a plump, bearded bureaucrat. A second purge, affecting several thousand more, took place: as counter-revolutionary activity began to spread, it was viciously suppressed. By the end of 1959 the Cuban press had bitterly attacked the United States and Cuba started importing large quantities of Russian oil, as well as receiving pledges of aid. One billion dollar's worth of American property on the island was expropriated and Russian submarines approached the Caribbean for the first time.

In January 1960 President Eisenhower asked Congress to cancel preferential treatment for Cuban sugar exported to the United States. By January 1961 Cuba was denouncing the United States in strident terms, and demanding the Americans reduce their embassy staff; it seemed they

were in physical danger. The United States then broke off relations with
Havana, as did most of Central America, and Castro made it plain that
he intended to export revolution. While the quarrel with America proceeded apace, so did collectivization of the island's economy, while the
press and broadcasting became organs of pro-Cuban, pro-Russian propaganda. A new peasant militia was intended to supplant the regular army.

One-party rule was firmly institutionalized under the United Party of
the Socialist Revolution until its formal unveiling as the Cuban
Communist Party in 1965. Castro proclaimed himself Marxist-Leninist.
In came a Soviet-modelled Marxist-Leninist system based on
'Committees for the Defence of the Revolution' to police neighbour-
hoods and grass roots organizations that took their orders from above.
Thousands of political prisoners were rounded up as many of Castro's
followers became disillusioned. Castro himself reckoned they numbered
around 40,000 in 1965, well above any other Latin American country;
they included Huber Matos, one of the revolution's leaders, who charged
Castro with betraying it.

What had started as a refugee trickle became a flood. Maybe 500,000
people left the country for Florida from a population of 9 million, in
large part because the Cuban economy was going to hell in a hand-
basket after virtually all industry was nationalized and food, flour, shoes
and clothing rationed. Shrewdly, Castro refrained from nationalizing
the sugar industry, but concentrated production, which fell by around
half, into the hands of individual peasants. Cuba's GNP declined to
around a third of the level achieved under Batista. Although the
Russians initially were no substitute for the American market, by 1963
they had agreed to buy some 5 million tons of sugar annually, paying
considerably more than the world price. Yet by the mid-1960s, the island
appeared to be on a steady downward spiral.

The Cuban missile crisis in 1962, which had forced the Soviet Union
to withdraw its missiles and 12,000 men from the island, dampened
Russia's hopes of exploiting Cuba's potential. Cuba's initial attempt to
spread revolution to the Latin American mainland was a failure, merely
provoking Latin American countries to join the trade embargo imposed
on the island by the United States. Only Mexico continued its relationship with Cuba. As the island's economic problems worsened, the Soviet
Union issued an ultimatum to Castro: institutionalize a Marxist-
Leninist system to consolidate Cuba's pro-Russian alignment; or go it
alone and possibly sink.

Castro faced a unique choice: an end to his regime, or socialism on the Soviet model. Non-aligned socialism was a distant prospect, because at that stage – President Johnson had sent the marines into the Dominican Republic in 1965 – reconciliation with the United States appeared impossible. Castro decided to seal the compact with the Soviet Union.

The Russians agreed to meet Cuba's economic needs by continuing to buy sugar and subsidizing the island, by the end of the 1970s to the tune of some $4 billion a year. This allowed the Cuban economy to restart, achieving a 6 per cent growth rate, roughly the average of Latin American countries towards the end of the 1960s. Castro could also provide a minimum standard of health and social security and further improve the country's literacy rate. Dorticos, considered insufficiently Marxist-Leninist, was dumped. Castro became President, strait-jacketed by Raul Castro in his capacity as commander of the armed forces, and by Carlos Rafael Rodriguez, the veteran Communist Party boss who had now become Vice-President.

The main price the Cubans paid the Russians was sending large armies – some 25,000 men transported in Russian aircraft – to bolster the beleaguered Marxist-Leninist regimes in Angola and Ethiopia. As this coincided with the remodelling of Cuba's constitution along Soviet lines, it was doubtless at Russia's prompting. The Cubans provided ideal cats-paws for such adventures: after Russian military advisers were expelled from Egypt in 1972, it had become clear what poor ambassadors they made. Russian soldiers in black Africa would have been an even greater intrusion. But many of the Cubans were black, from a tropical country with a climate similar to that of Angola, if not Ethiopia.

The Nicaraguan revolution of 1979 appeared to catch the Cubans unawares. Castro had seemed to prefer his new African theatre to Latin America. But the revolution persuaded the Cubans to supply a new stockpile of arms, funnelled through Nicaragua, to the guerrilla movements in El Salvador and Guatemala. In addition, training was given to guerrillas not just from those countries, but also from Honduras, Costa Rica and Panama.

Cuba by the 1980s occupied a special position. Its economy was wholly underpinned by the Soviet Union. It could not claim to be a successful socialist economy, even by its own austere standards, as its only thriving part, sugar growing, was mostly privately owned. Its authoritarian regime maintained the strictest and most pervasive controls in Latin

America; when in 1980 some Cubans took refuge in the Peruvian Embassy and were then allowed out of the country, there followed an armada of boat people to Florida, amounting eventually to some 100,000 refugees. When given just one opportunity to express an opinion on life in their tropical workers' paradise, many Cubans voted with their feet.

After Cuba's fall, Latin America looked ripe for Marxism-Leninism. Although throughout the continent, virtually every kind of society existed, none of them had achieved political stability, much less social equality. The countries themselves could broadly be divided into four stages of development. The main industrial society was Argentina, with over 90 per cent literacy, a per capita GDP of $650, well above that of most developing countries, little population pressure and highly urbanized. Two other countries in similar stages of development were Uruguay and Chile.

Next came the two developing giants. Brazil with some 110 million people and Mexico with 70 million were each racing into the late twentieth century with growth rates at around 8 per cent, well ahead of their high population growth rates of around 3 per cent. Both were endowed with large natural resources; Brazil had minerals, raw materials and commodities, and Mexico primarily oil. Outsiders saw them as countries with the economic potential to become like the United States.

The third category comprised more backward states with fewer natural resources and slowly and painfully established democratic traditions which were still fairly unsophisticated: Peru, Colombia, Venezuela, Bolivia and Ecuador.

The fourth were the really backward ones, Neanderthals like General Somoza's Paraguay in South America, and Guatemala, El Salvador, Nicaragua and Honduras in Central America. Poor and dominated by primitive political regimes, their armed forces held down the mass of their people in a primal economic swamp.

Communist prospects, at the beginning of the 1960s, looked to be excellent in each category for different reasons. Of the developed countries, Argentina had failed to establish stable institutions. The army vied continually with the populist Peronist Party for power. Many young people fiercely resented the army and joined the Peronists, but after the Cuban revolution Marxism-Leninism offered a way of breaking the mould.

In the late 1960s two clandestine armies preached the theory of urban guerrilla warfare: the Montoneros, who were formally Peronists, and the People's Revolutionary Army, avowedly Marxist-Leninist. When the army finally relinquished power to General Peron's government in 1974, these two armies had swollen altogether to some 10,000 men. Peron had won the 1974 election with a staggering 62 per cent of the vote, and the guerrillas claimed these as votes for the Left. A savage guerrilla war erupted, consisting both of urban attacks and, in the Indian region of Tucuman in the north, rural uprisings.

The extreme Right retaliated. Death squads in unmarked Ford Falcons became common in Buenos Aires, killing people they suspected of harbouring guerrilla sympathies or just those they merely disliked. Meanwhile, Argentina's economy ran riot: inflation soared, on a compounded basis, to 170 per cent at the beginning of 1976. Isabelita Peron, the general's widow, presided over the chaos, advised by a sinister right-wing astrologer, José Lopez Rega. Finance ministers came and went with bewildering speed, leaving the treasury ransacked. Strikes occurred daily. To many outside Argentina, it seemed that the country was on the brink of left-wing revolution.

Much the same happened in Uruguay, where the Tupamaro guerrilla movement, named after Tupac Amaru, the legendary Peruvian Indian leader, conducted a ruthless war of terror in once-peaceful Montevideo. The so-called 'Switzerland of Latin America' was plunged into economic ruin, overshadowed by a welfare state that had wildly shelled out subsidies. The ruling parties, the Colorados and the Blancos, were widely viewed as part of the old oligarchy, having little influence with the masses. Perhaps the Tupamaros could capture the popular imagination in a left-wing revolution.

In Chile, in the late 1960s, Eduardo Frei's Christian Democratic government had tilted leftwards, inaugurating land reform and other measures. The leader of the party's left wing, Rodomiro Tomic, allied with the Socialist and Communist parties, the one Marxist, the other Marxist-Leninist, to install a new type of radical left-wing government. This came about in 1970, with the election of Salvador Allende's Popular Unity government, installed by a combination of Christian Democrats, Communists and Socialists. This was the first Marxist government to be elected to power democratically anywhere and the first Marxist government on the Latin American mainland. Fidel Castro's triumphal visit to Santiago sealed its solidarity with the international communist movement.

In the second category of Latin American countries, the developing giants, the political scene was less favourable to Marxism-Leninism. In both countries the local Communist Party was a tiny minority. In Mexico, the ruling Institutional Revolutionary Party was in some ways the precursor of communist and Third World systems having evolved a one-party government based on coercion and patronage that had endured half a century. Marxism seemed unlikely to make much headway: the main opposition was a conservative party. In 1968 a left-wing student uprising was bloodily suppressed, with some 300 people killed in the capital's main square. After that all was quiet, although Mexico placated the left by initiating a close relationship with Cuba and adopting an anti-American posture.

Brazil was split between army conservatives and civilian populists. In 1963 Joao Goulart, a free-spending left-winger, plunged the country into such chaos that the army took over the following year. There were fears that army rule would radicalize the country behind the Left. But after an outbreak of terrorism in the late 1960s and early 1970s, the lid was screwed securely on.

In Peru, General Velasco Alvarado inaugurated a unique experiment in left-wing military dictatorship in 1968: he crashed his tanks through the national palace's gates to take power from the elected right-of-centre President, Fernando Belaunde Terry. Velasco had served in the Indian region; deeply affected by the misery and poverty there, he pushed through a degree of land reform and nationalization, as well as brutally suppressing all opposition, loyally backed by the Communist Party. This example of left-wing officers taking control of a country would not be repeated anywhere apart from Portugal and Ecuador, for different reasons.

Colombia continued, as usual, to sit on the edge of a volcano. Run by a conservative governing class that held democratic elections, power alternated between the Conservatives and the Liberals (they had fought a bloody civil war in the 1950s). Although half the electorate did not even bother to vote in general elections, Marxism showed few signs of winning support. In Venezuela, following the end of an armed insurgency in the early 1960s, an oil boom had defused tension. Part of the Venezuelan Communist Party broke away and formed a Eurocommunist Party under a reformed repentant guerrilla, Teodoro Petkoff, which won more votes than the Stalinist original.

In Central America, the ground looked more promising. There the weight of American intervention had long been felt; the region's extreme backwardness until the 1960s had allowed its countries to be controlled by pro-American military cliques, some actually installed by the United States. Nicaragua's President Somoza ran his country with the assistance of the 7,000-man American-trained National Guard. The wealth he had amassed made him hated, not just by peasants and industrial workers but also by the traditional middle class that regarded him as an upstart.

In El Salvador and Guatemala, cliques of brutal ruling generals presided, while economic growth roared ahead in the cities, raising city centres to the sky and creating a new middle class that could not understand its exclusion from politics. Honduras, under rather more benevolent military rulers, remained poor. The repressiveness of these local regimes and the misery of most people under them made them ideal for communist penetration. And indeed, in the early 1960s, guerrilla movements sprang up in the remote mountains of Guatemala and Nicaragua. But only a few hundred men joined them and they scored few successes.

It was, however, to Bolivia that Che Guevara, Castro's comrade-in-arms, was despatched to stir up revolution in 1966. This geographical freak of a country straddles Amazonian jungle, soaring mountains and a salt-lake desert. Its people, nine-tenths of them of Indian descent, live in stoic poverty on the high *altiplano* surrounding the city of La Paz, built in a mountain chasm. The infant mortality rate is Latin America's highest, GDP per capita the lowest. Having had more presidents, with an average tenure of around nine months, than years of independence, Bolivia was, in 1966, the continent's most politically unstable state. Although in the revolution of 1952 land had been parcelled out to Indian peasants, this had only made them poorer because the units were not viable. For Guevara, it would be straightforward to arouse them to fight against the miseries of their existence.

Far from it: men whose skimpy landholdings made them pocket capitalists rejected communist collectivism. Guevara's band of motley intellectuals fought in the remote highlands until the security forces killed him in October 1967. Castro shed few tears, secretly glad to be rid of Guevara, a political illiterate who questioned Cuba's totalitarian path. The revolution had run dry in Bolivia. But there was still potential all around the continent.

PART II

The Communist Universe

6

Middle Age

It is not possible to live long exclusively on revolutionary enthusiasm. The attempt of the revolutionary elite to perpetuate primitive Communism and enforce it as a permanent social state comes soon into conflict with life and with human inclinations towards individual differences, initiative, adequate material reward and a more comfortable and normal life. Suppression of human nature provokes revenge: general indifference towards work, low productivity, material poverty, and intellectual inertia . . .

The rulers being themselves human, share the same inclinations they want to suppress in others . . . So the revolutionary avant-garde gratifies the human inclinations of its own members and forces the primitive-communist way of life upon all the other citizens.

S. Stojanovic, from *Primitive Towards Developed Communism*, Belgrade, 1968

Khrushchev and Reform

Russia on the death of Stalin in 1953 was poised to make a great leap into the unknown. The years of terrible privation were over. Central planning had proved its worth in rebuilding a country shattered by upheaval and war – but could the system satisfy the peacetime needs of a new and more complex society? Now was Communism's chance to become a showcase of progress, to pull ahead of the capitalist system and provide a fairer society. There would be no excuse for failure. If economic progress and social equality evolved together, could the system's iron grip, necessary in times of drastic social transformation and war, be relaxed?

Two men were determined to prove that it could, that Stalin had been responsible for the failure so far to live up to the communist ideal: they were Georgi Malenkov, Stalin's preferred successor, an able, level-headed technocrat from within the government machine; and Nikita Khrushchev, a restless, dynamic, ebullient man of action who had risen through the communist bureaucracy to become the Party's First Secretary. Their rivalry was played out in an almost exact repetition of the shifting alliances that had followed Lenin's death. For Malenkov and Khrushchev first united to quash the ambitions of the weakest part of the Soviet power system: the security apparatus, which had become much too self-important, because of Stalin's extensive use of it.

The MVD – the Ministry of Internal Affairs – was thoroughly detested, having repeatedly terrorized the Party, bureaucracy and army. Its head, Lavrenti Beria, was struck down quickly. Under pressure, Beria introduced an amnesty on 23 March, just three weeks after Stalin's death and by 3 April had conceded that the 'Doctors' Plot' had been fictitious. Beria then allegedly attempted to seize power; whether he did or not will probably never be known. Russian army detachments entered Moscow to forestall any such move. By 10 July Beria had been dismissed, denounced as an 'agent of international imperialism' guilty of 'illegality and highhandedness'. He was executed in December.

A Committee of State Security (KGB) replaced the MVD. Many of the slave camps operating under the Organization of Corrective Labour Camps (Gulag) were closed and mass executions were abolished. The security apparatus remained as pervasive and efficient as ever. But the ultimate sanction was more rarely used; those suspected of anti-government sentiments were treated somewhat more leniently, marking the beginning of psychiatric, as opposed to purely physical, torture of dissidents.

Then the real contest began. This time the kingmaker, because it harboured few political ambitions, was the Russian army. The two great powers of the Soviet system, the bureaucracy and the Party, both led by able men, were at each other's throats. Malenkov's faults were honesty and overconfidence. In 1953 he appeared to be the favourite. But behind the scenes Khrushchev was installing his own men in senior Party posts, and after a spectacularly dismal harvest in 1953, by February 1954 he felt sufficiently confident to propose a wholesale upheaval in Soviet agriculture, clearly a failing sector by the time of Stalin's death.

Malenkov had proposed his own reforms for modernizing Soviet industry – stimulating consumer goods at the expense of heavy industry, and widening the choice of goods for ordinary Russians by the time of Stalin's death. Malenkov also wanted to sharply cut military spending, reducing the defence budget by some 9 per cent in 1954, and utilizing raw materials from the army's strategic stockpile. In agriculture he aimed for a modest increase in prices paid to the collective farms, and in foreign policy he sought an early version of détente to allow him to further reduce excessive military spending.

Although these were probably the policies to start the Russian economy growing again, this was irrelevant to the power struggle. The army bridled at the proposed cut in defence spending. Meanwhile, Khrushchev's radical agricultural proposals gained the Party's enthusiastic support. Khrushchev forged an alliance with the army in 1954, and by January was confident enough to attack Malenkov, without naming him, for 'incorrect reasoning, alien to Marxism-Leninism, a belching of the rightist deviation, a belching of views hostile to Lenin'. Khrushchev dishonestly proposed investing in heavy industry and defence as the priorities for a Communist state; consumer goods were merely bourgeois fripperies.

By the following month Malenkov, the most sensible and innovative man to dominate the Soviet Union, had resigned. The price for his removal was the installation of the Minister of Defence, Marshal Bulganin, as Prime Minister. Khrushchev regarded Bulganin as a lightweight and offered no objection. A supporter of Khrushchev, the able Marshal Zhukov, was, however, appointed Minister of Defence.

Yet Khrushchev was not there quite yet. The bitter Malenkov had joined with the main hangovers from the Stalinist period who, having originally sided with Khrushchev, were now alarmed by his reforms. With no real power base, but still commanding a majority in the Politburo, they included Molotov, the po-faced Russian Foreign Minister, Voroshilov, the lacklustre, inept and bureaucratic army chief from Stalin's day who was currently President of the USSR, and the veteran Stalinist, Kaganovich. When, with astonishing boldness, Khrushchev attacked Stalin's rule at a closed session of the Soviet Communist Party's Twentieth Congress in February 1956, they were furious.

The contents of this secret speech, once leaked to the West, came as a bombshell to the many not just in Russia who regarded Stalin as a world figure of heroic proportions, but to those in the West who saw him not just a Second World War leader but even as a father of his people. Khrushchev claimed that Stalin had brutally violated human rights, in effect murdering hundreds by illegal means and enfeebling the country through the great army purge before the war. He claimed that another murderous purge would have taken place but for Stalin's death in 1953.

The shock effect of Khrushchev's speech was felt immediately: not in Russia, where the degree of repression and residual loyalty to the Party remained too strong, but in Eastern European countries bursting with nationalist resentment against the hated Russian occupier. If Khrushchev was going to moderate Stalin's tyranny, let him start by dismantling the Russian Empire. Khrushchev had also denounced Stalin for quarrelling with Tito's Yugoslavia: this seemed to indicate that Eastern European countries could go their own way.

Following unrest in Poland, Wladyslaw Gomulka, a Party leader and nationalist jailed by Stalin, was promoted by the Party to be First Secretary. Khrushchev, stomping over to Warsaw in 1956 to threaten the Polish communists with invasion, found Gomulka simultaneously tough and placatory. He told Khrushchev that Poles would fight any such intervention, but insisted that Poland had no wish to leave the Soviet bloc and merely wanted control of its own internal affairs. Khrushchev returned only half satisfied.

In Hungary the Khrushchev speech took the lid off simmering popular unrest. The Hungarian pot was boiling so strongly that the Russians felt compelled to fire Rakosy, the Stalinist Hungarian Communist Party boss, and replace him with another nationalist ex-jailbird, Imre Nagy. After Nagy heretically asserted that Hungary was ready to leave the Warsaw Pact, the Russians decided that most countries in Eastern Europe would follow suit if Hungary got away with it, and after growling angrily invaded the country in October 1956. The bitter popular opposition they encountered was met with implacable brutality. The Politburo blamed Khrushchev for opening the floodgates of change and placed economic policy under the control of the state apparatus.

Khrushchev, nothing if not a fighter, promptly advocated the radical decentralization of industry and rallied his supporters in the Supreme Soviet against the elite of Stalinists and Malenkov supporters in the Politburo. In June the Politburo sought Khrushchev's resignation. He refused. The two sides wrangled for three days over the Politburo's right to sack him. Khrushchev argued that the Central Committee, which had appointed him and contained a majority of his supporters, would have to be convened for the purpose. The showdown was a grim, primal one, ended suddenly by a military coup.

Khrushchev's ally, the Defence Minister, Marshal Zhukov, strode past the armed guards at the entrance to the Kremlin and demanded the Central Committee meet. Zhukov's air force was already flying in the members from all over Russia. The Politburo had to give way and the Central Committee overwhelmingly endorsed Khrushchev: nine new names, including Zhukov, were appointed to the Politburo, swamping the opposition.

Khrushchev's ungrateful coup de grâce was, with true Stalinist duplicity, to fire Zhukov only three months later to prevent the army thinking that Russia could be ruled by military fiat. By 1958 Khrushchev had become both Prime Minister and Party Secretary. By 1959, a personality cult had developed, and his opponents – Malenkov, Molotov and Kaganovich – were shuffled away into obscurity. A dynamic reformer now guided Russia: unhappily, his reforms were precisely the reverse of what was needed.

Khrushchev's power base was the Party, and to safeguard his position, he had to establish the Party's superiority over the government apparatus. Therefore he first increased Party membership, particularly in the government and the army. By 1959, Party membership was up by 14 per cent on five years previously, to 9.7 million. Secondly, he decentralized power away from the Moscow-based bureaucracy to the regions, where the local communist parties had more influence. Corrupt local Party bosses moved in, tailoring industrial policy to their needs and those of their constituents with little regard for national objectives.

The Khrushchev plan replaced 140 ministries with 105 regional economic councils. After corruption mushroomed, Khrushchev backtracked, arresting many local officials. Going back to the drawing board, he strengthened the powers of the governments of the republics by setting up seventeen 'economic regions', while reducing the number of regional economic councils. Then he established several industrial councils to make the changes he wanted in Soviet industry, which the new local centres of power had rejected. It was reformism gone mad – tracking backwards and forwards like a yo-yo, leaving only disruption in its wake.

Khrushchev's bull-in-a-china-shop approach also affected Soviet agriculture. For a country with Russia's resources, the dismal failure of its agriculture to produce even enough for its own people was an appalling indictment indeed. He began with a gigantic project to open up the 'virgin lands' in northern Russia, Siberia, the northern Caucasus, the Volga region and Kazakhstan. Some 150,000 workers, lured by the offer of higher pay, would cultivate 100 million new acres. This involved a huge capital outlay and took a long time to yield returns, although the balance was probably, just, positive. Bad weather continued to plague these areas and production fell consistently short of targets, as it did when Khrushchev devised a scheme to produce more maize for animal feed; the Soviet stock of pigs, meat and poultry had never really recovered from the collectivization drive.

These were merely the hors d'oeuvres of Khrushchev's mission to upset everything. His goal was nothing less, as stated in a speech in 1961, than to 'overtake the United States in these five years in per capita output of farm products'. He decentralized, giving greater authority to the managers of collective farms, often just as inefficient as the old central bureaucrats. Having stripped the Ministry of Agriculture of most of its functions in the same year, Khrushchev discovered in the following year that he needed a central organization after all: so enter the All-Union Committee on Agriculture.

His best change was boosting farm incomes by increasing farm prices, which helped increase production; much of this new money, however, went into the pockets of the collective farm managers and local Party officials, and in 1961 he had to crack down to try and ensure it reached the farm workers. Khrushchev also wound down the celebrated Machine Tractor Stations, formerly the praetorian guard of the farm sector: their members, who had been better paid than other agricultural workers, had acted as a kind of supervisory elite on the collective farms. The latter were to buy the tractors; however, many lacked the money to buy them. Some 50,000 tractors and 220,000 harvesters were sold off, although the 2 million workers on the stations had to be found jobs.

At the same time, Khrushchev increased the size of the average collective so that by 1960 there were only 44,000 huge collective farms, each of 6,800 acres. The logic here was that bigger farms would take advantage of economies of scale, particularly as regards the new machinery. But disgruntled collective farm workers felt disinclined to work any harder in the new, bigger, even more impersonal units than they had before.

Khrushchev lacked the imagination – or was too afraid of his own Party officials – to try and exploit the peasants' willingness to work on their own private plots, astonishing oases of productivity in the Soviet economy. In the early 1960s it was reckoned that nearly a quarter of arable crops and nearly half of livestock production came from peasant plots occupying just 3% of the land, as did some 80% of eggs, 60% of potatoes and 46% of green vegetables. The government could not seize them, because the country desperately needed their produce. But Khrushchev believed passionately and wrong-headedly that well-organized, well-run collectives could become more efficient than private plots. He was wrong, as a succession of poor harvests would demonstrate.

Even on the cooked statistics, Khrushchev's over-ambitious aim of overtaking the developed West was ludicrously unrealizable. His intention in 1961 was to increase, in two decades, industrial production by 500%, farm output by 350% and per capita income by 250%. Industrial productivity was to rise by 350%. These Herculean goals were clearly unattainable even for the men elevated by Khrushchev. His one thoroughly attractive characteristic – a reluctance to use Stalinist repression to enforce his authority – helped make him the first absolute Soviet leader since the revolution to be deposed by his comrades.

He disappeared from view almost overnight: without warning, the Soviet press announced his resignation on 16 October 1964 due to his 'advanced age and the deterioration in the state of his health'. Khrushchev, no older than his successors, appeared to be in rude good health. His political obituary, written by *Pravda*, comprised a largely justified litany of 'hare-brained schemes, half-baked conclusions and wrong decisions and actions, separated from reality' he had embarked upon. He had 'bragged and blustered', had 'ruled by fiat', and had been inclined to 'the instant action that science and practical experience had already discarded'. Although his retirement was to be a comfortable one, he was unlamented; ordinary Russians had experienced only disruption under him, and nothing had come from it. In international terms, indeed, he had proved downright dangerous, bringing Russia almost to nuclear war during the Cuban and Berlin crises (when the Wall was built in August 1961 to stop the flow of East Germans westwards, provoking a tense standoff in October) without appreciably advancing its interests.

The 1950s marked the real end of the communist dream in Russia. As

Russian expansionism drifted towards stagnation, drastic reform was obviously necessary. Khrushchev was the wrong kind of manic reformer; virtually all of his changes made things worse. This was no coincidence; as a Party man, Khrushchev had initiated the kind of changes that the apparat considered suitable – reorganizing the system, setting up new bureaucracies to replace old, shuffling empires, redrawing the scale and structure of administration in truly grand, sweeping fashion. But the malaise in the system of control, the lack of incentives and bureaucratic inertia at both the local and national levels, meant that he achieved very little.

The only reforms that might have worked were expansion of the private sector, fewer controls and more rewards for industrial success. But this would have confirmed that the emperor had no clothes and that the collectivist system ran counter to the inclinations of most Russians. The Party would not do it: instead of jettisoning ideology and accepting that changes could be achieved through further private sector expansion, it chose to pretend that Russia didn't have one, thereby maintaining a hugely inefficient state sector. The Russian leadership was acutely fearful too, that in the wake of genuine economic reform and pluralism might come the pressure for political reform. They preferred to do nothing.

Levers of Power: Brezhnev and his Successors

To Khrushchev's successors, their master's fall proved that reformism of any kind was a dead letter; better gradual decline than one accelerated by impulsive attempts to reverse it. The new men, appointed by Khrushchev, were drawn largely from the second generation of Russian leadership, men who had been in the youth movement or junior Party posts at the time of the Revolution. One such was Leonid Brezhnev, who had made his way up the Party organization. Having enjoyed a very brief war career – which he later exaggerated – he was an outstanding organizer, with a gift for making friends at all levels in the Party that stood him in good stead throughout his life.

Brezhnev's bear-like face and his short and strong physique became a Soviet trademark. The Western leaders who met him encountered an outgoing, genial chain-smoker, with a bluffness and directness that could, when required, turn into stubborn obstreperousness at the negotiating table. But his sudden bursts of apparently impulsive anger were all carefully controlled, unlike Khrushchev's. He never really lost his cool and performed ideally as a steady-as-she-goes Party leader in a time of relative calm. His character was enough to win him some affection from the Russian people, while he gave nothing away and did nothing to rock the boat.

His counterpart, who in the early stages appeared to wield an equal amount of power, was Alexei Kosygin. This perfect example of the upper-level bureaucratic mandarin had enjoyed a successful career in economic planning and administration. His progress had been unremarkable until he was appointed Mayor of Leningrad in 1935, a post that brought him to the Politburo two years later. A loyal Stalinist, he was pushed off the Politburo in 1953 and did not return until 1960. His ascent, like that of so many in the Soviet hierarchy, was based on caution, good behaviour and conscientious hard work, although this had not prevented him from nurturing his own reformist ideas on the way up.

After the Khrushchev years, Brezhnev's instinct was to do the absolute minimum beyond trying to improve the lot of ordinary Russians through the sale of consumer goods. Kosygin, however, wanted to reverse Soviet decline. Khrushchev's ambitious targets had been hot air: in agriculture, average growth over the five years to 1963 was just 2%, compared with a target of 70% and a growth rate over the previous five years of nearly 8%. The 1963–4 harvest was a disaster: 1 million tonnes of grain had to be imported, costing some $1 billion. Industrial growth, according to the heavily inflated official figures, fell from around 20% a year in the late 1940s to around 8% in 1964. As regards the whole economy, growth had slowed from around 15% a year in the late 1950s to around 2.5% a year in the early 1960s. So the Soviet Union was falling behind the West, not catching it up.

Kosygin's sensible answer to the agricultural problem was to encourage private cultivation as far as the Party and its ideology would allow. Private plots were guaranteed, and restrictions on their use abolished. Collectives could, for the first time, buy livestock from the private farms. Farm production incentives for workers in the collectives were introduced. Investment in agriculture in the 1966–70 Five-Year Plan was hugely increased, with tractors and fertilizers being the first priority. In industry the Liberman reforms, named after a professor from Kharkov University, were an attempt to give managers an incentive to produce and greater freedom from central direction.

Both reforms, however, were limited. In practice little could be done to compel collective farmers to work harder, even through production incentives; they preferred the intensive production of private plots. In industry, decentralization provided short-term increases in production; but so much industrial capacity was being surreptitiously diverted to satisfy the private black market that there was little sustained growth in official output. In addition, Russia would run into the twin problems in the 1970s of a fall in demand for its exports due to the general world crisis, and the oil price increase. The latter's effects, although slight at first as Russia was self-sufficient in oil, eventually became acute in Eastern Europe, which had to buy it in hard currency.

Russian growth was also affected by the need to keep up in the arms race and from a reduction in the supply of capital goods as resources were transferred to the consumer goods sector: Russia could not afford to invest in both, unlike most Western economies. These marginal reforms, limited as they were, created such an outcry amongst bureaucratic vested interests that they were scrapped towards the end of the 1960s. Russian growth had ground to a halt significantly behind the West in virtually every field; to restart, the private sector had to be the motor. The Russian Revolution, only thirty years after Stalin's death, had run out of steam.

All that remained was the system, run by a group of ageing leaders, blatantly failing to act upon a communist ideology in which few believed except the ignorant or those that considered it preferable to any alternative. This monolith had become the prototype of many throughout the developing world, although not many subscribed to its ideals for more than purely cynical reasons.

The four pillars of the Soviet system made it, in some respects, easier to understand than a Western one: the Party; the government bureaucracy; the army; and the security apparatus. Below these were lesser elites and power structures, for example, the scientific and cultural elites. But these had no independent power bases; no one in either, not even the nuclear physicist Andrei Sakharov, father of the Russian atomic bomb, was immune if he stepped out of line or if someone with enough weight in one of the four ruling hierarchies had it in for them.

Conversely, none of the four over the thirty years since Stalin died had established an unquestioned supremacy, which made it very difficult for even a very senior member of one elite to strike at a member of another, unless very junior. He risked offending the bosses of this other elite and precipitating a major power clash. It was this diffusion of power, this pluralism of elites, which made Russia so difficult to reform. When Stalin died, the chosen men at the head of each elite vied for power – Malenkov for the bureaucracy, Khrushchev for the Party, Beria for the security services and, more passively, Voroshilov for the army. Khrushchev triumphed, and sought to consolidate his own position by becoming chief of both the Party and the government.

After Khrushchev's demise, his rivals decided forestall such a concentration of power by splitting the jobs between Leonid Brezhnev and Alexei Kosygin. Only in the last years did Brezhnev establish the authority that allowed him to all but eclipse Kosygin. Still, even he was held check by the army and security services.

The basic structure of Soviet power was thus slow moving and extremely simple. To achieve supreme power, to push through a policy, even a Communist Party secretary needed the support of at least one, and possibly two, of the other power structures. Within each power structure, there was naturally much infighting: each had its conservatives and reformists. Thus a Party secretary obstructed by those heading the other hierarchies might seek support from reformists beneath them to get his policy through. However, this was risky: it represented direct interference with the unofficial Soviet separation of powers, a challenge to the hierarchy not just within a particular power structure, but to the whole concept of hierarchy. The danger was that opposition might in turn be mobilized within the power structure of the man doing the interfering. This did much to cause Khrushchev's overthrow in 1964, and explains why Brezhnev, intending to last longer, refrained from canvassing support within rival hierarchies. He ruled by seeking support from the whole of one or more of the rival hierarchies for his policies, a slow and laborious process which resulted in governmental near-inertia. Nevertheless, he survived eighteen years to Khrushchev's eight.

The four powers of the Soviet state were very different. They each had their distinct identities, varied in their enthusiasm for reform and had different degrees of rigidity in their hierarchies. By a short head, the senior was still the Communist Party. It provided such political dialogue as there was, allowing the regime, in theory at least, to keep in touch with popular feeling; this gave it its authority at the summit of the Soviet pyramid. It also furnished the regime with its ideological buttress.

In its latter role, the Party had become largely redundant. The ideology, for most Russians, was something learnt parrot-wise at school like Latin lessons, with no relevance to real life. Marx was hardly taught at all; Lenin was learnt by rote, and students were positively discouraged from studying him too deeply, much less formulating their own interpretations of his work.

The cult of Lenin was the predominant personality cult in the Soviet Union, for Lenin alone was safe. Khrushchev had ripped Stalin's personality to shreds in 1956, and although partly reinstated by Brezhnev Stalin still scarred the minds of millions of older Russians. Khrushchev's cult never really got off the ground, and was quickly despatched to the breaker's yard after his fall. Brezhnev's cult, which grew towards the end of his period in office, was soon put on the back shelves.

Lenin represented the revolution at its most vigorous; his arguments could still justify the nearly fossilized Soviet state, and his strong features made him an eminently saleable public icon. The centre of the Lenin cult was, of course, his mausoleum, with its permanent queue of the curious – few Russians bombarded with his works throughout their lifetime could resist making at least one pilgrimage to see the man more responsible for their condition than any other. If they got inside they were hurried past a tiny, embalmed, waxen-looking body in the glass coffin – if Lenin it was. Some suggest the figure was indeed made of wax, symbolizing all too poignantly the Soviet attempt to keep alive a revolutionary spirit that by its very nature was bound to be short-lived.

Lenin museums existed in every small provincial town, Lenin statues adorned every village square, Lenin pictures hung in many Soviet homes, Lenin busts decorated many offices, Lenin friezes sprouted on the façades of official buildings. In the poorly educated countryside, there was evidence that he was widely respected. But in most urban areas, the Lenin cult went unheeded. Most schoolchildren regarded their studies' ideological content as a tedious chore – unless they wanted to get ahead. So few pupils were prepared to devote themselves to serious Party studies that those who did received promotion above their abilities.

Even among those who paid lip service to the ideology, or even fostered it, scepticism ran deep. True, Russians with promising Party careers were prepared to convince themselves that they were believers. Past the age of 30, however, it was hard to find Russians who did more than spout the requisite phrases; they preferred to talk of other things. By the age of 40, most Russians were even prepared to be jocular about the ideology. In the higher echelons of the bureaucracy, those sufficiently self-confident of their position and ability were prepared to admit, even to Westerners, that they did not rate ideology highly. They worked with the system because it was there.

Scepticism about, and indifference to, the Marxist-Leninist ideological message was a recent development. As late as the 1950s, the ideology was bound up with nationalism, always a potent force, and with the endurance of hardship: Russians had to believe in a promising socialist future, because otherwise there was nothing but despair. But in the late 1960s and early 1970s a generation emerged that, although living in cramped and uncomfortable conditions by Western standards, enjoyed some of the benefits of the consumer society and, rather than rebellious, were utterly uninterested in Marxism-Leninism.

Up to a point, this benefited the regime: youth protest was minimal, and directed against parents rather than the state. To some extent, the regime deliberately encouraged such distractions as supposedly 'safe' Western music to act as a useful valve for such feelings. Indeed rock music, mostly imported, became the opium of young people. Black market records and tapes circulated freely around the Soviet campuses, costing over $100 a copy, because the Soviet authorities tolerated it: the leadership's own children were among the most ardent addicts. Only those considered thoroughly safe performers, like Elton John and Cliff Richard, were allowed to grace Russian auditoria. The domestic pop scene tended to be a slightly tame copy of the West, epitomized by the most popular singer, the 40-year-old Alexei Koslov, whose complex compositions were sometimes too upmarket to be classified as 'pop'. And the authorities had a tendency to commandeer the better Russian popular singers to perform dull propaganda songs.

The safety valve seemed to work, just as the spread of consumer goods seemed to soften the potential for resentment against a system that most Russians considered far from perfect. As the American journalist Hedrick Smith wrote perceptively in *The Russians*, 'The hunger for Western music and the paraphernalia of the pop culture is evidence of a generation gap in Russia, a generation gap in reverse, at least among the middle class and the establishment youth. Whereas American youth rebelliously turned to jeans, copping out and the folk rock ambience in defiant rejection of parental influence, precisely what Soviet youth wants is affluence and the good life. They are in the vanguard of the new materialism. Young men will take summer construction jobs in Siberia if they can get 1,000 roubles in hard cash [officially $1,300 at the time, although the real value of the rouble was around 70 cents] and secretaries will scrimp on food to save money and blow an almost entire month's pay for such Western symbols of easy living as flared slacks, wigs, knee boots or platform shoes.'

As a Soviet journalist remarked: 'Our youth is alienated. They want to think over their problems without consulting us. They are introverts compared to us. We were extrovert. We started with the Spanish Civil War and we had the war against Hitler. We knew which side we were on. This generation acts as if ideology were irrelevant. A lot of them think it is irrelevant to them. They have not had any catalysis. They are not engaged. They are not committed.'

An older generation, which had grown weary and cynical of ideology, and a younger generation that took no interest in it had stripped the Party of half its legitimacy. Empty expressions of ideology fizzled on, of course. The nation, it appeared, enjoyed participating in mass events. At the May Day Parade, for example, hundreds of thousands turned out to watch the military march-past. In practice, they were bussed in by a system oiled with use. Students, factory workers and office workers were given the day off, provided they showed up dutifully to such occasions.

Almost everyone had to act as a 'volunteer' Party worker at some time or other. Many gave dull political speeches to people paid to listen to them, or were assigned to ensure that a small precinct turned out to vote for the single Communist Party candidate in the general elections held every four years. The turnout was usually as high as the authorities claimed because officialdom ensured that precincts of as few as forty people voted. Voters knew they could be in trouble if they failed to show up – and might be pestered until they did. But this minimal window-dressing of electoral participation at least allowed them to grumble to their shepherds, and some of the grumbles – about small things as well as big – were passed to the higher echelons of the Party.

It was wrongly assumed that the Party had no contact with the grass roots, that the top merely dictated to the bottom. In fact, as the Party's ideological role – which did precisely the latter – declined, its populist role grew. The Party's raison d'être was formerly based on the claim that it fired the people to greater achievement; protests by conservative state bureaucrats could thus be overridden. With the ideology clearly a dead duck, the state bureaucrats could decide most aspects of policy but for the Party's claim to be in touch with the masses and therefore an interpreter of which policies would, or would not, work. The Communist Party itself had, thus, become marginally more representative. Apart from the elections, which gave people a chance to air their grievances, most Party meetings showed no spirit of debate or imagination. But Party apparatchiks did seem increasingly to be aware of public opinion; and Brezhnev's emphasis on consumer goods production recognized the need to buy the acquiescence of the masses.

As in most political parties, there were two basic communist types: the usually Moscow-based urban Party sophisticate who sailed into a relatively good position because his contribution was valued, and the boss, usually from the provinces, who built up support and a power base by being well connected and popular in his locale. He provided an important link with ordinary people, and such an outsider could break into the Russian system and make his way to the top, although it was becoming more difficult. Many of the local bosses who fell victim to the corruption campaign represented the traditional methods of power-building, usually based around the promise of perks by a powerful man to his followers.

The Party was divided into cells of around a dozen people at the base, moving up into sections, district parties, provincial parties and finally the National Party. By the early 1980s there were some 15 million Party members, of which 45 per cent were middle class, 41 per cent were workers – although many of these had long since graduated to better things – and 15 per cent peasants. One of the Party's strengths was that it pervaded the other three power centres: its members were in the army, the bureaucracy and the security services, so that their loyalty to their own power bases was never complete. The Party's ability to raise men above their talents meant that men not up to their jobs, occupying their positions solely because of Party loyalty, staffed many parts of the state bureaucracy.

The Party, riddled with the internal fighting and competition by family connection common to most Third World political parties, was divided into three distinct factions. Those at the grass roots were predominantly populists; they wanted a Party more responsive to the needs of ordinary people and hence urged higher economic growth, spending upon consumer goods and the provision of better facilities by the state for their constituents. Party advancement was usually gained by selection from above; but ambitious men trying to climb up from the bottom usually tried to reflect the popular consensus.

In the Party's middle echelons were the ideologues largely patronized by Mikhail Suslov, the last of the zealots, a gaunt, severe hangover from revolutionary times; as already observed, this group had lost influence. It tended to oppose the indulgence in consumer spending, advocating growth through centralized planning, the increased provision of social services and, above all, an end to the still all-pervasive inequality in Soviet life. Its support was mainly in the universities and teaching professions, with some adherents in the provinces.

At the top, at least since Stalin's day, sat the Party managers, who usually owed their position to bureaucratic manipulation of the Party machine in a country whose vastness enabled a man with very little experience of the world outside to reach the summit. Such a man, for example, was Brezhnev's preferred successor, Konstantin Chernenko. Yet although senior Party men might represent their former ideological colleagues, they could not ignore the opinions of the other three parts of the power structure. This allowed them to act more pragmatically, rather than being bound by purely ideological considerations.

The danger for any Party secretary was losing touch with the grass roots, as Khrushchev did; once he had reached the top, the reformists within the government machine persuaded him to shake things up to boost economic growth as the only panacea to the contradictions within the Soviet system. In the process he ignored the need to cultivate the Party's grass roots and respond to their demands. He trod on a lot of toes, scrapping the pet projects of middle-ranking officials, so that his juniors formed an alliance with the other three power structures upset by Khrushchev's reformism and forced him out. Brezhnev learnt the lesson, and carefully built up his Party base through favours. He turned a blind eye to corruption while diverting investment to consumer goods projects, which the lowest level of the Party insisted that ordinary people wanted. Brezhnev more or less completely ignored the ideologues. He survived.

The Party was thus not a force for total immobility, as some people suggested. While it had tried to resist cherished projects being disrupted, it also tended to pull the Soviet machine in a more capitalist direction, towards satisfying people's hopes for a better life through increased consumer goods production. Indeed, Brezhnev's determination to satisfy these demands aroused the opposition of other branches of government – and ensured that Chernenko did not succeed him.

Brezhnev's formula for survival was simple; having won a loyal power base in the Party, he took care to satisfy the second most powerful of the Soviet centres of power, the armed forces, while doing what was required to appease the security services, the fourth and most junior branch. With Alexei Kosygin, the leader of the government hierarchy, his relations were always strained. The bureaucracy, contrary to the assumptions of outsiders, was always the most specialized, efficiency-conscious and modern of the Soviet power centres, and prided itself on being so. Central planning, of course, favoured the proliferation of huge ministerial empires, and of a sprawling bureaucracy in most regions. Locally and regionally the Party and the bureaucracy cross-fertilized parasitically with local Party bosses and, for example, local factory managers, forging often lucrative alliances that protected each of them.

The most famous Soviet corruption scandal, exposed in the early 1970s, involved just such cross-fertilization in the republic of Georgia. The man behind it was Otari Lazishvili, who had established a huge private business empire through his connections with, and pay-offs to, high-ranking officials, including the Party chief in Georgia, a Khrushchev crony, Vasily Mzhavanadze. The network extended into the central state ministries in Georgia, as well as factory management. Lazishvili's main source of income came from getting his factory management friends to fiddle the books so that, for example, a factory requiring 14 ounces of material to produce a plastic bag actually needed just one. The other 13 were creamed off to Lazishvili's large private factories, which helped to make him a millionaire many times over, owning two dachas with swimming pools. In his case, the corruption principally involved state rather than Party officials, but the Party was paid to turn a blind eye. In the end it was the ascent of a tough, ascetic Party chief, Eduard Shevardnadze, which broke the scandal, resulting in hundreds being dismissed or arrested.

Despite the command economy's inevitable corruption and inefficiency at a local level, the government machine at the centre was efficient, well run and staffed by professionals from the highest levels of the educational system who knew their business down to their fingertips. Their main objective was not to make an unworkable machine any more efficient, but to furnish the illusion that it worked. In this they succeeded well, shunning for the most part the ideological nostalgia of Party members.

Events such as fake openings of major new projects still years behind schedule were common. The Russian press hailed, for example, the opening of a power generator in Nazarovo in Central Siberia in 1968 as 'the beginning of a technological revolution'. Five years later a newspaper revealed that the project had not in fact opened because its steam-turbine generator had burnt out. More far-reaching, the official figures produced by the Soviet planning organization, Gosplan, were usually gross over-estimates. Hedrick Smith cites a poultry farmer who almost regularly returned false figures to show that targets – 100,000 eggs a day – had been met. Actual production was 70,000, the difference simply written off as 'broken eggs'. The authorities turned a blind eye, so long as they could maintain the façade.

It was estimated that between 1966 and 1970 only 26% of the number of cars planned, 50% of foodstuffs and cheese, 40% of trams, 58% of metal goods, 65% of textiles and 70% of electric power and steel had actually been produced. As this probably reflected the normal state of affairs, the official Soviet figures suggesting an adequate rate of growth during the bleak 1970s, as the West's economies ground to a stop, were nonsense; in reality the Soviet Union's economy had hardly expanded at all, although spending in the consumer goods sector, certain priority areas of high technology and on defence had grown.

The bureaucracy's failure on the economic front gave it its own distinct character. Although a minority of new men coming into the system sought to make careers for themselves through factory reorganization and improving production, many of them were discouraged by the inertia of the system and went into private enterprise. These underground private capitalists contrasted with others who sought a quiet life through fudging the figures or making cosy arrangements with Party bosses.

At the summit of the hierarchy, however, stood a highly meritocratic and results-oriented elite, the prime pushers for change within the Soviet system. They wanted to decentralize industry and introduce competition between factories, measures to gauge efficiency (this had been tried in part, with poor results) and, favoured by a radical minority, private competition.

Apart from this radical minority, the men at the top wanted no relaxation in the rules governing private enterprise, fearing that the market economy, both 'black' and permitted, which played a significant role in the agricultural, industrial, housing and retail sectors, as will be shown later, could mount still greater challenges to a centralized economy. Rather, tougher regulation of the market economy should go hand in hand with efficiency improvements in the planned economy. In this they differed with the Party, which was prepared to tolerate an underground market economy if it produced the goods, kept people happy and offered no political challenge. The bureaucratic chiefs, instead, chafed at the way the private entrepreneurs had emerged to satisfy the demand for consumer goods. They insisted that Soviet growth meant consumer sacrifice.

In this, the state planners were at loggerheads with the Party. The bureaucracy's chief within the Soviet hierarchy for years was Alexei Kosygin. In 1965 he launched his economic reforms aimed at decentralizing industry, which were quashed by a combination of his own inefficient middle managers and the Party. Kosygin was finally beaten by the 'Prague Spring' of 1967–8, which confirmed the leadership's worst fears, that economic reform would inevitably be followed by pressure for political reform. In April 1973 a new reform campaign began, spearheaded by some remarkable admissions of failure by the Soviet authorities, notably an article by Nikolai Smelyakov, Deputy Minister for Foreign Trade, who insisted that Soviet goods could not compete with Western ones. 'While our planning and distribution managers wrote treatises . . . the highly developed capitalist countries already occupied the markets,' he claimed.

The campaign supported Brezhnev's proposal for the setting up of large industrial companies called 'production associations'. These could trade internationally by being given considerable leeway to respond to international market forces. This was designed to improve Soviet exports and broaden the variety of goods that could be imported and made available to the Soviet consumer. The defeated, surly Kosygin dug in his heels, arguing that such units would become more powerful than the autonomous small-scale enterprises he had been advocating; he won the support not only of the lightweight Soviet President, Nikolai Podgorny, but also, and more importantly, of the army and the security services. Brezhnev's plan was shot down.

With Brezhnev cut down to size, Kosygin got his best friend who headed the bureaucracy – Andrei Gromyko, the Soviet Foreign Minister since 1957 – elected into the Politburo, also in 1973. Gromyko, viewed abroad as a dour, plodding apparatchik of the most inflexible kind, was certainly not a man open to new foreign policy ideas. But his consummately professional handling of Soviet foreign affairs had given virtually nothing away and his own department, compared to others, was glisteningly efficient. Until his rise to the Politburo, he carried out orders. Now, at last, he had a say in framing them, and his experience of the West and personal predilections suggested peaceful but tough-minded co-existence. Gromyko's diplomatic skills soon smoothed Brezhnev's fears that he was merely Kosygin's placeman; the Communist Party boss was, in the early 1970s at least, delighted by the outcome of his détente policies.

The Brezhnev-Kosygin struggle seems to have left them both spent and exhausted. No new ideas were tried, and when Kosygin died in 1980 Brezhnev paid an ungracious, tight-lipped farewell to him, getting his own man in the bureaucracy, Nikolai Tikhonov, appointed Prime Minister in his stead.

Even as the Soviet bureaucracy chipped inexorably away at the Party's control of power – although it was by no means able to force through its policies – the Soviet armed forces were making larger inroads. The Defence Minister, Marshal Grechko, joined the Politburo, violating a long-standing rule to keep the two separate. Under Stalin the army had briefly exercised a near total ascendancy over the politicians, but it was cut down to size after the war.

The armed forces' increased role derived from the Soviet leadership's internal and external paranoia. The former held that, as Party control of people's loyalties grew more tenuous, substantial and efficient armed forces helped check potential unrest among the people. The example of Poland, where a military dictatorship became necessary in 1981, had alarmed Russia's rulers. The external paranoia evolved from the Cold War, and the need to keep the Soviet's nuclear and conventional armed forces up to strength.

The nuclear priority drained huge resources from the economy, creating a Soviet military-industrial complex with even more economic clout and muscle than its equivalent in the United States due to the priority given to high technology defence spending. By 1980 Soviet military spending comprised around 14 per cent of GDP compared with 9 per cent in the United States (similarly the Russian space effort, which achieved remarkable results, although without putting a man on the moon, cost some $45 billion between 1958 and 1973, compared with $25 billion spent by the Americans). Throwing money at a problem could indeed produce results. Higher wages were paid in military factories – with higher standards expected. As one Soviet technician remarked: 'Military officers sit in each factory – in the big factories there are gen-

1. In the beginning . . . Karl Marx and Jenny around the time of the Communist Manifesto of 1848

2. The old order shattered: storming the Winter Palace, 1917

3. Revolutionary dictator:
Lenin and his family, 1919

4. Perpetual revolutionary:
Trotsky (*third from left*) in Red
Square, 1922

5. 'Rude and capricious': Stalin seizes power, CPSU congress, 1927

6. Stalin (*right*) with Rykov, 1930, one of the chief victims of the purges

7. Zhu De and Mao: architects of Communist survival in the 1930s

8. Mao and Chiang Kai-shek: before the final showdown

9. Fickle friends: Stalin and Mao, with Malenkov (*far left*) and Togliatti (*behind Mao*), 1949

10. Applauding the boss he later denounced: Khrushchev with Stalin

11. Standing alone: Tito in Belgrade, 1945

12. Unpredictable and irascible: Khrushchev

13. Red in the backyard: Castro and Vice-President Nixon, 1959

14. The suits take over: Ulbricht, Brezhnev and Gomulka

15. Best of friends: Dubcek, Kosygin and Brezhnev on the eve of the invasion of Czechoslovakia, 1968

16. Romanian loner: Ceausescu and admirers

17. The new inquisition: three victims of the Cultural Revolution, 1967

18. North Vietnam's frail man of steel: Ho Chi Minh

19. Some of Cambodia's victims

20. The Vietnam war: high-water mark of communism

21. Elected Marxist: Salvador Allende and the poet Pablo Neruda

22. Socialist who thwarted communism: Mario Soares during the Portuguese revolution, 1975

23. Prophet of Eurocommunism: Santiago Carrillo

24. Sandinistas Eden Pastora and Dora Maria Telles in Managua, 1981

25. Ethiopia's hard man: Mengistu Haile Mariam

26. Workers of Poland unite: Solidarity's Lech Walesa, 1980

27. Requiem for Maoism: Jiang Qing on trial, 1980

28. Deng Xiaoping: the great pragmatist

29. A man to do business with: Gorbachev and Thatcher (with Raisa and Denis on the left) on his first visit to Britain, 1984

30. Gorbachev at Westminster on the 1984 visit makes a point to the author (*left*) and Norman St John Stevas

31. Ice-breaking visit: Anthony Kershaw, Chairman of the House of Commons Foreign Affairs Select Committee (*front row, fourth from right*) with British parliamentary colleagues and 1917 Politburo veteran Boris Ponomarev (*on his right*) in the Kremlin, 1985

32. Evil empire no longer: Reagan and Gorbachev in the Kremlin, 1988

33. A helping hand: the Berlin Wall, November 1989

34. The killing is not yet over: the Tiananmen Square massacre, June 1989

35. The end of Soviet communism: Yeltsin celebrates victory over the coup plotters, August 1991

erals – and they operate with strict military discipline. They are empowered to reject substandard items.' He cited the example of fridges: 'Out of thirteen, the military representative would select one or two. Some would be thrown out as deficient and the rest would go to the civilian market.'

The amount spent on weapons systems was even higher than it looked, because of poor pay and conditions in the Soviet armed forces. Alexei Myagkov, a KGB officer who defected, recorded his own horrified reaction on joining the Soviet army for the first time as a 21-year-old lieutenant:

> In the armed forces I saw for the first time with my own eyes what it was like to be a simple soldier in the Soviet army, his miserable existence. The rigid discipline and conditions of life for a private were in great contrast to those of a private in the Western armies. During their service, Soviet privates live all the time in barracks. They are strictly forbidden to leave the location of their unit. In their sleeping quarters about sixty to eighty men are accommodated together. Each day a private is allotted duties to the last minute. Immediately after reveille, he has to fall in for physical exercise, after that washing, then he marches in formation to the mess-hall and break. After that he falls in for training, which continues for six hours. Then, after a midday meal, he again marches in formation, after which he is lined up again for further exercises. In the evening he is marched in strict formation to supper and bed. And before going to his sleeping quarters, he falls in for the evening roll-call; Sundays and other rest days differ from ordinary days in that instead of training, sporting competitions are held and in the evening artistic films are shown . . . on Saturday or Sunday only around 15 per cent of privates get permission to visit the town or village near to them for a few hours . . . from the beginning to the end of their service [most privates] have no possibility of visiting relatives. The private gets 3 roubles 80 kopek a month, with which he has to buy boot polish, a toothbrush and toothpaste, shaving gear and, for those who smoke, cigarettes. Soldiers are strictly forbidden to drink spirits or even beer.

An army staffed on the cheap, of immense size and power – little wonder that the armed forces had an expanding role in the Soviet state. That they also suffered from grotesque folie de grandeur was of little import: Victor Suvarov, a defecting officer, cited the example of Marshal Grechko, who became Defence Minister in 1967, for whom the high command of the north fleet had coastline cliffs painted grey: 'In all some 20 kilometres of coastline were painted. The sailors of two whole divisions and the men of a marines regiment laboured over this titanic work for several weeks and in the process used up the whole allocation of anti-corrosion paint supplied to the entire fleet for a whole year. The minister liked the colour of the rocks, and from that time forth the painting of rocks before the arrival of a high-ranking commander became one of the most remarkable traditions of our fleet.'

Such Pinafore displays demonstrated the self-confidence of the Soviet armed forces. When in 1982 equal numbers of civilians and military men were present on the podium at the May Day Parade in Red Square, Russians must have started wondering who really was in charge.

The answer, of course, remained the Party, partly because the military authorities, conscious of their limitations, were uninterested in providing answers to the complexities of Soviet economics. The army's ideas about economics, unlike those of the other services, were fairly uniform and extremely simple. Like the leading bureaucrats, the army supported the decentralization of industry, if this led to improvements in production, efficiency and quality control. Efficiency-conscious officers advocated greater factory discipline, more rigorous control of spending (except where it concerned their own), less emphasis on consumer goods manufacture and, like the bureaucrats, a reduction in the waste and corruption of the Party bosses.

Yet this was simply reordering the priorities within an accepted status quo; no new theory or reformist spirit would spring up in the stodgy military apparatus. Its officers, less intellectually equipped than the other holders of power, firmly upheld authority and tended to accept Marxist-Leninist tenets without question. Any relaxation in the state's control of production might challenge the authority of the communist system, and thus the state, of which they saw themselves as the ultimate upholder.

Above all the armed forces believed in nationalism, in the defence of Mother Russia and in ever-increasing spending to meet the constant conventional and nuclear threat from the West. Any prospective encirclement by China and the United States' allies in southern Asia and Europe should be firmly resisted; territorial expansion to fulfil Russia's raw material needs should, if necessary, be supported. If the army's ideas about domestic policy were obtuse, it had clear ideas about foreign policy.

The last of the four power structures was nominally the weakest, because it controlled the smallest number of men. The KGB, the state security apparatus and the dark horse of recent Soviet leadership battles was in some ways the most independent of the four branches of government, in that its members in the other three watched what went on. True, the Communist Party's members were also in the other branches of government, but the KGB was there in secret, with an astonishingly wide brief. Its main purpose was not to protect the state against outside espionage or even internal enemies, although both these functions were important, but to strengthen its own power at the other branches' expense.

KGB organs, being part of the state administration, were endowed with general powers and responsibilities. They published state regulations and ensured they were adhered to, guarded state secrets, controlled access to secret documents and liaised with other state organizations. They sanctioned entry to and exit from the Soviet Union by foreigners, regulated the issuing of permits for Soviet citizens to travel abroad and decided questions of Soviet citizenship.

An awesome range of powers to be exercised in the field reinforced all this. KGB agents were empowered by statute to:

> . . . carry on operational work with agents; to maintain 'safe' and local reporting flats; to organize eavesdropping activities; and to undertake secret photography. Two, to organize and carry out secret observation and to maintain agents. Three, to take special measures to curtail criminal activity. To set up secret control over both international and internal postal and telegraphic communications. To employ operational printing equipment in order to fabricate cover documents.
>
> Four, to check up on the behaviour of persons who have served sentences for particularly dangerous crimes against the state. Five, to check on the coding service, on secret communications and on security in all ministries and other official organizations, as well as in organizations subordinate to the KGB itself. Six, to carry out investigatory work on state and other crimes which fall within their competence; to detain or arrest suspected persons, to make searches, confiscations etc. Seven, to check documents of foreigners and Soviet citizens crossing USSR frontiers, to check on all printed matter carried and also on all loads transported either as hand luggage or ordinary luggage. To check that all foreigners leave USSR territory at the appointed time and to check on foreign persons employed in all means of transport.

KGB surveillance operated by having informers throughout the system. Many were ordinary workers from all walks of life, some attracted to the KGB for ideological reasons, others simply careerists. Blackmail or intimidation was commonly used to get people to enter the organization and then betray their colleagues. Here Myagkov describes the behaviour of Colonel Boychenko towards 'K', a potential recruit.

> Boychenko switched to open threats and blackmail. 'We have no desire to speak to you about unpleasant things, but you force me to do so. So, then, if you refuse to collaborate, we shall act as follows: firstly, we shall compromise you. I hope that you have not forgotten that you spent some time talking to Andrey about your acquaintances and friends and described them to him. And we recorded some of what you told him on a tape recorder. We have the possibility, armed with this tape, of persuading certain of your acquaintances that you have been collaborating for a long time with the KGB. If this were to happen, it seems to me that life in Bernau might not be very pleasant for you.
>
> 'Secondly, as I understand it, you possess a private workshop?'
> 'Yes.'
> 'And that son of yours is hoping to study in university?'
> 'Yes.'
> 'Well then, you know that we are in a position to ruin everything.' The colonel mercilessly hammered on his most painful spot. 'You will lose your workshop, your son will never study in university. As you see, the future of your family and its welfare lies in your hands. Well now, what are you going to say in answer to our proposal, yes or no?'
>
> All this time I had kept my eyes on K. His face was pale. Beads of sweat trickled down his forehead, his hands were shaking. He understood that he had no way out. He had to decide today, this very moment, the fate of his family. 'Yes,' he groaned from somewhere within himself.

However, according to Myagkov, the hackneyed method of sexual blackmail – the seduction of targets who could then be threatened with the resulting photographs – had fallen a little behind the times, due, as he remarks primly, to the general 'permissive trend of the last few years, with free love and amorality in matrimonial relations'.

> For instance a couple of years ago the KGB made an attempt to recruit one of the foreign diplomats in Moscow, who shall be nameless. A beautiful and clever woman was 'prepared' for him. The woman played her part well and said, apparently, that all was going well. The diplomat had been hooked. He fell under the influence of this woman and established sexual relations with her. Employees of the KGB's technical section managed to take 'classic photographs'. After all this had been done, the decision was taken that the case had 'ripened' and that the diplomat could be recruited.

One day when the diplomat turned up at the flat of his mistress, he was met not by his loved one, but by KGB men. Without wasting words, they went into action. At first an offer was made to the foreign 'Romeo' to co-operate on a voluntary basis. On his refusal he was shown 'interesting and unmistakable photographs' which would compromise him. But this time the trap was sprung in vain: the diplomat said he liked the photographs and would willingly accept several as a souvenir of his conquest, while the KGB could send the rest wherever it liked, to his wife and to his superiors. Learning from such failures, the KGB has lately been making use of this blackmail method less often and with greater caution. To compensate, other brutal methods are being used even more frequently.

The power of the KGB should not be exaggerated. True, as Myagkov explained, its agents felt themselves above the law. 'KGB workers have more freedom in their personal lives than any other citizen; they wield enormous power and enjoy total control of the citizens, to whom they appear impregnable . . . they are often uninhibited in their remarks about individual Soviet leaders and about the internal and external policies of the government. Yet one rule is strictly adhered to: all opinions and remarks must not go beyond the confines of the KGB.' The KGB was also a privileged elite, with excellent perks and much greater freedom to travel than ordinary citizens.

But, ultimately, the KGB was responsible to the Politburo, the representatives of the other three branches of government, and as the weakest numerically, it could not afford to antagonize any or all of them. So it successfully played off the branches against each other, and exploited the divisions between them. Its power, its secretiveness and the conspiratorial nature of its work gave the KGB some of the government's most able men who, because of the cynical nature of its operations, were those least hidebound by ideological or departmental prejudices. Such a man was the coolly calculating Yuri Andropov, head of the KGB since 1967, whose detachment allowed him to analyze what was wrong with the system, to decide what changes were needed to improve it – and, in his view, to save it.

Andropov made it to the top in November 1982 following Brezhnev's death not through compiling dossiers on his rivals in the Politburo, but because of the impasse between the Party, the state apparatus and the army as to which should take over. The Party was determined that no member of the Soviet bureaucracy should become Party secretary. Their leading candidate was Konstantin Chernenko; but the state bureaucracy, more powerful than in Kosygin's time, would have none of him, considering that he had Brezhnev's undesirable populist instincts without his intelligence.

Yet there was no obvious state candidate; Tikhonov, the Brezhnev nominee who had replaced Kosygin, lacked the support of his own juniors and Gromyko's post was considered too lowly. At least both the Party and bureaucracy agreed that no army nominee should become secretary, which would be tantamount to military rule. This process of elimination left the KGB chief who was acceptable to all because his slender power base would prevent him dominating the system.

The KGB's lack of obvious political prejudices meant it could suggest objective solutions to Russia's problems. But its size meant that any proposals were obstructed by more weighty powers in the Soviet state. Thus Andropov needed to assemble a coalition of followers from within the other three government groups to support his policies; this would not be easy.

Based on his speeches and writings, Andropov's views of the Soviet reform boiled down to the following: industry should be decentralized, greater incentives should be introduced and the regulations governing private plots in the farming sector should be eased. Increased efficiency in the public sector might sustain a very slow rate of growth in the consumer goods sector, to keep ordinary Russians happy, while increased investment expenditure should bring Russia's long-term growth prospects back into line. However, he feared the political consequences of any return of industry to the private sector. And while he knew that military spending was getting out of control and needed to be curbed, his good relations with the armed forces made him loath to implement this.

Hand-in-hand with economic reform, he believed in even tighter political control, which was essential for clamping down on popular dissatisfaction with the slow improvement in Soviet living standards – if indeed they were improving at all.

Andropov was not, as he was portrayed in the West, someone who would relax the system or adapt it to meet changing circumstances. His period with the KGB convinced him that the state could survive for a long time yet through combining repression with meeting the Russian urge for a better life.

Andropov's policy of 'efficiency with authority' won him the army's support, and his reforms friends in the bureaucracy. However, his reform plans were stymied because the Prime Minister, Nikolai Tikhonov,

Brezhnev's appointee, joined forces with Chernenko against him; furthermore, the army's Marshal Grechko, suspicious of his economic plans, preferred to abstain in central Politburo debates on economic matters.

To launch his economic reforms, Andropov had to neutralize or remove Tikhonov – or cultivate new friends to undermine Chernenko. The swift elevation of Geidar Aliyev, Andropov's crony and the former Party chief in Azerbaijan, to Deputy Prime Minister, put him in line for Tikhonov's job. Andropov probably intended him to replace Chernenko, opening the way for a thoroughgoing reform of the whole Party that might, in Andropov's view, sweep away Party waste, corruption and chaos and liberate new resources for the productive economy.

Andropov's illness in August 1983, followed by his death the following February, dashed his hopes of reform and meant the old men of the various power structures had to reconsider which was dominant, a problem compounded by a generational dilemma. Although within the Party apparatus Chernenko remained the leading figure, four younger men jostled for position beneath him: Mikhail Gorbachev, the most pragmatically minded among them; Grigory Romanov, a conservative realist; Vitaly Vorotnikov, the most ruthless and hatchet-faced of the four, a dour ideologue with considerable experience of running the Party machine; and Geidar Aliyev, Andropov's protégé, who was too young. The difficulty of selecting one of this next generation was threefold: first, they were impatient for change; second, they were too new and competitive for any of them to emerge as undisputed leader; if one did (Gorbachev seemed the likeliest), the others would probably gang up against him. Third and most importantly, whoever succeeded, the Party's supremacy over the rest of the system would be re-established.

The army was determined to prevent this, as were Gromyko and Tikhonov for the bureaucratic apparatus. Tikhonov, a friend of Chernenko, insisted that the latter was the only possible choice. He would not 'make waves' and would continue Brezhnev's policies, while not forgetting the populist 'errors' made during the latter's tenure of office. The wrangling was brief; the KGB, now headless, had little say. The main objection came from Marshal Ustinov, Grechko's successor as Defence Secretary and the army's leadership candidate. But neither Gromyko nor Tikhonov would accept military control of the Soviet system. So Chernenko, boxed in by a severely restricted mandate, took office in February 1984.

Chernenko, a tough and self-disciplined individual, had filled the almost impossible role of Brezhnev's acolyte for years in his struggle to the top. With shrewdness and intelligence, he had climbed from dirt poverty in the Siberian village of Bolshoya Tes via the Komsomol (the young communists), to become Party Secretary in Krasnoyarsk. In 1950, in Moldavia, he encountered the local Party Secretary, Brezhnev, serving him faithfully until his own admission to the Politburo in 1978.

In 1982 Chernenko had put himself forward as the successor to Mikhail Suslov as the Party's chief ideologue; standing on a mildly reformist platform, he advocated greater democracy within the Party. Although Andropov's stern insistence on discipline won the support of the army and the bureaucracy, Chernenko seemed to be more open-minded. He accepted the bureaucracy's argument that economic reform was necessary but personally favoured wider public consultation, an expansion of the 'popular' – in Soviet terms – power base of the Party and a reduction in defence expenditure in order to stimulate consumer spending.

But his chances of bringing this about were limited. His personality was stunted in Brezhnev's shadow, his succession too hedged about with the conditions imposed on him by the other partners in the Soviet governing apparatus, and his health too poor, for much change to be possible. He died in March 1985.

As regards the power structure, the Party had regained a slight edge in the struggle; yet the army and the bureaucracy retained a veto power; and the odds were that if the army and the bureaucracy jointly found a single candidate to succeed Chernenko, they could impose it over the heads of the young men in the Party. For these young men a difficult choice loomed: either to advocate wider democracy within the Party, thereby stealing a march on their rivals (the 'populist' course favoured by Gorbachev, Romanov and Aliyev), or to gain the support of the bureaucracy and the army by following the orthodox ideals of discipline and central control (advocated by Vorotnikov). The next round in the power struggle seemed likely to be decisive.

In the Soviet State

This was the state of the power structure on the eve of the most astonishing transformation since the 1917 revolution. The conflicts within it resulted in the often inexplicable turns of policy in Russia, and the even less comprehensible paralysis of the system. As can be seen, the Soviet system's great weakness was not just the enormous difficulty of changing anything in the post-Stalin age, but the way in which these high-level manoeuvrings between various bureaucratic empires virtually ignored the interests of the Russian people, who counted for very little, although they needed to be given enough to keep them quiet.

Russia seemed to be moving away noticeably quickly from the ultimate Marxist goal envisaged in the final stage of the dialectic – the true communist society. This implied the end of capitalism and of the class system, leading to total equality, the withering away of the state, freedom for the individual and internationalism. But in the Soviet Union, closet capitalism was on the march; the country, increasingly class-ridden, was developing into one of the most class-conscious anywhere; state power was all-encompassing; personal freedom was again under attack after a brief moment of relaxation; and Russian internationalism was a dead letter. To take each in turn:

The Soviet Union was not a socialist economy, but a mixed economy with central industrial planning. In the agricultural sector, by the mid-1970s, some 27% of all Soviet farm output – worth around $33 billion a year – came from private plots which occupied around 20 million acres, less than 1% of Russia's agricultural land. Some 25 million peasants operated as autonomous producers, and up to 62% of Russian potatoes, 32% of fruit and vegetables, 42% of eggs and 34% of meat and milk originated outside the state system.

Khrushchev had tried to crack down on private plots; Brezhnev reversed this, and they were here to stay. Furthermore, Brezhnev raised agricultural prices and considerably reduced compulsory state delivery quotas, enabling collectives to sell most of their produce independently. He also helped poorer families, most of whom earned around 80 roubles a month – just over $100 at the official exchange rate.

In industry the size of the black (private) market could only be guessed at: it was possibly at least 10 per cent of the economy, worth around $66 billion. Up to a quarter of the retail trade was outside state control. The private sector in industry expanded sharply in the 1960s and 1970s, although Andropov tried to curb it in the 1980s. Hard currency purchases of foreign technology – which the government judged a lesser evil than decentralizing the planning system – were mainly connected with production in the private sector. But corruption was so pervasive – for example factory managers applying for higher inputs than necessary in order to sell the surplus to middlemen – that the death penalty had been reinstated for 'economic crimes' in 1961.

By 1985 Russia and its 270 million people had, like most societies, three main classes, although the structured inequality of Soviet life was probably the most ordered in the world. The ruling class, tiny compared to other countries, consisted of senior government officials, the families of their predecessors and a handful of professionals who could command their own rewards. At its very summit stood the Politburo, and directly below it the Communist Party's Central Committee with two kinds of members, one earning $800 a month and the other $400 a month – between ten and five times the pay of the average worker. Much more important, however, were the perks that went with senior jobs: members of the Central Committee got all their houses and food free, and had it delivered to their homes or Central Committee head-quarters. A little lower down, members of parliament had private shops at which caviar, better vodkas and expensive wines were available. Even within the Central Committee staff there were three grades of employ-ees who went to different types of shops and cafeterias.

The ruling class also had access to cars, of which there were around three million in Russia in 1985. At the very top were Zil limousines, worth about 75,000 roubles (circa $97,500) each. The Chaika was for the next rank, worth around 33,000 roubles. The leadership also had special flats equipped with the latest Western gadgetry, their own hos-pitals, and country retreats. These were often large country houses, mis-leadingly called *dachas* (which originally in Russian meant a cottage or small country house) mostly clustered around the village of Uspenskaye near Moscow with many others in the enchanting village of Zhukovka on the Moscow River. They could travel, they enjoyed preferential access to restaurants, cultural events and Western films, and their children, educated at the best schools, were given a better start in life. Still, though, perks went with rank: when a leader lost his job or died, his family did not inherit his privileges – although his children had a better chance of a job with privileges than those from a family outside the elite.

The growing middle class, now as much as a third of the population, was labelled as the intelligentsia in Russia. It comprised middle manage-ment in factories and the bureaucracy, the professions, and some white-collar workers – anyone, in fact, occupying a position of responsibility. They enjoyed higher salaries – an average might be some 200 roubles a month – compared to an industrial worker's 80 roubles; they had friends who could grant favours; they commanded better perks; and they could get better housing simply by joining a cooperative through which, for a 40 per cent down-payment and 60 per cent mortgage, they acquired a property considerably better than the simple apartment every Russian had a right to. Much of the housing market was now in private hands – most peasants, for example, owned their own houses, with full inheritance rights – with the proportion increasing as the cooperative system spread. A cooperative property could not be inherited, but on the owner's death, the cooperative in effect repurchased the property by making a cash payment equivalent to its value. Furthermore money in Russia, unlike in Western Europe, could be inherited by a wife or child without being taxed.

The middle class had better clothes – the variety of thick coats and hats displayed style and wealth while middle-class children could be seen in elegant, Paris-chic clothes at the pay-at-the-entrance museums, at concerts and in smart hotel bars. Around 6 million Russians and their families belonged to the privileged elite with access to special shops, in particular the *Beriozka* hard-currency shops whose principal customers were foreigners. Russia was one of the few countries in the world that reserved better goods and foodstuffs for outsiders than for its own citizens.

When a middle-class family had a dacha in the countryside – a squat, wooden, two-up two-down box with a distinctive flat roof that sloped down at the sides together with a small plot of land – it had arrived. All of this represented a lifestyle the urban worker could only dream about. The peasants, who mostly still dwelt in ornately carved traditional wooden houses, were now dividing into those that had worked hard enough on their plots to join the ranks of the middle class, and the mere serfs who still worked on the collective farms.

Living standards at the bottom, extremely low compared to those of any Western working class, were sometimes comparable to those in a developing country. By the mid-1970s some two-thirds of Russians had television sets, some three-fifths sewing and washing machines and nearly half fridges. The average wage of blue-collar workers was around $87 a month; most of them had no prospect of buying even the cheapest car at around $5,000.

The delays in buying cars, and other goods, as well as their poor quality, were notorious; most Russians averaged some two hours a day in queues. But the shortages were not necessarily a sign of poverty but often merely the result of poor planning, with output being driven by production quotas rather than market demand. Sometimes they were merely the Russian equivalent of inflation – under Brezhnev, money pumped into the economy chased too few goods. With controlled prices, shortages resulted. Measuring real purchasing power is difficult, as on the black market the dollar was worth up to five times its official rate in roubles, which in theory could mean that Russians earned on average only around $20 a month. But the hours required to earn the money to buy certain goods provides the most accurate guide to purchasing power in the early 1980s.

A Russian worker took 27 minutes to earn a kilo of flour compared with 4 minutes in the United States, and 115 minutes for a kilo of beef as opposed to 102 in Britain and just 54 in the United States. Two kilos of sugar took 108 minutes in Russia, 20 in Britain and 14 in the United States and half a kilo of vegetable oil 47 minutes in Russia, 5 in the United States and 7 in Britain.

Seven kilos of milk took 147 minutes in Russia, compared with 30 in the United States and 55 in Britain. The same measure of vodka took 595 minutes in Russia, 61 minutes in the United States and 148 in Britain. A tube of toothpaste took 25 minutes to earn in Russia, 12 in America and 11 in Britain. Overall, the average Russian factory worker had to labour nearly 3.4 times as long as his American counterpart to buy the same weekly shopping basket.

In the consumer durables sector, the difference was even more striking. A fridge took 332 hours to earn in Russia, compared to 49 in America and 66 in Britain. A small car took 49.7 months in Russia – more than four years – 4 months in America and around 10 in Britain. And as for the fuel, 10 litres of petrol involved 173 minutes in Russia, 26 in America and 75 in Britain.

Only rents were substantially cheaper in Russia: it took 11 minutes to earn an hour's rent, compared to 40 in America and 25 in Britain. But Russian housing standards were poor. Most Russians did not have the minimum set in 1920 of 9 square metres per person living space; average living space was around half that in Western Europe. A quarter of Russian families still shared apartments; and in most families, more than one person occupied each room.

The Russian state health service, which absorbed nearly as much of GNP (around 6 per cent) as the American private one, worked very well by local standards: infant mortality was low and life expectancy, although falling, was around 70 years. There were some 24 doctors for every 10,000 people – the highest number in the world. However, hospitals were short of equipment and overcrowded, waiting lists were long (up to 5 years for non-emergency operations), medicines scarce, and hygiene and nursing poor.

Schooling strongly reinforced the Soviet class system: in 1970 over half of all Russian children under 14 had dropped out, and only 5.5 per cent went beyond high school. There were 6 schools for the very bright and the children of the important: in Siberia, from the 1 million annually technically eligible for entry to one of these schools, just 300 were picked. Working-class Russians were usually packed off to technical schools. Children were taught to be conformist and were constantly assessed. Most teaching was through straightforward rote learning and progress was performance-related, with enormous pressure on the Russian child to succeed.

The Soviet system of control, while not as pervasive as the West imagined, efficiently stifled any independent political initiative, and its authority over people's personal lives showed no sign of withering away, even as the private sector emerged from under the paving stones. After the supposed elimination of class conflict in the Soviet Union, the state's need to represent the interests of the working class against the exploiting class had theoretically vanished. In reality, the Russian state largely represented the interests of the new middle class, and now increasingly seemed to be, in Marxist terms, the principal instrument of class repression.

The emergence of the Russian middle class prompted the Soviet authorities to replace the liberalism of the 1950s and 1960s with sharper control, most obviously in the treatment of dissidents and the partial rehabilitation of Stalin as the embodiment of authority, nationalism and genuine popular affection. There were still some 500,000 members of the KGB. Some 2 million people served in labour camps, while there were between 10,000 and 20,000 political prisoners. The most common method of control was ending a person's prospects of promotion, or getting him transferred to a lesser job elsewhere: this usually ensured compliance.

In 1971 the main opposition newspaper, *The Chronicle of Current Events,* was closed and its editors and distributors arrested. Throughout the 1970s, the number of arrests of prominent dissidents increased while most of the best known were exiled, among them the author Alexander Solzhenitsyn.

For leading intellectual and cultural figures, the consequences of any refusal to adhere to the Party line had always been extremely serious. Yet in spite of this, there were always those who felt compelled to test the system's limits, whatever the consequences both politically and culturally, while the authorities always knew that they could stamp down hard on anyone deemed to be straying too far from their prescribed norm.

After Khrushchev succeeded Stalin in 1953, the cultural darkness lightened, so that a book like Ilya Ehrenburg's *The Thaw*, which dealt with the purges, could be published after the proposition was made that works should be judged by their 'sincerity' rather than their degree of conformity. Earlier Soviet writers who had been killed in the purges, such as Boris Pilnyak and Isaak Babel, were rehabilitated. A new edition of Dostoyevsky was published, works by foreign writers such as Hemingway and Graham Greene were allowed in for the first time and poetry flourished. Painting, hitherto straitjacketed by Socialist Realism was now allowed freer expression, architecture became less triumphalist, Western fashions in clothes and music began to creep in and the film industry thrived.

Yet the new tolerance had its limits: while Vladimir Dudintsev could see his book *Not by Bread Alone,* that highlighted the struggle of the honest individual against corrupt bureaucrats, appear in print, Boris Pasternak's *Dr Zhivago* – about the plight of individuals caught up in the Russian Revolution – was banned. Although it helped win for its author a Nobel Prize in 1958, a torrent of official abuse forced him to decline it and very probably contributed to his death in 1960. And authors like Andrei Sinyavsky, who wrote *The Trial Begins* in 1960, and Yuli Daniel, were compelled to smuggle their books out of the country.

Yet two years later Khrushchev personally approved the publication of Solzhenitsyn's *One Day in the Life of Ivan Denisovich,* based on the author's own experiences, which opened the eyes of the Russian people and later the whole world to the reality of life in Stalin's gulags. Yevgeni Yevtushenko symbolized the outspokenness of the new young poets with his *Babi Yar* (1961), a denunciation of Russian anti-Semitism and *Stalin's Heirs,* published in *Pravda* and memorably set by Shostakovich in his thirteenth symphony. In *Babi Yar,* Yevtushenko wrote prophetically: 'Some of those heirs have retired to cultivate roses, while in their secret hearts they believe they have only retired for a little while.'

He was right: following Khrushchev's downfall in 1964, the ice began to freeze again. Sinyavsky and Daniel were put on trial in 1966 and sentenced to labour camps. After 1963, Solzhenitsyn joined other writers by circulating his work as *samidzat* (illegally copied and distributed texts) inside Russia, although his books were published abroad as well. He suffered increasing official harassment; after *The First Circle* and *Cancer Ward* appeared in 1968 and 1969 respectively, the KGB seized the manuscript of *The Gulag Archipelago.* Yet in spite of this, the first parts were published in Paris in 1973. Solzenhitsyn – who had won the Nobel Prize in 1970 – was promptly denounced in the press, arrested and exiled to the West two years later.

Even an officially approved writer like Yevtushenko could fall foul of the authorities, and for some the creative and intellectual atmosphere became intolerable. Solzhenitsyn's companions travelling westwards included dancers (Rudolf Nureyev, Mikhail Baryshnikov and Natalia Makarova), musicians (Galina Vishnevskaya and her husband, Mstislav Rostropovich, who had supported Solzhenitsyn, Vladimir Ashkenazy and the violinist Viktoria Mullova), the Estonian composer Arvo Pärt, and the poets Irina Ratushinskaya (who spent seven years in a labour camp for her advocacy of human rights) and Josef Brodsky, a Nobel prize-winner in 1987, after he left Russia. This emigration did Russia's reputation in the West no good at all – not that ordinary Russians were ever allowed to learn anything about the real reasons.

The Czech film director, Milos Forman, revealingly reflected on cultural life under Communism: 'It's living in fear, which is boring – because you are afraid to lose a chance to go to school, to have a job, to do things . . . so you have to censor yourself what you say, what you do – you know – how you behave. But it's not an exciting kind of rebellion against the regime; it's a very boring rebellion because I guess any totalitarian system is basically very, very boring. [The bureaucrats were people] whose only pleasure in life was in power, and in nothing spiritual, just power, and I don't even know if they believed in it or not. They just did it to keep themselves in power and to keep everybody away who could disturb their power . . .

'Then there was a certain kind of relaxation of this strict ideological control . . . [and] everybody who had a little freer way of thinking was trying, trying pushing the boundaries, right? And they [the bureaucrats] became very sensitive. But it was a time when it was not very popular to ban films in an administrative way; so what they were doing usually when they saw a film and they didn't like it and they thought that it should be . . . banned, they arranged a screening for people, for working people, and they always planted . . . one or two people there who [said,] "OK, comrades, let's have a discussion about the film" . . . And now they attack the film, and finally the result was, "Well, the people rejected the film."'

At the heart of the increased repression in the Soviet Union was the onslaught on human rights. The 1975 Helsinki Accords, which had laid down basic human rights and freedoms, had not been considered especially significant by either the American or Soviet governments at the time; now suddenly, they became a major issue of controversy between the superpowers and drew an increasingly fierce response from the Russian authorities.

The issue was given a sharp push by two critical and coincidental global happenings: the inauguration in 1977 of an American President obsessed with the issue, Jimmy Carter, and the election in 1978 of the Polish John Paul II as Pope – one of whose primary concerns was to liberate his own people from the atheistic doctrine of dialectical materialism.

In 1977, with the West's espousal of the human rights provisions of the Helsinki Accords, Helsinki Watch committees were set up around the Soviet Union, with the support of President Carter, and the crackdown grew fiercer: many of those involved were put into mental hospitals to be drugged, while others were sent to labour camps, imprisoned or exiled. The human rights advocate, Yuri Orlov, prominent in the Helsinki Watch movement, was sentenced to seven years' imprisonment while Anatoli Sharansky was convicted of treason and sentenced to thirteen years hard labour. Jewish would-be émigrés from the Soviet Union, encouraged by Helsinki's pledge to respect people's rights to emigration, applied in ever-increasing numbers to leave, and the total permitted to do so soared from 14,000 in 1975 to 50,000 in 1979, although the figure fell back after tighter restrictions on this Jewish exodus were introduced. In 1980, the international symbol of Russian dissidence and a former member of the scientific elite, Andrei Sakharov, was internally exiled to the city then named Gorky 260 miles east of Moscow where, under the harsh living conditions imposed upon him, his health sharply deteriorated. The treatment of Sakharov was appalling to behold, but not as bad or as quick as that of thousands of unknown dissidents.

Not until the advent of Mikhail Gorbachev would conditions ease.

Russia had become one of the world's most xenophobic societies. Its people, sheltered from contact with the outside world, heard only the 'official' view of world events, constantly portraying the Soviet Union as peace-loving and reasonable, and the United States, Western Europe and China as aggressive and encircling. Ordinary Russians firmly believed this: they had a strong sense of patriotism, remembered their own history – Russia has traditionally been invaded and has not acted as aggressor – and knew no better.

The commitment to spreading revolution was by now underplayed, as was any example of expansionism which might undermine the general 'peace-loving' image: a prominent Soviet economist insisted to the author, who had asked him about Afghanistan, that there was no Soviet army there, merely a 'limited contingent of Soviet troops'. When asked how this differed from an army, he had no answer.

Ordinary Russians, proud of their country, eagerly believed that life in the West, although better goods were available, was dangerous, insecure and criminal, compared to their own static, ordered existence. This old-fashioned nineteenth-century style nationalism had no connection with proletarian internationalism.

World revolution was subordinated to Russian national self-interest: thus the quarrel with China; the Russians ordering Western European Communist parties, particularly the French, to faithfully reflect the changes of Russian foreign policy – most famously at Stalin's rapprochement with Germany in 1939, whereupon Western European parties reversed their attitudes to the Nazis overnight; and the decision to deny aid to Allende's Chile on the grounds that the Marxist experiment there was doomed.

By 1985, Russia was truly stagnant. Ordinary Russians were spared the pressures and rewards of a Western way of life; with nothing to strive for, they worked to keep their family and were assured of a standard of living at the same level as most of their fellow citizens. In practice, only one sector of society had a greater sense of security than its equivalent in the West: the employed working class, which had an absolute right to a job, however nominal. Further up the scale, society was intensely competitive because the class structure that had emerged meant that those unable to advance were likely to be condemned forever to the bottom of the pile.

The competition started at school, where for pupils the constants were supervision, striving and pressure for exam results. In such an atmosphere, only the most gifted – and the children of the governing class – could obtain better jobs. It continued in offices, where inefficiency and subservience to political interests bred advancement through the personal favouritism of the bosses. It existed in the shops, where an article in short supply became a prize possession to show off to the neighbours. Promotion and perks in jobs were desperately sought after, because they represented status and could lift ordinary Russians out of the drabness of their existence.

If this class-divided society had emerged, why did the Soviet Union go to such lengths to cover it up? Ordinary Russians clearly paid little attention to the barrage of propaganda spewed at them from every side, or Radio Moscow's invocations to vote in elections: 'The reason why so few members of the Supreme Soviet lose their seats is that they are chosen initially from the best qualified and worthiest members of the population,' blared the unlistened-to loudspeaker at a railway station.

The people were as bored of propaganda as by the government's rigid refusal to permit any statement of opinion that in any way criticized the state or to allow the import of foreign newspapers. The country was virtually sealed off, its own press a daunting catalogue of economic achievements. There was little mention of crime or, in the absence of criticism, any subject that might interest the casual reader. Only the genuinely committed ideologues believed.

While political freedom in Western democracies gave ordinary people at least the impression that they could express dissatisfaction with their rulers, ironically in communist Russia the system resembled the Divine Right of Kings, the doctrine enshrining the natural, God-given superiority of a monarch and his consequent right to rule. The façade of equality in a system remarkable for its inequality helped provide legitimacy, because it gave people the rationale for accepting a political and economic system that tied them to the bottom rung of the ladder. Furthermore the Russian communist leaders, who chose not to submit themselves to election by the people, could claim that only the Communist Party could bring this vision of a totally equal society into being.

If the façade of equality was the first element of legitimacy, the second was nationalism: the eulogizing of all things Russian. 'Russian cooking is well known to be the best in the world,' trilled the loudspeaker in Moscow's main tourist hotel. The militarism in the streets, the regime's wallowing in history which selectively deified the imperial past by the preservation of Russia's ancient monuments, the glorification of imperial art and literature, the decrying of non-traditional art forms – these were part of the same nationalist ethos. Nationalism spurred Soviet efforts in the space race and the arms race, and the attempt to get iron and steel production to equal that of Britain in the 1950s. The Party expressed the will of the nation, and all Russians supported the nation. Strident Russian rhetoric, designed largely for internal consumption by politicians anxious to maintain power, was taken too seriously in the West.

The third element of legitimacy was control, although now of a less extreme kind. In the years of suffering and privation, people accepted the dictates of authority without question. In the years of greater prosperity, the middle class was less cowed in matters other than political. Middle-class Russians wanted a more colourful life, represented by pop music, discotheques, better clothes, consumer goods, cars. The totalitarian state was bending before the complexities of modern industrial society and of consumerism, to the extent that growing demand had increased the number of cars on the streets from 55,000 in 1965 to 3 million in 1985. The Russians lacked the hard currency to import jeans, so Soviet firms were set up to produce them. 'The Russians are capable of great efforts for short periods,' a senior Party official told the author: the next effort would be in the consumer goods field.

Only in politics was the prohibition on dissent absolute, and the penalties still fearsome. This was not as unpopular as people in the West tended to assume. Most ordinary Russians the author spoke to at the time regarded their leaders as incompetent or worse; but they were apprehensive of alternatives. The system provided lifelong security and public safety. Another senior Party official cited as the worst defect of Western society the pervasiveness of crime. 'In Russia there is some,' he added, 'but much less. Old ladies do not have their handbags snatched.' This was explained by the grip of an authoritarian society, and the controls that prevented Russians moving from city to city or from country to city, which excluded the potentially criminal unemployed population that flooded the cities of most other developing countries. The absence of crime was popular among Russians of all classes. The country in many ways resembled a much fiercer version of Franco's Spain; authority was respected, although people grumbled about it.

Like Franco's Spain, only to a much more pronounced degree, Russia was also an incompetent over-centralized society. The system of central planning, however refined over the years, was impossibly laden with vested interests, political motivations and corruption in order to bypass the bureaucracy. Maybe the most crucial difference between Soviet and Western policy-making was the lack of accountability at every level except to those immediately above an official. The press, when it carried rare criticism of a national or local policy, was usually grinding an axe for a particular faction within the hierarchy.

Yet the voters, contrary to outside impressions, had a modicum of choice at local level. A popular local man could be chosen to stand over the Party's candidate, provided he espoused all the goals of the Soviet system; even this was rare, however. Public scrutiny of the Party was non-existent. Economic performance was not subject to comparison, and quality control in industry was largely missing. The bureaucracy was biased against any new ideas and innovations that appeared to challenge the existing order – even though they might actually refine and improve the system.

In most Western countries the main spur to change came from debates in the media, the expression of public opinion, and politicians launching new initiatives. In the Soviet Union the political elite's position was so shakily based on the pretence of a mutual crusade that it had become the most conservative institution of all. Further, as a middle class emerged, the Party struggled to keep it from realizing the extent to which its sophistication was outgrowing the political system. Thus the treatment of dissidents remained as stiff as ever, the exclusion of Western political material absolute, and the controls that confined Soviet art to its gauntly socialist 'realism' rigid.

Against the system's frigid impersonality – its inertia, its outdatedness in a modern industrial society and its restrictions on individual liberties – the Russians had evolved a number of defences; these included the intimacy of family life, which in closeness and making do with a few treasured possessions is among the warmest in the world. The high Russian divorce rate was evidence not of the absence of family life, but of the stress such intimacy – usually grandparents and children shared the same apartment – can impose.

The system also made Russians a very discreet people; but privately they criticized its abuses in most levels of society. The existence of a private farming sector that accounted for a third of agricultural output as well as a bureaucracy-bypassing black market in industrial goods were signs of the endurance of the human spirit; all attempts to remould it according to Marxist doctrine had failed.

7

Perpetual Revolution

'Look you, the world is turned upside down.'

Mao Zedong

The Sino-Soviet Divide

The first public break in the forward march of world Marxism-Leninism took place with a characteristically enigmatic speech delivered by Chairman Mao in Moscow at the conference marking the fortieth anniversary of the October Revolution in November 1957. To the tiers of grim-faced Russians and their foreign guests, Mao's words caused a ripple of surprise. He spoke about the east wind prevailing over the west wind. The Soviet press chose to interpret this as a rebuke to the West. In practice, it was an attack on the Western form of Communism – the Russian model.

The split between the two great communist giants – respectively the largest and the most populous nations on earth – came dramatically quickly after the signing that same year of a Sino-Soviet Treaty of Friendship, Alliance and Mutual Assistance, at which Russia pledged to protect China from outside attack and promised non-interference in its internal affairs. Yet the two countries had never really trusted each other: the Russian communists had consistently misread the Chinese situation, saying that the time was ripe for revolution in 1930 – much too early – but not after the Second World War, advice which the Chinese wisely ignored. The Russians had urged a seizure of power in the cities, as in their October revolution. But these were Chiang Kai-shek's strongholds, and Mao was right to rely on the countryside.

The Russians had also wanted the Chinese communists to subordinate their struggle to the cause of Russia's fight against Hitler, thereby preserving good relations with Chiang. Mao had to fight Russia's own supporter, Wang Ming, for control of the Party. Mao had paid obeisance to Stalin, who had patronizingly perambulated him around the achievements of the Russian Revolution; but although admitting his authoritarian methods, Mao privately detested the overbearing Russian dictator who was puzzled by him. 'What sort of a person is this Mao? He claims to be a Marxist, but he does not understand the most elementary truth of Marxism. Perhaps he does not want to understand.'

Mao tolerated this because he needed Russian military equipment, but was determined to strike out as his own man at the earliest possible opportunity. But he had to wait; in the face of American hostility – not recognizing China, and sending military help to South Korea and Taiwan – China inevitably looked for continuing support from Russia.

The Russians gave China credits of $300m; negotiated to hand over to China the Changchun Railway, Lushun (Port Arthur) and Dalian (Dairen) in north-eastern China and to return some Japanese property seized in Manchuria. As late as 1957, Mao was extolling the alliance with Russia: 'This is a great alliance of two socialist countries, we share the same history and the same life-story with the Soviet Union and the entire Socialist camp.' Even after Khrushchev's unsuccessful visit to China in 1959, in which the tough man of action took issue with the steely, subtle theoretician, China and Russia claimed to be getting along splendidly.

Under the surface the position was very different. The Chinese got less from the alliance than they had hoped. They urged that continuing revolution around the world should follow in China's footsteps. The Russians urged caution. The Chinese sought Russian help in recovering Taiwan; the Russians refused to supply the necessary weaponry. Chinese hopes of sophisticated technology and armaments from their traditionally suspicious neighbour came to nought.

Moreover, Soviet economic aid came at a price. Between 1950 and 1960, some 10,000 Russian trainers had been sent to China and a similar number of Chinese teachers to Russia. Around 11,000 Chinese students went to study in Russian universities. But the Chinese payment in return included grain, edible oils and foodstuffs worth some 21,900 million roubles including 5,760,000 tons of soya beans, 2,940,000 tons of rice and 900,000 tons of meat. On one reckoning Chinese exports in kind to Russia were worth four times as much as Soviet aid. The Russians were thoroughly unwise to take this semi-colonial attitude, apparently not appreciating that the Chinese did not consider themselves a dependent nation.

By 1958 the Chinese were grumbling about the way the Russian relationship was developing. Many senior Chinese argued that they should have a larger army, not improved weaponry, to compensate for their inability to obtain the latter from Russia. The Russians suddenly broke off their defence agreement with China in 1959, after only two years. The behind-the-scenes reason was the Chinese demand to be supplied with nuclear weapons, to which the Russians replied that if they were, they would be placed under Soviet military control.

The first hints of the extent of the quarrel broke in 1959 when the *People's Daily* lashed the Russians for 'being scared out of their wits' for suggesting that China 'change her habits and give up her struggle for revolution'. Many commentators have suggested that behind the obvious subjects for disagreement lay the Russian fear of the 'yellow hordes' in the south, which made a conflict inevitable.

There may have been some such subconscious feeling. But the real rationale was a straightforward power struggle. First, the Russians, viewing the Chinese as their revolutionary offspring, were determined to control the direction of the world revolutionary movement, just as they controlled Eastern Europe. But they could never hope to occupy China, and therefore could not order the Chinese to do their bidding.

Second, the Chinese, and in particular Mao, who was regaining his influence throughout this period, sincerely believed in world revolution, and despised the Russians both for their doctrine of 'socialism in one country', and their conservatism. In fact, the Khrushchev years marked the beginnings of the relaxation of Cold War tensions between Russia and the United States, and the Chinese suspected a Russian readiness to sell out in return for a quiet life. The ideological break was consummated when Mao regained the initiative in Chinese domestic affairs and embarked upon the Great Leap Forward of 1958, repudiating Soviet-style economic policies. The Chinese now decided to assume the mantle of leader of world Marxism-Leninism, said Mao, his own version of which 'was to displace Khrushchev's revisionism, which was akin to that of the leaders of the First International after 1864', with the Gate of Heavenly Peace – Tiananmen – and not the Kremlin as its symbolic heart. By late 1959 the split was so wide that the Russians failed to support the Chinese in their bitter quarrel with India. The Chinese damned the Russians as 'revisionist' and openly attacked the Soviet

Union's climbdown during the Cuban missile confrontation with the United States.

By 1964 the polemics had become vicious: Khrushchev was denounced for appealing to 'personal material interests', and for establishing a new 'aristocracy' in Russia. The Russian regime had 'reduced the ideal of Communism to efforts to stuff one's belly with a plate of goulash'. By November 1965, the antagonism between Marxism-Leninism and Khrushchevism was irreconcilable. The two countries were openly competing in the Third World, with China funding a number of revolutionary movements and attacking the Russians for supporting only those that served its narrow nationalist self-interest.

In 1964 the Chinese even tried to prevent Russian participation in the Afro-Asian Conference in Algiers. The Chinese seemed to be going out of their way to be provocative: in March 1963 they insisted sharply on a revision of their border treaties with Russia. The Russians denounced the Chinese for border violations: and when they accepted there should be talks about disputed islands on the Amur River on the Chinese north-eastern border, the Chinese upped the ante. In 1964 Mao said ominously that China had not yet 'presented its account' for the area to the east of Lake Baikal, which had been taken over by Russia only a century before and which included Vladivostok and the Kamchatka Peninsula. Five years later, tensions over the border issue spilled over into armed clashes between the two sides along the Ussuri River, a tributary of the Amur. There were even fears that war was imminent.

The split was rooted both in ideological competition and traditional national rivalry. Even so, it seemed highly unlikely in the mid-1960s that the result would be a rapprochement between the United States and China. But as the United States began to pull out of Vietnam, China's fear of America dwindled sharply and Washington's perceptions were changing as well. By the end of the 1960s the Nixon administration was reaching out to China through a number of intermediaries. Then, in January 1971, it was announced that President Nixon would visit China by spring of the following year. Henry Kissinger, his National Security Adviser, was already there.

China drew up four principles of co-existence, to which the United States subscribed. These were that 'countries, regardless of their social system, should conduct their relations on the principles of respect for the sovereignty and territorial integrity of all states, non-aggression against other states, non-interference in the internal affairs of other states, equality and mutual benefit and peaceful co-existence. International disputes should be settled on this basis without resorting to the use or threat of force.' In addition 'both [China and the United States] wish to reduce the danger of international military conflict; neither should seek hegemony in the Asia-Pacific region and each is opposed to efforts by any other country [i.e. Japan] or group of countries to establish hegemony.'

This staggering leap in Chinese foreign policy marked the triumph of national over ideological interests after Russian relations had gone sour. It was a turning point in post-war world history, at once nullifying the danger of the Soviet Union interpreting the communist victory in Vietnam as carte blanche to spread revolution to the Third World; the Chinese would join the United States in containing Soviet ambitions. China's leap from ideological fanaticism to foreign policy pragmatism did, however, pose one danger for the United States, namely that in the future the same pragmatism might induce it to make common cause with the Soviet Union.

The Sino-Soviet divide, followed by the American alignment with one of the two great communist powers, dealt a devastating blow to Marxism-Leninism's internationalist idealism. This preached that national differences were merely a product of competition between bourgeois imperialist interests, but clearly nationalism went far deeper than that. Furthermore for one Marxist-Leninist country to require capitalist support against another suggested that the revolution was far from being a continuing world process. The original split between Russia and China had been ideological: an impatient young revolution versus the conservatism of the old one. When China sided with America, however, the split was not ideological, but principally a conflict of power interests.

The primacy of nationalism over Communism was no mere freak of the Sino-Soviet relationship. Within a couple of years it sparked off open conflict in South-East Asia. The Sino-Soviet split influenced this: China and Russia had both competed to support the North Vietnamese with arms and aid. As China moved closer to the United States, however, Russia sought to outflank China by increasing its support for the country to its southern flank, which had an army of more than 100,000 men, thereby distracting Chinese forces from the northern border with Russia. By March 1973, Zhou Enlai was already anxiously advising the North Vietnamese to 'maintain an equilibrium between Soviet and

Chinese influence'. After a visit in 1975 by Le Duan, the Secretary-General of the Vietnamese Communist Party to Beijing, no joint communiqué was issued; in Moscow, his next destination, the Russians provided some $2 billion in aid.

While Chinese-Russian relations were deteriorating, in Cambodia the Chinese supported Pol Pot's 'Kampuchean' regime in its attempt to remain independent of Vietnam; in addition, the authorities in Phnom Penh started accusing the Vietnamese of planning to annex a large part of the seas off Cambodia.

In September 1977, Kampuchean government forces launched a major cross-border attack against the Vietnamese. Following continued shelling of their border towns, in January 1978 the Vietnamese launched a limited thrust into Cambodia, then withdrew. The following December the Vietnamese invaded again, using 100,000 troops and some 20,000 tame Khmer insurgents. In a swift and successful operation Phnom Penh was captured and a puppet pro-Vietnamese regime installed. The Vietnamese became bogged down, however, trying to weed out the Khmer Rouge and assorted armed gangs from the hills and jungles of the northern and western borders.

The Chinese were not prepared to watch the rape of Cambodia without reacting. By mid-1976, relations between China and Vietnam were almost non-existent. The Russians made Vietnam a full-fledged ally in 1977, supplying two destroyers and four squadrons of Mig-21 fighter jets. By May 1978, there were 5,000 Soviet advisers in the country. The Vietnamese joined Comecon (the Communist economic development organization, founded in 1949) in June, and by November had signed a treaty of friendship and co-operation with Russia. The Vietnamese started cracking down on the ethnic Chinese population: some 160,000 Chinese were expelled north, and Chinese shops and property confiscated. The boat people, more than half of them Chinese, started a mass exodus in August 1978: altogether, around 163,000 people fled.

Old border troubles flared anew. In February 1979, shortly after the successful Vietnamese invasion of Cambodia, some 85,000 Chinese troops crossed Vietnam's northern border at twenty points, encountered stiff resistance and withdrew. The invasion, 'limited in time and space' as the Chinese put it, had made its point: the Chinese would use military force if the Vietnamese overstepped the mark. Tensions between the two diminished, and China appreciated the spectacle of Vietnam bogged down in a war in Cambodia.

Thus, soon after the victory in Vietnam, rivalry between the two major communist powers plus the traditional loathing of the Vietnamese for the Cambodians and the Chinese for the Vietnamese had asserted themselves. Sino-Soviet rivalry fissured the communist movement around the world: in Europe the Eurocommunist movement as a whole started stressing their differences with the Russians, and asserting that their relations with the Chinese were henceforth on an equal plane; the Italian communist leader, Enrico Berlinguer, even visited Beijing. In Africa the Chinese vied with Russia for ideological mastery of independence movements, gaining a foothold in some East African countries and, a little later, in Zimbabwe. Here the Russians supported the independence movement of Joshua Nkomo, although that of Robert Mugabe, backed by the Chinese, was the eventual winner. Communist internationalism and solidarity had become superpower competition, with scarcely a whiff of any revolutionary flavour.

The ascent to power of Yuri Andropov as Soviet leader offered the prospect of a Sino-Soviet rapprochement. Although low level talks got under way, disagreements about the border disputes, Afghanistan and Cambodia continued to divide the two communist giants. Meanwhile the Chinese relationship with the United States had been regularized, with regular visits by senior officials in both directions. However, some disagreements persisted, particularly due to President Reagan's commitment to Taiwan and the American reluctance to sell China sophisticated arms. But in the triangular superpower relationship, China's interests seemed to lie in closer links with the United States rather than Russia.

The Cultural Revolution

China in 1966 would make one last attempt to prove that the revolutionary ideal still lived and that political action could, after all, change human nature. Mao Zedong shuddered as he looked across the Soviet border; there revolution had lapsed into a conservative, unequal and underdeveloped society in which the only evidence of socialism was a centrally planned economy shot through with corruption and private enterprise. To Mao, as he expressed it, there was still a chance to enthuse the masses and particularly the young into overthrowing the conservatism of their elders to create a society genuinely moved by the goals of equality and work for the common good, in which the profit motive and greed played no part. In fact the Cultural Revolution was a cynical power ploy to prevent Mao being ousted after the disaster of the Great Leap Forward.

There is little doubt that Mao conceived of himself as a traditional emperor, according to Li Xiaojun:

> At times Mao went so far as to speak of himself as an emperor. In his poem 'Snow' he lists one by one those monarchs who had founded a new dynasty – for example Qin Shi Huang Di, the First Emperor; Han Wu Di, founder of the Han Dynasty; and the first emperors of the Tang and Sung dynasties. He acknowledges their military accomplishments, but then compares them unfavourably to himself, saying that they are inferior because they lack his literary talent. Again, when on one occasion Mao welcomed the commanders of the eight great military regions of China, he said: 'I receive the dukes and princes of various areas.' And these were not tongue-in-cheek remarks, for when Mao met the French writer André Malraux in his later years, he remarked frankly that he was the last emperor in the succession of Genghis Khan and the Kangxi Emperor [reigned 1661–1722].
>
> In his last meeting with Edgar Snow, the greatest Western apologist for Mao and his revolution, Mao said 'I am a monk holding up an umbrella,' which when understood in its allegorical sense means 'I defy all laws human and divine'. (Chinese allegorical sayings are not always easy to explain in translation. Here the import of the words 'I am a monk holding up an umbrella' is as follows: the word 'monk' implies 'without hair', the word 'umbrella' implies 'without sky'; and in Chinese the words 'hair' and 'sky' have the same pronunciation respectively as the words 'law' and 'divine'. The saying is an elaborate pun. So Mao's meaning was that he was a person who never followed rules, but did exactly as he wished.)

The Cultural Revolution, a period of madness, started as a military coup presided over by Mao and organised by Lin Biao but quickly got out of control. A group of radicals, the Gang of Four, headed by Mao's wife, Jiang Qing (Chiang Ching), used the popular forces unleashed by Mao and Lin Biao as a stepladder to power. They believed that once a revolution had started under the banner of extremist ideals, there would be an opportunity to seize control of its direction.

The Cultural Revolution, as the name implies, began as a backlash against the urban-based intellectual elite that dominated China's cultural and in particular educational life. Specifically it was a play, *The Dismissal of Hai Jui* by the Beijing historian Wu Han that was seen as a thinly veiled attack on Mao for his excesses during the Commune Movement and Great Leap Forward of 1958, which provoked the Maoist backlash. When Peng Zhen, the Beijing Party boss, defended the liberal writers who had come under attack from the Maoists, Mao moved from quasi-exile in Shanghai to Beijing to take charge in May 1966 when the Cultural Revolution burst into life with a demonstration at Beijing University. Liu Shaoqi, Zhou Enlai and Deng Xiaoping – Mao's principal rivals – were each forced to make a public self-criticism for mishandling this. Mao then called upon universities across the country to rise up against Party committees. Liu Shaoqi was later nearly kidnapped by Red Guards.

A purge was ordered of the leading journalists, educationalists and members of the artistic community. Jiang Qing, a former actress, was appointed to the Central Cultural Revolution Committee to reorganize the army's famous opera troupes, which were the spearheads of the Party propaganda machine. 'Paris Communes' were set up in Shanghai, Beijing and other major cities to recreate the revolution from the bottom again. Operas and plays were now turned into Maoist spectacles, extolling the virtues of Maoist workers, peasants and Red Guards. 'Liberal' and 'bourgeois' writers were prime targets. Education was to be controlled by the poorer members of the community to promote their children, who were to have authority over teachers; and the rural communes were once again to be given primacy over not just cultural life but the country's large industrial complexes. The denunciation and browbeating of teachers by their students became a symbol of the excesses of the Cultural Revolution along with the stridency of cultural events and the chanting Red Guards with their little Red Books.

The world was gripped by the images of extremism: the millions clutching their 'little red books', the stridency of cultural events, the denunciation and browbeating of teachers, the endless parades of revisionists in dunces caps and the wild demonstration at the Chinese Embassy in London, when diplomats attacked the police with dustbin lids and sticks to display revolutionary fervour and safeguard their jobs. Agriculture was disrupted in many provinces and production in factories fell sharply as the Red Guards took control, particularly in Shanghai, where the radicals controlled the Party machine. 'Long marches' of Red Guards trekked to distant parts of China to enforce their ideals of equality upon settled communities barely touched by the Chinese revolution. In February 1967, the establishment of the Shanghai People's Commune, with its own autonomous 'proletarian organ of administration' was announced in Shanghai, the heartland of the Cultural Revolution. At that stage the commanders of China's armed forces, supported secretly by the wily Zhou Enlai, informed Lin Biao and Mao that they would not preside over China's disintegration; they insisted the Cultural Revolution be halted. The Shanghai Commune was disbanded and a Party-nominated Revolutionary Committee replaced it. In Mao's subsequent speeches to the Red Guards he called on them to tone down their militancy; he had hesitated on the very brink of civil war. An attempted coup was staged when Mao visited Wuhan in July. He escaped in a nightshirt and slippers.

In fact, the disruption was relatively short-lived; although up to 400,000 may have been killed, Lin Biao ended the Cultural Revolution as quickly as it had begun. In 1968 the Red Guards were disbanded and in April 1969, the Ninth Congress of the Chinese Communist Party triumphantly announced that the Cultural Revolution was over, formally stripping Liu Shaoqi of all his posts and calling for a return to stability. This marked Lin's premature bid for supreme power. Having unleashed the fury of the mob, he decided to suppress it through what was, in effect, a military takeover.

In 1968 he had compelled Mao to accept that the Red Guards were out of control and had betrayed movement's original aims. Lin Biao had seized power from the Chinese Communist Party, which had been subservient to the army for a long period during the revolution and was now purged. The army claimed it was only restoring order – after having unleashed the revolution in the first place.

The 'Three Part Committees', a coalition of army officers, workers' 'leaders' charged with restoring order to the shop floor and orthodox Party members were set up to provide China with a new and stable governing structure. The army dominated these committees, and its men spread through into the countryside where bloodshed frequently resulted as fighting flared up between tough-minded army commanders and young revolutionaries. Mao at first appeared to object to the military seizure of power, denouncing the army's excesses. But by the Ninth Party Congress it seemed that he had once again lost control to Lin Biao.

At the congress, Lin was officially proclaimed Mao's successor, and propounded in communist terms an unprecedented heresy – the theory of the importance of the individual in politics. He argued that once in a while a man of unsurpassed genius like Mao appears who transforms

history and should rise above day-to-day politics. Lin in effect proposed
to kick Mao upstairs, while imposing a military dictatorship on China.
Lin also proposed to revive the Chinese presidency, in abeyance since
Liu Shaoqi 's overthrow.

Mao was not taken in: at the second session of the Central Committee
of the Party, held in Lushan, the strikingly beautiful mountain resort of
the court-favoured poets above the Yangtze valley, Mao denounced the
theory of the individual's role in politics, as much on classic Marxist-
Leninist grounds as on historical ones. It had been responsible for
tyranny throughout history, he insisted, and had inspired Liu Shaoqi .

The debate seemed to be an abstract of Marxist-Leninist theology. Yet
the power struggle in China turned on one simple issue unconnected
with Marxist-Leninist theory. Mao had tolerated the army's plans in
order to depose the conservative bureaucrats who had stripped him of
effective power. Now the army, having used him as an instrument to take
control from the Party, was in turn pushing him aside. He was fighting
back. Quite soon he understood that the only solution was an alliance
with those same communist bureaucrats he had pushed out four years
earlier.

Zhou Enlai, the low-profile mandarin who had somehow survived
the Cultural Revolution by keeping on good terms with Mao and with
Lin Biao, was the man to carry this through. Zhou had been largely supportive of Liu Shaoqi 's conservative policies; but – consummate politician that he was – he favoured propagating those ideals cautiously. He
recognized the needed to bend with the wind of the Cultural Revolution
in order to survive and reverse it.

Zhou saw that the only way to frustrate an army takeover was an alliance between the Party, Mao and the people Zhou most disliked – the
left-wing revolutionaries alienated by Lin Biao's attempts to restore
order. The split between Mao and the army was already common knowledge. Zhou knew he had to move quickly to pre-empt a military coup
d'état. So the 'Train Plot' of September 1971 was staged. So much seems
improbable about this plot that it is hard to believe that a man as able
as Lin Biao (the architect of both the final victory over the Nationalists
and the first triumphant Chinese offensive in the Korean War) could
have been involved in it. Mao was to be blown up in a train travelling
from Beijing to Shanghai while crossing Henan province. But the man
supposed to plant the bomb confessed and Mao changed trains as an
additional precaution. Lin Biao, supposedly on holiday at a seaside

resort near Beijing, was horrified to find that the plot had failed, and hurried his family aboard a plane to Russia. The aircraft had too little petrol and crashed. The wreckage was only discovered months later.

The rest of the story is comic-book stuff. To murder Mao – Lin's most dangerous single rival – and then blame right-wing or left-wing extremists for doing so as a pretext for imposing military control was a textbook way of carrying out a coup. But Lin Biao had far better opportunities to kill Mao – for example by infiltrating one of his men into the military security detachment that guarded the Chinese leader. Lin himself had excoriated those in China who supported rapprochement with the Soviet Union – so it seems unlikely he would have chosen such a destination for his aircraft. Lin's followers had drawn up a bitter criticism of Mao:

> The living standards of the masses, the cadres and the troops have declined. Resentment is on the increase. The people might dare to be angry, but they dare not express their anger; sometimes they don't even dare to feel anger. The ruling clique has degenerated and is decrepit, muddleheaded and incompetent, and it is utterly isolated from the people . . . It has changed the political life of the Party and state into a patriarchal system of feudal dictatorship and autocracy . . . (Mao) is not a real Marxist-Leninist, but the worst feudal tyrant in China's history . . .
>
> The ruling clique knew . . . exactly what the masses most desired and most feared. By playing on these hopes and fears the ruling clique has exploited the masses heartlessly.

For Lin to take off in an aircraft without fuel seems crazy. More probably, Lin was rounded up by forces loyal to Mao within the Party while vacationing and, without his own soldiers' protection, was then executed. The airplane story is likely to have been concocted for fear that the news of the killing of so high an official – no senior man, not even Liu Shaoqi, had been executed in China since Mao came to power – would excite popular emotions.

The main worry of those who had connived at Lin Biao's murder was an army rising in fury at its leader's murder. But all remained quiet: the Chinese army was a conservative body, with little time for Lin or for the Cultural Revolution that he had helped to set in motion.

Zhou finally had to ease his newfound allies, Mao and the revolutionary zealots around him, from power and set China back on the course from which the Cultural Revolution had diverted it. He established a wary modus vivendi with the Left because Mao, increasingly frail and exhausted, would not abandon his radical streak. As the author Roger Garside observed, Mao was a chastened man at the end of the Cultural Revolution: 'A tree that has been struck by lightning retains the appearance of strength for a while, but puts out no new leaves; its roots wither and its branches and trunk begin to crack and decay. So it is with Mao.'

Mao's famous poem on the eve of the Cultural Revolution was about a roc which 'wings fanwise, soaring ninety thousand li and raising a raging cyclone . . . Gunfire licks the heavens, shells pit the earth'. It then describes the sparrows – his contemptible opponents – trying to scale to a jewelled, peaceful palace as 'farting nonsense'. Rejected and defeated, Mao had to accept that he had misjudged the Chinese, who wanted nothing so much as a quiet life. Yet he clung to his left-wing revolutionary cronies, headed by a woman he himself regarded as a strong-willed fanatic, Jiang Qing, as fiercely as to the heartbeats of a dying life.

The power of the Left largely paralyzed any attempts by Zhou Enlai to regulate the economic and social chaos set in train by the Cultural Revolution. In foreign policy, Zhou could operate with relative freedom, largely because his opponents held no strong views on it other than regarding fossilized conservative Russia as the antithesis of everything the Cultural Revolution had stood for, worse even than capitalist America. Zhou was able to persuade the Politburo that China's national interests should dictate the choice of friendship between ideologically unattractive superpowers.

During this period he worked out the policy that in 1972 saw the dramatic visit to Beijing by President Nixon. Zhou knew even by the early 1970s that he would not live much longer: in 1972, aged 74, he was informed that he had cancer. His only hope of leaving China in competent hands was to prepare the way for a successor who would finally crush the Left. In 1973 Zhou persuaded Mao to allow Deng Xiaoping back onto the Politburo. By 1975, at the time of the Fourth National People's Congress – the first since 1964 because the splits within the Party had been too deep to allow one earlier – Deng was approved as China's effective prime minister, in charge of day-to-day planning, while the ailing Mao hovered above and the dying Zhou watched parentally.

The Fourth Congress was the highpoint of Zhou 's rule: he repulsed a concerted attempt by Jiang Qing and her supporters to gain a majority of the senior posts in the state bureaucracy. Zhou also announced that the government's priorities were defence, and science and technology. With this agenda, China resembled any developing country;

Marxism-Leninism, much less Maoism, had been forgotten. Mao stayed away from the congress – ostentatiously receiving foreign visitors to publicize his disapproval.

Deng Xiaoping

Deng set a furious pace on assuming his new position. Short in stature and with a penetrating sense of humour and an absolute lack of the pompousness that characterized most of the other Chinese leaders, he was a practical down-to-earth man who rejected virtually all ideology. He grumbled on taking office that 'people are obliged to talk about class struggle every month and every day and the class struggle cannot be relaxed even for an hour'.

Deng's views were anything but revolutionary. He complained about the armed forces, which 'have become a power behind the throne', the officers 'thick-skinned, disunited, arrogant, soft and lazy'. Education was also a shambles, in Deng's view. 'The level of college education at present is even worse than that of the secondary technical schools in the past. College students are far from being real college students. It is a real mess.' And he was scathing about the 'culture' represented by Jiang Qing: 'The national operas today are no more than a gong-and-drum show. Go to a theatre and you find yourself on a battlefield.' Deng made no secret of his wish to demote those who had risen to power during the Cultural Revolution. 'As for the comrades who have risen by helicopter or rocket, they aren't good enough. They can go down again, while retaining their ranks.'

Deng was fond of quoting one thought of Chairman Mao. 'In the last attempt the impact upon the people . . . of any Chinese political party depends on whether and how it helps to develop the productive forces.' On another occasion he exclaimed: 'No more criticism of the theory of productive forces; if it goes on, production will not rise . . . it doesn't matter if we place the emphasis on profits . . . maintenance of equipment is bad, our technology is backward.'

The management of the economy was the target of Deng's most withering criticism in a report published in 1975 entitled 'On the Accelerated Development of Industry'. 'Management is in chaos; work productivity is low; production quality is poor, maintenance is expensive, costs are high and breakdowns are frequent.' Deng's answer was that responsibilities should be defined; there should be a hierarchy of authority; and discipline should be reintroduced. On foreign trade, Deng argued that exports be increased to allow more imports of advanced technology. Foreign contractors should be allowed to open up China's oil and coal reserves, which in turn would boost export earnings to pay for imports. This broke with the Cultural Revolution's policy of an inward-looking China.

The death of Zhou Enlai in January 1976 was the first key event in a crucial year in post-war Chinese history and also marked the start of Deng's final struggle with the Gang of Four. The funeral was notable for as genuine an outburst of spontaneous grief as China had seen since the Communist Party first came to power. Ordinary Chinese understood what Zhou had done for them in restoring order to their lives after the mayhem of the Cultural Revolution. For days afterwards Tiananmen Square was packed with people weeping – not so much in sorrow as apprehension that the Left might stage a comeback.

The fears proved justified: an edict was promptly issued forbidding further displays of mourning for Zhou. The newspapers, largely controlled by the Left, almost ignored the dead statesman. Deng disappeared, after delivering a public eulogy to Zhou on 15 July. Soon newspaper attacks on Deng's views appeared. 'Chairman Mao has taught us: never forget classes and class struggle,' insisted one editorial in the *People's Daily*. By 6 February, the newspaper was accusing 'Party people in authority of taking the capitalist road' – the Left's favourite expression when denouncing the Right. Zhou 's Four Modernizations came under attack and were said to be hiding 'a complete set of revisionist programmes and lies'. By mid-February it was clear that Hua Guofeng, who had become acting prime minister, had supplanted Deng at official receptions. Hua, a tall, amiable lightweight who straddled both sides of the Party, had survived because he aroused no one's hostility. Deng recognized in the weeks after the funeral that he was too controversial to fill the top post, and his rearguard action was fought to keep the extreme Left from gaining control, rather than for his own retention of power. Hua, a smiling, all-things-to-all-men apparatchik, was an ideal choice. Deng next tried to persuade the oracle of Chinese politics, Mao, that the only way of avoiding civil war was to support him – because the forces of the Right that Deng represented would fight rather than let the revolutionary Left regain control once more.

The struggle this time was a grim one, conducted against the

backdrop of China's worst recorded natural disaster, the Tangshan
Earthquake in July 1976 that claimed 500,000 lives. Strikes erupted
around the country: in Wuhan, the giant heavy machinery plant closed
for five months, as did a motorcycle factory in Luoyang and the tractor
factory in Nanchang. Railway workers went on strike, throttling the life-
line from eastern China to the autonomous region of Xinjiang. Peasants
broke away from their communes. Gangs of men armed with sticks
broke into state granaries and looted banks. Other groups broke into
armouries and formed rival factions that fought one another. The
country was on the brink of anarchy.

On 9 September came the news of Mao's death, which went largely
unmourned, unlike Zhou's. His people did not miss the man who had
made China's revolution and kept it ceaselessly alive in the teeth of wiser
counsels. And while some feared that Mao's death would mark the
beginning of full-scale civil war, others believed that at long last the
opportunity had come to restore stability to China.

Deng was of the latter persuasion. In a ringing call to arms at the
resort of Cong-Hua he summoned his supporters to the fight.

> Either we accept the fate of being slaughtered and let the Party and the
> country disintegrate, let the country which was founded with the heart
> and soul of our proletarian revolutionaries of the old generation be
> destroyed by these four people [the Gang of Four] and let history regress
> one hundred years, or we still struggle against them as long as there is any
> life in our body. If we win, everything can be solved. If we lose, we can
> take to the mountains for as long as we like or we can find a shack in other
> countries, to wait for another opportunity . . .

Deng believed he commanded the stronger forces, including the military regions of Guangzhou, Fuzhou and Nanjing, now that Mao was dead.
As for Hua Guofeng, the compromise candidate for Party Chairman and
the vital figure in the struggle, leaders of the army, the state and the Party
made clear to him that Jiang Qing and the Gang of Four must be removed
to prevent civil war. At Mao's funeral Hua made cryptic references to 'plotting', in a speech that clearly worried the Gang of Four leaders.

On 6 October 1976, Jiang Qing, Mao Zedong's widow, was reading a
book on a sofa in her bedroom. By the standards of a film star or political leader in the West – and she was the equivalent in China to both –
her lifestyle was modest. Her home was comfortable without being over-

large and featured a series of decorative pools draped with lotus blossoms, a small private cinema, in which she watched the foreign films denied to her people, and silk sheets on her bed. She was rumoured to have a lover. By the standards of ordinary Chinese, undergoing absolute austerity, rigorously bound to a sexual ethic that forbade the slightest display even of intimacy, she lived on a pinnacle of bourgeois decadence. Ironically, with her frosty look, slight frame and severe spectacles in middle age, she was the public figure identified with the very opposite. She also had a reputation for personal vindictiveness: a beautiful rival, Liu Shaoqi 's wife Wang Guangmei, once wore a pearl necklace at an official reception. During the Cultural Revolution she was compelled to wear a necklace of table tennis balls.

Jiang Qing's bedroom was unlocked and someone entered without knocking, which mildly annoyed her. What alarmed her much more was that the intruder commanded a small contingent of soldiers. 'On the orders of the first Vice-Chairman of the CPC Central Committee and President of the State Council, Comrade Hua Guofeng, we are here to arrest you and put you under examination in isolation,' he declaimed. According to the officially leaked account, she shouted for her guards, but the officer who had come to arrest her now controlled them. According to her enemies, her handmaidens – who had resented her arrogance for years – spat on her as she writhed in self-pity on the floor. The account does not quite square, however, with the dignity and defiance she would show later at her trial.

The story of Jiang Qing on the way up had something of the Eva Peron magic to it: a beautiful young actress, she had arrived in Shanghai in the 1930s where her beauty, rather than her acting ability, had gained her parts and lovers. Non-political, at least to begin with, she moved on to Chongqing, the Nationalist capital in Sichuan province, where she thought success would come more easily. After having difficulty finding parts, she went to Yan'an, met a famous guerrilla commander from the hills, Mao Zedong, and in 1939 became his third wife. By most accounts Mao loved her for her physical attractions rather than her mind, and the marriage was never particularly close. After years of illness, he gave her the minor responsibility of reforming Beijing's theatre and opera, and she soon became a political tool for those who wanted to climb the Party ladder by making use of the Chairman's authority.

She had three principal allies. The first was Wang Hongwen, a good-looking, playboyish young man who had meteorically risen from factory floor troublemaker to Vice-Chairman of the Chinese Communist Party while still less than 40 years old, which made him a child in Chinese political terms. Wang's strident criticisms of his factory managers had been his main qualification for high office at a time when the Cultural Revolution glorified such negative qualities. His main role in his senior Party post was running the popular militia, a huge but poorly trained force consisting mainly of workers taking time off for military training. In the event, the popular militia were to prove a paper tiger; but by the end of the Cultural Revolution there were worries that it possessed the strength and firepower to take on the People's Liberation Army, the most conservative force in China.

On the night of Jiang Qing's arrest, Wang Hongwen arrived at Huairen Hall in Zhongnanhai in Beijing for a meeting of the Chinese Communist Party's Politburo Standing Committee, the powerful internal organ controlled by the Gang of Four. The room was empty. Suddenly, security guards sprang out from behind a screen, punched him to the floor and handcuffed his hands behind his back. The Chairman of the Chinese Communist Party, Hua Guofeng who had ordered the arrests, was watching on closed-circuit television.

Jiang Qing's second ally, Yao Wenyuan, was a vitriolic propagandist. He had risen to power during the Cultural Revolution, dispensing cultural and ideological purity in the Chinese press and broadcasting with crude vigour. Yao went along gently enough when a group of guards came to arrest him at his home on 6 October. The last member of the Gang of Four probably carried the most political weight. Zhang Chunqiao served in the highest position of government of any of the four, as a vice-premier; he also, more than the others, appeared to conform to the puritan ethic he sought to impose on China. Zhang was arrested without resistance in the same hall as Wang Hongwen.

Thus was destroyed, quietly and without resistance, the power of the group that had sought to defy political gravity by imposing a concept of perpetual revolution upon a country profoundly weary of upheaval. The main fear of the leadership group that had ordered the arrests was that Shanghai, the capital of revolutionary sentiment in China, might rise up when they heard that the Gang of Four had been arrested. Their chief allies in the city, headed by Ma Tianshui, were summoned by the communist leadership to Beijing; there they sent a coded telephone message to their followers in Shanghai – 'my old stomach trouble has come back' – to reveal that the Gang had indeed been arrested.

In Beijing, the Shanghai leaders were shown evidence that the Gang of Four had no support in the country at large; their own past shortcomings would be overlooked only if they prevailed upon their followers not to rise up in the Gang's defence. Ma returned dispiritedly on 13 October, to tell his comrades to bow to the inevitable. Edicts were rushed through to allow posters – the main vehicle of political announcement in China – to go up around the city condemning the Gang of Four.

No one, not even the Gang of Four's most vitriolic opponents, could have anticipated the events that followed. On 18 October the streets of Shanghai went wild. For a full week, millions of people poured out to give vent to their relief that the horror, dislocation and misery of the Cultural Revolution were past. The Shanghai Party leaders were compelled to join in the demonstrations – which were largely a repudiation of their own policies. Witnesses insisted that the demonstrations could not have been stage-managed as they expressed too much joy and exultation for them to be anything but spontaneous, On 21 October, with the Gang of Four's capital fallen, the demonstrations spread to Beijing. Huge processions of people with firecrackers, drums and cymbals toured the streets. Women danced sensuously in the evening, to entertain the weary but jubilant demonstrators – in stark contrast to the preceding years, when all such exhibitions were frowned upon.

So ended, in Beijing's largest demonstration for thirty years, man's boldest attempt gain control of human nature in the cause of Marxism-Leninism. For all the human failings of the Gang of Four, they represented something much larger than they understood. To most Chinese their main motive seemed all too clearly to be the acquisition of supreme power, leapfrogging the conservative older and higher echelons of the revolutionary leadership surrounding Mao. Few people seriously heeded the call to perpetual revolution, least of all the men they tried to supplant, led by the formidable, down-to-earth tough man of the Party, Deng Xiaoping. He once commented of the Gang of Four, 'They sit on the lavatory, but can't manage a shit.' Yet the Gang represented the tail end of the principle that motivated Mao himself to the very end of his life, and whose non-fulfilment led him to die a disappointed man: perpetual revolution.

Mao, not the Gang, had borne the prime responsibility for the Cultural Revolution, the last of the disruptions he had inflicted upon the Chinese people in pursuit of his impossible dream. In China, the achievement of political power in 1949 had been only the first stage in

Mao's struggle to transform the largest society on earth, which he only relinquished at his death thirty-seven years later.

On 24 October, around 1 million people flocked to Tiananmen Square to celebrate. Hua made a ritual condemnation of Deng at the beginning. In response he got a bouquet: Deng praised him as the Communist Party's 'wise leader'. Hua was not inspiring: having promised a campaign to educate the tens of millions deprived of schooling during a decade of no examinations and beatings of schoolmasters, very little money materialized. He declared grandiosely that ten new oil fields would be developed. None were found.

But Deng's rehabilitation would be slow. Even though he had many supporters, a significant number of Politburo members still hesitated to allow him the post of Prime Minister and First Vice-Chairman of the Party, from which they knew he, not the weaker Hua, would dominate Chinese politics. A long public debate developed. Through posters ('Democracy Wall') and a mass press campaign, Deng's supporters vied with the small left-wing group at the top. In the event, Deng's men gradually moved into power, slowly easing their opponents out.

The year 1977 marked the turning point for the new pragmatism. Competitive exams were brought in, and schooling was designed to be selective. Bonuses for those working harder were restored in industry. The traditional art forms were once again permitted. On 10 November the Central Work Congress brought together all the leading members of the Party. Middle-of-the-road officials were accused of opportunism and weakness in not attacking the excesses of the Gang of Four. Chen Xilian, the commander of the Beijing military region and the Gang's main military protector, was accused of 62,000 miscarriages of justice involving the deaths of some 20,000 people. Hua was demoted from 'wise leader', and accepted the principle of collective leadership.

The public confirmation of Deng's authority came in a speech in June 1978, in which Deng ostensibly laid claim to the mantle of Mao the pragmatist. 'There are comrades who talk about Mao Zedong's thought each day, but often forget, abandon or even oppose Chairman Mao's fundamental Marxist view and method of seeking truth from facts, proceeding from reality in doing everything and integrating theory with practice.' In the autumn of 1977, People's Congresses assembled to dismiss hundreds of officials who had risen during the Cultural

Revolution; they were replaced with men from the past. Hu Yaobang, Deng's close associate, who had become Director of the Party's Organization Department, masterminded the purge.

By November, 1978, Deng felt secure enough to relax the rules governing political censorship in order to do two things: to test what Chinese really felt and to begin cutting the Mao legend down to size. Deng of course denied any such intention, saying ingenuously, 'in the beginning we made an attempt to stop the campaign. We thought the masses would oppose attempts to attack Mao's name. The leaders were opposed to it and I am not supporting it. But we shall not check the demands of the masses to speak.'

On 'Democracy Wall', they were certainly speaking out. One poster accused Mao of 'mistaken judgement in class struggle', another of 'metaphysical thinking in his old age'. Orators near the wall made more and more daring speeches even criticizing Communism itself. 'We should ask ourselves why the US, Japan and Western Europe have such advanced economies. Is it a result of the kind of constitutional system they have?' Another involved the issue of human rights, appealing to America's President Carter. 'We would like you to pay attention to the state of human rights in China. The Chinese people do not want to repeat the tragic fate of the Soviet people in the Gulag Archipelago.' One poster advocated the Chinese be permitted to have 'sexual relations when and with whom they liked'.

The flowering was brief. In March 1979 it became apparent that Deng was being leant on within the Politburo to put pressure on those 'abusing' the new freedom. Deng made his position clear: 'You say you want to dissolve the human rights congress, to blame the masses for storming government offices, to suppress counter-revolution and even to close down Democracy Wall. If that is what you want I will go along with majority opinion . . . But I have to make clear that . . . the result will definitely be unfavourable. Counter-revolution can be suppressed, sabotage can be restricted, but to wind back down the old practice of suppressing differing opinions and not listening to criticism will make the trust and support of the masses disappear.'

Deng bowed to his colleagues because he needed their support in the continuing persecution of the Gang of Four, who were brought to trial in 1980, signifying that the Party as a whole had decided to exorcize the Left beyond hope of rehabilitation. Jiang Qing was now irretrievably branded a criminal. She and her colleagues had their death sentences commuted, out of traditional Chinese deference for the lives of those at the very top.

Another reason for the attack on freedom of expression was the fear that the Left might take advantage of it. Regulations were published that same March to control disorder: 'Slogans, posters, magazines, photographs and other materials opposed to socialism, the dictatorship of the proletariat, the leadership of the Communist Party, Marxism-Leninism and Mao Zedong's thoughts are formally prohibited.' Wei Jingsheng, editor of the magazine *Exploration* and the main advocate of democracy, was arrested on 29 March. The crackdown was on nothing like the scale of previous political purges, and some measure of debate was allowed to continue. The Chinese revolution had mellowed in middle age.

Political calm descended on China under the genial grip of Deng Xiaoping, who quickly laid the ground for his own succession. Hua Guofeng was slowly eased out as Party Chairman, and Deng's protégés promoted. In 1981 Hu Yaobang became Party Chairman and Zhao Ziyang, the Sichuan Party leader, the effective prime minister. Deng formally dropped his Party posts and was content with a background role, letting the younger men – in their sixties! – get on with the job.

Perpetual revolution was over. Thirty years after Mao's great victory, the attempt to remould human nature had been discarded. Rarely in history can such upheaval have been wrought by the ambitions of one man, by the selfish but romantic vision that had allowed him to pursue his plans for revolution well into his dotage. The Russian experience had been one of grim realism, the vicious Stalin succeeding the pragmatic Lenin and causing appalling turmoil by attempting to turn Russia into a modern country. Mao was no grim realist, but rather a man who was never content to let reality dictate the course of events. When his ideas had wrought their havoc, pragmatic bureaucrats like Deng had to pick up the pieces, offering nothing less than the pragmatic politics which were common to many morning-after revolutions throughout the Third World – in Egypt, Algeria, Tunisia.

The Chinese experience was different in another sense. After Stalin had come the disruptive bureaucratic reforms of Khrushchev, which so manifestly failed that the Soviet leadership became paralytically inert. Deng, on the other hand, was not afraid to try radically new policies or challenge the economic canons of Marxism-Leninism in the name of greater efficiency. Of course, China had much further to go than Russia: its industrialization and modernization of agriculture in 1980 lagged far behind that of Russia in 1950. But there was a real prospect of China moving further towards a capitalist future. This was rendered easier, also, by China's lack of a Russian-style institutional conflict of powers – the Party, the bureaucracy, the army and the security services – that froze reform. The thirty years since the civil war had marked the struggle of revolution against consolidation. The security services had always been controlled by the Party, and had never been developed, as they were by Stalin, into a separate arm of personal power. The army, defeated in its attempt to run the government under Lin Biao, had been reduced to impotence by its divisions for and against the Gang of Four: while essential to the maintenance of order, it knew better now than to challenge the Party's authority, although it remained extremely powerful. The conflict of Party and bureaucracy had been between Mao, who represented the revolutionary spirit, and Liu Shaoqi, Zhou Enlai and Deng Xiaoping, who represented the pragmatic spirit of the bureaucracy – even if they were all senior Party men. When such men gained control of the Party, the bureaucracy was content.

Thus Deng, when he finally assumed power, was almost unchallengeable: he controlled the Party, the army and the bureaucracy supported him, the country was calmer, and the security forces were under control. And unlike Soviet Russia, a fifth power existed in the Chinese state – that of the younger generation, first harnessed by Mao's Red Guard movement, but now thoroughly disillusioned by the extremism of that period.

Deng also tried to jog the new government into relaxing the repression – of cultural and political life, and of freedom of expression, although not too far. The opening of this political safety valve seems to have had a moderating effect, unlike the crudely heavy-handed KGB attempts at suppressing all dissidence.

Perhaps the most significant difference between the Russian and Chinese revolutions was the role played by public opinion. While the mass Chinese demonstrations were largely stage-managed affairs arranged by one clique against another, the genuine political battle between Maoism and the consolidators of the revolution had been fought out in public, with both sides mobilizing their forces and open confrontation ensuing. Unlike the hidden conflicts between cliques at the top of the Soviet leadership, in China the sudden disappearance of senior men, the abrupt reversals of policy in order to stake out a position, the show trials and the all-pervasive security, the fight for the country's future – all of these had taken place almost in the open, although the political debate was always conducted within the overall framework of Marxism-Leninism.

While both sides of the political spectrum in China encompassed people who, given half a chance, might have argued for something other than Marxism-Leninism, ultimately, it was the public preference for the Zhou line that won the battle against Maoism. This genuine element of popular expression gave the Chinese revolution, for all its excesses, more vigour and vitality than the Soviet system and provided an alternative model to the stiff rigours of 'democratic centralism', although it was too chaotic a model to be copied by any other Third World revolution. But when the Chinese communists abandoned centralism, they abandoned one of Lenin's most cherished precepts.

In the Chinese State

At the end of the 1970s, the great majority of Chinese still lived in the countryside. The revolution had affected living conditions, but the speed and depth of this varied considerably, and the illusion in the West of a new rural prosperity was no more than that. In the richer produc-ing areas, the revolution had a considerable impact; in the poorer, very little. By the calculation of a Chinese communist magazine, some 200 million peasants earned less than the equivalent cost of a 330lb ration of rice a year – also about 100 calories less than the United Nations esti-mates of the annual safety barrier below which people are undernour-ished. Average daily calorie intake was 2,000 per person, the same as in India – or in China in the 1930s. Prosperity varied wildly: the richest 20% of peasants had about 36% of per capita income; the poorest 20%, 9%. Some 27% of Chinese peasant incomes were less than $33 a year, while half were between $33 and $67. At the extremes, 1% earned more than $63, while some 29% earned between $10 and $27 a year – which even the Chinese regarded as the minimum for subsistence. In fact large areas of China were no better off than before the revolution.

The main communist success was doubling grain production – but the population had also doubled. Still, campaigns to eliminate rats, fleas, mosquitoes and sparrows (which eat grain) helped to reduce infant mor-tality rates from 200 deaths per 1,000 births in 1949 to around 40 per 1,000 in the 1970s – an improvement, however, no greater than in other developing countries. Famines became less frequent, but still recurred. It was reckoned that as a result of the disastrous consequences of the Great Leap Forward, an estimated 6.5m people died of malnutrition.

Village life revolved around the production teams, numbering some 5 million. In most villages the traditional thirty or forty principal families dominated this reincarnation of the old village structure. Most attempts to abandon private cultivation were reversed by Deng. Mao's policy of trying to make regions self-sufficient in grain production, which resulted in a catastrophic decline in Chinese food production, was also stopped. China's low agricultural productivity remained astonishing. Average output of grain per worker in China, according to Deng himself, was around 2,200 lbs, compared to 111,000 lbs in the United States.

Most peasants had been bypassed by the revolution: they had to struggle by on smallholdings much as they did under the emperors, and even sending their children to the local primary school cost $4. It was reckoned that the Chinese earned less than any other villages in Asia relative to what they paid for industrial goods. The low prices were to some extent offset through intensive cultivation of private crops: peasants earned around 70 per cent more for private produce than they received from the state.

Old village practices had, if anything, been encouraged. In December 1978 prices were raised for many crops, private plots were recognized, and peasants were given more independence to plant what they wanted. Above a fixed quota peasants could keep their produce – an ingenious system that ensured production of what the state needed and more: production rose dramatically. Yet the description given by an American visitor cited in Fox Butterfield's brilliantly perceptive *China: Alive in the Bitter Sea* remains all too true of life in rural China today:

> The American discovered that the best-fed people in the village, the men who did the hardest labour and earned the most work points, ate a diet that consisted of only about 2 pounds of wheat flour a day. Once or twice a week they also got some pickled vegetables and perhaps an egg; once a month they might get a small piece of fatty pork. While he and his wife stayed in the village the police brought in special food in a jeep for them every morning. As a gesture of courtesy, the American's in-laws held a banquet for the local cadres. Again, the police delivered extra rations . . .

The final and crowning course was fish. The Yellow River was only two miles away, and many of the nearby fields had fishponds in them, but when the American later asked the peasants about the last time they had eaten fish, they shook their heads and said they couldn't remember. 'Only the cadres are allowed to catch fish,' one elderly man with a wispy goatee told him.

The poverty in the countryside was to some extent explained by China's crash industrialization programme, copied from Stalinist Russia. In thirty years, more than half of all investment went into major industries, especially steel, while 8 per cent went to agriculture and 5 per cent to light industry. This small-scale industrial revolution in a poor country yielded staggering initial results. Between 1950 and 1980 some 350,000 factories were built at a total cost of $213 billion and China's annual growth rate, officially, averaged 10 per cent after 1953. The country became the world's biggest producer of tungsten and cotton textiles, the third biggest coal producer, the fifth biggest steel producer and created its own high technology and armaments industry

To pay for this colossal investment, not only profits, but real living standards, were kept low: consumption was discouraged, and workers saw a sharp fall in living standards between 1965 and 1980, partly due to the way in which industry functioned. Many factories worked at only 20 per cent capacity. The system of central control smothered productivity. Under state direction, the bureaucracy set targets for each factory and provided the necessary materials. There was no incentive to exceed the targets, but every incentive to use up a factory's allocation so as to get as much the following year. For many years factory managers had virtually no independence and could not fire workers. This encouraged absenteeism, low productivity and pilfering. In 1980, according to official statistics, some 23 per cent of factories operated at a loss.

In 1979, the counter-revolution started: Deng launched his long-awaited industrial reform. Heavy industrial investment was to be cut back and production of energy, consumer goods and agriculture encouraged. Some 6,000 farms could keep around 20 per cent of profits earned under the state quota. Forty thousand more could determine prices – previously a sacred right of the central planners. These experimental farms would have to market their own produce, not simply hand it to the state, and would have to borrow capital, not be supplied with it by the government. This switch away from investment spending to consumer spending was something of a success. But Deng ran into furious resistance from vested interests in seeking to reorganize the bureaucracy, and by 1981 the reforms appeared to have run out of steam.

The most powerful achievement of Marxism-Leninism by the 1980s was the establishment of a minimum standard of living, education, housing and welfare in the cities (although, as already mentioned, not in the countryside, in much of which conditions remained as before the revolution). Minimum was the operative word – few Chinese apartments, for example, were equipped with more than a communal latrine and one source of cold water. The attempt to make Chinese rural society more equal had resulted in the virtual abolition of the richer peasants as a class; even so, middle peasants enjoyed a standard of living as much as ten times higher than that of the poorest, although any improvement in production and encouragement of the private sector would most probably heighten inequality in the countryside, rather than diminish it.

In the cities, the same carefully crafted system of bureaucratic privilege existed as in the Soviet Union although, China's being the more recent revolution, it was less entrenched. As in Russia, living standards for the mass of the people were roughly the same, but the middle class minority enjoyed an inequality that was all the more absolute because it derived from the state. Social status was determined by prominence in the state hierarchy, not by profession, earnings, personal worth or culture, and was all the more fiercely pursued. China even had the same special food stores for senior Party officials as existed in Russia – number 53 Donghuamen Street, a five-storey building with blacked-out windows, was the main one in Beijing.

The Party itself had a highly structured set of ranks, concealed by the obligation to wear identical dress – Mao tunics and baggy trousers. There were some 38 million Communist Party members who, with their dependants, made up a middle class of around 180 million in a country of 1 billion people. The grade 24 clerks at the bottom of the pile were paid around 40 yuan a month (just over $18, at the official exchange rate). A deputy minister was grade 8 (receiving 280 yuan, or $128), provincial governors grades 6 and 7 and cabinet ministers grades 4 and 5. Deng spent a long time in grade 2, whereas Mao and Zhou were in grade 1, earning 400 yuan (just under $185). This, of course, was deceptive. Salaries were small by comparison with the perks enjoyed, which were meticulously allotted according to grade, even down to types of office chair (leather chairs only went to those of grade 13 or above). At a higher level, chauffeur-driven cars and access to special restaurants could be expected when the appropriate grade had been attained.

For senior Party figures, home comforts could be considerable – a large suburban house, modern bathrooms, a swimming pool. Labour being plentiful, officials had servants – a general, for example, might expect to have a maid, a chauffeur and an orderly. Inequality and hierarchy, although nothing like as extreme as in Russia, were essential to social order. Rank, largely a matter of political loyalty and seniority, existed throughout society: there were 12 ranks of professor, with monthly salaries of between 56 and 360 yuan, and 18 ranks of engineers and workers, earning between 34 and 110 yuan. The basis existed for a very conservative and hierarchical society in the future – and the seniority system explained also why Chinese communist leaders, like their Soviet counterparts, were usually so old.

Such a system in China could be expected to cause simmering discontent among the young, who could only rise through the system very slowly. It was to just such sentiments that Mao appealed during the Cultural Revolution. Yet the Cultural Revolution had one significant side effect: most of the participants hated it, finally creating a solid base of anti-Communism among those who by the 1980s had reached their late 20s and early 30s. Furthermore, some 17 million young people were sent from the cities into the countryside during it, and most detested the experience. Thereafter their main objective was a quiet life, and they comprised the bulk of the constituency that swung the political debate Deng's way.

But a new generation came into being since then, and most observers regarded them as cynics, much in the Russian mould. They seemed to be disillusioned with Marxism-Leninism and crudely aped Western culture – although not rock music. Fox Butterfield cites a questionnaire given to a group of journalism students in one university; it revealed that a third supported Marxism, half believed in 'fate' or in nothing at all and a handful believed in Christianity.

These university students were China's brightest and best, for Chinese education owed nothing to communist ideals about the abolition of class differentials: it was ruthlessly meritocratic, streamed and elitist, rooted deep in old Confucian traditions of hierarchy. (Not that Mao did not seek to change it: in the 1960s college entrance exams were abolished, curricula were simplified and students were told to attack, often physically, their teachers. But his changes were scrapped after the Cultural Revolution, and the old ways returned.)

Education had become, once again, extremely conservative. Visitors to schools usually attested to the pupils' astonishing discipline and respect for teachers. When one visitor entered a school in a remote area, she was astonished that the 8-year-olds did not turn to look at her but gazed stolidly ahead, as their teacher had instructed. The government's expansion of the numbers of schools was a genuine achievement; approximately 210 million pupils were attending by the 1980s. All children attended primary school, and 88% reached initial secondary school, although only 50% completed their secondary education and a minuscule 3% reached university. Even in Russia, the equivalent figure was around 23% (and in the United States, 35%).

In a comparable developing country, the Philippines, nearly 20 times proportionately as many people had a university education. China spent a paltry 2% of GDP on education, far behind Russia with 7.6%, and the United States with 6.4%, or even countries like Bangladesh and Somalia. The tiny amount allocated to education explained China's awesome illiteracy rate, which according to the New China News Agency in 1983 extended to some 140 million people.

At the apex of the pyramid were the privileged few. The 285,000 who went to university in 1980 were drawn largely from the existing Chinese elite. In 1979 it was reckoned that of 2,000 who went to Beijing University some 40% came from a Party or army background – that is, from only 2% of the population. Some 11% came from 'intellectual' backgrounds – another 2.5% of the population. Sons of the intelligentsia and the Party's top brass had access to 'Key Schools' – veritable Etons, which had a 90% success rate when it came to entry to university. This highly structured and competitive system – and the ruthlessness in denying better education to the masses – meant that those at the top felt highly motivated and privileged enough to support the regime and not make waves. However, the high rate of unemployed young people who, contrary to the claims of the system, were classed as those 'waiting for work' was a potentially simmering source of discontent. It was impossible to get fired, but it was hard to get a job. Mao had pushed the surplus urban population into the countryside and after his death, thousands of young people returned, going on the rampage for jobs in Shanghai. Still, the poor urban unemployed did not pose much challenge to the regime.

The system of control deterred all but the boldest. Because of the political tumult, comparable only perhaps to the Stalinist period in Russia, the number of those recently affected by repression was much greater than in Russia. The vast majority of Russians went about their ways in a surly, orderly way, aware of, but untouched by, the repressive apparatus. In China most families had, at one stage or another, suffered.

The numbers, as in Russia, were awesome. In the land reform of 1949–51, it was estimated that some 3 million former proprietors and supporters of the old Nationalist government had been killed; Mao himself reckoned that some 800,000 'enemies of the people' had died up to 1954. As many as 4 million were arrested during a further anti-communist revolutionary campaign in 1955–6, with many imprisoned for long periods or executed. In the 1957–8 Anti-Rightist Campaign, which followed the brief blossoming of the Hundred Flowers movement, millions more were sentenced to labour camps or to gruelling work in the countryside. In 1978 91,000 leftovers from this campaign were released from jail.

The Cultural Revolution was a fresh nightmare: according to a *People's Daily* estimate, some 100 million people were affected – be it through investigation, losing their job, imprisonment or execution. At least 400,000 people, maybe twice that, were killed. The indictment of a former minister of security provides a cameo of the persecution during the period. In 40 days he was alleged to have been responsible for the killing of 1,700 people, the searching of 3,600 houses and condemning 85,000 people from Beijing to forced labour.

The numbers sentenced to indoctrination or labour camps in China since 1949 are incalculable, possibly millions. There were two types of camps: re-education camps and reform camps. Re-education camps were principally for prisoners with shorter sentences, of up to three or four years, and inmates were supposed to do lighter work. The camps were said to have a regime less physical than psychological, compared with the brutality of Soviet labour camps. The most common form of maltreatment was brainwashing, forcing prisoners to confess and condemn their crimes until they accepted their guilt and the Party doctrine. Camps existed outside main cities and in most provinces.

Beijing's camp, called Clear Stream Farm, had around 3,000 prisoners. There were also forced labour factories and whole regions that were effectively labour camps. A notorious one near the Russian border was the 'Lake of Emergent Enthusiasms', with up to 40,000 inmates; conditions were Siberian. Close to Tibet, remote Qinghai province, China's bleakest and wildest region, was studded with camps. One sprawled over 500 square miles, and included nine branch camps. To escape these security fortresses was futile: with no shelter and no villages, fugitives would merely die of exposure. Fox Butterfield describes the experience of a Presbyterian minister:

> In the coal-mine camp where he was sent, the convicts worked from 6 a.m. to 6 p.m. seven days a week, with one day of every week for political study sessions. In the early days he was there, the prisoners' rations were based on how many buckets of coal they chipped away each day. Beginners got only 35 pounds of food a month, barely enough to keep them alive. 'We worked harder than anyone in a regular factory or a mine in China,' the minister recalled. '. . . For the first few months my hands were a bloody mess and my back and arms ached all the time, but there was no medical attention.'
>
> The diet consisted of small pieces of steamed cornmeal mush for breakfast, a watery soup or gruel with some vegetables for lunch, and more cornmeal for dinner. The prisoners got meat only twice a month, little chunks of fat which they happily devoured since it was the only animal protein or oil they received . . . and every inmate except those sent to solitary confinement ate the same meagre diet.

At the peak of the repressive system was the Public Security Ministry, responsible not only for political trials, executions, and the labour camps, but also for the vast control apparatus. The Central Investigation Department, a small organization, dealt with foreign espionage. The three main organs of control were the regional police, the *danwei*, and the country's ubiquitous Street Committees.

The *danwei* was simply every person's 'work organization' that, in the huge faceless society that is China, gave him his identity – more so than his name did. Usually based in a person's place of employment, it acted as a substitute family. It arranged his children's clothes, his housing, even his rations. The *danwei* had to approve marriages, or movement from one city to another: the police had checkpoints outside these to make sure that people did not leave their cities illegally. The *danwei* compiled a dossier on each individual; there was no escape for the average Chinese from this system of continuous assessment throughout his life.

The Street Committee watched over people when they were away from work, at home. It could search apartments without warning, monitor the minute aspects of daily life – including bedtime and visitors –and try to impose family planning. It could report people to their *danwei*, so that those who behaved irregularly at home were often denied promotion at work, and it had access to a part-time reserve, the urban militia, or the police: few ordinary Chinese were rash enough to cross these committees. In the cities the system of files, according to Fox Butterfield, 'ensures that every person's education, work, friendships, and misdemeanours, including anonymous accusations are recorded and may secretly cause him trouble in promotion or police harassment'. The Chinese describe the files as 'a shroud that wraps you all your life'.

The same system operated in the countryside with an added refinement: there were more than 100 million loudspeakers in China, most in peasant houses, with broadcasts of Party music and information that could not be turned off. Indoctrination, surveillance, hierarchy: the system was cosy enough for the mute conformist, but smothering for those with independent minds.

The one-party system and the centralized state structure all remained in place, despite Deng's attempts to allow free enterprise in industry and agriculture. These instruments of political control were too useful for any government to dispense with: China was ruled by hierarchical authority, through a class system as rigid as anything under the emperors, and much more so than its fellow Asian developing countries, where a man with nothing could get to the top through initiative.

To be among the ruling 3 per cent in China was to be privileged to a degree that existed in almost no other country. Privilege and coercion went hand-in-hand with inefficiency: by the standards of most Asian developing countries, China lagged sadly behind, conditions for the peasant majority of the population remaining unchanged from centuries ago. The progress of the past thirty years could not be gainsaid: China had found its own way to development – a slow, brutal, turbulent way – which left it lagging well behind its Asian peers.

The Death of Chinese Communism

By the mid-1980s China's economic reform process was clearly no outright espousal of private enterprise. Despite massive privatization being permitted in China's coastal provinces, huge state enterprises continued to coexist alongside this, while most of the interior remained untouched by the changes. Although China's economic growth had, by the standards of the past, been phenomenal as a result of Deng's reforms – around 10 per cent a year for a decade – the country had started from an incredibly low base due to decades of misgovernment. China's economic reforms were certainly more radical than in the early years of the Gorbachev experiment in Russia because Deng, who authorized them, had more power than the Soviet leader; but equally the opposition within the communist hierarchy was deeply entrenched and colossal vested interests protected their industrial and commercial empires and networks of families and cronies.

Deng had charged the two principal reformers, Hua Yaobang and Zhao Zhiyang, with China's economic revival; but like Gorbachev in Russia they would conclude that economic reform would be blocked and diluted unless the Party was radically reformed. As long as they retained Deng's backing, they could get their way. But when both challenged the unquestioned domination of the Communist Party, they encountered huge opposition and lost Deng's support. This made it inevitable that economic reform in China would be limited.

Brave, tough, energetic and in some ways extremely likeable, Deng's personal moderation was in complete contrast with the awesome excesses, personal, and political, of his predecessor, the even less principled Chairman Mao, whose protégé he had been early in his career. But he suffered from a huge downside: he was essentially authoritarian. According to Nikita Khrushchev: 'I do not remember what [Mao] said about Liu Shaoqi and Zhou Enlai, but he did not like either of them . . . The only comrade Mao praised was Deng Xiaoping. I remember that Mao pointed out Deng and said to me: "Do you see the short man over there? He is very clever and promising!"'

As a pragmatist Deng supported economic reform because he believed it might deliver the goods after decades of upheaval and dogmatism; but he also believed in the power of the Party, and was no friend of democracy. The Cultural Revolution's excesses had instilled in him, as in hundreds of millions of other Chinese, a horror of disorder and political upheaval.

In 1979 it had suited him to support the 'Beijing Spring' and the display of free speech on 'Democracy Wall'; but with his assumption of power after Hua Guofeng's fall, he quickly clamped down again while deciding that economic reform could begin. Zhao Zhiyang dubbed this process 'crossing a river cautiously by feeling for underwater stepping stones'. The reform process tried to exploit the benefits of Western economic thinking without absorbing its ideology. The first steps were necessarily cautious, although they undoubtedly brought great initial benefits.

Zhao began with the countryside, where he expanded a pilot experiment in his own Sichuan province to the rest of China – the so-called 'responsibility system'. Under this, the peasants were allowed to retain small plots for their own cultivation, although these formally belonged to the collective. This was popular, although almost as inefficient as the old collective system, because millions of tiny plots were created. Peasants were permitted to legalize their previously illegal small cottage industries such as crafts and textiles. Prices of agricultural produce were also raised slightly, but not sufficiently to cause protest in the cities or really stimulate agricultural production.

Compared to the previous system of full-scale collectivization in huge agricultural units based almost entirely around grain production, with livestock farming and cottage industries almost entirely prohibited, this was a genuine improvement. According to one senior Party official, in most places peasants – 'beggars on the land' – had previously subsisted on between 50 per cent and 80 per cent of the minimum necessary intake of food, and starvation was common: in 1984, 20 million had died of famine.

But the great peasant mass remained miserably poor by international standards because the reformers dared to go only so far. They feared upsetting Party leaders by permitting 'private landowners' to return; they feared upsetting the urban masses by raising the price of food too high. The result was a significant but modest improvement in living standards in the rural areas – where the overwhelming majority of Chinese still live – combined with very rapid economic development in some urban areas, which further highlighted the backwardness of the countryside. To this day the government's main fear is of massive peasant unrest – notoriously the trigger for the fall of dynasties – that could imperil China's whole economic experiment.

Moreover, conservative economists, headed by Chen Yun, favoured massive investments in infrastructure and construction alongside the reformers – which produced serious inflation in China during the 1980s. Most of the construction work was in fact premature and resulted in overcapacity; huge sectors of the economy which remained desperately poorly equipped, underfunded and lacking in research and development, were neglected. This further variant of the Great Leap Forward had some market credibility; but the model was heavily lopsided. Chen Yun argued that a command economy was like a bird held in the hand, unable to breathe; a free economic system would allow it to fly away, so better to keep it in a cage with room to move.

The result was a messy compromise, unbalanced as between city and country. It delivered considerable economic progress compared with what went before, retained the state as the driving wheel and motor for the economy and created boom cities alongside a morass of economic backwardness. When inflation was stamped on in the early 1990s, unemployment rose sharply and inequalities dramatically increased. By using the brake and accelerator simultaneously, a jerky progress was achieved which nevertheless did considerable harm to the social fabric and was potentially unsustainable. By thus hindering reform, conservative warnings of doom threatened to become self-fulfilling; they seemed likely to create the kind of social unrest and country/city confrontation that would require a further clampdown.

The limits of Chinese reform became all too apparent in the late 1980s. Hu Yaobang's outspokenness and advocacy of moderate political reforms to unblock the conservative opposition to his economic reforms – shades of Gorbachev – had long irritated the hardliners: in 1986–7 they had their chance. A wave of protest erupted on student campuses, demanding freedom of speech and free elections. Tens of thousands broke through police cordons to reach Tiananmen Square, echoing the beginnings of relaxation in Russia. This time, they departed peacefully. But the demonstrations provided the pretext for the hardliners, now supported by the army, to force out Hu Yaobang and destroy the most prominent liberals in the Party, including the respected Fang Lizhi, who argued that the whole Marxist-Leninist experience of the past thirty years had been erroneous and proved wrong by events, and that democracy had to be fought for.

Deng could not save his protégé, Hu. Zhao Ziyang, the new Party Secretary, was now in the firing line. On 16 April 1989 Hu Yaobang, the students' hero, died. Following his funeral amid emotional scenes, student demonstrators occupied Tiananmen Square in their tens of thousands. As the numbers swelled, Deng, suffused by memories of the Cultural Revolution, declared that this 'chaos' must be ended. Zhao, who had returned from a visit to North Korea, managed to persuade most of the demonstrators to disperse, but enough remained to thoroughly embarrass the government during the historic visit to Beijing of the Soviet leader, Mikhail Gorbachev who, although mainly kept well away from the crowds, was occasionally greeted with shouts of acclaim.

The day after the visit ended on 19 May martial law was declared, as Zhao's hardline opponents secured the support of Deng and most army chiefs (except for a few veterans who, admirably and surprisingly, opposed the spilling of blood). In fact, following Zhao's instructions, most of the demonstrators had gone home and the remainder posed no threat to public order. Thus it was clear that the proclamation of martial law was merely a pretext by Zhao's anti-reformist enemies to oust him and he was placed under house arrest in the Forbidden City. Li Peng, the leading hardliner, a dour apparatchik in the mould of Erich Honecker, the East German communist leader, carried the decision to its unnecessary and appalling conclusion simply to rub in the triumph of the hardliners. On 4 June occurred the massacre that so shocked the world.

At 10 p.m. on the previous evening, units of the 27th and 38th armies moved into central Beijing. Those that tried to block them were shot or crushed. In western Beijing fighting broke out near the Shoudu iron and steel works, in the Xi Dan shopping complex, and at several other locations. Some 500 were killed in these battles that took place away from the television cameras. Another army column approaching through the eastern part of the city met less resistance. The tanks surrounded Tiananmen Square, while thousands of infantry poured into it from the Forbidden City and from tunnels underneath it. Many protestors were killed, others surrendered and those herded into the narrow side streets were killed, beaten or arrested. The images of the massacre, carried by live television across the globe, shocked the world: the lone protester in front of the tank was particularly evocative. China's image never fully recovered, even after a decade.

The Chinese Red Cross estimated that around 2,600 people died. The true figure will never be known: the bodies in Tiananmen Square were buried on the spot or disposed of outside the city. The key point was that the diminishing rump in the square presented no threat to public order, and so the massacre was unnecessary. One Party faction carried it out to enforce its supremacy over another and to ensure that the reformists were thoroughly routed; as in the Cultural Revolution, the victims had been bystanders in a power struggle. So Deng, who seemed to have restored China to sanity after the madness of Mao, was finally to be condemned by history as a despot.

The massacre also demonstrated that brute military force was essential to prop up the hollow edifice of a system in a state of decay as great as that of the Soviet Union under Gorbachev. While the structure of communist power remained as lethal and formidable as ever, the buttress of support behind it had crumbled into ruins. After the Cultural

Revolution, ordinary people became increasingly disillusioned. While the fat cats and bureaucracy continued to hoard their economic empires and privileged status, an alternative economy was growing, from which massive profits and large fortunes were being amassed. Gambling, prostitution, consumerism and commercialism were intruding as obscenely and unequally upon the rim of the huge impoverished interior of the world's most populous nation as under the Kuomintang; indeed the communist leadership was profiting by them.

Chinese Communism, always something of a cynical masquerade to the men at the top, was a reality by virtue of the fact that hundreds of millions had, at least for a time, believed in it. But Tiananmen demonstrated that the Party had abandoned all pretence of representing the peasants and workers, or standing for equality and social justice. Now it stood nakedly exposed as a sanguinary defender of privilege, inequality and kickbacks which it defended against young idealists by using the men with guns to mow them down; once it had unleashed tens of thousands of them onto the streets in the name of revolution.

In the cities, to the eyes of visiting Westerners, the economic transformation has been astonishing. The sheer extent of the construction in the region around Hong Kong, or the glittering structures of modern Shanghai, suggest a country that has undergone an industrial revolution. The reality is a little different: the state has divested itself of many offshoots and many of the small government enterprises are now run on 'production contracts' – essentially independent entities able to buy, sell and make profits according to supply and demand.

But the state retains ownership of larger industries, and keeps charge of even the most independent enterprises through the strict control of credit. Many potential foreign investors have been discouraged by the close surveillance practices to which they are subjected and widespread corruption and red tape. The most successful outsiders have proved to be the extensive expatriate Chinese population and the Japanese, skilled at wending their way through the system's complexities.

While Chinese economic liberalization may by now render the return of the command economy inconceivable, the economic strategy still comprises such a profusion of deals between free marketers and communist centralizers that the goal of raising China's economic development to match its Asian neighbours seems desperately far away. China's average living standards remain anything up to fifteen times below those of neighbouring Taiwan or Hong Kong, now a special province of the mainland. Westerners who enthuse about the past two decades of modernization neglect this.

The problem, of course, remains political: the colossal vested interests among the holders of power, and the corruption and cliquery that spring from this represent major barriers against genuine reform, as do the millions of Party hacks who comprise a huge parasitic army of political commissars shadowing every aspect of economic and daily life, since they know they would become superfluous if it lost its leading role. Add to this the byzantine complexities of the Party's organization and internal feuding, pithily summed up by Li Xiaojun:

> The Party structure exemplifies the Chinese saying: 'What I create itself defeats me', for some parts of the Party are so independent of other parts, and the parts stand in such opposition and tension to one another, that it is virtually impossible for the whole to be controlled properly by whatever faction is in ascendancy at the topmost levels. This – usually to the deep alarm, occasionally to the amusement, of those with inside knowledge of Party affairs – has often resulted in absurdity, contradiction and turmoil, most of it hidden not just from the outside world but from the Chinese people themselves.

A further colossal obstacle is the army, intimately bound up with the Party since the civil war, possessing vast economic power through military-related industries and exerting a direct influence on politics that had no parallel in Soviet Russia. Worse, unlike Russia, the armed forces remain key power brokers at a time when the Party has lost much of its authority. Military men occupy top political posts and during one phase of the Cultural Revolution virtually ran the country. The army, divided into quasi-autonomous military regions, remains deeply conservative: economic reform is only tolerated in that it offers the promise of greater prosperity, national wealth and military spending. In politics it ardently opposes reform. On national issues – for example whether to attack Taiwan or to repress Tibet – it has a huge, perhaps a dominant, say. As regards foreign policy, the need to keep easily ruffled military feathers on side is a major inhibition, highly evident in the seizure of the American spy plane in 2001 when Chinese President Jiang Zemin took several weeks to persuade his generals of the only practical course of action – to hand the American crew back.

China lags behind Russia in several key respects. Compared with Russia China remains an extraordinarily closed society. The press is still rigidly censored, satellite television tightly controlled and access to the Internet restricted, not always successfully. In the long run this Canute-like attempt to stem the rising tide of outside information in order to preserve its authority and protect social conformity cannot succeed.

Its economic leap forward is, like Russia's, of comparatively recent vintage. But this author is deeply sceptical of the claims that China will emerge as an economic superpower second only to the United States in the near future: the Chinese model has produced sharp economic growth in certain coastal provinces, but the statistics for the country's economic boom are grossly exaggerated according to recent studies. The key state industries remain hugely parasitical, and the strains of inequality between town and country, public and private sector, the few and the many, may prove too much for society to withstand. Its political institutions remain those of a tightly-knit communist autocracy that has recently been deprived of any ideological pretension that it is about the promotion of equality. Instead, inequality is the order of the day. Increasingly, therefore, the leadership has itself resorted to banging a nationalist drum to preserve its authority.

Worse still, among young Chinese nationalism is perhaps the most potent current ideology. This has nothing to do with the rediscovery of ancient Chinese civilization but rather with the nouveau riche self-assertiveness of a people who seek global political status to match their new-found global economic importance; with communist ideology laid bare as a sham, and with little sign of the rulers permitting democracy to make headway, nationalism is almost the only ideology thrusting young Chinese can still rally around. 'Patriotic education' was launched by the government in 1946: it teaches that America used biological weapons against China in the Korean war, that it has 'inflicted' national humiliations – *guo chi* – on China, and that the Japanese are 'devils'. Such nationalism is often anti-American, because big brother so often seems to be looming over China's shoulder – its bombing of the Chinese embassy in Belgrade, its spy planes patrolling just off the Chinese coast, its arming and encouragement of Taiwan and support for Japan.

But it is by no means exclusively so. China's nationalism closer to home can be even more bullying: the oppression of Tibet and the Uyghurs of Xinjiang, 2,500 of whom have recently been arrested as 'Islamic terrorists' accused of killing forty people in a decade, hardly a serious threat; the consistently uneasy relations with India, Vietnam and Japan; the attempts to intimidate the Philippines over the Spratly

Islands, the claims to the South China Sea and the steadily escalating war of words with Taiwan. The Taiwanese standoff could easily lead to war, and a pretty nasty one at that: just because this has not happened yet after so many decades of sabre-rattling does not mean that it won't – in particular because a now-democratic Taiwan is viewed as an ever-increasing political threat to the mainland. Nationalism is only one of the major problems that China faces today. Population control is another, with the one-child family policy showing significant, if limited, success.

Jiang Zemin's designated successor, Vice-President Hu Jintao, who succeeded to the leadership in 2002, is a protégé of Deng Xiaoping. Jiang, however, has sought to stay on by retaining some of the levers of power. The outgoing Prime Minister and former economic tsar, Zhu Ronji, has recently outspokenly criticized his own party which some interpret as an attempt to dispute the succession. Hu and other 'fourth generation' leaders like the reformist Vice-Premier, Wen Jiabao (who has succeeded Zhu), are aware of the widespread feelings against the dominant Shanghai faction, and the danger of resentment in China's western provinces that lag far behind the coastal belt. Massive layoffs by state enterprises that are already causing widespread discontent, peasant unrest, an inability to resolve the economic contradictions, the fear by those within the system that they and it may be doomed (possibly leading to a new Gorbachev-style generation taking control), all these threaten the current regime.

The country's Maoist rump is seeking to exploit this discontent by attacking pro-Western Politburo members, private businessmen and multinational corporations. With China's entry into the World Trade Organization, the dislocation to the economy and the disparities between the coast and the interior are likely to increase. Yet, without greater economic liberalism China will fall still further behind its neigh-bours. While a fresh Maoist backlash seems unlikely to gather much support, the simmering tensions beneath a Communist Party that has entirely lost its legitimacy remain very serious.

On that terrible night of 4 June 1989 in Tiananmen Square, Chinese Communism died; all that remained was a hollow shell of Chinese armour, its reflexes still energetically thrashing about with a bloody sword. The alliance of Party bosses and military figures that succeeded Deng under Jiang Zemin, a mediocre political fixer, and his successor, Hu Jintao, could last a few more years yet. But fall it will, as assuredly as the regimes in the Soviet Union and Eastern Europe before it.

8

Enforced Revolution

'In brief, it means that at present, while retaining the essential centralism, we should place the emphasis on developing more and above all democratic foundations, and this not only in the upper Party echelons.'

Alexander Dubcek

The Great Oppressions: Hungary and Czechoslovakia

Hungary was the only Eastern European country where Communism was even halfway accepted by the governed, primarily because Janos Kadar, the shrewd Hungarian Party boss, had a genuine streak of nationalism: in January 1980, for example, he declared, 'We belong together whether we like each other or not; we are the sons of the same people. We have one country. We live together. We stand or survive together . . . Communists are not worse Hungarian patriots than the non-Party people. We too were born Hungarian. We live here and we shall die here.' That kind of patriotic emotionalism contrasted sharply with the drab socialist platitudes uttered in much of the rest of Eastern Europe.

So did Kadar's economic policy, brought in quietly after the 1956 uprising that brought him to power. The most obvious expression of this was in agriculture. Kadar introduced cooperatives in 1958–9; very different from collectives, they were run by the most prosperous peasants in the villages, and within them private plots were encouraged. Roughly a third of all agricultural produce came from small – and efficient – private producers and soon a quarter of total Hungarian exports came from agriculture, whose overall production had jumped fourfold. The government sensibly provided the credits and machinery needed by farmers: with around 1.8 million private plots Hungary's markets were brimming with products.

In addition, the Hungarians even allowed a small artisan and private shopkeeper class, numbering around 200,000 people, to remain in existence. The Hungarians, unlike the Russians, turned a blind eye to the black economy: the Communist Party daily *Nepszabadsag* admitted that around three-quarters of Hungarian producers earned some income from it, and private developers built around 35,000 to 40,000 private houses – over two-fifths of all residential accommodation. The Hungarians also defused tension by allowing genuine trade unions to become part of the fabric of society: the unions frequently used their veto under a labour code of 1967, although in the late 1970s there were attempts to reduce this power.

The final element in the Hungarian equation was flexibility as regards the socialized part of the economy – the large industrial enterprises. At the heart of this was the insistence that producer prices should accurately reflect the cost of inputs: fixed prices of inputs and products were abolished. Industry still remained, by and large, much too cumbersome: some two-thirds of all companies had more than 2,000 workers and were unwieldy and bureaucratic. The authorities tried a more flexible approach, setting up industrial cooperatives that allowed, in effect, profit sharing among the local workforce. Yet this concept, dubbed 'socialist enterprises', never got off the ground. The Hungarians also permitted foreign investment and partnership with foreign companies. The adventurousness of Hungary's system meant that the country's national income rose by 3.5 per cent annually between 1950 and 1980. This achievement stilled discontent, and the security apparatus became a little more relaxed than elsewhere in Eastern Europe.

When the general economic crises of the late 1970s and an increase in the price of Russian oil hit Hungary, it borrowed $8 billion from the West – no small sum for a country with only 10 million people. Growth fell back; incomes in 1979 were up by just 3 per cent, while prices were rising by 15 per cent. Food prices were ratcheted up sharply by some 50 per cent, both to rake in extra income from exports and cut back on unrealistic government subsidies. Yet it was a measure of the Hungarian acceptance of a system that provided a better standard of living than elsewhere in Eastern Europe that these steep price rises caused no disorders. After 1956, Hungarians had learnt the facts of life: they had to accept the Communist Party, and behind it Russia dominance. It seemed that

Kadar was giving them as much freedom as was possible within these limits.

In January 1968 Alexander Dubcek replaced Antonin Novotny, a dour, hard-faced, pragmatic conservative, as First Secretary of the Czech Communist Party. Under Novotny the country had stagnated although it had a passable industrial base and a reasonably efficient agricultural sector in which the proliferation of private farming plots allowed a comfortable surplus to be generated. Czechoslovakia's natural agricultural wealth made it a country that was easy enough to administer economically to provide a minimum standard of living. But its national identity, unlike Poland's and Hungary's, was not too strong. Czechoslovakia's brief period as an independent quasi-democracy had been ended by Hitler's occupation of the Sudetenland, and then Germany and Poland's dismemberment of the rest. Russian occupation was disliked, but most Czechs tolerated it.

Dubcek's arrival in the seat of power changed all that. He was that rare breed, a genuine communist idealist who believed in socialism but believed equally passionately that it must be supported by a majority of Czechs. Three things followed: firstly, the hard police state enforced by Novotny was unnecessary; second, the Party should become democratic and even submit itself to genuine elections; and third, Czechs could be independent of Russia because Soviet fears that a non-aligned Czechoslovakia would reject Communism were groundless.

Nineteen sixty-eight was the year of student protests in France, Italy and West Germany, and Dubcek's most able supporters, apart from the reforming group within the Party hierarchy, were student leaders. In March the students attempted to reach out to Czechoslovakia's workers, the main bulwark of Novotny's orthodox regime. Philosophy students from Charles University in Prague made an outright appeal to the unions, insisting that Dubcek's was the only way to save socialism and denying that he favoured the restoration of capitalism.

The reformers did not, however, stop at politics. Dubcek approached a radical economist, Ota Sik, to draft proposals for enterprise councils elected in each plant to supervise their management, making the workers, in effect, the company directors. The aim was to win wider support for the greater degree of competition Dubcek wanted to introduce. Under Sik's proposal, remuneration would be tied to results. Inefficient plants would be allowed to close down, although former employees could be granted jobs in state enterprises. In June 1968, the old trade union organization, ROH, was broken up, its twelve main branches becoming thirty-two, to reduce its power and make it directly representative of the workers. The intention was also to temper the unions' expected resistance to the increased importance of market forces. Despite the self-control plan, most workers were initially suspicious of the Dubcek experiment, largely imposed by a middle-class elite.

Reforms flowed in torrents from the Dubcek regime. His keynote speech was delivered on 22 February, on the twentieth anniversary of communist rule in Czechoslovakia; standing next to Leonid Brezhnev, he declared:

> In the early 1950s our people lived through one of the greatest changes in all their history. Never before had it been possible to effect within such a short historical period such deep changes in the socio-economic, political and ideological life of the country. Unfortunately, the size of the errors and shortcomings which the then leadership of the Party regrettably failed to avoid corresponded to the scale of these truly gigantic processes. There were many setbacks in inner Party life, the consequences of some of which are still felt by us.
>
> In the atmosphere of false suspicion these problems and very serious socio-political problems were compounded by such negative phenomena as violations of socialist legality from which not only communists suffered ... We must remove, along both state and Party lines, all the injustices being done to people, and we must do so consistently and without reservation.

This was blasphemy enough. But the solution proposed by Dubcek must have seemed anathema to Brezhnev beside him:

> For the Party to carry through its leading role in the present situation means first and foremost to create the necessary preconditions for the growth of greater initiative, to provide greater scope for the constructive national change of opinion, to make it possible for every communist to be informed thoroughly, objectively and in good time about events in his own country and abroad, so that he should find a point of view with regard to the Party's policy and, particularly, so that he should participate not only in effecting, but also in forming, the Party's policy and its actions, especially in the sphere in which he is employed.
>
> In brief, it means that at present, while retaining the essential centralism, we should place the emphasis on developing more and above all deep democratic foundations, and this not only in the upper Party echelons,

but especially lower down, in the organization and among the membership.

This amounted to three revisionist theses in one: the Party should allow more internal debate; the Party should become more democratic; and the government's actions should involve greater consultation.

Novotny, still President of the country and controlling a large part of the Party apparatus, the secret police, the army and many of the unions, used these statements to try and depose Dubcek. Dubcek retaliated by making known that a senior general was under investigation for the alleged theft of $20,000 worth of government stock. The general promptly defected abroad. Over the next few days appalling stories of blackmail, corruption and theft emerged, involving the son of the President, a Party first secretary and other generals. The Central Committee secretary responsible for ideological affairs was replaced. By 15 March Novotny, forced to dismiss the interior minister and the prosecutor-general, faced numerous resolutions from provincial parties demanding his own dismissal.

The attack on the President opened the floodgates. Small groups left the official Czechoslovak youth federation to form independent bodies; newspapers began to break away from the Stalinist-controlled publishing groups; unions started to defect from the official structure and the railroad engineers set up their own union. In early March there were press tributes to Jan Masaryk, the last defender of Czech democracy. Hundreds of people turned up by the graveside to honour him.

Dubcek professed to be shocked by the liberalism of the 'March days'. Journalistic activities, he claimed, 'have sometimes attained an impulsive character'. His chief aide, Josef Smyrkovsky, was simultaneously preaching the opposite: 'At the present time we are bothered by much worse things which are a thousand times more serious than that some journalist says a few words which are more than he ought to have said.' On 22 March Novotny was forced to resign the presidency, and Dubcek was promptly summoned to a hastily-called Warsaw Pact summit at Dresden where he was told in no uncertain terms that his candidate for the presidency, Smyrkovsky, was unacceptable. The Czechs compromised by accepting Ludwig Svoboda, a veteran Czech military hero who had fought alongside the Russians during the Second World War.

Nevertheless, the liberalization continued. Various senior officials, fearing prosecution for their excesses during the 1950s, committed suicide, including a well-known torturer, Josef Sommer. The liberals pressed for the holding of the Czech Communist Party's Fourteenth Congress well before time, to reform the Party. At public meetings an end to the Party's monopoly was demanded. By April, Dubcek had published the Action Programme of the Party, subtitled, 'The Czech Road to Socialism'. This attacked the 'suppression of democratic rights and persecution of the people, violation of the laws, licentiousness and misuse of the power of the Party in the past'.

It attacked also the 'direction of the economy from the centre', which had caused 'slow increases in wages . . . stagnation of living standards . . . the present state of the transport system, poor quality goods and the public services'. Socialism must be built by giving scope for the various interests of the people to assert themselves. The programme even attacked egalitarianism because 'it promotes careless workers, idlers and irresponsible people to advantage as compared with dedicated and diligent workers, the unqualified compared to the qualified'.

The Communist Party, it insisted, was not a 'monopolist concentration of power . . . it employs the voluntary support of the people'. There should be periodic opinion polls and a free press. The secret police apparatus should be used only against foreign interests and 'not be directed and used to solve internal political arguments and controversies in socialist society'. *Pravda* lambasted the programme, suggesting that anyone who doubted the Communist Party's rightful monopoly of state power was an enemy of 'socialist realism', a nationalist and a revisionist.

In May there were extensive Russian troop movements on the border, possibly in response to a public meeting on 3 May, in which a number of speakers had denounced Communism itself. Dubcek visited Moscow the following day, and endured a further tongue-lashing about his anti-socialist excesses. However, as the danger of an anti-communist political party being formed increased towards the end of May, the interior minister insisted that 'opposition political activity' was still banned.

In mid-May Ota Sik outlined the government's economic reforms. Western capital would be welcomed. Industries would be decentralized. Enterprise managers would be forced to compete for commodities and markets by adjusting their prices. In addition, private enterprise would be allowed to flourish and consumer, not heavy, industries would be encouraged. In agriculture Ota Sik pointed out that 'the countryside had been deprived of its young'. Sik's criticism was withering: some two-thirds of agricultural workers were more than 47 years old. A Czech worker had to work around 117 hours to earn enough to buy a transistor radio, he claimed, while a West German worker needed only 12 hours. Some two-thirds of the nation's machinery, he insisted, was obsolete.

By July, Brezhnev was fed up. He publicly denounced 'apologists for the bourgeois order' who are prepared to 'pose in pseudo-Socialist clothes in order to weaken the solidarity among socialist countries'. The Russians again mobilized their troops along Czechoslovakia's borders. This time the Russian move backfired. The Czechs responded with firmness, refusing to budge from their reforms. The Russians wavered momentarily. The troops stayed put, and *Pravda* drew a parallel between Czechoslovakia in 1968 and Hungary before 1956. The Czechs then demanded the Warsaw Pact be reorganized, so that all members were regarded as equals. Dubcek received a flood of letters supporting this proposal. At a Warsaw Pact meeting in mid-July, the Czechs were bluntly informed about the power realities in Eastern Europe. The final communiqué insisted that pact members be vigilant against imperialism which, 'using means peaceful and unpeaceful gains a grip from the inside or from the outside on the socialist system and alters the correlation of forces in Europe in imperialism's favour'. It further demanded that the 'healthy forces' in the Czech Communist Party, 'namely the socialist ones, be activated to mobilize the country for the struggle against the forces of counter-revolution'.

Dubcek cocked a snook: 'We think the cause of socialism is not advanced by the holding of conferences at which the policy and activity of one of the fraternal parties is judged without the presence of their representatives.' The Russians were livid, but still hesitated. They demanded that the entire Politburo of the Czech Communist Party attend a meeting with the Soviet Politburo. The Czechs replied that any such meeting must take place in Czechoslovakia. The Russians fumingly agreed: the meeting took place at Cierna Nad Tisou, a village near the Soviet and Hungarian borders. Every morning, the Russians arrived in fifteen sleeping cars pulled across from the Ukrainian town of Chop; every evening they returned to the Ukraine.

The venue for these bitter and heated talks was a railwaymen's club. The Russians failed to drive a wedge between Dubcek and the hardliners on his party's Politburo: the Czechs had decided to present a united front. On 2 August Dubcek returned to tell his countrymen: 'We kept the promises which we had given you, and we returned with the same convictions with which we had departed for the talks.' He ended this ringing declaration with one of the statements that history places in the mouths of politicians that ring hollow for years afterwards, comparable to Chamberlain's 'Peace in our Time' declaration. 'I was asked on my return to the airport if our sovereignty was threatened. Let me say frankly that it is not.'

The pressure on Czechoslovakia suddenly eased. The hardline ruler of East Germany, Walter Ulbricht, visited the country and uttered no threats. The Soviet Politburo went on holiday. Détente with the West proceeded apace. Only vitriolic attacks by *Pravda* against the Czechs sounded a discordant note: 'The enemies of the working class in Czechoslovakia continue openly and insolently to attack socialist concepts. Unfortunately, these attacks did not receive their proper rebuff,' the newspaper insisted. On 20 August it declared that communist parties should 'ensure that imperialist conspiracies are nipped in the bud'.

The same afternoon, Russian leaders were flown in from holiday to a formal meeting of the Central Committee to endorse the invasion of Czechoslovakia. At 11 p.m. Russian, East German, Polish and Hungarian troops poured in through some twenty border crossings, and the dumbstruck border guards let them through, while dozens of Antonov-12 fast-reaction troop transports airlifted light tanks and thousands of soldiers into the country.

The people of Czechoslovakia awoke the following day to find tanks on the streets. Instead of futilely attacking overwhelmingly superior forces, they took the only course open to them: they accepted the plea of Radio Prague to 'keep calm. Let your weapon be passive resistance. Don't be provoked into bloodshed.' Thousands gathered in the streets to block the passage of Russian armour.

The Russian soldiers, who believed they were liberators, were confused and ordered the tanks to halt. Barriers of overturned buses and cars blocked their path. The crowds tried to reason with the crews, then started jeering at them. The tanks began rolling slowly forward, shooting first over the heads of the demonstrators, then at them. In Wenceslas Square in Prague, and in Bratislava, the process was repeated. But resistance went on, direction signs were pulled down and Czechs fled the country in their thousands.

Thankfully, the human cost of the invasion was relatively small – around 70 people killed and some 1,000 wounded. The Russian ambassador at the United Nations blithely told the world: 'The armed units of the Soviet countries, as is known, entered the territory of the Czechoslovak Socialist Republic on the basis of a request from the government of this state, which applied to the allied powers for assistance with armed forces.'

But the Czech government had done nothing of the kind. Dubcek was attending a tense and angry meeting of the Czechoslovak Presidium at the time of the invasion. 'It is a tragedy,' he exclaimed, breaking down. '. . . I had no suspicion, not even the slightest hint that such a step could be taken against us.' Few doubted his sincerity, and even the pro-Russians in the leadership rallied to his call for national independence. Dubcek stayed in his post, and was only seized hours later by armed guards who none too gently tore a telephone from his hands. Smyrkovsky was also arrested. Both thought they would be killed.

But President Svoboda, whom the Russians needed to provide a legal cover for the invasion, refused to dismiss his Party Secretary, telling the Czech Stalinists who urged this on him to get out of his office. As the Czech Communist Party met secretly to proclaim its opposition to the invasion, as hidden radio stations and printing presses multiplied across the country, Svoboda was flown to Moscow. There the old soldier threatened to commit suicide if the Russians pushed him too far. The Russians offered Czechoslovakia massive economic aid, a bribe also rejected. At long last the Russians were compelled to bring Dubcek and his arrested colleagues into the talks.

After four days of browbeating, during which the Czech contingent's only knowledge of events in the outside world was what the Russians told them, agreement was reached. The Czechs salvaged what they could, but had to accept that the Action Programme was dead and that their government's efforts would focus on 'guaranteeing efficient measures to strengthen socialist power, the directing role of the working class and the Communist Party, the interests of developing and strengthening fully relations with the people of the Soviet Union and the eastern socialist commonwealth'.

This was outright surrender. When Dubcek returned on 27 August, broken in spirit, he presided over the final crushing of freedom. In September he was allowed to keep his post of First Secretary, but an executive committee was set up to run day-to-day affairs. Shortly afterwards, Dubcek lost his other posts, was humiliated and eventually became a gardener, while Gustav Husak, the tough collaborationist Slovak Party boss, became First Secretary. He purged the Party thoroughly, although he did not persecute his opponents, and the police state, although harsh, did not revert to Stalinist repression. Rather, it relied on the acquiescence of the Czech people in the face of overwhelming military power.

The 'Prague Spring' was an Eastern European milestone. At the time of the 1956 Hungarian uprising, the Russians could still just argue that socialism had had insufficient time to grow proper roots in Eastern Europe, and that the revolt pitted crude nationalism against enlightened, liberating Communism. By 1968, after nearly two decades of socialist rule, Czechoslovakia's rejection of the Russians could not be ascribed to ignorance of the system. The Czechs had demonstrated that they hated foreign domination and favoured democracy.

The surge in Dubcek's popularity has been widely interpreted as signifying real support in Czechoslovakia for 'socialism with a human face'. It certainly reflected the relief felt by Czechs as the repression was eased; but the strident anti-communist criticism that broke out suggested that many Czechs had no loyalty at all to the Communist Party. The flowering, in a supposedly socialist society, of support for alternative power centres blew a raspberry at the Marxist-Leninist ideal that as a society developed, it would lose its political divisions because class divisions would disappear. Czechoslovakia demonstrated that political divisions would reappear immediately the straitjacket was unfastened. Fear, not the communist system, had restrained them.

Now Russia, not socialism, ruled by armed force. As in Hungary in 1956, the Russians had gone into Czechoslovakia, for one reason: insubordination from within the local Communist Party. Should the Czech example of internal Party reform be repeated throughout Eastern Europe, political liberalization might have ultimately led to the deposition of the Party itself. Whereas in Poland three years later the reform process would start from outside the Party, so that the Russians thought they could rely on local forces to resist strikes and student movements, the Czechoslovakian episode could have led to the unravelling of Communism in Russia itself. Now, with authority re-established and democratic centralism reasserted, the world was shown, once again, that Marxism-Leninism ruled the peoples of Eastern Europe by force of arms, not legitimacy.

'It All Started in Gdansk . . .': Poland

On 14 August 1980, a little bespectacled lady, Anna Walentynowicz, a militant member of the small Free Trade Union, was sacked by the managers of the Lenin shipyard at Gdansk in Poland. The union, which had tried unsuccessfully to initiate a strike a month before, rushed off 6,000 newsletters demanding a strike for her reinstatement and a wage increase to match the appalling rise in the cost of living.

Workers took part in a mass meeting by one of the factory gates. The local manager climbed on a bulldozer to urge the men back to work. Another man, well built, with a strong face, humorous eyes and a bushy moustache that was to become famous the world over, joined him. Long a well-known union activist, Lech Walesa was nevertheless respected for his moderation, and for the grim courage with which he had fought the government for years, culminating in his sacking from the shipyard four years before. After an angry speech, Walesa persuaded the workers to lay down their tools. A strike committee was set up to talk with management, who now faced an extensive series of demands including the pay rise that had previously appeared in the Newsletter, early retirement and improved food supplies. The following day the strike spread to the Paris Commune shipyard and then all over Gdansk. The demands became more overtly political. Solidarity had been born.

Why did the dismissal of a single female employee prompt Walesa and his fellow strikers to brave imprisonment and the anger of one of the most tightly controlled political systems in Eastern Europe? The answer lay in Poland's economic crisis that had been brewing up since the mid 1970s. Among its causes were agricultural underproduction in the countryside, the government's concentration on ambitious industrial projects and its neglect of the farming sector. One result of this was an insufficiency of meat to satisfy mounting demand. The only answer was to raise its price – something the government was loath to do for fear of provoking urban workers. But in 1976, it suddenly decided that not only would the price of meat rise by 70 per cent, but that the price of sugar should double and that of butter and cheese be raised by one-third.

This threat to living standards led to an explosion of strikes, which forced the government to increase wages. But as industry grew increasingly less competitive through lack of investment and growing labour costs, Poland was trapped in a vicious spiral. Only higher wages could buy off such unrest, which in turn contributed to industry's growing inefficiency, which meant productivity lagged behind money supply and caused further inflation that further fed union demands. The country's trade balance also plunged into the red, but that was soon overcome by borrowing abroad. By December 1979, foreign debt totalled some $18 billion; as it mounted, so did the interest bill, causing a diversion of Poland's resources into servicing the debt, which further squeezed living standards.

But the Polish Communist Party's problem was that it had no mandate to enforce austerity; indeed, since the war, all its attempts to acquire a genuine popular legitimacy had failed, except, as we shall see, in 1956 under Gomulka, when it served as an expression of Poland's national interest. In one of Europe's most fiercely Catholic countries the Church, along with what remained of the middle class, was hostile to the Party, and it was widely regarded as merely a tool of the Soviet Union and not representative of the Polish people at all. Only through economic growth could the Party hope to stave off the growing anger. When growth petered out, a thunderclap became inevitable.

The Polish Communist Party had born the Russian stamp ever since 1941, when Soviet aircraft parachuted a group of communists into German-occupied Poland to form the Polish Workers Party. The London-based government-in-exile had a national army of around 200,000; the Workers' Party numbered no more than 50,000. But the Russians 'liberated' Poland in 1944 and set up a Committee of National Liberation; they refrained from liberating Warsaw where the nationalist forces staged an uprising. The 'Warsaw Ghetto' massacre followed, in large part the fault of the Russians who then assisted the new government to suppress anti-communist resistance in the countryside.

Wladyslaw Gomulka, the Party Secretary, was no cardboard Stalin, however: originally a factory worker, he was strongly patriotic. But he lacked support in a rurally based country with a large middle class and a substantial landed gentry. At first, in 1946, Gomulka tried to appeal to the middle class; social change in Poland, he promised, would be 'evolutionary'. State power would be based on 'parliamentary democracy . . . The dictatorship of the working class or of a single party is not essential . . . Poland can proceed and is proceeding along her own road.'

Gomulka's moderation was exposed as a sham when the middle classes started fighting back: Stanislaw Mikolajczyk's Peasant Party, almost certainly more widely supported than the 'godless' communists, was violently harassed: its rallies were broken up and its leaders jailed. In January 1947, in a rigged election, it won just 10 per cent of the vote and Mikolajczyk left Poland. The Polish Socialist Party, which had originally collaborated with the communists, was purged and then absorbed into the Workers' Party. All industries with more than fifty workers were taken over: by 1946 the state controlled over 90 per cent of industrial production. As in Russia, state-directed post-war reconstruction went remarkably well. Impoverished peasants were transferred to work at low – but by their old standards, high – wages in the new industries.

Gomulka, although a hard-line dictator content to deny his own people democracy to preserve his own authority, soon sought a degree of independence. Some $40m was borrowed from the United States in 1946. In 1947, Stalin decided to take Gomulka in hand. At a Cominform meeting in Warsaw, Gomulka was ordered to nationalize private farms. Yet he knew that private farming was at the heart of any fragile consensus that still existed in the country, and refused. This was heresy – nine months before even Tito had dared to try it. In 1948 Gomulka was booted out by the revolutionary minority in his party led by Boleslaw Bierut, a hard-line Stalinist supported by the Soviet armed forces stationed round the country.

The clampdown began. The Polish army was expanded to 400,000 men, Eastern Europe's largest armed force. Officials who supported Gomulka were purged. Russian military advisers swelled the ranks of the Polish officer corps. Marshal Konstantin Rokossowski was made Minister of Defence. A Russian of Polish origin, he had been one of Stalin's wartime commanders: Poland's armed forces had become merely an appendage of the Russian armed forces. Four-fifths of trade union leaders were purged. Life for the Polish worker, recently emancipated from peasant life, was hard.

Neal Ascherson, much the most perceptive recent analyst of Poland, writes of this period in *The Polish August*: 'The workers, in title the rulers of Poland's new society, were now its most helpless and exploited section. Deprived of the normal means of self-defence, they were regularly herded to triumphal demonstrations. Their submissiveness was ensured by a system of confidential files kept by the state on their behaviour and attitudes; most personnel officers were in the service of the security police. As in other Eastern European economies subjected to Stalinism, standards of work and honesty collapsed. In spite of the close surveillance and penalties, there was widespread absenteeism, theft of materials for the black market and falsification of production statistics.' The rulers justified all of this – if they admitted it at all – as the price necessary for advancing Poland towards genuine socialism.

Even the new Stalinists, turning Poland into an industrial society, held back from full-scale collectivization. They knew that the peasants would fight for their land. By 1955, only around 9 per cent of Poland's arable land was collectivized. Although peasants were forced to supply the urban market, the rural scene remained astonishingly static. The Security Office (UB) was severe enough, ordering the arrest of Gomulka in 1951 and the detention in a monastery of Cardinal Stefan Wyszynski, the Primate of Poland. The Party meanwhile adopted the standard model; its national directorate became grossly over-centralized, while on the fringes local Party organizations found ways round central directives.

This phase lasted until Khrushchev's attack on Stalin in 1956. Bierut coincidentally died just two weeks after the speech and Khrushchev hurried to Warsaw to tell the Poles who should succeed him. However, the country was abuzz with activity. In Poznan, after a day of workers' strikes and violence, at least 80 people were killed. The strikes revealed to the Polish communist leadership what should long have been obvious: that only terror had kept the peace in Poland over the previous six years. Given any relaxation, Poles took to the streets.

Within days, Gomulka was being urged to return to the leadership. Khrushchev was determined to prevent this: Soviet troops moved to the Polish border, but astonishingly the Polish Party mobilized the army to stand by and resist an invasion. Gomulka was conciliatory; he was not prepared to follow Russian diktats in internal affairs, but he would keep Poland in the Warsaw Pact and support a continued Russian connection. The spectacle of Khrushchev trying to bully Gomulka, and failing, strengthened the Polish strongman's authority as a national leader standing up to the Russians. His further changes won him widespread support. He announced the reform of the secret police and offered the workers self-management. He made plain his sympathy with the plight of Hungarians being suppressed by the Russians, but ordered Poland to do no more than send them food and medical supplies.

Cardinal Wyszynski, the wily Polish Primate, came to his assistance. 'Poles know how to die magnificently,' he told them. 'A man dies but once and is quickly covered with glory. But he gives long years in trouble, hardship, pain and suffering. That is a greater heroism.'

Gomulka became an embodiment of the national spirit. When he left for Moscow in November 1956, to negotiate the new basis of Polish-Soviet relations, large crowds turned out to pray for his success.

His achievement was considerable: Poland, alone among Russia's satellites, was allowed to administer itself without interference. Polish trade became less dependent on Russia. The police state was eased. The workers won the right to educate people in Catholic schools. The press won freedom – for a while. Peasant communes, sharing out the land, replaced the collectives. Workers Councils, properly elected for the first time in Polish history, sprang up throughout industry.

But the Warsaw spring reverted back to winter. In the elections in January 1957 there were more candidates than seats available: people would clearly use the freedom given them to oust Workers' Party candidates. Gomulka made a strong appeal to support the Party as the sole guarantor of Polish independence: in the end, fewer than 10 per cent of those elected were non-Party candidates. From then on the regime hardened perceptibly.

Gomulka personally was an authoritarian. Although he pushed reforms that permitted decentralization, he understood sooner than the Russians that such measures, under state control, would only increase inefficiency. By December 1958, the Workers Councils had disrupted production sufficiently for the government to be able to pass the Workers Self-Government Act that, as so often, would do the precise reverse of what its name implied. The workers were bypassed.

Gomulka also sought to weaken Cardinal Wyszynski's position. Church institutions were closed and religious education gradually eased out of the schools. Wyszynski's overt opposition to the government's policy became even more pungent. 'A systematic social organism has been set up to fight against God,' he thundered. By 1968, Gomulka's regime, ever more firmly entrenched, had lost its popular support and was viewed as a repressive, if pragmatic and non-ideological government. Street fighting broke out after Gomulka clamped down on a newspaper that poked fun at the Russians, and the government reacted toughly over the following weeks. Gomulka also sent Polish forces to help with the occupation of Czechoslovakia.

One of the striking features of the 1968 crackdown was the government's success in mobilizing the workers against the students; the Party leader, for all his faults, had shrewdly ensured economic growth in the consumer goods sector, visibly raising most Poles' standard of living.

However, emboldened by this victory, Gomulka overloaded the Polish economy, which had been slowing down. Technocrats were brought in, economic incentives were increased, and spending was switched from social programmes to investment. The aim was to increase exports to fund food imports. Poland's agricultural production problems seemed almost permanently insoluble, but the government was prepared to anger Polish workers by attempting to tackle the issue head-on. The low level of food prices gave the peasants no incentive to produce anything above a minimum for themselves, and Gomulka shrewdly understood that to nationalize farming would mean an insurrection in the country-side. The only answer seemed to be price increases: December, 1970, saw flour prices up by 16%, sugar by 14% and meat by 17%. The public reaction was explosive: furious crowds roamed the streets and the police fired on them. Several dozen workers were killed; strikes paralyzed Gdansk and a dozen other cities. Gomulka suffered a stroke and was replaced by Edvard Gierek, a nondescript and conciliatory Party Secretary from Upper Silesia. In the Warski shipyard in Szczenin (Stettin) he urged the workers to call off the strike, hinting that if it continued it might provoke Soviet intervention. 'I say to you: help us, help me . . . I am only a worker like you . . . the fate of our nation and the cause of socialism are in the balance.' The message hit home.

Gierek and Gomulka's styles were exact opposites; Gierek, a quiet, humble man, sought practical solutions to problems that Gomulka's passionate oratory and frosty imperiousness had failed to solve. Gierek reversed the policy of switching investment from consumer to industrial goods; indeed he printed and borrowed money in a dash for growth. By 1972 national income had risen by 10 per cent; by 1973 Poland was the third fastest-growing country in the world; and by 1975 real wages had risen by 40 per cent. The effort could not last: inflation and borrowing soared dizzyingly. Furthermore, the government's efforts to increase private food production had not worked, so it began to backtrack. When the government felt it had to raise food prices in 1976, this provoked a furious outbreak of rioting by the workers, notably in Ursus and Radom, which the authorities dealt with very harshly. Poland was like a volcano, this explosion in 1976 foreshadowing the 1979 eruption.

After 1976, the government bought off the strikers by abruptly dropping the price increases. But the strikes had worried the government so much that they sought to ease fears by awarding substantial pay increases and by encouraging the private sector: private farmers were allowed to buy more land and tractors. The state meanwhile switched subsidies from heavy industry to agriculture, which now received a fifth of all state investment. Huge quantities of grain were imported – 8 million tons in 1977 and 7 million tons in 1978. Food bottlenecks were eased, with production rising some 15 per cent in 1977, but food subsidies continued at the rate of around 70 per cent. The switch away from industrial investment soon took its toll. National income had already fallen by around 2 per cent in 1975 and industrial production by 5 per cent. The inexorable rise in inflation and borrowing as workers' wages rose and productivity dropped, combined with no increase in agricultural production largely because the peasants sat on their surplus produce, made a crisis inevitable.

Meanwhile underground unions were set up – the main one being KOR – the Committee for the Defence of Workers Rights. The government, warned by the Russians and foreign creditors that the boom could not continue, jammed on the monetarist brakes. The mixture of a sudden fall in living standards, a recent workers' victory and a weak central authority was explosive enough, without the added impetus of one other event.

In October 1978, astonishingly, Cardinal Karol Wojtyla was elected as the first Polish Pope. The leadership sent a warm message of congratulation and invited him to visit Poland. He arrived in June 1979 to be greeted by around a quarter of Poland's population. He urged peaceful reform, and criticized 'colonialism' but attempted to still the tensions beneath the surface. Yet he could not undo the symbolism of his election: it had been a stirring declaration of Poland's moral independence. To hatred of the regime was now added the patriotism represented by the Pope.

The first stirrings of dissent were felt in Party meetings as members protested in 1979 against food shortages and corruption in private life. In February 1980, Gierek tried to staunch the rising tide of criticism by admitting failings and promising better things to come. He could not, however, alter the grim economic picture. By July he had to introduce a further round of meat rationing. This was the last straw; it fell not to the Church, whose role had been restricted by Cardinal Wyszynski to mediating between government and people, but to ordinary workers in factories to undertake the only protest the government could do little to counter: downing tools.

The Ursus tractor factory outside Warsaw was the first to grind to a halt. The aircraft factory at Mielec in south-eastern Poland followed. By 8 August a hundred and fifty firms had been affected by stoppages. By 15 August the Gdansk and Gdynia shipyards had ceased to work. The main force behind the organizing committee that called the workers out in Gdansk was the man who had endured no fewer than one hundred arrests in the course of years of public agitating about the crackdown on the workers in 1970: Lech Walesa.

Even Walesa appeared astonished by the support for his strike movement of August 1980, and did his best to calm the workers' anger. But the tinder caught. The MKS (Inter-Factory Strike Committees of Gdansk and Gdynia) took the name 'Solidarity' from their official newsletter and gradually other strike committees began to affiliate. Within days, the Polish Prime Minister, Edward Babiuch, had been dismissed as a scapegoat for the crisis. The government started negotiating with the strikers.

By the end of August an agreement had been negotiated; in Gdansk, Walesa recognized 'the leading role of the Party' and in return got an acceptance of legitimate unions that would collectively form 'an authentic representative of the working class'. The unions could have their own headquarters and issue their own publications. Censorship would be eased. Mass could be broadcast on Sundays. The agreement called for economic reform, in which the unions would have a say. Regarding the original strike demand – a significant pay increase and shorter working hours – the government promised only to find 'ways of compensating for the cost of living' and to examine 'principles and means of introducing free, paid Saturdays'.

Gierek vanished after the agreement and suddenly suffered a well-timed 'heart attack'. Stanislaw Kania, a shrewd man with a deceptively tough exterior, took over as Party Secretary, having defeated a hard-liner, Stefan Olszowski, and ordered the latter's supporters in the Party to be purged. Kania's approach was to meet the unions half way, but he would preside over a spreading strike movement that his party could not control.

The Gdansk agreement thoroughly alarmed the Russians, who demanded that the Party demonstrate that it still had the monopoly of power in the country; conceding authority to the unions might otherwise set a precedent throughout Eastern Europe. For Brezhnev the sticking point had come. When Solidarity registered as a trade union in

October, according to the Gdansk agreement, the judge insisted that the union formally recognize that 'the Party exercises the key role in the state'. Walesa was furious, and further strikes seemed imminent. Kania flew to Moscow, and secured Brezhnev's grudging acceptance of a reference to the Party's 'leading role' in an annexe to the Gdansk agreement.

After registration, Solidarity could boast a colossal membership of 8.5 million, of which some 750,000 were Party members – roughly a third of total Party membership. Following more strikes in November, the Russian armies in East Germany, Czechoslovakia and western Russia took up front-line positions around Poland's borders. Diplomatic messages cannonaded from the West, threatening the Russians with every sort of economic and cultural reprisal short of war if they invaded. At a Warsaw Pact meeting, the East German interior minister, virtually acting as a prosecuting counsel, accused the Polish leader of leading an 'anti-Soviet offensive'. Like judges with their minds made up, the Russians watched in silence.

Kania returned to warn Poles that 'the future of our nation lies in the balance. The persisting unrest is pushing our fatherland to the brink of moral and economic annihilation.' This momentarily chastened Walesa and other Solidarity leaders. However, in the countryside, an even more militant organization had come into being: Rural Solidarity, with 500,000 small proprietors as members, who insisted that peasant farming be protected. By January 1981 the government had grudgingly accepted their legal existence.

The grim arm-wrestling between Solidarity and the government continued into 1981, with two public outbreaks of strikes in February and March, the second of which brought further rumbles from Russia. A bitter power struggle took place between Walesa and the more militant members of Solidarity. In June, Russian growls grew to a roar as the Polish Workers' Party Congress met to consider internal 'democratization'. Infected by Solidarity's example, the delegates were elected by secret ballot, demanded changes in the agenda and voted seven-eighths of the members off the Central Committee. A new statute was drawn up, recognizing the secret ballot and limiting a Party official's tenure in the same position to ten years.

The impetus for total political change had become unstoppable. Solidarity members suggested that even the new democratic Workers' Party lacked the legitimacy of their own organization, which could claim to represent a fair chunk of Poland's people. Walesa fought vainly to restrict Solidarity's demands to the economic sphere and out of politics. In November talks took place between Walesa, the new Polish Primate, Archbishop Glemp, and the new Party Secretary, a dour military figure, General Wocjiej Jaruzelski. Kania, a spent force, had been booted out the previous month. Solidarity stubbornly refused to accept Jaruzelski's proposed reforms.

By the end of the month it became clear that the government, having abandoned any hopes of a compromise, wanted to provoke Solidarity into extreme action to justify a crackdown. On 2 December Solidarity called a general strike for 17 December. But on Sunday 13 December, Jaruzelski proclaimed martial law, suspended the unions, arrested the entire union leadership together with Gierek and other senior Party officials, and placed thousands of union leaders, journalists and intellectuals in detention camps. A military Council of National Salvation was set up, a state of war declared, civil freedoms suspended and military tribunals established with powers to even sentence offenders to death.

The declaration of martial law marked a turning point in post-revolutionary communist history. It marked not only the blatant use of armed force to suppress an uprising by the workers against a state supposedly acting in their interests, but also the eclipse of the Communist Party's authority. After thirty-five years, the Party had so signally failed to enforce its authority or even embody popular support that the army was compelled to do the job for it. Although much of the army had little sympathy for the Party's objectives, it had one overriding reason for taking over: on 11 December Marshal Kulikov, the Russian commander of Warsaw Pact forces, had given an ultimatum to Jaruzelski: if he did not act, the Pact's forces would.

Jaruzelski persuaded his senior commanders that only the installation of an authentically nationalist and Polish military regime would prevent a bloody invasion. The Russians had delivered their ultimatum because the Communist Party had gone too far. To win a measure of popular support, it had followed Dubcek's party in Czechoslovakia and attempted to become democratic. That was unacceptable. Jaruzelski's brief was to sweep away Solidarity, and to reconstruct the Party along Stalinist lines.

In the event, he refused to do the latter, and the Soviet Union was forced to follow along, as the cost of an invasion would have been enormous. The Jaruzelski coup marked the first termination of Communist Party control in an Eastern European country. However unattractive the new military regime, it showed that communist rule was not only reversible, but that it could be challenged by the forces of order themselves. As the appeal of the Marxist-Leninist idea dwindled, the system relied increasingly on naked, armed power; and the army, not the Party, had the monopoly of force.

In fact, force was probably the only solution to the Polish problem as the impetus for change had come from the workers. The Polish case was a freak, because the demand for national independence coincided with an economic crisis provoked by the inefficiency of the communist production system, both in industry and agriculture, which left workers' demands for decent living standards unsatisfied. If the workers had reached a social pact with the Party and army, they could have exchanged pay restraint for political and economic reforms. This was attempted first by Kania, Walesa and the Church. But for the Russians, such political reforms were unacceptable and Walesa could not persuade his unions to accept this idea: they wanted the impossible – political reform together with higher wages, reduced working hours and workers' control, which would have made industry ever more inefficient. In reality, the economic system required comprehensive reform, with the introduction of genuine incentives to produce and compete.

This left only one alternative – the imposition of sacrifice at gunpoint. If Poland's army did not take action, the Russians were ready to move. So there was bitter irony in the way the soldiers forced strikers back to work in Poland, just as they had under the Tsar in Russia in the years preceding the First World War. The tradition of an authentic army strongman like Jaruzelski went back to the pre-war regime of Marshal Pilsudski. Jaruzelski surprised most people in one respect: he pressed that the Polish armed forces themselves take control without outside help. Poles were more prepared to take orders from a soldier than from the Communist Party. In addition, Jaruzelski displayed an uncanny judgement of just how he could coax the genie back into the bottle and drew a measure of support, perhaps surprisingly, from many Poles who realized that labour indiscipline could not continue indefinitely. During the sixteen months that Solidarity had been functioning, economic disruption had worsened the plight of ordinary people.

Over the two years following the imposition of martial law in Poland, confrontation deteriorated into stalemate. The government arrested thousands of Solidarity activists, censored the press and ordered workers back to work. In the harsh winter of 1980–81, many workers, told they would not be paid if they failed to show up, had no choice. Resistance in the factories now comprised malingering and works-to-rule. The authorities threatened to send home workers that joined in such action.

Poland somehow staggered through that bitter winter into summer with a slow return to normality. Large demonstrations took place, which were tear-gassed and water-doused by police. Sheer brute force, plus the understanding of ordinary Poles that their already miserable economic lot would become even worse if they continued resisting, whittled down the spirit of Solidarity. When Lech Walesa was freed in 1983, his spirit appeared unbroken. But the government had taken the calculated risk that he had lost his following; ordinary Poles would not endure another grim struggle of heartbreak and misery on his behalf.

Martial law was lifted in July 1983. By December, the anniversary of its imposition had passed off almost without incident. Poles still had portraits of Walesa on their walls and still met in unofficial groups to discuss ideas. Among ordinary workers the Church, whose priests fearlessly criticized the government from their pulpits, became the main centre of opposition. But the authorities had squeezed its critics out of most government and academic jobs.

Solidarity bulletins and illegal printing presses were repressed vigorously. Some 2,500 people were imprisoned for political offences. The Communist Party still seemed in a terminal state of decline – with Party membership 250,000 lower than before martial law. The Party's hardliners, criticizing Jaruzelski for being too soft, cut little ice. The general meanwhile toyed with setting himself up at the head of a mass movement on Latin American military lines.

On 17 June 1983, the Poles welcomed Pope John Paul II in Warsaw like a temporal, rather than a spiritual, leader. More than a million people turned out to hear Karol Wojtyla on his second visit to Poland since becoming Supreme Pontiff, cheering his every word. The sea of faces turned towards him not in spiritual awe, not even in hope, but just in tribute to the man they recognized as their leader. The Pope was blatantly political in his speech, talking of 'the terrible injustices of history', and calling for 'victory in truth, in freedom, in justice and in love'. The people made two-finger salutes in honour of Solidarity, the banned Polish trade union; banners proclaimed 'Welcome, father of Solidarity'.

Many outsiders assumed that the fervour was primarily religious, or that support for Solidarity was simply an expression of trade union sentiment.

Poles, sure enough, are deeply religious in a private way; but the expression of religious fervour was for most ordinary people a means of asserting national independence through the grim years of Soviet domination. Solidarity sprang up, originally, as a trade union force. But the 10 million people that joined it in its first heady months of existence did so to express a national protest, not out of support for union rights. Solidarity's leader, Lech Walesa, found that one of his earliest fights was resisting the demand of his followers that political objectives – the lifting of censorship, the right to form political parties – be appended to the immediate trade union objectives: the right to strike and to decentralize industry.

It was the Pope, not Walesa, who first ignited the fires of active Polish nationalism. In 1979, his first triumphant visit to his homeland demonstrated that the Roman Catholic Church that the Pope now headed was more powerful and better supported in the world outside than the Russian-installed Communist Party in Poland. The Pope's election caught the imagination of a nation that, twelve years after an authentic worker revolt had been bloodily suppressed, was facing an even harsher economic crisis than the one applying then.

A remarkable report commissioned shortly afterwards by the Party revealed how little support the regime had. It concluded that 'during the entire post-war period, Poland did not develop any universally respected or truly workable rules and mores to govern its social life'. The report complained about 'sham planning and the sham implementation of plans, sham accomplishments in industry, science, the arts and education, the sham declaration and fulfilment of pledges, sham concern for social welfare . . . Sham socialism, sham freedom of choice, sham progress.' The report could hardly have been more damning. Even the ruling Communist Party of Edward Gierek was prepared to admit the truth behind the façade.

In the light of this, the wholesale rejection by the workforce of communist ideology is not so surprising. Many outside Poland suggested that the workers still believed in Communism, although they considered its application in Poland flawed. Lip service was indeed paid to Communism by some moderate strike leaders in an effort to pacify successive Polish governments and the Soviet Union. But Walesa himself would not offer the system formal support or even define himself as a socialist. Among shop floor workers, the main allegiances were the nation, the Church and family, in that order. Foreign-imported Communism ranked nowhere.

The significance of the Polish upheaval could not be exaggerated. It revealed the bitter irony – which sent intellectual shock waves through the communist movement of Western Europe – that the one power in the workers' state strong enough to confront the oppression of the system was the workforce itself. It proved that endlessly drumming communist ideology into a people did not guarantee it would take hold. Most significantly of all, it exposed the Communist Party as a shell, having to rely upon, and eventually be replaced by, the traditional instrument of coercion, the armed forces; and army rule, unlike Party rule, had few pretensions to immortality.

For the first time a communist system had shown that it was vulnerable; the initial Soviet hesitation in congratulating Jaruzelski for the imposition of martial law was because the Russians were loath to welcome a military leader who, even from dire necessity, had pushed the Party to one side.

9

Schisms

'Lenin used to speak of the state in the first phase of socialism keeping much of the content of bourgeois law. But the state with which we are dealing has gone further than Lenin foresaw in this sphere. It has kept not only some of the content of bourgeois law but has provided examples of distortion and degeneration which at other times could only be imagined in imperialist states.'

Santiago Carrillo

The Eurocommunist Heresy

What had happened to the communist revolutionary flame in Western Europe, where Marx considered his ideology had the best chance of success? The Spartacist uprising had failed in Germany in 1919, and there had been flickerings in the 1920s and 30s. Although communist parties polled fair-sized percentages among the industrial voters to whom they specifically appealed, in Italy, France and Spain, where the communist minority succeeded in hijacking the Republican cause during the Spanish Civil War, the Party had invariably been crushingly defeated by the Right; thereby ironically assisting the likes of Mussolini, Hitler and Franco gain power.

After the Second World War, with the Right discredited, the Left had its chance to recover. In West Germany the Communist Party was outlawed by the constitution, and in Spain and Portugal, right-wing authoritarian regimes lingered on. But in Italy and France the opportunity seemed to exist for significant progress. The first post-war election results were not discouraging: the Italian Communist Party won around 19 per cent of the vote in 1946, just short of the Socialist Party, and the

French Party, 20 per cent. The communists assumed that as these countries became industrialized and the balance of electoral power shifted from the peasantry to the urban working class, communist support would grow inexorably.

Two things frustrated communist ambitions in Western Europe: the Cold War nurtured the suspicion among Western electorates, including the working classes, that communist parties were subversive Russian agents; and as industrialization brought greater prosperity, the working classes grew more bourgeois and acquisitive. Those owning cars, television sets and consumer durables knew perfectly well that they could lose much more than their chains from political upheaval.

Thus Western European communist parties began to try and distance themselves from the unappealing Soviet model. This was easier said than done. In Italy the spur was Khrushchev's attack on Stalin in 1956. Palmiro Togliatti, the Italian communist leader, a brilliantly eloquent, tough little intellectual who had succeeded a rather reflective Marxist-Leninist, Antonio Gramsci (who died in prison under Mussolini) attempted to furl the Russian umbrella. In 1964,when Togliatti died at Yalta on the eve of delivering an attack on the Russian system, his 'Yalta Testament' was the first Western European communist declaration openly to criticize the treatment of Soviet dissidents.

In France, Maurice Thorez, leader of the French Communist Party since 1930, was cut from a different cloth. A wartime exile in Russia, on his return to France, thanks to an agreement between the Soviet Union and General de Gaulle, he once more took charge of the French Communist Party. He grabbed the reins from those who had led the wartime resistance to the German occupation and offered a pro-Russian brand of Marxism-Leninism that de Gaulle had no fear would be electorally attractive.

Even after 1956, the French Party, heavily financed by the Russians, refused to change. In 1961, when two young members of the Central Committee, Laurent Casanova and Manuel Sirbin, suggested the Party express its support for democracy, two young Stalinists, Georges Marchais and Roland Leroy, promptly replaced them. Marchais became General Secretary in 1972, with Leroy as his deputy, and they continued to impose a thoroughly Stalinist imprint on the Party.

But events would not fit French communist assumptions. Thanks to its thoroughly unappealing doctrines, the Party had been stuck at around 20 per cent of the vote. In 1968, a student uprising touched off a worker revolt that the communists did their best to damp down. But the student left posed a challenge to which the Party had to respond. Those joining the Party were dull, orthodox hacks, and if more lively radicals emerged on the extreme Left, they might drain away communist support. In its Champigny manifesto, the Party grudgingly accepted that political pluralism might be necessary. However, the concept of the dictatorship of the proletariat was not abandoned until February 1976.

The Spanish Party was another that climbed aboard the Eurocommunist bandwagon, led by a feisty little ex-journalist with a leathery worker's face and a puckish grin, Santiago Carrillo. Carrillo's remarkable life included being Commissar of Madrid as a 21-year-old during the Spanish Civil War (he governed with the utmost brutality) and thirty-six years in exile in Paris, while his associate, Dolores Ibarruri, 'La Pasionaria' (the passion flower) so called because of her fiery speeches rather than her looks, spent a similar period in Russia.

In Paris, Carillo, who succeeded Dolores Ibarruri as Secretary General in 1960, slowly worked out his own brand of 'Eurocommunism'. The Russians were dismayed, and supported the defection from the Party in the early 1970s of two hard-liners, General Enrique Lister and Eduardo Garcia. However, the two turned out to have no Party following at all.

Other parties – the British, the Belgians, the Japanese – followed in Eurocommunism's wake. Only in Portugal, where a left-wing military clique supported by the Communist Party had thrown out the right-wing dictatorship of Marcello Caetano did the Party stay true to Stalin. It reasoned that the workforce in Portugal, Western Europe's poorest country, would support primitive communist ideals and could be persuaded to believe in the myth of Russia. The Portuguese communist leader, Alvaro Cunhal, had been born in the old mould. This white-maned, bright-eyed zealot with a high staccato voice who, theatrically, kept away from the windows during the 1974–5 Portuguese revolution for fear of being shot at, had spent his exile in Czechoslovakia after some thirteen years of prison in Portugal. Almost alone of leading communists in Western Europe, he supported Russia's invasion of Czechoslovakia in 1968.

Surprisingly, he was right about Stalinism's electoral appeal in his country: the 16 to 18 per cent the Party polled in successive elections was certainly impressive, as was the dominance of the communists over the Portuguese labour movement, Intersindical, and the peasant co-operatives in Portugal's southern region, the Alentejo.

Ironically, it was the leader of what would be the least successful Eurocommunist Party who articulated the movement's ideology. Carrillo's book, *Eurocommunism and the State*, which appeared in 1977, was a bombshell. Not only did it propose a new, democratic form of Communism as an article of faith, it criticized the Russian regime as a spent force and no longer the model for communist movements around the world. The philosophy of Carillo's Eurocommunism was rooted in democracy:

> Socialism, in order to extend and transform itself into a world economic system, which does not imply one single model or subordination to one state or group of states, or the lessening of independence and originality of each country, or even the disappearance of differences of interests between this or that state – must recover for itself democratic and liberal values, the defence of human rights, together with respect for dissenting minorities.

He went on to accept the existence of a private sector in the socialist state.

> The coexistence of forms of public and private ownership means acceptance of unearned increment and the private appropriation of part of this, i.e. the existence of a mixed system. Society has the means to ensure that this unearned income is not exorbitant, by means of taxation, and that it is nevertheless sufficient to encourage private enterprise . . .

Having asserted that this 'mixed economy' would lead to a plurality of political parties whose beliefs would represent the various interest groups involved, he considers the implications:

> All this means that the class struggle is going to manifest itself openly, although the social consensus will logically be greater than that which exists in present-day society in which the hegemony is exercised by monopoly capital . . .
>   Let us take a look at the socialist countries which have carried out their revolution along a classical road . . . examples of inequality still continue. There are vital problems, such as the standard of living and the supplying of the population with goods and foodstuffs, which cannot be considered solved. Problems of productivity, of participation, are on the agenda. And there remain the great unsolved questions of democracy and social contradiction which a one-sided propaganda hides but does not solve.
>   That type of state which has arisen in the Soviet Union, which is not a capitalist state since it does not uphold private property, but which is not

the state Lenin imagined either – with the worker exercising power directly – how is it to be fitted in with the Marxist conception of the state? Lenin used to speak of the state in the first phase of socialism keeping much of the content of bourgeois law. But the state with which we are dealing [Soviet Russia] has gone further than Lenin foresaw in this sphere. It has kept not only some of the content of bourgeois law but has provided examples of distortion and degeneration which at other times could only be imagined in imperialist states.

Even if orthodox Communism had its limitations, Carillo warned that 'we do not put aside the possibility of regaining power by revolutionary means, if the dominating classes close the democratic processes'. Eurocommunists promised that if elected, they would return to opposition if voted out. But they never believed that electors would ever reverse their verdict – a hangover from the theory that the tide of history is irreversible. Lucio Lombardo Radice, an Italian communist, went further; he argued in 1977 that Eastern Europeans would want to keep socialism if they were ever freed from the Russian yoke. 'Would any part of the people want . . . a retreat from a higher form of society to a lower? . . . It is entirely unhistorical as well as unreasonable to suppose that they would want to turn the clock back.' Events in Poland two years later would prove him spectacularly wrong.

For Carrillo, Western society was far from democratic. 'Even in the most democratic capitalist state everything is organized to defend the interests of the dominant class.' In his view the best way to end this exploitation was not, as the French Communist and the British Labour parties then argued, nationalization of the means of production, but worker participation in industry and decentralization of power to the regions. Italy's Communist Party favoured more state planning, not further nationalization.

Carillo also showed a traditional apparatchik's distrust of institutions like a free press and broadcasting, claiming they were 'the most dangerous opiates of the people. We must fight to acquire dominant positions for revolutionary ideas. This applies equally to the church, to education, to culture, to the system of relations of the political forces, the means of information etc.' Carrillo's analysis of what had gone wrong with Marxism-Leninism was perceptive. The thrust of his book was that industrialization, rather than reinforcing an ultra-concentration of capital, had diffused power into many people's hands, creating a large constituency of bourgeois supporters. The urban working class, far from a majority in most countries, often ended up as a minority, outnumbered by the old peasant class and the new professional and service classes. The urban working class was also becoming more bourgeois in its attitudes.

Modern technology, he claimed, had now once again concentrated power in the hands of an ever-smaller minority of monopolist capitalists. Because most of the professional classes were outside the exploiting minority, they had joined forces with the working class who should welcome the former as allies; if democracy was what the professionals wanted, so be it. Less explicitly, the Italian Communist Party had long urged an alliance with the bourgeoisie, through the 'historic compromise' coalition between itself and the ruling Christian Democratic Party.

Carrillo's views drew an angry response from Russia. In June 1977 the Russian magazine *Novy Mir* (New Times) attacked his book for its 'crude anti-Sovietism'. That was hardly accurate: while most Eurocommunists now rejected the Soviet model, they were much less critical of Russian foreign policy. For example, Sergio Segre, the Italian Communist Party's international boss, stated flatly in the mid-1970s, 'I don't think anyone in Western Europe says that the Soviet Union is casting aggressive eyes towards Western Europe,' while Lucio Lombardo Radice claimed that 'it is extremely difficult to foresee under what conditions a warlike emergency could occur. The Italian Communist Party would probably not want to commit itself to either side. It would be for peace. It would certainly oppose anti-Sovietism.'

Although the Italian Communist Party's foreign policy planners accepted the existence of NATO, they considered Russia was usually right and America, wrong. For Giancarlo Pajetta, the Italian Party's foreign policy boss, America was a greater evil than the Russians:

> In American society civil rights are unknown, and not just for repressed Puerto Ricans and Blacks, who are squashed like cogs in a machine in which they don't participate . . . Many Americans are also dissatisfied with their lives . . . They can't identify with their democracy – only half the people voted in the last presidential election. A Russian participates with greater interest and feels that things are more his own than an American worker, where only the elite has voting rights and a high standard of living.

A leading French communist told the author: 'The Russian domination of Eastern Europe is not comparable with the power of the

American multinationals in Western Europe. The Russians uphold revolution the world over, with no hope of financial gain – witness the aid going to Cuba and Vietnam.'

By the middle of the 1970s, the Eurocommunists, while differing strongly with the Russians, were treated with justifiable scepticism in Western Europe. They were still receiving Russian money and had not yet passed the three major tests that would convince most people that they were committed democrats. These were: firstly, easing their support for Russian foreign policy; second, abandoning the rigid Leninist concept of democratic centralism; and third, severing their remaining financial and organizational links with Russia.

In 1979, however, Eurocommunism as such broke up. The three main parties – the Italians, the French and the Spanish – went their separate ways. In Italy that year, after three years of cooperation just short of government with the Christian Democrats, the communists walked out after failing, in their opinion, to be given their fair share of power. Many people expected the Party, in abandoning its historic compromise tactic, to revert to intransigent opposition and friendship with Russia. Instead, the Party proved its sincerity by continuing its evolution.

Its trade union wing continued to obstruct the government's anti-inflationary policies – although not to the point of making Italy ungovernable. But the Party's criticism of Russia grew increasingly sharp. At the end of that year the Italian communists vigorously attacked the Soviet occupation of Afghanistan; in 1981 they used the military takeover in Poland to denounce Russia harshly. The Russian Revolution, said the Italian communists, was no longer Communism's guiding model. They argued that their links with Russia were no closer than those with China or with any other communist movement. The Russian 'special relationship' was at an end. 'We refuse to identify a guiding force in international Communism,' Giorgio Napolitano, the Party's Deputy Leader, told the author. It was a declaration of independence.

The Italian Party, the largest in Europe, survived these years of opposition with difficulty: its vote in the 1979 general election fell from 34 per cent to 30 per cent and slipped a fraction further in 1983. The Party's leader and author of the historic compromise strategy was the dourly bureaucratic Enrico Berlinguer, from a well-off Sardinian family. Berlinguer clung to his position by steering carefully between its factions, moving the Party no faster than it wanted to travel.

Berlinguer's short stature, sardonic, elfin looks, and controlled passion when speaking made him the best known figure in Italian politics during the 1970s; but he was respected rather than liked by those stolid workers, representing millions of their fellows, who witnessed him haranguing the crowds in Rome's Piazza San Giovanni.

Beneath him, the Party was split three ways; the Right had long been headed by a grizzled veteran with a background in liberal politics, Giorgio Amendola, who created the whole idea of the historic compromise. His successor, Giorgio Napolitano, was a man with a considerable presence, which made him the main challenger in the early 1980s to the rather jaded Berlinguer. But while Napolitano represented only one wing of the Party, Berlinguer was safe. In 1982, Napolitano conceived a 'left alternative' alliance with the Socialists, as opposed to the corrupt Christian Democrats.

The Party's Stalinist wing was led by Armando Cossutta, an unimpressive, dour-faced Senator who argued that the Party must keep close to its Soviet origins, a view swamped at the 1983 Party Congress, which significantly permitted what appeared to be a real debate. Cossutta's support, however, was derisory. The third group was the Party's radical liberation wing, headed by the charismatic Petro Ingrao, some of whose followers had broken away in 1969 to form the far-left Manifesto group. By appealing to this group, which also favoured a left-wing alternative, Napolitano hoped eventually to gain a victory in the Party.

In France the Communist Party went the other way. Faced by its inability to advance electorally, the Party did its utmost to prevent its allies, the French Socialists, whose support was growing, from wresting power from the Right. The Party leader was Georges Marchais, a flamboyant, loud-mouthed orator, whose iron grip on the Party, enforced by democratic centralism, tolerated nothing except the most rigid orthodoxy. He turned the Party towards Eurocommunism in 1976 without even convening the Party's Central Committee and moved them back again in 1979 with equal lack of consideration.

The Party's new Stalinist bent did not stop it rather feebly joining the Socialists' push to victory in the 1981 election, which gave France its first government of the Left in twenty-two years. But it did cause them to do badly at the polls: they fell from 19 per cent to 17 per cent, to a point where the new Socialist President, François Mitterand, felt it would do no harm to include communists in the government for the first time since the war. The United States accepted this with only a murmur.

In Spain, the authentic Eurocommunism of Santiago Carrillo ran up against a far superior force: that of the Socialist Workers Party, led by the young and dynamic Felipe Gonzalez. In the first Spanish general election for fifty-one years, that of 1977, Carrillo's Communist Party polled just 10 per cent of the vote. This was not impressive, but Carrillo could claim that after the Party's suppression under Franco, it had lacked sufficient time to organize. Carrillo himself came under fire for not practising what he preached: his party was rigidly controlled from the top, and he was reluctant to abandon democratic centralism, arguing that the Party's main available weapon was discipline.

However, at the 1982 general election, the Socialists swept into office following the collapse of the Union of the Democratic Centre government that had run Spain since Franco's day. The communists were trampled in the stampede: their vote fell to 9 per cent. Carrillo resigned as Party leader, making way for the younger Pablo Inglesias, in an attempt to rejuvenate the Party's image. Clearly, Spanish Communism was not being killed by Carrillo's personality but because for most voters Eurocommunism seemed little different from the socialism preached by Felipe Gonzalez. Only the communists' trade union wing, the Workers' Commissions, led by a trenchant, earthy labour leader, Marcelino Camacho, who had spent years in the political underground under Franco, appeared to represent a significant force by contrast with the ineffectual socialist trade unions.

The Spanish shared the dilemma of all the Western European communist parties, and indeed of the European Left as a whole. For three decades, the existence of substantial communist parties embracing pro-Russian positions had prevented the Left from coming to power in Italy and France. 'We can't win with the communists, and we can't win without them,' was the despairing socialist wail. As the communist parties started to evolve away from Russia, their policies increasingly resembled those of socialist parties, and as they lost their distinctive character, they lost support. This made voters less frightened of electing socialist parties to office.

But the communist seats in government in France, no more than a token gift from the socialists with their absolute majority, brought little satisfaction to a party on the skids. The Eurocommunists faced a crisis of identity: they needed a new one to replace the old Stalinist one. Before his death in 1979, the author asked Giorgio Amendola to define what made the communists distinct from the socialists: 'We are a party of discipline and of the workers.' Yet as communist discipline frayed at the edges, and as the workers turned to socialist policies that represented a softer brand of Marxism, the Party was seeing even these two basic ingredients slip away.

The Eurocommunist dilemma went to the heart of Marxism-Leninism. Communism had suffered some debilitating setbacks in Western Europe in the 1980s. For the Party 18 per cent of the electorate in Portugal and 9 per cent in Spain after four decades of right-wing rule was remarkable enough. For the Italian Communist Party to be unable to progress further after breaching the 30 per cent barrier in the 1977 general election – even though Italy continued to be misgoverned by the same sprawlingly inefficient Christian Democratic government that had run the country since 1946 – was even more astonishing. And the French Communist Party's retreat in recent opinion polls to only 12 per cent of the vote, as its ministers ineffectually rode on the coat-tails of a socialist government, signalled that these parties might be in terminal decline.

These setbacks were compounded by a deep recession in Western Europe, when the defects of the capitalist system ought to have become apparent to all. For communists, the awful truth appeared to be that during economic growth, industrial workers were attracted to bourgeois parties, and come recession, they preferred safety. Revolution held no appeal; neither did nationalization, increased government expenditure (indeed, the socialist governments of Bettino Craxi in Italy, Felipe Gonzalez in Spain, Mario Soares in Portugal and François Mitterrand in France were implementing austerity policies which involved reduced welfare spending) or the suppression of democracy.

Western Europe had become too prosperous for Marxism-Leninism to take root. The creed only appealed to poor, backward societies where people had very little to lose from revolution and would swallow a simplistic Marxist message. Also, as Russian-dominated Eastern Europe grew more prosperous, so people and industries strained for greater freedom from control and it became increasingly clear that history was on the side of the West, progress gave birth to pluralism – the exact opposite of the Marxist credo. How would Lenin have reacted to the blunt declaration by Manuel Azcarate, of the Spanish Communist Party, that history had bypassed the Russians? 'We will not treat Lenin as a once-and-for-all absolute . . . Therefore at the Ninth Congress of the Communist Party of Spain, we changed the wording we had hitherto used to define our party; we reviewed the formula describing ourselves as a Marxist-Leninist party. We shall no longer have Leninism as the fountainhead of our inspiration.'

Marxism-Leninism was being tossed, in Trotsky's immortal phrase, into the dustbin of history.

Southeast Asia: The Victors Fall Out

The Vietnamese and Cambodian revolutions were quick to turn sour, not just because of Vietnam's war with China and its invasion of Cambodia. The main barometer of discontent in Vietnam was the flow of boat people in the early years of Communism, risking their lives in the stormy South China Sea rather than staying in their workers' paradise.

After January 1979 some 25,000 Vietnamese escaped in boats, while another 45,000 left under official auspices. It was reckoned that a further 1 million people wanted to board the Air France jets that left regularly from Ho Chi Minh City (as Saigon had been renamed) for Bangkok. Altogether, after 1975, around 1.5 million refugees left Vietnam, Cambodia and Laos. By 1983 there were some 50,000 to 80,000 Vietnamese working in Eastern European countries; they were not forced to go, but even competed for places, so grim had life become in the south. As one prominent Vietnamese leader, Tua Hung, admitted to an Australian visitor in 1980: 'We will be poor and we will be hungry until the end of the century.'

As the fiercely hierarchical Communist Party enforced hard-line Marxism-Leninism on South Vietnam, disillusion spread so quickly that a vigorous debate began within it about how best to move forwards, following food riots, violent disorders and plummeting production. By 1978 grain output had fallen to an all-time low of 13 million tons. So reluctantly, the Party allowed a degree of economic liberalism, freedom to small traders and incentives to agricultural producers: this enabled harvests to recover to around 16 million tons by 1982.

By 1982, industrial production had risen by 12.7 per cent. Per capita income in Vietnam, which had fallen from $250 a year in 1975 (after the ravages of war) to an appalling $150 in 1982, began to pick up slightly. The new economics supremo, Vo Van Viet, was behind the reforms: they included piecework for factory workers and 'production contracts' for peasants, under which they could keep everything produced above a certain quantity. Factory managers could buy raw materials on the free market and peasants were actively encouraged to cultivate private plots. This 5 per cent of the land yielded some 60 per cent of agricultural income.

Differential earnings were allowed to continue; for example, trishaw drivers by 1983 were still earning some 2,000 dong (then approximately $33) a month and street traders some 4,000. Economic liberalization meant there was more money available to pay higher salaries, and by 1980 the government admitted that it controlled less than 50 per cent of income in South Vietnam. For newer Party leaders like Le Duc Tho, this was a fact of life, but others, such as the ailing Le Duan, Vietnam's communist boss, told the Party Congress in Ho Chi Minh City in December 1983, that 'we must immediately reduce bourgeois trade and readjust private trade', and denounced 'speculation, theft of state property and illegal practices'.

The speech precipitated a minor drive to collectivism and the rounding up of 'bourgeois elements' into re-education camps. But even the apparatus of control and the presence of 300,000 or so Vietnamese in labour camps could not obscure the impossibility of feeding South Vietnam outside a free market system. Even so, by 1983 Vietnam was devouring some $4 billion a year in Soviet aid.

By the same year, Cambodia had become an annex to Vietnam, acting among other things as its rice bowl – even though its own population was starving. The Vietnamese officially encouraged their own people to settle there. 'All state institutions and people's revolutionary committees' were instructed to 'assist and support Vietnamese settlers in Kampuchea,' in a circular issued by the Vietnamese in April 1983. The local inhabitants were to assist the Vietnamese in 'rapidly expanding the movement of the Vietnamese people'. Some 189,000 Vietnamese troops, meanwhile, stayed in the country.

Cambodia remained trapped in a three-way civil war: the armed bands of the Right and the Khmer Rouge rump occasionally fought each other and continued their spasmodic resistance in the north and on the Thai border, across which the Vietnamese intermittently pursued them. The government of Heng Samrin, a former Khmer Rouge commander who had changed sides and joined the Vietnamese, was wholly underpinned by Vietnamese armed power: it enforced a spartan, austere and barely functioning Marxism-Leninism. One visiting journalist, Brian Eads of the *Observer*, reported graphically in May 1983, that Phnom Penh:

. . . resembles something between a refugee camp and a mammoth rubbish dump. No one has the time or inclination to remove the noisome slurry of human waste, which maroons a hospital where children die like flies of intestinal diseases. There is a curious mixture of torpor and energy, squalor and self-indulgence . . . On paper, scores of industries have been revived. In fact, government factories seldom function . . . If there are happier notes to be sounded, it is in areas where the regime has recognized its inability to cope. The markets are filled with foodstuffs and consumer goods smuggled into the country. Public transport involves cycles and motorcycle-drawn carts. There are shops, restaurants and a variety of services, all the work of private enterprise.

If life under the Vietnamese was better than under the Khmer Rouge, this was not saying much. By 1983 the population of Phnom Penh had returned to around 600,000. Some 25,000 in the country suffered from severe malnutrition. The Soviet Union had to provide some $500m in aid, while international relief agencies coughed up $350m. In the bleak American phrase, the country was a basket case.

Arab Socialism

The Arab world seemed ideal for Marxist-Leninist growth. In the east the United States had drawn a line against Soviet penetration of Iran after 1940, forcing the Russians to pull out of Azerbaijan in the north. The superpower contest in Iran helped to contain any southward expansion of Russian influence and, as subsequent events would show, Iran nurtured anti-Western Islamic reaction, rather than socialism, in its bosom.

However, most of the Arab world appeared more vulnerable: feudal potentates ran the majority of countries and people lived in conditions little changed since the Middle Ages. Yet across the region, small groups appeared, drawn from the armed forces and the small upper classes; they were influenced by Western ideas of progress and Eastern European ideas of equality, each suggesting that despotism was out of date. Most of these ideas revolved around two concepts, as in Africa: the one-party machine, and some vague socialist creed.

The groups justified the one-party idea on the grounds that Western multi-party systems eventually led to corruption, election rigging and patronage. In reality, the lack of electoral competition was primarily intended to allow them to stay in power unchallenged. Nevertheless, they sought legitimacy by claiming to be both nationalists and socialists, and by establishing local branch organisations around their countries to provide patronage and the enforcement of one-party power. The model of one-party socialist government that grew up in most Arab countries was a characteristically Third World one; only in Lebanon did a multi-party system represent the country's complex mixture of rivalries and clans, and it broke down, horribly, in the 1970s.

The Soviet Union began to pay attention to the Arab world in the 1950s. From the start, the Russians could challenge the feudal status quo, which the West had little alternative but to defend, although they represented an ideology as alien as the old colonial one. In most Arab countries, the local revolutionaries would happily take arms and money to overthrow the old hierarchy, but had no intention of allowing themselves to be run by the Russians if they could help it.

The Palestinian issue was another reason for the Arab world to look to Russia rather than the West for friendship. Since Israel's foundation in 1948 a diaspora of educated refugees had washed around the Arab world, unsettling local regimes and insisting they back the Palestinians in exchange for a quiet life. This was one cause the Russians quickly espoused, recognising its potency.

During the 1960s, the communists appeared to be making substantial inroads in the region. This alarmed many in the West, who could not differentiate between local elites making use of Russian help and actual Soviet penetration and control. The Russians provided advice on setting up Soviet-style one-party systems: in many countries communist parties were encouraged to join the local socialist parties. In 1965, for instance, the Egyptian Communist Party dissolved itself and agreed to join the Arab Socialist Union, the party of the colonels who had toppled King Farouk. The Russians hoped that military aid – Egypt owed Russia some $11 billion by the early 1970s – and the provision of some 15,000 mainly military advisers would transform Egypt into a client state. Egypt's President, Gamal Abdel Nasser, allowed them to believe this, but the country was too large for Russia to swallow.

The Russians also made an enemy of Anwar Sadat, failing to back him when he was the apparently nondescript interim President during the struggle to succeed Nasser. After the 1973 war with Israel had given Egypt back a measure of national pride, Sadat slung out the Russian advisers, and renounced both the debt and the Soviet-Egyptian Treaty of Friendship and Cooperation. The Russians could do nothing; by the end of the 1970s, a country which had gobbled up 43 per cent of all Soviet aid to the Third World between 1954 and 1971 had become the main recipient of United States aid.

Egypt had been Russia's main hope in the Arab world. Its lesser priorities had been Syria and Iraq, the latter a coutry where the Baath Socialist Party, founded along Pan-Arab socialist lines, had overthrown the pro-western Hashemite dynasty that exerted a benevolent, but very loose, rein. In each country, the Baath Party was joined by the local Communist Party. In Iraq in 1972 a 117-strong 'Progressive National Front' government was formed, including two Communist Party members, and both parties ran together in the one-party elections held in 1973.

In 1972 the Syrian Communist Party emerged from its underground struggle to form an alliance with the ruling Syrian Baath Party: two communists were brought into government and communist newspapers were allowed. Some 5,000 Soviet military advisers arrived in Syria, which in 1974 signed a cooperation and friendship treaty with Russia. As Syria's hostility to any kind of Middle Eastern peace settlement grew, it became more obvious that President Hafez al-Assad, a ruler from a minority sect, was relying for his survival on security forces trained in Eastern Europe. By the end of the 1970s, there was room to question the Syrian government's freedom of manoeuvre: in its international alignments and repressive one-party control, Syria seemed to have become all but a Marxist-Leninist satellite.

No room for doubt existed in Yemen. In 1967, the British, under pressure from terrorist attacks – some 480 incidents took place in 1966 alone – announced their withdrawal from Aden. This left a vacuum that the small pro-Soviet group in the Crater filled with alacrity. Two groups vied for control of the country: the Egyptian-backed FLOSY (Front for the Liberation of South Yemen) and the Marxist-Leninist National Liberation Front (NLF). The NLF broke with FLOSY in 1967, and the two fought it out in the streets of Aden, while the British army stayed outside the Crater. In July the British re-established their authority.

By then the British withdrawal had been brought forward to November, and the NLF quickly swept away the traditional rulers left naked and defenceless by the British. The country continued to simmer for years: the Marxist-Leninists had difficulty imposing their rule upon the rebellious tribesmen of the south, and a curious cycle began.

Oil-wealthy Saudi Arabia attempted buy off successive South Yemeni leaders; but when the latter tiptoed away from the Russian connection, they were overthrown by the NLF's hard-line Marxist-Leninist group, led by Abdul Fattah Ismail, who successively toppled the country's first and second presidents. In the process, the army was thoroughly purged; a 'Red Guard' force was set up, and urban-based mobs seized land-owners' property.

Several thousand Russian military advisers, approximately 2,000 East Germans and even a force of Cubans were sent to South Yemen. The Soviet air force took over the former Royal Air Force airfield at Khormaskar outside Aden; communications and surveillance equip-ment were installed on Socotra Island off the Yemeni coast; and a naval and air base was built at Mukalla, in the Hadramaut. The Soviet coloniz-ation of South Yemen became complete in 1978, when Ismail's men, supported by 5,000 Cuban troops, assaulted the presidential palace while a Soviet warship shelled it and overthrew Salim Rubayyi Ali, the President, who had been inching away from the Russians.

South Yemen was a jumping-off point not just for the Cubans' sub-sequent campaigns in Ethiopia and monitoring Red Sea shipping, but also for the infiltration of men into neighbouring North Yemen and Oman, where the Omani army put down the insurgency with British and Iranian help during the 1970s. In North Yemen however, a guerrilla insurgency continued to sputter amid the dirt-tracked, stunningly beau-tiful fields of *qat*, a mild narcotic chewed by most Yemenis, as carbine-equipped tribesmen dwelling in crazy-angled ancient skyscrapers tried to keep the cities free of guerrillas. North Yemen's poorly equipped army that ran the country could not suppress the guerrilla threat, although it prevented it spreading. By the 1980s, South Yemen seemed, to all intents and purposes, to be a Russian colony: as in Afghanistan, any aspirant ruler had to obey the Soviet diktat. However, the Russians had to leave under fire after an insurrection by anti-communist tribesmen in the mid-1980s, and the region lapsed into tribal chaos.

The expulsion of the Soviet military advisers in Egypt and the halting of the export of revolution from South Yemen was followed by a gradual diminution of Iraq's dependence on the Soviet Union. The country's emerging strongman, Saddam Hussein, decided that he no longer needed the 4,000 or so Soviet military advisers as a power base. When the oil price boom multiplied the country's wealth fourfold, he turned to Western-style technology and development to replace the Soviet aid that had turned Baghdad into a drab Eastern European clone city at the heart of Araby.

The Iraqis were also at loggerheads with their Baathist Arab neighbour, Syria, to whom the Russians turned, because of their strategic position next to Israel. Thus, no sooner was the ink dry on Iraq's treaty of cooperation with Russia in 1974 than Saddam Hussein purged the local Communist Party and then, cardinal sin, invaded Iran in 1981 without telling the Soviet Union. Relations with Russia became very strained in the 1980s, while Iraq's links with France, Italy and the United States went from strength to strength – until Saddam decided to invade Kuwait, misreading what he believed was American tacit acceptance, and was turned into an international pariah.

Meanwhile, the Soviet Union used Syria as a troublemaker. The Russians reckoned that they could only profit from a continuation of the Arab-Israeli dispute; American support for Israel antagonized Arab states, and through the Russian position as a superpower and their influence in the region they could insist on being involved in any overall peace settlement. Therefore the Syrians, with Soviet support, obstructed any agreement with Israel over the contentious issue of the Israeli occupation of Syrian territory on the Golan Heights and, after Israel's move into Lebanon in 1982, continued fighting by Syrian-supported elements prevented a comprehensive peace settlement in Lebanon throughout the following year.

Syria subsequently kept its troops in the country as part of a deal to leave the country alone, although Syrian self-interest, of course, ensured that keeping the Lebanese pot boiling would prevent Israel's formal annexation of the Golan Heights. But the Russians played a major role, too, in stiffening Syrian attitudes – although they also helped restrain them from direct engagement with the American peacekeeping force in late 1983.

Afghanistan

Christmas Eve 1979 was just another day for the citizens of Kabul, overwhelmingly devout Muslims. The snow lay deep and crisp and even on the remote, rugged mountain range of the Hindu Kush, visible to the northeast; otherwise it was light for the time of year and the day a fine one. The townspeople went steadily about their business in the bazaars, haggling angrily on their haunches over pipes and – for the better deals – cups of pungent coffee. Buyers stomped ritually in disgust before being summoned back with a shout and the final offer to clinch a deal. Then both men would leave without so much as a goodbye, making the point that they considered their side of the bargain to be a shoddy one, while both, inwardly, smirked.

The residential quarter of the city lacked the muddled bustle of the bazaar. Very little of old Kabul remained: dull Eastern European-style functional apartment blocks housed the middle classes, while the upper class owned comfortable, secluded, one-storey villas with patios and gardens set behind walls. In the surrounding villages dwellings were more traditional: mud-brick buildings and the land that went with them sheltered behind thick walls, the size of the enclosure testifying to the wealth of the owner which, in the case of major Afghan tribal chiefs, might include a small village. In a country riven with feudal practices, property and blood feuds and, more recently, guerrilla warfare, the enclosure kept enemies out and women in, out of sight. Everything the latter needed was provided within the walls, so that they should not be exposed to the lustful, sinful gaze of men outside. Afghanistan that Christmas Eve remained one of the world's backwaters: around 16 million people whose tribally based Islamic way of life had remained less touched by progress than any in the Islamic world except North Yemen.

Apart from demolishing the old centres of Kabul, Herat and Ghazni, economic growth had barely grazed the surface of the country, leaving the small towns and villages in which most Afghans lived undisturbed in their colourful, centuries-old squalor. The small, sly children, the black-swathed women sometimes wearing vivid embossed shawls, the earnest men with worry lines gouged into their faces by the elements, sporting Abraham-Lincoln beards and natty white turbans with long tails, could have walked straight out of the age of Tamerlane in the four-teenth century. Where the heady rise of oil wealth had transformed Iran and the Arab Gulf states to the west in two decades, where departed col-onizers had ordered life in the Indian subcontinent to the east, the Afghans' fierce independence in a land bereft of widely developed mineral wealth had allowed the country to retain the old mores.

Yet no country, not even Afghanistan, which in three conflicts arrested the expansion of British influence in the nineteenth century, could shut the door on the twentieth century forever. Among the first to open it were hippies from the West in the 1960s, trundling in ramshackle vehicles across the country and sampling its marijuana and opium en route to meditative nirvanas further east. Within Afghanistan, twentieth-century ideas took root among that fraction of the country's tiny ruling class that had travelled outside the country.

In a country so primitive, the ideas were rudimentary. A mere handful of people, like the Western-educated Ahmed Said Ghailani, were inspired by democratic ideals, although none of them imagined they could be applied in Afghanistan for many years to come. The larger minority was inspired by the primitive egalitarian sentiments of the Afghan Communist Party. To anyone with a minimum of education and a little knowledge of the world outside, their message of progress through feudal emancipation, the spread of education and industrial development was almost irresistible.

To the north, moreover, lay the Soviet Union, from which almost any power within Afghanistan had to seek approval. King Zahir Shah, ruler of Afghanistan for forty years, was legendary for his gentle inaction. A keeper of falcons and a collector of books and cars, he had wisely presided over his jealously independent and competing tribal chieftains by doing nothing. The writ of central government barely ran in Afghanistan. The King adopted a similar approach to the Soviet Union, conceding most of its demands for favourable trading arrangements.

During the 1950s and 1960s, the King attempted to balance Russia's influence by seeking American aid to develop southern Afghanistan. The United States constructed the southern ring of the highway that ran in a circle around the country, the Russians rushing in to build the northern end. Suspiciously strong bridges were erected – to support tanks, it was later alleged. But America was not really interested. The State Department appeared to think that the King was exaggerating Russia's interest in his kingdom to extract as much money as possible. Washington was sceptical about the Soviet Union's motives in moving any deeper into a nation with so little to offer economically, and by the end of the 1960s American aid was drying up.

The State Department planners at the time were probably right in their assessments of Soviet intentions towards Afghanistan but failed to pinpoint the internal dynamic for change. Because the system of government by a gentle and doddering monarch was so anachronistic and its writ so limited, the King's ambitious, tough-minded cousin, Mohammed Daoud, easily staged a Soviet-backed palace coup in 1973. Daoud was no communist revolutionary, but he shattered the old structure and had to seek the backing of the Afghan communists, whose leader, Mohammed Taraki, had overthrown Daoud by April 1978. Another country, on Russia's very border, was on the road to revolutionary 'liberation'.

The *Sowr* (April) revolution soon turned sour. In the countryside, communist cadres, preaching equality and the emancipation of women, were met with an angry silence from large and small landowners alike, who were wedded to tradition. Worse, villagers started murdering the cadres. The government despatched small contingents of soldiers to the villages where this happened, and the Islamic fanatics among the villagers began to organize themselves to fight the soldiers.

In 1979 Taraki's ruthless Minister of the Interior, Hafizullah Amin, used the government's failure to handle the growing insurgency as the pretext for a coup, ousting and murdering Taraki. A reign of terror began, in which Amin's army-based Khalq (the masses) faction – named after its newspaper – butchered its Parcham (the flag) opponents while seeking to extend its control of the countryside.

Yet the more political prisoners were crowded into Kabul's notorious Pul-I-Charkhi jail, the fiercer the Islamic reaction. Amin, never a man to be restrained by conviction, soon concluded that while the Afghan revolution remained a Marxist one, its chances of survival were small. The Russians alleged that his government had established contacts with the Americans that would have resulted in a flow of Western arms and aid; the murder of Adolph Dubs, the American Ambassador in Kabul in February 1979 is still shrouded in mystery. Amin also turned to a West German firm to prospect for oil and gas near the Soviet border. Certainly, the Russians could not have accepted any actions by Amin – including, for example, negotiating with the guerrilla opposition – that might have reduced their influence in a country directly on their borders and about to join the communist fold.

The Russians believed they could comfortably mop up the guerrillas in a few months. They would enforce revolution by arms. On Christmas Eve 1979, 40,000 troops were airlifted in, and 45,000 soldiers entered by road shortly afterwards. In a gun battle in the presidential palace that night, Amin was killed and replaced by the leader of the Parcham faction, Babrak Karmal, who 'summoned in' the Russians – when in fact they were already there.

Four years later, despite the killing of some 200,000 civilians, Afghan resistance was as strong as ever; the Russians and their allies intermittently controlled only around 10 per cent of the countryside and the centres of the big cities, and some 4 million Afghans had fled the country. The Afghan people, it seemed, hated the forces of progress and 'history'.

Why Afghanistan? This was the first time since the annexation of Eastern Europe that the Soviet Union had used overwhelming armed force to occupy another country.

The invasion flouted the Yalta Agreement, under which a tacit limit to the Soviet sphere of influence had been recognized reluctantly by the West. It destroyed any lingering hopes for the process of détente begun by the Nixon administration in the early 1970s. America's President Carter declared that the invasion had shattered his illusions about Soviet behaviour and intentions overnight, and it also resulted in a boycott by over sixty nations, led by the USA, of the 1980 Moscow Olympics, which the Russians had intended to use as an international showcase for the Soviet way of life.

The invasion ruined the Soviet Union's carefully nurtured image as a peace-seeker not just among Western European electorates, but particularly in the Third World, where the Russians now began to be described in terms as derogatory as those formerly applied to the United States.

The United Nations General Assembly overwhelmingly condemned the invasion and called for the withdrawal of Soviet troops. Cuba's Fidel Castro not only failed to secure the seat on the United Nations Security Council traditionally reserved for the chairman of the group of non-aligned countries, but was also unable to muster support for a pro-Russian line at the latter's summit in Havana. The Islamic and Arab world, where for years the Soviet Union had mounted a special effort to win friends, found the Soviet massacre of Muslims fighting a 'holy war' against the occupation forces abhorrent.

Another Russian pretext for intervention was self-defence. As a majority of the Soviet population in the Central Asian republics were likely to be of Muslim descent by the year 2000 owing to the Muslim birth rate, there were fears that this might threaten the political stability and territorial integrity not just of the Asian republics but of the Soviet state as a whole, should Islamic militancy gain a foothold following the Iranian revolution in 1978.

In practice these fears were greatly exaggerated: the Russians viewed the revolution in Iran with delight, as it removed a pro-American pawn on their southern border that had blocked their possible access to the Gulf. Any ripples from the revolution within the Soviet Union were easily contained through the medium of Russia's own tame and co-operative Islamic leaders. The Sunni Muslims of Russia's Asian republics considered themselves a great deal more advanced and sophisticated than the obscurantist Shia sect in Iran, with its primitive fatalism and pessimism.

Soviet control in southern Russia was also exercised very differently from that of the Shah in Iran. The Russians skilfully blended Islamic ideals with socialist equality. The upper class Muslims supported the changes brought about by the Soviet system, whereas in Iran the Shah ruled alone, dominating a very narrowly based bureaucratic hierarchy, and in open conflict both with the clerics and his own middle class. Moreover, the Soviet army was constantly visible in the southern Russian republics, its conscripts rotated to ensure a permanent and substantial non-Islamic element. In Iran, it was ultimately the army's failure to support the Shah that led to his downfall.

Whatever fears might have been aroused in Russia by the Islamic revolution in Iran – which the local Communist Party, the Tudeh, was instructed to support to the hilt – were dwarfed by the strategic loss of Iran to the United States. That an Islamic victory in backward Afghanistan would have any effect on the sophisticated Muslims of southern Russia was too far-fetched to be plausible. Indeed, only after Soviet troops had actually entered the country might Russia have feared that a withdrawal would look like a defeat by an Islamic movement.

The main reason for the invasion was probably the one attributed to the Russians in the West – to consolidate an apparently strategic pawn which had fallen into their hands by gradual penetration over the years, bringing them a step closer to the Gulf and the Indian subcontinent. In the east, Afghanistan commanded the approaches to the subcontinent, threatening Pakistan. In the new 'Great Game' between Russia and China, Pakistan was China's ally while India was Russia's. Grabbing Afghanistan brought Soviet troops to Pakistan's border, which helped prompt that country to divert at least three divisions from its eastern border with India. This delighted India, which refused to condemn the Soviet occupation of Afghanistan as shrilly as other Third World countries.

Furthermore, the Pakistanis began to construct a large and hugely expensive network of interconnecting roads along the remote western foothills, largely subsidised by $3 billion in military aid from the United

States. The Pakistanis, moreover, were intimidated into muting their own criticism of the Soviet Union. The country's military ruler, General Zia-ul-Haq, had his own reasons for domestic nervousness: although his army had subdued the country, political passion boiled just beneath the surface.

Most dangerous was the threat of separatism by the country's Baluchi minority. Baluchistan lay between Afghanistan and the Indian Ocean, a remote, semi-desert country crossed by few roads. The tribesmen had traditionally resented the central government, and were bought off with generous lashings of economic aid. When a new party emerged from the new urban elite, the Workers' and Students' Organization, which was both pro-Soviet and separatist, Pakistan faced two dangerous scenarios: another war with India, with the Russians coming to the help of their allies and helping to dismember Pakistan, or an uprising in Baluchistan which, if the Pakistanis found it difficult to subdue, could furnish the Russians with a pretext for seizing the province.

To the west, Russia also gained considerable strategic advantages from her occupation of Afghanistan. It opened up a new route for a Soviet thrust towards the Gulf through Iran, bypassing most of the country's mountainous north. The air bases in western Afghanistan were only a few minutes flying time from Iran's main cities for Soviet fighter jets – and not much longer for Soviet troop transports. Now Soviet aircraft could easily reach the Gulf in the event of a major conflagration, such as an uprising in Saudi Arabia that American troops might be required to quell. A major Soviet objective, repeatedly emphasised by President Brezhnev, was to 'demilitarize' the Indian Ocean by expelling American ships necessary for the maintenance of Gulf security out of the area.

Also, the Soviet Union was almost certainly running short of oil. Although the world's biggest producer, pumping more than eleven million barrels a day, Russia could only exploit its huge Siberian reserves with Western technology to which it was denied access. Eastern European countries, formerly supplied with Soviet oil, now had to use their precious foreign currency reserves to buy abroad. Moreover, access to Gulf oil would mean cheaper supplies for southern Russia. Russia's oil thirst provided a strong motive for invasion, and military experts were alarmed by Russia's decision to develop a north-south railway system close to Iran's border, connected to the main east-west link for transporting weapons and supplies.

*

The Russian occupation of Afghanistan quickly settled into a pattern. It soon became clear that the Russians could do no more than hold the main cities and venture out in force to secure strategic highways and villages. The biggest of these operations were in the Panjshir Valley against the forces of Ahmad Shah Massoud, a quietly-spoken resistance leader. The Russians would normally send in an advance force of the Afghan army to bear the brunt of the early casualties. (The latter were normally Afghan conscripts and there was a flood of desertions among them.) Within two years of the invasion, the Afghan army had dwindled from around 80,000 men to 20,000, forcing the government into a conscription drive that proved to be a complete failure. Russian jets and helicopter gunships meanwhile would pound guerrillas perched on the sides of the valley, forcing them up to the tops, allowing the main Soviet forces to advance. The Russian and Afghans would withdraw at nightfall, having 'captured' the valley. The insurgents would then reoccupy it.

Unable to inflict serious casualties on the guerrillas during these engagements, the Russians attempted to intimidate the civilian population. Around Kabul and most major cities the Russians pulverized the many villages that acted as rest centres for the opposition, particularly those by the sides of roads that sheltered guerrillas waiting to ambush armoured convoys.

Perhaps 200,000 Afghan civilians were killed in these Soviet forays. The guerrillas initially were fairly hesitant, picking off individual tanks and small truck convoys in remote areas. As the war proceeded they grew bolder, assaulting towns and even the inner cities. Sometimes the Afghan army and the Russians lost all control of major city centres. For example, when an insurrection initially took place in Kabul's bazaar area, the Russians refrained from intervening; but later they did so, with increasingly murderous results. When the guerrillas took over the centres of Herat and Kandahar (as happened more than once), the Russians attempted to bomb parts of the cities. It soon became apparent that the Russians had decided not to deploy sufficient forces to properly subdue the entire country (probably as many as 500,000 men). They limited themselves to increasing the number of soldiers there from 85,000 to 110,000 chiefly to safeguard their essential strategic interests. The principal one comprised a few key lines of communication: the road around the centre of the country could not be adequately defended all the time, but could be kept open for armed convoys, and the one from Kabul through Jalalabad to the Khyber Pass witnessed repeated Soviet offensives. The most vital link was the highway from the northern town of Mazar-i-Sharif to the Salang Pass and Kabul. The Russians concentrated from the beginning on keeping this open, but on occasions the guerrillas succeeded in gaining control; indeed they may have been responsible for an explosion in the Salang Pass in 1982 that resulted in several hundred deaths. Major Soviet garrisons were built at Faizabad, Kabul, Jalalabad, Gardez and around the country. Major Soviet air bases were established at Baghram, Kabul, Jalalabad and Asadabad in the east, and Kandahar, Shindand and Herat in the south and west. The western airfields brought Russian aircraft to within striking distance of the Gulf.

Meanwhile the Russians pursued diplomatic efforts to prevent the Afghan insurgents getting arms from Pakistan which, by 1982, sheltered some 4 million Afghan refugees – a quarter of Afghanistan's 16 million population and one of the greatest refugee exoduses in history. The refugees set up resistance organizations based around the decaying former British colonial city of Peshawar; the leading ones were two Islamic fundamentalist groups, the Hezb-i-Islami and the Yunis Khalis group.

Among the non-fundamentalists, the main bands were led by Pir Syad Ahmad al-Gailani and Sijbatullah Mojaddedi, both from the tiny Western-educated elite. These groups commanded many of the localized resistance movements in eastern Afghanistan; however, the country's heartland was occupied by Hazara tribesmen, who obeyed nobody's dictates. The insurgents of the west operated out of Iranian territory.

Most of the arms going to the insurgents were antique Lee-Enfield rifles or muskets hammered together in the Pakistani tribal area. The Mujaheddin (literally, 'those fighting a *jihad*', an Islamic holy war) also increasingly used arms captured from Russian and Afghan soldiers, and received some assistance from the Chinese. The Americans, for their part, only began supplying arms on a large scale under the Reagan administration: a few Sam-7s, in particular, the weapon the Afghans most wanted, found their way in to combat Russian Su-77 helicopter gunships.

This supply of arms infuriated the Russians, who at first threatened Pakistan with dire retaliation and in some cases chased guerrillas across the border. The Pakistanis, for their part, tried to throttle back the supply of arms. But with 4 million refugees on their soil, they could hardly be expected to police the wild, rugged mountain part of the tribal area.

In November 1982, Yuri Andropov's signals to Pakistan's President Zia suggested that a deal was in the offing. However, after UN-brokered talks between the Russians and the Pakistanis began, the gap was clearly as wide as ever. Essentially, the difficulty was that the Russians knew that immediately they withdrew, Karmal's puppet regime in Afghanistan, kept in power by Russian troops, would collapse; even the Communist Party was bitterly divided, with Karmal's Parcham wing under attack from the majority Khalq faction. The likeliest outcome of a Soviet withdrawal would be a Khalq takeover, followed by negotiations with the opposition to bring them into government, or a continuing guerrilla war. Either way, the Soviet Union would face a hostile government.

In one sense Afghanistan had become Russia's Vietnam, in another sense, not. Russia was stalemated, incapable of military progress and supporting an increasingly discredited regime that controlled less than 10 per cent of the country. In terms of legitimacy, Russia had far less excuse for its occupation than the Americans had had in Vietnam. However, the Afghans possessed much less firepower than the Vietcong.

It was Mikhail Gorbachev who finally extracted the Russians from their Afghan venture, starting the move towards a Russian withdrawal in 1986. This commenced in 1988 and was completed the following year.

The aftermath of the Russian departure from Afghanistan left a country beset by warlords from rival regional ethnic groups. When the Sunni fundamentalist Taliban movement came to power, dominated by the Pashtun (the country's largest ethnic group), a brutal peace was re-imposed upon the central provinces at least. But following the Taliban's decision to admit Osama Bin Laden's Al Qaida terrorists on their expulsion from Sudan, the country was paralyzed by overseas, particularly American, hostility and the uneasy relationship between the two fundamentalist groups. Following Al Qaida's attacks on the United States on September 11th 2001, an allied-supported insurrection by several tribal groups under the umbrella of the Northern Alliance took Kabul and expelled the Taliban following massive American bombing. The old Communist Party, which had first unleashed civil war upon Afghanistan, is now all but annihilated.

Latin America: Exporting Revolution

By January 1978 the Marxist failure to ignite Latin America seemed overwhelming. No mainland country had followed Cuba in setting up a

Marxist-Leninist regime. One by one, revolutionary hopes had been dashed. In Uruguay in 1973, the army had stifled the Tupamaro guerrilla movement with a ferocity that left the country aghast. Military rule was barely disguised by the constitutionalist presidency of Juan Bordaberry; by 1975 Uruguay had some 3,000 political prisoners, the highest proportion of political prisoners per head of population in any Latin American state. Refined methods of electric shock torture had become a fact of life.

In Brazil, the army takeover of 1964 was followed by nearly two decades of uninterrupted military rule during which death squads provided an effective response against a wave of terrorism that began in 1968. Mexico's one-party system stayed spectacularly unruffled while Bolivia lurched from coup to coup as usual, although the far Left had little say in any of them, apart from a brief left-wing military interlude under General Torres at the end of the 1960s.

In Argentina the military junta that took over from Isabelita Peron in 1976 instituted a savage campaign against the far-left guerrilla armies, which now had 10,000 men at their disposal. Pitched battles took place in Tucuman province. The army used terror tactics against the Indians that sheltered the terrorists, compelling them to withdraw their support. Guerrilla camps were mopped up. In the cities, some 15,000 people 'disappeared'. Paramilitary squads of the far Right carried out the murders, so that the army could claim that it was uninvolved.

Security forces belonging to each of the armed services and each of the provincial governors competed to eliminate the Left. The winner was probably the navy's security service, run by the good-looking and utterly ruthless Admiral Emilio Massera, who fancied himself as the next Peron; mutilated bodies dropped from aircraft were washed up on river banks, remote lakes and even on the edge of the River Plate. By 1978, the army was victorious, after what it acknowledged had been a 'dirty war'. Guerrilla attacks had dwindled to almost none. The Left was either dead, or in exile.

The Left's most spectacular defeat took place in Chile. Salvador Allende was the world's first democratically chosen Marxist president, albeit on a minority vote; he had won a bare plurality – 36 per cent – against the right-wing Jorge Alessandri's 35 per cent. Next came the Christian Democratic Rodomiro Tomic, well to the left of his party, with 28 per cent. Tomic swung his support behind Allende, which gave him a mandate to govern, but not to introduce a full-scale socialist revolution. Allende denied his radical intent in his message to Congress in

May, 1971: 'Our revolution will follow a pluralist model, which Marxist ideologists have been able to visualize but which they have never been able to turn into practice . . . I am sure that we will have the energy and capacity to create the first socialist society that will bring together the three ideals of liberation, democracy and the multi-party system.'

The reality was very different: pro-Allende journalists, in a seminar on social responsibility in the mass media, proudly proclaimed that 'there can only be real liberty of expression in a society where all the means of communication are controlled by the state'. Nationalizations proceeded at a gallop: by the end of 1972, 80% of industrial production and 75% of agriculture was state-owned. The nationalisation of copper brought problems: in 1971 production fell by 5% in the giant open-cast mine at Chuquicamata, 7.5% at El Salvador and a startling 17% at El Teniente, the world's largest underground copper mine. Some 3,500 farms were seized, covering some 12.5 million acres – including many below the 200-acre unit the owners could supposedly retain. Agricultural production fell sharply, causing Chile's farm imports to double from 193 million tonnes in 1969 to 400 million in 1972.

Both the conservative Nationalist Party and the Christian Democratic Party began to challenge Allende through their control of Congress, which pushed through an anti-nationalization amendment in February 1972. Allende vetoed it. In July two election results, in which Allende supporters were resoundingly defeated, demonstrated the government's unpopularity. By October right-wing inspired strikes were spreading across the country. The movement began when southern truck drivers resisted a state takeover: most were owner-drivers, determined to fight socialism. The strikes soon spread to students, white-collar workers, seamen and pilots.

The government asked the army, which had traditionally stood aside from Chilean politics, to restore order: censorship was imposed and strikers' meetings broken up. The strikes collapsed after the army commander, General Carlos Prats, was installed as Minister of the Interior. Early in the New Year, violence flared up again with clashes in the working-class areas of Santiago. In the March 1973 general election the Popular Unity government gained support from the left of the Christian Democratic Party, winning some 43% of the vote; the right-wing Nationalist Party also picked up support from the Christian Democrats, getting 21% to the latter's 29%, thus giving the right-of-centre parties 50%.

Between March and September, Chile plunged into chaos. Extremists were trying to push Allende leftwards and disorders broke out in the slums. Allende, through the good offices of the Interior Minister, General Prats, tried desperately to get the army back into his cabinet. But the Council of Senior Generals voted against joining by sixteen to six. At the end of June a colonel tried single-handedly to stage a putsch, ordering a number of tanks to drive to the Interior Ministry and Defence Ministry. The army high command suppressed the revolt quickly, and the colonel surrendered to Prats.

By July the truckers were on strike again, as were the shopkeepers, taxi drivers, and the professional unions. Meanwhile guerrilla attacks and bank robberies, many staged by the extreme Left, spread. By mid-August, the Christian Democrats and the Nationalists were allies again, denouncing the government for violation of the constitution, accusing it of attempting 'to seize total power with the programme of subjecting everyone to the most rigorous political and economic controls, and of seeking by this means the installation of a totalitarian rule absolutely opposed to the system of democracy that the country upholds'. In this situation the armed forces 'must be a guarantee to all classes and not just to a section of the country or a political clique'.

The senior generals privately advised Prats to resign as Commander-in-Chief. Having lost their confidence he stepped down in favour of General Augusto Pinochet Ugarte. On 10 September the tanks moved in: after a brief but bloody battle, in which the Moncloa Palace in Santiago was bombed repeatedly and blasted by tanks, it was captured. Allende stayed there to the end, and was probably shot by the army, although officially it was said he committed suicide. Resistance continued for several days in various pockets of the country and up to 3,000 people were killed in the ensuing butchery. The military coup was harsh, but not instigated from outside. The Chilean army had acted of its own accord and had not required the support of the Americans to move, although it received it.

Chile's attempt to humanize socialism failed because the Communist Party and its Socialist allies in Chile were too radical; having achieved power by democratic means, they had not respected the limits of democracy, being intent on installing an irreversible Marxist revolution. If the left was to hold power with a genuine mandate to bring about the kinds of changes it wanted, it needed much more than one third of an electoral vote.

*

The lesson of Chile was not lost upon Italy, where the communists began to seek the acquiescence of the middle classes. Non-democratic communists everywhere, in particular Central America, realised that overcoming an existing power structure meant not just obtaining formal power but also gaining the support of the armed forces – or getting them dissolved altogether.

Allende's fall dealt a considerable, but not terminal, blow to the Latin American communist movement. His murder had been magnificently symbolic. The ruthless right-wing military dictator who replaced him added fuel to the fire of global communist propaganda. For communists, the fight went on: the dictatorship, they reasoned, would merely radicalize the population and sooner or later the Latin American masses would throw out the oppressors and embark on revolutions.

Over the years, however, this signally failed to happen. In successive countries, as opposition to military dictatorships gradually grew, the old bourgeois parties picked up support, not the extreme Left. The Dominican Republic returned to democracy under President Guzman, a social democrat, the Left picking up a fraction of the vote. In Ecuador another social democrat, Jaime Roldos, won the first decisive election after the generals returned to barracks in 1978. In Peru, Fernando Belaunde, whom the army had pushed out in 1968, won a thumping majority in the 1980 presidential election, with the Left taking less than a third of the vote.

In Brazil, the main winners, as the country gradually returned to democracy in the 1980s, were the conservative Social Democratic Party and the opposition Brazilian Democratic Movement, with its tiny Marxist fringe. The Communist Party was nowhere in sight. In Argentina, the two front-runners in the elections of 1983 were the Peronists and the Radicals, Argentina's traditional parties, both under moderate leadership that isolated the Marxist-Leninist Left. During military rule it became apparent that disorder had led to military intervention, and increasing prosperity in most countries resulting from rapid economic growth made the prospect of violent revolution less attractive. Even in Latin America, prosperity and progress were bypassing the communists, leaving too small a pool of potential militants.

In Chile, a country that had experienced a Marxist regime, the main opposition force turned out to be the Christian Democrats, with the Nationalist Party a little way behind. The country's socialist parties were by 1982 seeking to jettison their Marxist pasts and to emulate Felipe

Gonzalez's Socialist Workers Party in Spain. The Communist Party remained out on a limb, commanding no more than 15 per cent of the vote in opinion polls.

It was a bleak picture for Marxism-Leninism in South America. One remaining hope was that the debt crisis of the 1980s, which resulted in plummeting living standards for Latin Americans, would radicalize the population. More likely, populist movements would pick up the pieces.

Managua, in Nicaragua, is one of the strangest capitals on earth and not really a city at all, because its centre was destroyed in an earthquake in 1972; when the city was rebuilt, new houses were constructed away from the seismically sensitive area in the middle to form an urban ribbon around the outskirts. The centre of Managua, where thousands of bodies were ploughed into the ground after the earthquake, presents a desolate, eerie spectacle. Huge, half-wrecked shells of buildings that the government lacked the equipment to pull down stand like giant gravestones to the holocaust. A bruised parliament building and a cathedral without a roof overlook the main square of the city, which in turn overlooks a giant lake in which two volcanoes puff lazily. The spectacle is beautiful, although disturbing.

On 22 August 1978 this tranquillity was disrupted when forty men, led by Eden Pastora, 'Commander Zero', a legendary guerrilla from the country's Sandinista National Liberation Front, broke into the Chamber of Deputies, a rubber-stamp parliament of appointed supporters of the country's gangster-dictator, Anastasio Somoza, to hijack it at gunpoint. Craggy, with film-star good looks, Pastora possessed heroic courage and genuine leadership skills, although his political views were somewhat muddled.

His second-in-command was a 20-year-old slip of a girl, 'Comandante Dos', Dora Maria Tellez, small with short curly hair and blazingly determined eyes. The guerrillas secured nearly all their demands – the release of political prisoners, payment of a $12 million ransom, safe conduct out of the country – from the humiliated President Somoza. The Sandinist insurrection had begun, re-igniting the flames of Latin American revolution that seemed to have been doused after Fidel Castro seized power in Cuba in 1959.

The revolution quickly came to the boil. Somoza was the latest and most disliked of a long line of family rulers that had amassed some two-fifths of the country's GNP. The regime was propped up by a National

Guard of 7,500 men, acting as a murderous private army for Somoza's personal interests. By grabbing much of the international relief following the 1972 earthquake and rebuilding Managua largely on his own land, Somoza had made many enemies among the country's tiny but influential middle class, who were further incensed in January 1978 when Somoza's thugs gunned down its most respected member, Pedro Joaquin Chamorro, editor of the newspaper *La Prensa*.

The Sandinist revolution had started out twenty years before, led by Carlos Fonseca Amador, a dreamy-eyed Marxist-Leninist who named it to commemorate an anti-American bandit fighter in the 1920s, Augusto Cesar Sandino. Fonseca was killed in 1968, but his co-founder, Tomas Borge Martinez, carried on the movement. Borge ran the movement's Prolonged Popular War (GPP) faction, closely aligned with Fidel Castro's Cuba. The GPP believed that the using guerrilla tactics in the hills against the National Guard was the only way to stage a successful uprising in Nicaragua; however, for a long time the GPP's cause seemed hopeless.

With the seizure of the Chamber of Deputies, the country's terrorized population realised that Somoza was not invulnerable: middle-class youths flocked to the Sandinists, forming a new faction, the Terceristas, around two hard-line Marxist-Leninists, Daniel and Humberto Ortega. Daniel was a brilliant political theoretician and a tub-thumping orator, Humberto the quiet one, a skilful military organizer. Most of their new followers were not Marxist-Leninists, simply Somoza haters. A third faction of the Sandinist movement, the Proletarios, gathered around Comandante Jaime Wheelock, a youthful radical who argued that Somoza could be overthrown only with the support of the urban working class.

The war got under way in earnest in late 1979 as the guerrillas seized cities, relinquishing them when the overworked National Guard (recently swollen to 14,500 untrained men by Somoza) moved in. After the guerrillas took a succession of cities around Managua – Leon, Esteli, Matagalpa – Somoza's men wheeled crazily all over the place in an effort to reoccupy them. The regime's fate was sealed when the Proletarios called on their urban supporters to rise. The slum quarters of every major city, including Managua, erupted into fighting. Somoza's air force savagely bombed the outskirts of his own capital to try and throw the rebels back. The bombing was in vain; the dictator fled on 18 July, thence to embark on a Caribbean cruise, flaunting his pilfered wealth before his starving and long-suffering people before retiring to lechery in Paraguay and an assassin's bullet a year later.

The Sandinist revolution was slow to lower its black and red mask and reveal its ideology. When asked to define the revolution's ideology, Borge told the author that it 'is unique. We are a revolution that derives some inspiration from Cuba and some from other revolutions.' Refusing to describe it as Marxist-Leninist, he believed that eventually the domination of the old ruling classes would be replaced by the domination of 'the People'. At first, too, there was quiet hope in the West that the Sandinist movement would be genuinely nationalist, socialist and democratic, because it was young and popular and had drawn considerable support from a broad spectrum of opinion in Nicaragua – the middle classes, the peasants and the industrial workers.

But the Marxist-Leninist element soon came to the fore. The Ortega brothers forged a tight alliance with Borge's GPP group, leaving the huge bulk of the Terceristas out in the cold and the Proletarian faction isolated on the left. Eden Pastora was given a lowly job as Deputy Interior Minister under Borge's eye. Independent trade unions and peace organizations loyal to the Proletarios were banned and their leader, Wheelock, was compelled to adopt a laid-back radicalism.

The revolution's direction became clear as the Sandinists shelved their promise to hold a general election within months of coming to office and postponed voting, first until 1983 and then until 1985, explaining that time was needed to organise the poll. But Borge happily pointed out that elections were not that important. 'Nicaragua already has real democracy, brought about through social improvement, through our anti-illiteracy campaign. We do not reject the idea of going through the motions of formal democracy, but it is of course inconceivable that the Sandinists would not win the elections.'

A long-running battle began between the government and *La Prensa*, Nicaragua's sole independent newspaper, which was banned whenever it voiced even moderately independent criticism. At length, a group of pro-Sandinist journalists attempted to take over the paper and, on being frustrated, walked out to found their own. Nicaragua's Human Rights Commission, based in a seedy downtown block, was besieged by long, patient queues waiting to tell harrowing tales of the tortures still inflicted by the Sandinists upon prisoners and of relatives denounced and arrested as counter-revolutionaries. Around half of the country's economy remained in private hands; but, increasingly, private industrialists were accused of acts of economic sabotage and their factories expropriated. Large areas of land were nationalized on the grounds that they were being badly cultivated by their owners.

Most revealing of all was the growing Cuban presence in the country. Approximately 20,000 Cuban military personnel were thought to have entered the country by the end of 1980, helping to construct a naval base and a large airfield on eastern Nicaragua's Miskito Coast. Cubans staffed the telecommunications network in downtown Managua. The Intercontinental Hotel, a large triangular building dominating the Managua skyline, which had housed Howard Hughes until he was tilted out of the city by the 1972 earthquake, became a favourite Cuban haunt, particularly the Colonial Bar, with its potted plants, ice-cold beer and blissful air conditioning. A whole floor was allocated to the Russian Embassy, with burly Sandinist-supplied security guards chasing off anyone with the temerity to get off the lift there.

In April, 1980, the two moderate non-Sandinist members of the junta the Sandinists had levered into power when they took over resigned: Violeta Chamorro, widow of the murdered newspaper proprietor, who had maintained a dignified refusal even to criticize the regime, and Alfonso Robelo, the leading social democrat on the junta, a young businessman who complained that the Cubans had bugged his office. The Sandinist revolution, far from blazing a new Latin American trail, seemed to be tilting towards the old Soviet model. And yet it did so hesitantly. The private sector was not expropriated immediately: Castro advised the Sandinists that sugar, the one working part of the Cuban economy, should remain in private hands. The Sandinists were also terrified, to begin with, of offending the Catholic Church headed by the Archbishop of Managua, Cardinal Miguel Obando y Bravo, a towering personality whose influence among Nicaraguans was undisputed. The church/state dispute merely simmered until, early in 1982, the Nicaraguan bishops issued a pastoral letter denouncing the Sandinists' forcible resettlement of some 13,000 Miskito Indians because they objected to having atheistic socialism imposed upon them.

The Sandinists launched a vigorous counter-attack. 'We are not afraid of their cassocks,' declared Borge roundly. An aide of the Archbishop was stripped by Sandinists and accused in front of a jeering mob of having been caught 'in flagrante delicto' with a girlfriend. Shortly afterwards the Sandinists declared that martial law had been imposed and civil liberties had been suspended for a month, which became eight months and then a year. Nicaragua was still a freer society than most socialist countries, but it had passed the point of no return.

The Sandinist revolution was the only classical, old-style Marxist-Leninist revolution since Castro's in Cuba. Its causes were the astounding backwardness of Nicaragua and Somoza's excesses; his regime was a classically incompetent military dictatorship relying on too small an army to repress the population. The emerging middle class ultimately drifted away from him.

There was also a profound dose of anti-Americanism in the Nicaraguan revolution, described by one ambassador in Managua to the author as 'Iranian' in its extremism, the Nicaraguan model thereby following the stereotype of modern revolutions. The drift towards authoritarianism, the rapid militarization of the country – within three years, 55,000 men were under arms compared with 7,000 under Somoza – and the refusal to submit itself to popular endorsement, showed how the Nicaraguan regime followed a classic Marxist-Leninist path for an underdeveloped country.

Nicaragua became the exemplar for, and exporter of, revolution through armed force to its equally backward neighbours. The arms that suddenly started trundling out of the country started a brush fire of revolution in El Salvador and Guatemala. In El Salvador, the various strands in a small guerrilla movement united to form the Farabundo Marti National Liberation Front (FMLN), which swelled to 6,000 men and began to pose a major challenge to the government. The FMLN were supported by some social democrats, like Guillermo Ungo and Ruben Zamora, who headed the small front organization, the Democratic Revolutionary Front; but its hard-line leaders – Cayetano Carpio and Joaquin Villalobos – were orthodox Marxist-Leninists.

The insurrection prompted the Americans to support a band of officers who overthrew General Carlos Humberto Romero's repressive military dictatorship and installed, eventually, a civilian front government under a Christian Democrat, José Napoleon Duarte. Duarte, however, proved unable to control the Right's excesses. The incompetent 18,000-strong Salvadorean army struggled to find the guerrillas in rugged hill country, where they could more or less roam at will. The war settled into a stalemate, with the Americans funnelling arms and aid to the government, and the Cubans supporting the guerrillas.

In Guatemala four separate guerrilla organizations, all of them to some extent Marxist-Leninist – the Guerrilla Army of the Poor, the Revolutionary Organization of the People in Arms, the Guatemalan Workers Party and the Revolutionary People's Army Organization – assembled an army of around 5,000 men to fight the appallingly oppressive government of General Romeo Lucas Garcia, whose death squads were commanded from an office within the presidential palace. Lucas Garcia retaliated by staging bloody army sweeps in the countryside and massacring entire villages, until deposed by the more moderate General Efrain Rios Montt. Rios Montt proved much more adept at dealing with the guerrillas: he ended death squad killings in the cities, which encouraged the local moderates to come out of hiding. In the countryside he ruthlessly pursued the guerrillas but also offered them amnesties as well as food and employment-generating projects for the peasants. Guerrilla violence was kept to a just bearable level.

In Honduras, a small army of terrorists attempted to take over the country after a series of attacks in 1982, but was quickly stamped on by the army. Central America was, by the end of 1983, a perfect validation of the theory that Marxism-Leninism only appealed to backward societies.

PART III

The Collapse

10

The Redeemer

'We want to introduce incentives into industry – within a Leninist framework of course.'

Mikhail Gorbachev

The Last of the Behemoths: Andropov and Chernenko

The reports of Yuri Andropov's condition and personality in the summer of 1983 were conflicting, as they always are about very sick men. Those like the French Foreign Minister, Claude Cheysson, were deeply impressed by his cold, hard, calculating-machine-like intelligence, the hooded, imperturbable eyes, the smile that gave nothing away, the remark that went to the heart of the matter, the absence of a sense of humour. The West was initially apprehensive that the Soviet Union was controlled by a man with a formidable and imaginative intellect who would wrong-foot his adversaries. And then the reports trickled through of the way the tall man stooped, the parchment-yellow complexion, the trembling hands and the long periods in which he seemed unable to comprehend what was being said. Just eight months after succeeding Leonid Brezhnev, it seemed that Yuri Andropov was a sick man.

Andropov was 69 when he took office on a chilly early winter day in Moscow in November 1982. In the first few months he seemed well enough. But by June 1983, he was moving with considerable difficulty. When he met President Koivistoe of Finland that same month, aides supported him on both sides and his hands shook uncontrollably. At a meeting of the Supreme Soviet Andropov spoke while seated – something Brezhnev, even at the end, had rarely had to do.

The first visit by a major Western leader was that by the West German Chancellor, Helmut Kohl. But Andropov not only failed to turn up at the airport but also ducked the inaugural banquet. Andrei Gromyko, the Foreign Minister, claimed that Andropov was absent for 'humanitarian' reasons, notwithstanding suggestions that Kohl's outspokenness in the Soviet Union had warranted the snub.

In fact, health was the cause. Only when Andropov was comfortably seated were television cameras allowed to film the Soviet leader when the two men met. Even so, Andropov's left hand was shaking and German officials noted that he was 'clearly burdened by his physical health' – although his mind was apparently working overtime. Rumour had it that he was on a kidney machine.

Rather than bad luck, it was a commentary on the Soviet system of government that an ailing man of 69 could succeed the 74-year-old Brezhnev. Ironically, Andropov represented the reforming wing of a Soviet Communist Party that seemed to have been, in the twenty-seven years since Khrushchev first tried and failed, impervious to reform.

Andropov's decisive succession appeared to have resolved the struggle between the efficiency-conscious bureaucracy and the populist-minded Party. The ease of the transition astounded outside observers. It had been widely predicted that Brezhnev's death would lead to a power struggle between Andropov, representing the state apparatus, and Konstantin Chernenko, Brezhnev's preferred heir, representing the Party. Politically, Chernenko accepted the bureaucracy's argument that economic reform was necessary but personally favoured wider public consultation, an expansion of the 'popular' – in Soviet terms – power base of the Party and a reduction in defence expenditure in order to stimulate consumer spending. But when it came to the question of Brezhnev's successor, Andropov's stern insistence on discipline and 'efficiency with authority' (see below) won the support of the army that, for the first time, decided to play the kingmaker in Soviet politics and back him and not Chernenko, as did the KGB and the bureaucracy.

The army's role in Soviet politics had grown steadily during the last five years of Brezhnev's rule and reached its apotheosis with the appointment of the Defence Minister, Marshal Dmitri Ustinov, to the Politburo – under Russia's unofficial separation of powers, a separate part of the constitution. Joining Ustinov was Andrei Gromyko, the Foreign Minister; although nominally too low a figure in the bureaucracy to attain Politburo status, Gromyko's power derived from his long service and wholesale domination of the Soviet foreign policy machine in a period when no member of the Politburo could deny its importance.

It was these men who made Andropov Party Secretary. As a former head of the KGB, Andropov's power base was too slender for him to aspire to leadership of the Soviet Union in his own right, since Khrushchev had chopped the sprawling tentacles of Stalin's security services. There is a story of a dry intervention by Andropov as Chernenko addressed foreign policy issues at a Politburo meeting during Brezhnev's last months. 'You know nothing of the subject,' the KGB leader was reported to have sniped. This lack of any experience of the world outside Russia caused Ustinov and Gromyko to judge the tough-minded old-style Party boss as unfit to lead a global superpower.

Andropov was not, as he was portrayed in the West, someone who would relax the system. His period with the KGB convinced him that the state could survive for a long time yet through combining repression with meeting the Russian urge for a better life. Based on his speeches and writings, his views on reform boiled down to the following: industry should be decentralized, greater incentives should be introduced and the regulations governing private plots in the farming sector should be eased. Increased efficiency in the public sector might sustain a very slow rate of growth in the consumer goods sector, to keep ordinary Russians happy, while increased investment expenditure should bring Russia's long-term growth prospects back into line. However, he feared the political consequences of any return of industry to the private sector. And while he knew that military spending was getting out of control and needed to be curbed, his good relations with the armed forces made him loath to implement this.

Hand-in-hand with economic reform, he believed in even tighter political control, which was essential for clamping down on popular dissatisfaction with the slow improvement in Soviet living standards – if indeed they were improving at all.

However, Andropov's plans for reform would remain stymied as long as Chernenko had the support of his ally, the mild-mannered Prime Minister, Nikolai Tikhonov, Brezhnev's appointee; furthermore, Marshal Ustinov, the Defence Minister, was suspicious of Andropov's economic policies and preferred to abstain in Politburo debates on such matters. Thus, to bring about the changes he wanted, Andropov had to neutralize or remove Tikhonov – or cultivate new friends to undermine Chernenko. Furthermore, Andropov did not acquire the added kudos of the largely ceremonial post of President of the Soviet Union until June 1983 (something that took Brezhnev thirteen years). But he showed every sign of asserting his authority decisively from the moment he took office.

He made it clear, from the start, that his objective was reform. Previously the reformers had generally been people like the former Prime Minister, Alexei Kosygin, who had never risen to the commanding heights of being Party Secretary, so Andropov's intentions alarmed a host of vested interests who, during the subsequent months, took advantage of the President's declining health and fought to prevent Chernenko being ousted or neutralized in the way intended by Andropov's supporters.

Andropov's initial actions were, to say the least, modest. The principle one was to inaugurate a commission under Nikolai Ryzhkov to suggest ways of reforming the economy. The head of the Russian planning agency, Gosplan, was despatched to inspect the Eastern European economies to see whether any lessons from them could be applied to Russia. In addition, Andropov launched a major anti-corruption drive to try and undercut the main bases of support of the Brezhnev and Chernenko camps. Still, it remained to be seen whether any firm reform proposals would actually be drawn up, let alone implemented.

Chernenko busily rallied support among those who supported minimal change. At first, in the early months of 1983, an attempt was made to keep him muzzled: he was prevented from attending the meeting in East Berlin to commemorate the 100th anniversary of the death of Karl Marx, the Lenin Birthday celebrations in Moscow on 22 April and, most pointedly of all, the traditional May Day Parade. Andropov also appointed Gromyko, as well as his main protégé, Geidar Aliyev, the rigorously anti-corruption former Party chief in Azerbaijan, as his deputy prime ministers to cramp Chernenko's ally, Prime Minister Tikhonov. This probably put Aliyev in line for Tikhonov's job, and ultimately made him a leading candidate to replace Chernenko, thus opening the way for a thoroughgoing reform of the whole Party that might, in Andropov's view, sweep away Party waste, corruption and chaos and liberate new resources for the productive economy.

But at an oft-postponed meeting of the Central Committee held on 14 and 15 June, the new Soviet strongman failed to remove Chernenko from two key posts: as head of the Central Committee's General Department, where he controlled most Party appointments, and as the Party Secretary responsible for ideology. During this meeting Chernenko also managed to obstruct any new nominations by Andropov to the Central Committee.

Chernenko's continuing role was underlined when he proposed Andropov for the presidency, as he had for the Party secretaryship immediately after Brezhnev's death. His speech took a markedly different line from that normally emanating from the Kremlin. In appealing to the West to maintain 'peaceful coexistence and détente' and omitting any reference to economic reform, Chernenko appeared to be seeking the role of true defender of the values of the Brezhnev regime: that such a difference of opinion surfaced in public at all suggested that the shrewd, if unsophisticated apparatchik was far from a spent force. Was pluralism tentatively entering the highest reaches of the Soviet government?

The answer was yes, but the reason was unexpected. The fears about Andropov's health meant that the hierarchy was holding Chernenko in reserve should Andropov die. Only Chernenko could stave off the challenge of the younger generation jostling for position at the top. The Kremlin's old guard, split into its rival power bases, were united about one thing: the veterans must retain power. The four old men behind Andropov – Gromyko and Tikhonov for the bureaucracy, Ustinov for the army and Chernenko himself for the Party – were afraid of generational change.

In August 1983 Andropov disappeared with, it was claimed, a cold. Only months later was it admitted he was suffering from anything more serious. 'Why,' a senior Soviet official asked the author petulantly when he inquired after Andropov's whereabouts the following New Year, 'do you persist in asking these questions? The health of the Soviet leader is trivial, not a serious matter. Matters of policy are serious, but not these personal matters.' A month later, Andropov was dead of kidney disease.

Konstantin Chernenko was appointed Party Secretary after Andropov's funeral on 14 February 1984, at which he had been a singularly unceremonious master of ceremonies. He could hardly deliver his farewell speech, let alone raise his arm in salute. In his first policy speech on 2 March, Chernenko lost his place in his prepared text, and stumbled over words; he was sweating profusely and even appeared to have trouble breathing. One possible explanation of his manner was his diffidence and nervousness in public, when his career had been spent in silence, acting as Brezhnev's major-domo. In fact he was himself ill. The old man stumbled on for a year, virtually incapable of handling affairs of state, clearly installed as caretaker because of an unresolved power struggle between subordinates. Being terminally ill was his chief recommendation: it meant that the question of the succession could be postponed, although while he was in power, Soviet policy was paralyzed.

The Soviet Crisis

During that transition year of 1984, the Soviet Union had finally to confront its ghosts, abandon delusions and face reality, which meant confronting four central issues: the economy; international isolation; the war in Afghanistan; and the role of the Party. To take economics first: no member of the Soviet governing class with access to the real figures for the Soviet economy instead of the interminable tannoy ones announced to ordinary Russians could harbour any illusion: it was in terrible condition. Excluding a few 'shop window' areas, on which resources were lavished, such as defence-related industries, the space programme, some areas of medicine and a few selected areas of industry, the rest of the economy was simply grinding to a halt.

The economic crisis was a central reason for Andropov's election. Brezhnev's populism in encouraging consumer spending had devastated industrial investment, which from growing at 7 per cent in the mid-1970s fell to 1.5 per cent in 1981, improving only a little in 1982. This pandering to the masses alarmed the army, which was concerned by the evidence of the Brezhnev government's financial irresponsibility and was eager to hang onto its share of government spending (a whopping 14 per cent of GDP).

Worse still, the banks were closing in. According to a memorandum circulated within the senior bureaucracy two years later, the Soviet Union owed the West the colossal figure for those days of some $30 billion– a figure projected to rise to some $350 billion by the year 2000.

The memorandum noted that this would entail spending about three-quarters of Russia's export earnings on debt servicing, and echoed the opinions of independent Western observers:

> The results of this analysis show that our country has reached a limit beyond which lies an insurmountable lag in economic and scientific-technical development behind the advanced industrial nations. The Soviet Union lags ten to fifteen years behind the capitalist countries in its

economic development, and this lag is growing. The USSR is now on the path to becoming one of the under-developed nations.

I was in the Soviet Union around that time, and can vouch for the last statement with a scrap of anecdotal evidence: at Leningrad airport, my luggage was hand-wound down to the luggage area below – something I had not seen even in the most primitive Third World airports, let alone the second city of a world superpower.

The second stark factor facing the new Soviet elite was international isolation. Soviet foreign policy had failed just as comprehensively as economic policy. The great hopes following America's defeat in Vietnam had yet to materialize. In the east Soviet expansionism had been checked by Chinese hostility, which had also blocked further Soviet gains in South-East Asia. In Latin America revolutionary causes were running into the ground. In the Middle East disillusion with Russia was as great as with the United States. In Western Europe popular communist movements were in retreat; and in Africa the Soviet Union was mired in unwinnable colonial wars. Added to all this, the international condemnation of Russia for human rights abuses merely served to make an already bleak picture even bleaker

A further major battle now impinged on the Soviet consciousness: the Soviet deployment of modernized intermediate-range SS-20 missiles targeted at Western Europe thoroughly alarmed NATO's European members. The German Chancellor, Helmut Schmidt, in particular, argued that the missiles should be included in the Strategic Arms Limitation Talks governing intercontinental missiles stationed in the United States and the Soviet Union. But the latter refused, encouraging European fears of a deal being cut above their heads that would leave Western Europe vulnerable to a Soviet nuclear strike, a massive Soviet conventional attack (there was a huge disparity in conventional forces between Eastern and Western Europe), or simple blackmail: would the Americans really risk nuclear annihilation to come to the aid of their European allies?

Despite widespread popular protest in Western Europe, the Americans agreed to deploy Pershing II missiles as well as newly developed cruise missiles in Western Europe to counter the Soviet SS-20s. In retrospect the Russian modernization of its SS-20s was probably regarded as a cheap means of gaining an advantage over the West – but little had prepared them for the vigour of the Western reaction.

Now much worse beckoned, from the Russian point of view. With Ronald Reagan succeeding Jimmy Carter in 1981, the nearly bankrupt Soviet economy faced an arms race without limits. Reagan announced a $33 billion increase in defence spending, a jump of some 50 per cent, amounting to 7 per cent of GDP. Reagan declared, 'So far as an arms race is concerned, there's one going on right now, but there's only one side racing.'

In 1983 he launched the concept of 'Star Wars', the Strategic Defence Initiative, to develop a comprehensive system of global defence based on lasers in space to intercept incoming missiles. If successful, the Americans would keep the option of a first strike against the Russians while denying it – and indeed any prospect of successful retaliation – to the Russians. The alarm that the prospect of a further massively expensive twist in the arms race induced among Soviet leaders, particularly the new generation, cannot be exaggerated. Eduard Shevardnadze, the future Foreign Minister, estimated that 50 per cent of Russia's GDP was being devoted to defence spending – in itself an explanation for this potential immensely wealthy country's backwardness. Even so, Russia was barely keeping up with the United States and its allies on defence. Now, with an economy plunging to Third World levels, Russia would have to spend billions more, while the American offer to share Star Wars technology adding an ironic extra twist to this ruinously expensive race.

I was an official guest of the Soviet government as a member of the House of Commons Foreign Affairs Select Committee soon afterwards, and virtually every senior general and official I met returned remorselessly to the need to persuade America to abandon Star Wars. The Russians were, frankly, terrified of the cost of Star Wars, and feared that President Reagan intended to go ahead with such a system. Undoubtedly the Reagan administration's position was to some extent a bluff: the technology was barely developed, the cost to the United States, although bearable, would be staggering, and many argued that such a system was impossible to perfect. Even so, the Russians could not afford to call Reagan's bluff for fear of self-immolating their ailing economy, which would deliver the coup de grâce to their own development. My own suspicion was that Reagan was terrifying the Russians into talking, but had no illusions about Star Wars, and only intended developing it on a very small scale. In my opinion it was one of the most successful bluffs in history.

Another consideration for the Soviet Union was the war in

Afghanistan, embarked upon with such certainty when the military establishment's influence in Russia was at its peak. It had gone on for years and was clearly unwinnable, with Soviet casualties proportionately approaching American levels in Vietnam and with tens of thousands of families afflicted by bereavement. In a country without a free media, information was much more patchy than in America during the Vietnam War; but nevertheless it spread remorselessly, by word of mouth. In addition the invasion of Afghanistan had tilted much of the non-aligned world against the Soviet Union, dramatically reversing its previous anti-American stance. The effect of the war upon Soviet society was almost as profound as Vietnam had been upon the United States.

Finally, the new Soviet elite had to look afresh at the significance of the Communist Party. It still formally represented the people, and change could only take place under its auspices and within the context of Marxist-Leninist ideology. But if the new generation, young, moderate and rational, could open up the Party and loosen its control from top to bottom, this might induce a genuine debate about the best way forwards – which, in those days, was as much as rigid Party control would tolerate on the question of reform.

Once again, it should be emphasized that this was the third generation of Soviet communists since the 1917 revolution. The first, represented through most of the early period by Stalin, was brutalized, traumatized and terrified by tyranny, mass upheaval, and war. The second was so desperate for security and easy living under conditions of very modest prosperity – nevertheless far more than their parents had enjoyed – that they ejected the talented and moderate, but overactive and erratic, Khrushchev to secure this. As the Soviet Union coasted gently into decline, their children, now a substantial middle class, were impatient for a turnaround – and unsurprisingly many Russians preferred not to have their grim, impoverished lives interrupted and even hankered after a new Stalin. The emergent middle class of fifty-somethings, although a small proportion of the Soviet population as a whole, was however now at last achieving control.

Confronted by an economy on the verge of collapse, a seemingly determined, belligerent America resolved to run it into the ground, a war wasting thousands of young lives and an inert political system, the old men at the top of the Politburo representing the four traditional pillars of the Soviet system – the Party, the bureaucracy, the armed forces and the security apparatus – now at last had to choose.

To recap: Brezhnev, representing the most stultified and corrupt Party bosses, had joined with the armed forces (a political-military-industrial complex) to (peaceably) elbow aside the architect of Khrushchev's fall, Kosygin, blunting his administrative reforms for nearly two decades, so that a weak Prime Minister, Nikolai Tikhonov, was unable to carry them out. As the Brezhnev era drew to a close, amid widespread cynicism towards the Party's corruption and lack of responsiveness (although no one supposed it would lose its total monopoly) Brezhnev increasingly depended on the armed forces and to a lesser extent the security apparatus, allowing the former free rein to resolve the Afghanistan problem through military means.

When this turned to disaster, the reformists within the bureaucracy and the KGB (by no means convinced of the wisdom of invading Afghanistan) united behind Andropov, who sought an end to the arms race and economic regeneration. Andropov was the first Soviet leader since 1917 not to head the Communist Party (apart from the brief Malenkov interregnum) and his accession signalled the complete disrepute into which it had fallen after Brezhnev: he was in fact used to block the rise to power of Konstantin Chernenko, an old-style, corrupt, once formidable but now ailing Party leader in the Brezhnev mould. However Andropov's attempt to end the arms race and even to renounce using force in controlling Eastern Europe (he had been the Soviet Ambassador in Hungary during the invasion in 1956) was met with deep suspicion in the West, and coincided with Reagan's early years in office.

With Andropov's sudden death, it proved impossible to block Chernenko, who was supported by the discredited armed forces and the most conservative elements in the Party. But the old guard were losing their grip: most of the bureaucracy, now loyal to the veteran Andrei Gromyko, the KGB and the reformist elements in the Party, as well as officers sickened by the disaster in Afghanistan, rallied behind a former Andropov protégé, the Politburo's youngest member and a senior Party figure, Mikhail Gorbachev, aged just 54.

Gorbachev Takes the Reins

Gorbachev was one of five fast-rising representatives of the younger generation of the Politburo. The others were Vitali Vorotnikov; Yegor

Ligachev; Eduard Shevardnadze; and Boris Yeltsin. Vorotnikov, an unashamed defender of the ancien régime, was unacceptable to the reformist wing. Ligachev was an able, pragmatic conservative, slightly younger than Gorbachev. Shevardnadze had made too many enemies from his anti-corruption campaigns against the old guard in Georgia. Yeltsin was too raw and untested. Only Gorbachev and Ligachev were really in the running.

To this day, one can only speculate how within the heart of the Soviet system someone of Gorbachev's views rose to the very top and whether he harboured his secret reformism while he did so, preparing to dismantle the colossal apparatus, (the most formidable totalitarian system ever constructed) that nurtured him. To anyone who knew the country before Gorbachev's accession to power, that the system would be dismantled so quickly, or that a Soviet leader of all people would be the agent of change seemed inconceivable

However evident the rot by 1985, however creaking and foundering the Soviet economy, however derided Brezhnev, Chernenko and the gerontocrats, however triumphal Reagan and his advisers, the system – apparently cast in concrete – seemed only capable of superficial change. Only the most prescient could have believed that the system was on the verge of collapse or that within five years the Soviet domination in Eastern Europe would have ended, the Soviet Union itself would have been dismembered and Russia would be on the verge of democracy. All this would be down to one man. Was this intended, or accidental? The answer seems no clearer today than at the time.

Mikhail Sergeyevich Gorbachev was born on 2 March 1931 in Privolnoe, southern Russia, the son of a collective farm tractor driver and thus of impeccably proletarian origins. Clearly extremely bright as a young student, he won a place at the most competitive and elitist of Russian educational institutions, Moscow State University, where he displayed high intelligence and, as far as can be discovered, entirely orthodox communist political leanings. He returned to Stavropol in southern Russia and joined the Communist Party at the age of 21, soon leading the Komsomol (young communists) of the town. There he met the attractive, formidably intelligent and outspoken Raisa Maximovna.

With his experience in agriculture, he joined the Stavropol Agricultural Institute at the age of 35, also becoming Secretary to the Stavropol City Communist Party. He was obviously bright to have advanced so far so fast, but had pursued a largely provincial career. Within a year he had been elected to the Supreme Soviet, the rubber stamp parliament, an honour that reflected his superiors' perception of his abilities, and a year later to the Central Committee of the Party, its real parliament.

Now he could shine. As Party Secretary in Stavropol with considerable freedom of action, he made friends with an exact contemporary, Boris Yeltsin, who held the same position in the industrial region of Sverdlovsk; they would barter agricultural and industrial produce under the command economy. But unlike Yeltsin, Gorbachev had become a figure of substance on the Central Committee and was talent-spotted by Andropov and Gromyko, among others, his mentor being Alexander Yakovlev, the brilliant academic head of Moscow's most influential think tank, the Institute for the Study of World Economy and International Relations. Up to this point Gorbachev, although intellectually curious and open-minded, showed no sign of unorthodox thinking; it must be a matter of speculation whether he nurtured secretly radical instincts, or whether the reform-minded Yakovlev sowed the seeds of reform in his institute.

In spite of his humble background and provincial origins, Gorbachev was charming, well dressed, sophisticated and had a mind like quicksilver. Although certainly groomed as a potential Soviet leader from the age of 40, his abilities were his own. In 1978, at the age of 47, he became Secretary of the Central Committee and was given charge of all Soviet agriculture, one of the most important – and difficult – briefs in the country; collective agricultural production had long been stagnant while the non-state sector was thriving. A year later he became an alternate member of the most powerful body in the Soviet Union, the Politburo, and the year after that, at the age of just 49, a full member.

This dazzling ascent shows that a powerful element of the gerontocracy was determined to promote him – not because he wished to dismantle the Soviet system but because he was intelligent and energetic and best embodied the impatience of the younger reformers. He reflected the ideas of both Andropov and Yakovlev: first, drastic economic reform; second, an end to the ruinously expensive arms race; third, a withdrawal from the unwinnable war in Afghanistan and a rejection of the use of force in international disputes; and fourth, a measure of greater internal accountability within the Party. This did not of course extend to ending the Party's monopoly in Russian politics, much less the break-up of the Soviet Union. But it was intensely radical nevertheless by Soviet standards – with meaningful economic reform requiring all three other conditions to be fulfilled.

Gorbachev presented this as requiring much greater discipline and effort within a Leninist context – which would have appealed to both the old and the new guard. The Soviet Union had hit the economic buffers, and needed a hyperactive reformer to take control. Although Gorbachev had ascended the Party hierarchy, his sponsors were Andropov and Gromyko, respectively at the head of the KGB and the bureaucracy; of the last survivors of the 1917 revolution, the wispy-moustached, but still bright-as-a-button, Boris Ponomarev also backed him.

The demise of Chernenko in March 1985 meant it was time for the new generation of the Party to be elevated. The ultra-traditionalists, who wanted the minimum disturbance to the status quo, backed the conservative Ligachev. But Gorbachev was supported by his own generation as well as by Gromyko and Ponomarev, and as he appeared the more dynamic and discipline-minded of the two by securing approval for the introduction of limited incentivization in industry, the succession seemed assured by the end of 1984.

On 3 December he introduced a revolutionary new word into the Russian political dictionary – *perestroika* (restructuring):

> Perestroika means a resolute mass initiative. It is the comprehensive development of democracy, socialist self-government, encouragement of initiative, criticism and self-criticism in all spheres of our society. It is utmost respect for the individual and consideration for personal dignity. Perestroika is the all-round intensification of the Soviet economy, the revival and development of the principles of democratic centralism in running the national economy, the universal introduction of economic methods, the renunciation of management by injunction and in administrative methods, and the overall encouragement of innovation and socialist enterprise.
>
> Perestroika means a resolute shift to scientific methods, and ability to provide a solid scientific basis for every new initiative. It means the revolution with a planned economy.
>
> Perestroika means priority development of the social sphere aimed at ever better satisfaction of the Soviet people's requirements for good living and working conditions, for good rest and recreation, education and health care. It means unceasing concern for cultural and spiritual wealth, for the culture of every individual and society as a whole.
>
> Perestroika means the elimination from society of the distortions of

socialist ethics, the consistent implementation of the principles of social justice. It means the unity of words and deeds, rights and duties. It is the elevation of honest, highly qualified labour, the overcoming of levelling tendencies in pay and consumerism.

This is how we see perestroika today. This is how we see our tasks, and the substance and content of our work for the forthcoming period. It is difficult now to say how long that period will take. Of course, it will be much more than two or three years. We are ready for serious, strenuous and tedious work to ensure that our country reaches new heights by the end of the twentieth century.

He was setting out an agenda. A week later, at a conference in Moscow on ideology, Gorbachev also first referred to *glasnost* (openness) as 'a compulsory condition of socialist democracy and a norm for public life'.

When he came to Britain the same month, I observed Mikhail Gorbachev across a table for three hours when the Soviet Foreign Affairs Committee, of which he was Chairman, met that of the House of Commons, of which I was a member. I doubt whether anyone present, seasoned British politicians like Sir Anthony Kershaw, Peter Thomas, Norman St-John Stevas, Ian Mikardo, Jim Lester, Ivan Lawrence, Denis Canavan, Mick Welsh and Nigel Spearing will ever forget that meeting: we sensed we were witnessing the beginning of a revolution, although none of us anticipated just how far it would go.

A number of things immediately struck me. Although he only held a junior office, Gorbachev totally dominated his delegation, which included senior Russian generals who would speak only if he asked them to. Highly articulate, completely self-confident and in command of his brief, he had a mind and ease of manner and delivery that would have shamed most Western democratic politicians, let alone the wooden Russians we had met previously. He was formidably intelligent (our experience as a committee was that the older ones would spout propaganda at length, often reading, while the younger ones would hardly speak at all; Ian Mikardo would do a weary gesture of a gramophone going round as one of the former started up). Points were bounced back at us with complete intellectual ease.

Perhaps most remarkably, he had a highly developed sense of humour and irony, often cracking jokes or making humorous asides. When, western-style, we all tried to get in a question simultaneously he remarked of Anthony Kershaw, 'you are obviously a very democratic chairman'. This easy bantering was the exact reverse of every senior Soviet figure we had encountered before. Indeed, although precise and to the point, verbosity was his main problem as a speaker (famously, his Russian mimics would end long, repetitive statements with the phrase, 'that's the first point'). My own diary records that Gorbachev, although unsurprisingly cautious and orthodox in his views (he had not after all yet succeeded Chernenko) made clear that his priority was economic development through an end to the arms race.

> The foreign policy of a nation is inseparable from developments on its domestic scene, from its socio-economic goals and requirements. As K.U. Chernenko . . . put it recently, the chief aim of our plans is, proceeding from the results of Soviet citizens' work which becomes more and more efficient, to raise the prosperity of the nation by boosting the living and cultural standards of the people. Our party and state in general emphasize economic advance through efficiency and intensive growth factors. We concentrate on the early introduction of the latest achievements of science and engineering in industry and agriculture. Using the fruits of the current revolution in science and technology, we are tackling targets to be reached by the year 2000. The Soviet Union needs peace to implement its huge development programmes.

I believed he was being honest about this, and that it was the cost of a Star Wars arms race that was propelling Russia to the negotiating table. His opposition to Star Wars was total, and he revealed to us that Russia was ready to negotiate not only 'the non-militarization of space', but also the question of 'reducing nuclear arms, both strategic and medium range'.

Gorbachev was tough about one thing (ironically, in view of later developments): the post-Yalta boundaries of Europe:

> The peoples of our continent paid dearly for realizing that under no circumstances shall they indulge the forces which have not given up attempts to change the post-war territorial realities in Europe . . . These realities have been sealed in the allied agreements on the post-war European set-up; major bilateral treaties and the Helsinki Final Act [also known as the Helsinki Accords]. Sticking to the documents would halt those who would throw in doubt the results of the Second World War and post-war developments and the inviolability of frontiers in Europe. There can be no ambiguity on this score.

Gorbachev told us frankly that 'we want to have prosperity through efficiency and growth' and argued that this depended on progress in foreign policy. In answer to a question about Ethiopia, he spoke warmly of 'Comrade Mengistu' and insisted that it was wrong to suggest that Russia 'has limited itself to delivering arms to Ethiopia' during the famine there – tacitly acknowledging that these comprised the main Soviet exports to that country. When Islamic militancy in southern Russia was raised, he looked studiously through his gold-rimmed spectacles. 'We have achieved great changes in the Asian republics, in pursuing equality. On the other hand,' he claimed, 'there has been adherence to Islam there.' But he added, 'It is wishful thinking to suggest that allegedly big processes (Islamic fundamentalism) are under way.' Islam had reacted principally against imperialist aggression. 'We are on the side of this. But we do not support Islamic fanaticism. We even condemn it.'

Norman St-John Stevas asked him about human rights. He went into a controlled tirade. 'The only clergymen put on trial have been guilty of violations of specific laws. We have only taken action against anti-Soviet groups. We have only taken action against those clerics who do not respond to our spiritual values. We have always reacted to violations of the law.' He went on to call these 'insignificant issues'. And if it came to discussing human rights violations, 'there are 2.3 million unemployed in your country'.

He returned to his central theme – the need to control Star Wars – when nuclear weapons were mentioned again 'If space weapons are deployed, verification will be very difficult. It will be impossible to verify which warhead is fixed.' He said the Soviet Union was ready to discuss both strategic and medium-range weapons.

His response to Norman on human rights had been loud, but wholly calculated, very different from Khrushchev's celebrated altercation with George Brown. His other answers had been informative and reasoned. Afterwards, when I asked him directly about economic reform, he replied, 'We want to decentralize industry and introduce industrial incentives in industry, as well as new technology – just like your ICI [he had just visited an ICI plant] – and then added, as an afterthought – 'within a Leninist framework, of course.' Like everyone present, I had no doubt that he knew he would be chosen to succeed Chernenko, and that the latter was at death's door. A few days later he cut short his visit to attend to the ailing Soviet leader, who died on 10 March.

Gorbachev was proposed as General Secretary by Gromyko, and seconded by Tikhonov, the Prime Minister, a conservative who had earlier opposed the nomination. The new young leader moved with extraordinary speed and vigour in pursuit of his four main aims – economic revitalization, an end to the arms race, withdrawal from Afghanistan and greater democracy within the Party. In addition he echoed Andropov's almost unnoticed view that force should not be used against client states.

The goals were truly radical – but emphatically did not include the end of the monopoly of the Communist Party in Russia or the introduction of competitive, pluralist elections. Gorbachev's priority was to achieve peace, thus saving huge amounts of money, and to radically incentivize the economy. He set this out in his book *Perestroika* (published in the UK in 1987) calling for the 'most radical programme of economic reform of our century . . . since Lenin introduced his new economic policy in 1921':

> The reform is based on dramatically increased independence of enterprises and associations, their transition to full self-accounting and self-financing, and granting all appropriate rights to work collectives. They will now be fully responsible for efficient management and end results. A collective's profits will be directly proportionate to its efficiency.
>
> . . . We will free the central management of operational functions in the running of enterprises and this will enable it to concentrate on key processes determining the strategy of economic growth. To make this a reality we launched a serious radical reform in planning, price formation, the financial and crediting mechanism, the network of material and technological production supplies, and the management of scientific and technological progress, labour and the social sphere. The aim of this reform is to ensure – within the next two or three years – the transition from an excessively centralized management system relying on orders, to a democratic one, based on the combination of democratic centralism and self-management.

All this was radical enough. But perestroika and glasnost were not to be allowed to derail the primacy of socialism and the Party, as he made clear:

> We are not going to change Soviet power, of course, or abandon its fundamental principles, but we acknowledge the need for changes that will strengthen socialism and make it more dynamic and politically meaningful. That is why we have every reason to characterize our plans for the full-scale democratization of Soviet society as a program for changes in our political system . . .
>
> It may seem that our current perestroika could be called a 'revolution from above'. True, the perestroika drive started on the Communist Party's

initiative, and the Party leads it. The Party is strong and bold enough to work out a new policy. It has proved capable of heading and launching the process of renewal of society . . .

. . . The restructuring concerns all, from rank-and-file communist to Central Committee secretary, from shop floor worker to minister, from engineer to Academician. It can be brought to a successful end only if it is truly a nationwide effort. But in any case, everyone must work honestly and conscientiously, sparing no efforts and abilities. Such a movement will gradually involve more and more people.

Glasnost was an essential accompaniment to perestroika. Gorbachev condemned excessive secrecy: 'We have grown accustomed to many practices when there was no openness. This applies to both the rank and file and high officials.' The Russian people, he continued, '. . . must know the truth. One mustn't be afraid of one's own people. Openness is an attribute of socialism. But there are still some people, in the higher echelons too, who speak about socialist ethics for all and of a surrogate kind for themselves: that is, something that suits their selfish ends. That won't do.'

However, this was easier to say than put into practice; for example, Gorbachev's concept of press freedom, while a large step forward from blanket censorship, was limited. Gorbachev immediately embarked upon a whirlwind of activity, purging the Party structure and launching a deeply unpopular campaign against alcoholism. By 1986 he felt strong enough to undertake major economic reforms, declaring that major loss-making factories would be allowed to go bankrupt and limited private enterprises would be permitted – no more than an acknowledgement of the huge black economy.

In November 1985 he had held an emergency summit with President Reagan at which the two men got along but without real progress. In January 1986 he proposed to the startled Americans the elimination of all nuclear weapons by the year 2000; both sides should also remove all intermediate range nuclear missiles in Europe. This was received with deep scepticism in the West.

At a private meeting in the Kremlin in mid-1985, when I raised the issue of the Soviet invasion of Afghanistan, Boris Ponomarev, the Politburo member, told me unequivocally that 'Russia wishes to withdraw; the sooner the better'. The decision had already been taken in principle, although I found disbelief when I reported this back home. In July 1986, Gorbachev announced the Soviet withdrawal from Afghanistan, the country's biggest defeat since the Second World

War, comparable to America's humiliation in Vietnam. Meanwhile, Gromyko, the Foreign Minister, had been elevated to the presidency, where he continued to act as a prop to Gorbachev on behalf of the conservative wing of the bureaucracy. One of Gorbachev's chief reforming allies, Eduard Shevardnadze, became Foreign Minister, while another, Yakovlev, was given charge of the media.

At the end of 1986 Gorbachev startled the world by announcing that the internal exile of the world's most celebrated dissident, Andrei Sakharov, was over. Earlier in that same year, another prominent dissident, Anatoli Sharansky, had been permitted to leave the Soviet Union for Israel after nine years in prison. Gorbachev's espousal of perestroika and glasnost meant an easing of the harsh restrictions on artists and dissidents. Most of the several hundred dissidents jailed by Brezhnev were released. Religious freedom was at last fully permitted. Books were published criticizing not just Stalin but Brezhnev and corrupt Soviet bureaucracy in general. By the end of the Gorbachev era, virtually all political prisoners had been released and there were almost no restrictions on cultural expression, while press criticism flourished.

In October a second summit with Reagan took place at Reykjavik. In the presence of an astonished American Secretary of State, George Schultz, Gorbachev proposed the complete withdrawal of intermediate nuclear missiles in Europe and the elimination of all strategic nuclear weapons over a ten-year period. Even more astonishingly, Reagan agreed, with Schultz's full support; this was no mistake by an ageing leader, but represented the policy of the American State Department at the time. It entailed, effectively, the withdrawal of America's nuclear umbrella over Western Europe – which appalled America's European allies. However Gorbachev unwisely also insisted that Star Wars development be confined to the laboratory, and Reagan, whose baby this was, refused, invalidating the whole agreement.

Once again, it seemed that Gorbachev was a dynamic, vigorous, young and entirely different kind of Soviet leader – but one ultimately unwilling to break free from the system that had incubated him. To cold war warriors in the West he was deeply sinister – a man who appeared to present a new face for the regime while espousing the old ideals. His public relations were a triumph, particularly in the West. In place of remote, shuffling, elderly leaders here was a man unafraid to visit workers' homes and hospitals with only a tiny entourage and ask pointed questions. The Tsarist remoteness of Lenin, Stalin and Brezhnev had

been replaced by something of the approachability of a Western politician. Martin Walker of the *Guardian* recalls one such visit:

> He blithely breaks all the political rules in his walkabouts. In his tour in
> Moscow's Proletarsky district, he arrived with just two cars. Nor was he
> escorted by the Moscow Party boss Victor Grishin, a breach with trad-
> itional protocol akin to the Queen pottering about the City of London
> without having informed the Lord Mayor. Indeed I gather that Mr
> Grishin only came along on the second day because Mr Gorbachev was
> hearing so many accounts of bad housing and unreliable food supplies
> that he told an aide: 'Grishin ought to be listening to that.'
>
> His visit to the kindergarten was unplanned. He had seen a young
> couple in the street, gone to talk to them, learned that they were going to
> pick up their child, and asked to come along. After chatting with parents
> there, Mr Gorbachev invited himself to the young couple's home for 'a
> glass of tea'.
>
> He came well briefed. In the virtually obligatory visit to the hospital he
> asked the doctors what problems they had. None at all, they choroused.
> Everything just fine. He began to probe . . . Then the doctors began to
> say what everyone in Russia knows, that shortages of medical supplies are
> endemic.
>
> 'So why not tell me so in the first place?' Mr Gorbachev asked. There
> was silence, and then a young doctor said: 'It's too hard to remember
> everything we don't have. The list is so long.' Then Mr Gorbachev went
> over to the group of nursing aides peering round the door, and picked out
> an elderly woman. 'How much do you earn, Granny?' She got 110 roubles
> a month, about two-thirds of the average wage, and she had been working
> there for thirty years. Mr Gorbachev began to ask her how she got by, and
> one of the hospital officials said that of course she could always get a part-
> time job. Mr Gorbachev froze him with a look. 'You had better start
> paying them enough.'

But that was all he appeared to be: public relations. His masterful
peace offensive had, it seemed, caught the American leadership on the
hop, but had progressed no further; his economic reforms were soon
effectively stalled – with Russians grumbling bitterly about his vodka
ban; the press was somewhat less tightly controlled and Sakharov had
been released as a gesture. The withdrawal from Afghanistan was a major
step – but not a sign of the new spirit of reform, rather an acknowledgement of Soviet defeat and disengagement from a costly and unwinnable
enterprise. In reality, for ordinary Russians, nothing fundamental had
changed.

II

Whirlwind

'Life punishes those who come too late.'

Mikhail Gorbachev

The Unravelling

Sceptical Western observers failed to realize that Gorbachev was indeed sincere in his reform proposals – but that he was locked into a bitter power struggle, as they were being blocked by the system of collective leadership developed during the Brezhnev years. The General Secretary was not a dictator, as in Stalin's and Khrushchev's time; there was a separation of powers as well as checks and balances, even a degree of pluralism, in the leadership, American-style, which in this case was condemning it to inertia. Gromyko, representing the old men in the bureaucracy, had combined with the conservatives in the armed forces and the KGB to back the minority anti-reformist wing of the Party led by Yegor Ligachev, a man almost of Gorbachev's generation.

Gromyko, the latter's patron, furious both at being kicked upstairs to the largely ceremonial position of President and at the radical changes in Soviet foreign policy, was no longer Gorbachev's ally. Gorbachev realized that speed was essential to prevent his reform programme being paralyzed, or even his replacement by Ligachev. The only solution was the one he had avoided because it would create too many enemies within the Party – radical political reform.

Gorbachev later maintained that his frustration at the blockage of economic reform propelled this decision, and there is no reason to doubt this version of events: he had not taken power as a politically radical and subversive pluralist, but as an orthodox communist determined to improve the system within the framework of a one-party state. Clearly, no one knows what he thought at the time; but this author suspects that a man of his intellect was well aware of the possible consequences of political reform (although not their full extent) and even secretly favoured them; there were plenty of diehard opponents to alert him to the dangers.

His conversion to political reform at the end of 1985 marked the turning point after which the Russian Revolution began to crumble through the disintegration of the entire power structure. (This would, incidentally, have a massive impact on China, where full-scale economic reform was undertaken to prevent the collapse of the Party's political authority, as was to happen in Russia.)

In January 1987, he took the first tentative step, proposing that senior Party officials should be elected by secret ballot, to enable his supporters to replace the apparatchiks undermined by the radicalism at the top. This placed the old guard in an impasse: they were horrified by his proposed reforms, but challenging the General Secretary's authority just after his appointment would attack the lynchpin of the system they were defending.

At about this time the first of several rumours concerning an attempt on Gorbachev's life began to circulate. Gromyko, faced by this dilemma, decided in June to support the General Secretary. Throughout the year Gorbachev and his supporters would steadily capture the higher echelons of the Party.

While this was going on, he decided on an entirely typical and ultimately fatal manoeuvre, although he could not foresee it at the time. In 1985 he had appointed Boris Yeltsin, his old friend from Sverdlovsk, to run the Party machine in Moscow, replacing the dinosaur-like Viktor Grishin. Yeltsin promptly embarked on a populist campaign of denouncing Party bosses for their corruption and perks, while riding the Moscow underground (the best in the world) and hobnobbing with ordinary people. This horrified the old guard; it seemed that a subversive was running Russia's capital city.

Gorbachev was also appalled by Yeltsin's crude populism, clearly designed to appeal to a working class constituency (in a possibly democratic Russia) just as Gorbachev epitomized the newly dominant middle classes. In addition, Yeltsin publicly charged that Gorbachev was under his wife, Raisa's, thumb – an unprecedented display of *lèse-majesté* towards the head of state. Gorbachev decided to authorize the public humiliation of Yeltsin before the Moscow Communist Party apparatus. As successive speakers denounced Yeltsin, the latter seemed entirely broken; Gorbachev from the podium, laid a consoling hand on his shoulder. It had been a humiliation worthy of one of Stalin's purges and would have crushed a lesser man.

Gorbachev felt that by dismissing an over-eager subordinate and thus consolidating his authority, he had secured the grudging respect of conservatives; firing Yeltsin demonstrated that he was not a dangerous radical. It was one clever tactic too many, although one Gorbachev must have considered essential as a sacrifice to the old guard to enable his reform programme to proceed. Gorbachev had no way of knowing that he had now created his deadliest foe – indeed, his political assassin.

As Gorbachev consolidated his authority, he personally attacked Stalin, and by implication the crabbed generation of conservatives that had ruled in his shadow ever since. Stalin, he announced, committed 'unforgivable crimes'.

> The guilt of Stalin and his immediate entourage before the Party and the people for the wholesale repressions and acts of lawlessness is enormous and unforgivable. This is a lesson for all generations.
>
> Those were real crimes stemming from an abuse of power. Many thousands of people inside and outside the Party were subjected to wholesale repressive measures. That, comrades, is the bitter truth . . .

He went on, significantly alluding to Khrushchev, that 'the failures of the reforms undertaken in that period were mainly due to the fact that they were not backed up by a broad development of democratization'. He had wielded the sword of democracy to cut the Gordian knot of obstruction to his rule – without realizing that the sword could be turned against him. Even at this stage it seems unlikely that Gorbachev appreciated the full consequences of political reform upon the Soviet Union and the monopoly of the Party.

At the end of 1987 he had his first real foreign policy success. Early in the year he had revived the proposal for withdrawing intermediate range nuclear forces from Europe, but this time neither linked to an end of America's development of its Star Wars project nor the inclusion of the British and French nuclear forces. At long last another summit was held in Washington. After careful preparation, the INF deal was agreed, although no progress was made on strategic long-range nuclear missiles. Gorbachev's reception by the American public was ecstatic:

'Gorbymania' was born. His moderation, approachability and above all his ability to communicate intelligently and decisively were so far removed from the old style of Soviet leadership, and even it seemed of Western leadership, that Americans adored him. But it was widely noted, too, that he was more popular abroad than at home.

This was because the problems in the Soviet Union were more entrenched. With the economic reform programme stalled, the hopes of ordinary Russians had reverted to deep cynicism; meanwhile Gorbachev's confrontation with the huge Soviet apparatus had provoked furious conservative accusations of bringing about the disintegration of the Soviet system. By early 1988, after nearly three years, Gorbachev's leadership seemed to be drifting.

In fact in the previous year he had carefully prepared a strike against his enemies. In May 1988 he announced his reforms were being opposed at the apex of the Communist Party – thereby acknowledging his power struggle with Ligachev. The same month President Reagan, visiting Moscow for the first time, was charmed by his encounter with ordinary Russians – but this was no substitute for little progress on disarmament.

Gorbachev had other things on his mind. In June he convened a Communist Party Congress for the first time in half a century, thus bypassing all its usual structures. Using an institution packed by his own supporters, he announced that real power was to pass from the Party to an elected parliament, naturally still dominated by the Party (otherwise the congress would not have approved it).

In October, reinforced by the decisions of the congress, he moved still more decisively: Gromyko was dismissed as President and, a little later, Gorbachev took his place. Ligachev was given the agriculture portfolio, a significant demotion. The hard-line KGB chief, Viktor Chebrikov, was replaced by Vladimir Kryuchkov, and, in a break with tradition, both the KGB and the Defence Ministry lost their traditional seats on the Politburo.

At a stroke, Gorbachev had elbowed aside his main enemy in the Party and shorn it of its power, established his political supremacy over the bureaucracy, represented by Gromyko and the Prime Minister Nikolai Rhyzkov, and lowered the status of the KGB and the army, both of which had suffered a significant loss of prestige with the disaster in Afghanistan. The calling of the congress to bypass both the Central Committee and the Politburo was masterful, worthy of Lenin himself. And it was bold, because Gorbachev was elevating his own personal power above all the traditional centres of Russian power, which left him dangerously exposed. What claim had he to authority other than leadership of the Party, which he had now cut adrift? He had been elected to his present office only by the Party's apparatchiks, whom he now treated with contempt. He was an emperor without clothes.

His only alternative was to anchor his authority in popular legitimacy, as a constitutional president responsible to an elected parliament – neither of which yet existed. It was a deeply dangerous gamble, and a measure of his extraordinary courage and self-confidence that he undertook it. By proposing that power devolve to an elected parliament he was initiating the end of the monopoly of power in the world's largest country. For a moment his conservative opponents seemed too stunned to react, while the radical opposition, increasingly dominated by the bitterly resentful Yeltsin, had been wrong-footed and dared not raise its head.

Gorbachev ended this extraordinary year with another bold move; in an address to the United Nations in New York, he astonishingly pledged to reduce unilaterally the Soviet armed forces by 500,000 in two years and to withdraw 50,000 troops and 5,000 tanks from Eastern Europe. He also announced major reductions in Soviet troops along the Chinese border. Less widely reported, but even more important, was his repudiation of the Brezhnev doctrine asserting Russia's right to intervene in Eastern Europe.

> It is obvious that force and the threat of force cannot be and should not be an instrument of foreign policy . . . Freedom of choice is . . . a universal principle, and it should know no exceptions . . . The growing variety of options for the social development of different countries is becoming an increasingly tangible hallmark of these processes. This applies to both the capitalist and the socialist systems.

This was a momentous declaration and one carefully noted in Eastern Europe.

The year ended with the first significant signs of unrest inside the Soviet Union: growing tension between Armenia and Azerbaijan after rioting by both communities in each republic. The conservatives took this as the first indication of national disintegration following Gorbachev's relaxation of central control. They were right.

Eastern Europe: All Fall Down

The following year, 1989, saw the reaping of the harvest sowed by Gorbachev during the previous year. Following his astonishing United Nations speech, he systematically brought about the downfall of the old stooge dictatorships of Eastern Europe, compelled to support the Soviet Union for so long, to the incredulity of the old men who ran them and their long-oppressed subjects. If these countries asserted that this was when they suddenly rose up and won their independence, the reality was different: Gorbachev gave it to them.

To Gorbachev, representing the post-Stalin generation, this was simple humanity and common sense: only repression and violence could keep these gerontocractic and unreformed systems in power. The Soviet Union was no longer willing to apply that violence, particularly after the suffering of the Soviet army in Afghanistan, nor to encourage their local proconsuls to do so.

Underlying this was Gorbachev's confidence that the fall of the communist regimes in Eastern Europe would not trigger a Western occupation of their countries and present a military threat to Russian territory – the latter arguably prompting Stalin's annexation of Eastern Europe. Gorbachev's decision and his avoidance of bloodshed in achieving this peaceful revolution would be his finest hour.

When the door of their prison cells was suddenly unlocked, the Eastern Europeans only opened them tentatively and with apprehension. The country that ten years before had been so brutally beaten after its quest for freedom, was the first to test the new climate, followed by an old jailbird whose escape attempt had occurred more than thirty years earlier.

When Mikhail Gorbachev telephoned Poland's new Communist Party chief, Mieczyslaw Rakowski, on 22 August 1989, his words were unambiguous and displayed no Soviet weakness: he told the Polish communists, in effect, to get lost. The Party leadership was 'not accomplishing anything' – and Russia would not block the formation of a new government by the Polish opposition movement, Solidarity.

With that statement, the Soviet hegemony in Eastern Europe was over. Gorbachev wasn't reacting to recent events in Eastern Europe, because as he saw it there had been nothing to react to – indeed, Solidarity, like other Eastern Europe opposition groups, had been baffled by what they saw as Russian inertia. But now he was making a decisive Soviet intervention in favour of freedom: and with the doors opened, everyone could pass through – hence the speed of change in just four months.

How could Solidarity topple so swiftly the military regime installed amid repression and terror just a decade earlier? The process had begun three years earlier, when the regime was forced to accept that Poland's economy was unsalvageable without the workforce's cooperation. General Jaruzelski had imposed martial law in 1980 to avert Brezhnev's threat of an outright Soviet military intervention – and with Jaruzelski's assumption of power, the Communist Party had lost its legitimacy for the first time in an Eastern Europe satellite state to the forces of order, the last resort of any state.

By 1986, Jaruzelski's economic policies, which were primarily directed towards over-dependence on trade with the Soviet Union, had failed. So some modest free-market incentives were introduced and in the following year a referendum was staged to support this, even though it meant three years of economic sacrifice. Surprisingly, the government failed to secure a majority – and even more surprisingly, the vote was genuinely valid. Once more Solidarity struggled back into the limelight, announcing workers' cooperation in exchange for democratization:

> The Polish referendum proves that the restructuring of the economy, of societies, and of public life cannot be achieved against the wishes of society . . . We are ready to enter [into an 'anti-crisis'] pact for the common good, but on one condition: that our right to express and represent our interests is respected.

Solidarity now flexed its muscles again. When food prices were increased by some 40 per cent in 1988, strikes and protest crackled across the country and a further wave erupted in August. Jaruzelski, with a surprisingly acute political sense for a soldier, was well aware of the evolving situation in Moscow, and realized that it was time to talk. He offered direct negotiations with Solidarity and even its legalization in exchange for an end to the unrest. Controversially, and bitterly opposed by many activists, the movement's legendary leader, Lech Walesa, agreed.

In October Rakowski, the most liberal-minded of the Polish communist leaders, became Prime Minister. Although a tough negotiator, he was bludgeoned by Jaruzelski into participating in a 'roundtable' discussion – to emphasize the equality of the partners – with Solidarity, the Church and other non-government bodies. In exchange for legalizing

Solidarity, it was confirmed that the unions would support the reform programme and that the Communist Party would remain in office.

On 6 April a historic agreement provided for a free press, freedom of association and an independent judiciary. A bicameral parliament was to be set up with 65 per cent of the seats in the dominant lower house being reserved for the Communist Party and its allies, and just 35 per cent for the opposition. The second chamber, the Senate, would be freely elected. Four years later the votes for both would be entirely free. It was the formula for a gradual handover of power.

The government staged the elections two months later, before the opposition could organize. Astonishingly, Solidarity won 99 of the 100 sets in the freely elected Senate, and every seat they contested in the lower house. It was the reverse of a traditional communist rigged election, with an all but unanimous vote for the opposition: the people had completely rejected the People the first time they had freely been given the opportunity. In this climate tension mounted, and Walesa sought stability by ensuring that Jaruzelski was narrowly elected President of the new lower house.

As no communist could form a government, Walesa urged the traditional communist satellite parties to join Solidarity in forming one; thus he neatly turned the roundtable on the communists. A respected Catholic intellectual, Tadeusz Mazowiecki, became Poland's first non-communist Prime Minister and was so overcome with emotion that he fainted on taking office. The communist fall was secured with Gorbachev's telephone call, in which he said he would intervene only if Solidarity took action against the Soviet Union; asked about the suggestion of Romania's tyrant Nicolae Ceausescu that the Russians should intervene – an astonishing remark for a leader who had established himself by declaring his autonomy from Russia – Gorbachev replied contemptuously, 'Ceausescu fears for his skin.' When Poland found the cell door unlocked, it was the first to walk through.

Next came Hungary. By contrast with the combative Poles, the country had spent the three decades since the 1956 uprising cannily and carefully improving its prison conditions. Greater economic incentives permitted by the regime promoted modest growth in the 1960s, subsequently disrupted by oil price increases. Hungary's response to the latter was to borrow, and the foreign debt swelled to around $9 billion by 1979. To ease its way, the country became the first Eastern Bloc country to join the IMF and the global market. In 1980 the Seventeenth Congress of the Hungarian Socialist Workers' Party had daringly advocated greater democracy and recognition of the 'secondary economy'.

The latter policy had dramatic effects: for example, the 10 per cent of restaurants in private ownership were soon enjoying profits equal to those of all the remaining 90 per cent in state hands. Enterprise business work partnerships – in effect, embryonic small businesses – mush-roomed, with more than a quarter of a million people participating and supplementing their ordinary wages by half. In politics the reformist wing of the Communist Party headed by Imre Pozsgay successfully pressed for elections in 1982 in which, although the Party retained its monopoly, there was a genuine choice between candidates.

In 1986 Gorbachev visited Budapest and seemed impressed by the Hungarian reforms. Emboldened, Pozsgay published his *Turning Point of Reform*, cataloguing the deficiencies of Hungarian economy, denouncing central planning and advocating Hungary's full entry to the world economy and freedom of prices and wages. The head of the Party, Karoly Grosz, responded by moving further down the reform path and away from underneath the umbrella of the ageing and failing Hungarian leader, Janos Kadar. In 1988 the latter was deposed as General Secretary of the Party and given the honorary role of Party President.

Grosz replaced him, and told Gorbachev that he wanted a Hungary that was 'open, integrated into the world' but which provided for democratization only 'in the context of a one-party system'. The cau-tious Hungarians were exactly mirroring progress in the Soviet Union. Pozsgay was put in charge of relations with the latter and, as in Russia, permitted a new flurry of criticism as well as allowing the formation of independent political organizations.

In January 1989 Pozsgay published a report of his 'Central Committee Historical Commission' which pulled no punches by describing the 1956 uprising as 'a popular uprising against an oligarchic system of power which had humiliated the nation' and asserting that the socialist path was 'wrong in its entirety'. On 15 March the hero of 1956, Imre Nagy, was commemorated in a mass demonstration of more than 100,000 people and by 16 June, again in a massive demonstration of popular respect, he was re-interred in official splendour as a national martyr.

By then Grosz had called for a roundtable discussion with opposition groups, but the latter's refusal to attend paved the way for Grosz's replacement by Pozsgay, who successfully started a dialogue in June. The

Party no longer sought to retain a complement of seats in parliament, sensing the failure of such a move in Poland. Free elections were agreed upon, which eventually took place in the spring of 1990. But it was too late to save any vestiges of the old regime. Even under the reformer Pozsgay the communists polled just 9 per cent. The winners were Democratic Reform, a Christian Democrat-style alliance, with 44 per cent of the vote, while their allies won some 18 per cent. The more free-market oriented Free Democrats won 23 per cent. This staggering repudiation of the communist past was not quite as overwhelming as in Poland, but demonstrated that even the most reform-minded communists could command no more than a tenth of the support of the people in the absence of guns to enforce their role; once again, the reform process followed Gorbachev's decision to turn the key in the lock.

As Poland broke and Hungary tiptoed out of their cells, a country that had so far slept in a corner also stirred. For thirty years, a wily and crooked dictator, Todor Zhivkov, had run Bulgaria with iron-like control combined with Balkan shrewdness and pragmatism. Zhivkov claimed to have tried reform as early as the 1960s and was not notably vicious, except to his enemies abroad: Georgi Markov, whose broadcasts were beamed into Sofia, had been murdered with the poisoned tip of an umbrella in London in 1978. Bulgaria, with its huge percentage of Russian speakers had slavishly followed the Soviet lead, even lending its security services to carry out the Soviet Union's dirty work – allegedly also in the assassination attempt on Pope John Paul II (although there is no conclusive evidence for this).

Zhivkov, corrupted by years in power, had balanced cozying up to Russian leaders with just the right amount of individual initiative to present himself as a 'reform' communist. For example in 1982 he initiated his 'New Economic Mechanism' and in 1986 proclaimed the 'scientific-technological revolution'. In 1988 came *perevstroistvo* and glasnost, Bulgarian-style. While these declarations were pure window-dressing, the harsher reality was Zhivkov's sudden campaign against his country's 1 million-strong ethnic Turkish minority, about 10 per cent of the population, insisting they change their Islamic names. Hundreds were killed and 300,000 fled to Turkey. Coupled with Bulgaria's parlous economic state – the foreign debt had dizzyingly ascended to some $9 billion – the country was beginning to depart the norms of civilized conduct. The campaign against the Turks was almost certainly an attempt by Zhivkov, sensing that his quasi-medieval regime was foundering, to reinvent it as one inspired by nationalism.

A group of senior politicians decided to try and challenge it. Stoyan Mikhailov argued in the Politburo that Zhivkov's reforms were a sham, but in July 1988 Zhivkov threw him out, together with his mildly reformist heir apparent, Chudmoir Alexsandrov. Meanwhile sympathetic opposition groups began to form among the intelligentsia, hitherto Zhivkov loyalists.

With the latter lashing out increasingly wildly, crushing demonstrations in the autumn of 1989, and installing his unpopular son Vladimir as Minister of Culture, three elderly courtiers in the palace decided to act – the Defence Minister, General Dobri Dzhurov, a veteran former Prime Minister, Georgi Atanasov, and the Foreign Minister for nearly two decades, Petur Mladenov. Given the close official contacts between the Soviet Union and Bulgaria, these moves must have taken place with the Russians' complicity – even possibly at Gorbachev's prompting. Bulgaria, an example of gangster Communism, had become an embarrassment.

On his way to China, Mladenov may even have called in to see Gorbachev. Atanasov visited the Soviet Embassy on 4 November and Mladenov was emboldened to denounce Zhivkov for condemning Bulgaria to wallow 'in the same pig's trough as the rotten dictatorial family regime of Ceausescu [in Romania]'.

On 10 November the four plotters decided to present an ultimatum to Zhivkov to quit, sending four army units into Sofia to help him decide. He promptly resigned and Mladenov took over. The new President ordered that Zhivkov be expelled from the Party, that the Communist Party lose its leading role in society and that a roundtable discussion the following month should lead to free elections the following year.

The opposition came together as the Union of Democratic Forces under Zhelyu Zhelev, but although his radicalism secured 24 out of 26 seats in Sofia, it alienated the traditionalist peasantry in the countryside; the reformed communists, remarkably, ended up with 52 per cent of the vote to the UDF's 36 per cent in June 1990. However Mladenov was forced from office the following month, after it was revealed that he had favoured using tanks against demonstrators. In Bulgaria's case, the Soviet keyholder himself had summoned this sleepy, corrupt old jailbird to his feet and out of the prison door.

*

Eastern Europe's most spectacular peaceful revolution was now simmering. Erich Honecker's East Germany was a paradoxical society: rigidly disciplined and centralized under a command economy that existed with nowhere near such thoroughness elsewhere in the Eastern bloc, it was the only Warsaw Pact member that seemed to make Communism work. Officially recognized as one of the world's great industrial and sporting powers – all those proudly trumpeted Olympic medals – it enjoyed a standard of living well ahead of its partners to the east.

But wealth is relative and most East Germans judged their success against West German standards. With West German television continually beamed into the East, and with the multiplicity of contacts across the border, most Easterners accepted that they enjoyed nothing like a comparable standard of living; the rigid enforcement of the police state and the all-pervasive Stasi secret police and security network could not keep out the truth. Thus while the dour, pedantic, schoolmasterly Honecker believed with some justification that he ran a successful country – at least by comparison with his eastern neighbours – ordinary East Germans begged to disagree.

In early 1989 this workers' paradise was disrupted by a stream of would-be emigrants from East Germany into Hungary, which could not logically exclude them since it had welcomed thousands of Romanian citizens of Hungarian origin from persecution in Ceausescu's Romania. This was the first real crack in the dyke of the dammed-up floodwaters of freedom of Eastern Europe. With the Hungarian regime rapidly liberalizing, it was only a matter of time before its border with Austria was opened, and the East Germans were able to flow into the West – 11,000 doing so in September. Meanwhile thousands more crowded into the West German Embassy in Czechoslovakia seeking asylum.

Honecker, still unaware of the whirlwind spinning towards him, was more concerned with staging the fortieth anniversary celebrations of the creation of the German Democratic Republic on 7 October as gloriously as possible. He excoriated Gorbachev's reform programme, considering his country vastly superior and more economically successful than the Soviet Union, and the impetuous young Gorbachev as someone lacking the experience and wisdom of a communist elder statesman like himself.

On 7 May a traditional East German election saw the communists triumphantly returned to power with 98.95 per cent of the vote. A month later East German television glorified the massacre in Tiananmen Square as 'the heroic response of the Chinese army and police to the perfidious inhumanity of the student demonstrators'. Thus Honecker, by praising tanks rolling over unarmed students, demonstrated his contempt for Gorbachev and the cracks opening up in Eastern Europe. The country's opposition was fragmented, small-scale and cowed by the brutally effective Stasi, so perhaps he had some justification for his optimism.

But a truly spontaneous popular uprising without leaders or parties was totally unexpected. Its origins were to be found in a sermon traditionally delivered on Monday afternoon in St Nikolai's Church in Leipzig. On 25 September some 8,000 gathered there and marched through the city centre; on 2 October the numbers had swollen to 10,000. This was extremely brave, in view of the regime's expressed support for the Tiananmen Square massacre and its ruthless efficiency.

When Gorbachev arrived in East Germany in advance of the anniversary celebrations a couple of days later, a handpicked crowd of Party activists cheered him with the cry, 'Gorby, save us!' Gorbachev, who had embraced Honecker on arrival with a Judas kiss, said he was 'disgusted' by the East German handling of the crisis. 'Life punishes those who come too late,' he remarked pointedly to Honecker.

A day after he left on 8 October, the Leipzig demonstration was due to resume, this time targeted specifically against the Fortieth Anniversary celebration itself. Honecker ordered the security forces to take all necessary measures, thereby authorizing the Tiananmen Square solution. But it is believed that Leipzig's military and security chiefs sought advice from Moscow and were told that Gorbachev would not support repression. In the event 50,000 people walked through Leipzig peacefully; this was the tensest moment yet in the unravelling of Communism in Eastern Europe, which could have provoked massive bloodshed. Once again Gorbachev had waved his wand and peace had prevailed.

As important, and unprecedentedly, Honecker's own officials had defied him. Over the following weeks the Party resolved to replace the out-of-touch leader with his protégé Egon Krenz, an office-based bureaucrat with an undertaker's smile and no charisma at all. Krenz, in spite of his inauspicious background, realized that the game was up, purged the Party, offered reforms and opened the Czech border. Gorbachev greeted him coldly in Moscow, however, for having done too little, too late.

Meanwhile the number of demonstrators swelled to 300,000 in

Leipzig in early November, and 500,000 in East Berlin on 4 November. 'We are the people' was the slogan, in response to the Communist Party's claim to represent the people, which soon changed to 'We are one people,' alluding to German unification. The dignity and orderliness of these huge demonstrations were the most impressive things about them. On 9 November Krenz's government announced that 'private trips can be requested without fulfilling requirements'. This curious and possibly mistaken statement soon electrified East Berlin, where crowds gathered by the Wall.

On the night of 9 November they demanded of the nervous guards the right to cross over. The guards had no clear instructions, and a few brave men and women began to move through, followed first by hundreds and then thousands. It was an historic moment; Easterners and Westerners embraced and chipped away with makeshift instruments at the hated wall, the symbol of German division since its construction in 1961. Around 5,000 people had successfully found a way across this symbol of German – and European – division since its construction since 1961, while roughly the same number had been captured trying and 191 had been killed. The East German government fell and was replaced by one led by Hans Modrow, leader of the Communist Party's reformist wing; the entire Politburo also resigned. Following the inevitable 'roundtable' talk with the opposition, which had only come into being two months before, a 'government of national responsibility' was patched together by February 1990.

When Modrow, responding to intense popular pressure, proposed a unified and neutral Germany, the West German Chancellor, Helmut Kohl, promptly rejected it. When free elections were held in March, the West German parties swept East Germany, Kohl advocating immediate reunification, the Social Democrats' Oskar Lafontaine pressing for delay. The Christian Democrats won a resounding 48 per cent of the East German vote to the Social Democrats' 22 per cent. Surprisingly, the communists gained 22 per cent, their best showing in Eastern Europe and perhaps a reflection of the country's relative economic efficiency.

It was not enough to sway the East Germans. When the offices of the Stasi in Berlin were raided by mobs, they discovered some 125 miles of shelving containing files on some of East Germany's 17 million people. Unification presented huge problems, but was rushed through with astonishing speed. Kohl unwisely agreed to swap East and West German marks (the Ostmark and the Deutschmark) at one to one for many transactions, such as wages, pensions and small savings, ignoring the Bundesbank's advice to exchange them at two to one. In fact the Deutschmark was worth at least seven or more Ostmarks, but the one-to-one exchange raised the spectre of an inflationary explosion that had to be damped down by high interest rates, a problem that persisted for several years and adversely affected the entire European economy. It also rendered East German industry wholly uncompetitive.

Gorbachev seemed surprised by the speed of reunification after his decision to liberate East Germany. He had to accept Western demands that Germany remain within NATO, although no NATO troops would be stationed in the former East Germany; the 370,000 Soviet troops and their dependents stationed there would be withdrawn in convoys and covered trains. It was a spectacularly symbolic ending of the Soviet Empire in Eastern Europe and the military confrontation that had kept Europe at daggers drawn for the past four decades. The entire East German regime was effectively vaporized, with Honecker, Krenz and the celebrated spy chief Marcus Wolf facing prosecution. A senior West German general brutally summed up the process to me: 'East Germany is not being unified with the West; it is being absorbed.'

I was in Germany on 3 October 1990, when two at last became one. The occasion was one of the most moving of my life, as hundreds of thousands of young people took to the street, fireworks exploded and the national anthem was sung, burying the terrible history of a nation under odious dictatorship for twelve years, then divided against itself for forty-five. I recorded:

On 4 October 1990, I joined the orderly human torrent that poured through the Brandenburg Gate to a Germany no longer split after forty-five years of division. It was one of the biggest street parties the world has ever witnessed. Two million West Berliners flowed through the neoclassical baroque edifice, past the balloon sellers in the city's most celebrated street, the Unter den Linden. Behind, in the shadow of the Reichstag, Russian uniforms and caps were on sale for a pittance, as the departing occupiers tried to earn a few marks to take back with them to their economically devastated homeland. Beyond lay the stately drab edifices of East Germany's showpiece, now thronged with würst and sauerkraut sellers catering to the crowds.

The day was free of clouds, blue-skied above the rejoined throng below; the mood was unecstatic, subdued, friendly, with families taking an afternoon promenade – not a celebration. You could tell the Westerners by the expensive open-necked casualness of their clothes, in contrast to the Easterners' shabby suits or jackets and ties. The Westerners were a little edgy, as if they knew that freely crossing the magic threshold, which few had ever expected in their lifetimes, was not the fulfilment of a dream but entry into an uncertain looking-glass world where all was parallel but inverted, and would take decades to reorder. There was guilt at witnessing the conditions of down-and-out, dignified poverty in which their blood relatives had lived for so long, as well as apprehension about the cost of taking them under the West's wing and contempt for their submissiveness . . .

I passed Berlin's ornate Komische Oper [Comic Opera] where a champagne bottle had been inserted into the crook of the arm of a sculpted nymphet on the façade . . . I skirted looming, dreary bronzes of Marx and Engels in a park, where a silly street-theatre was being staged by Euroenthusiasts – on second thoughts perhaps it struck exactly the right note of mockery for that life-freezing, apocalyptic pair.

Far from the placid crowd, I took the overground [railway], open for the first time, back across a city which had been divided for two generations. The acned Bronx-like tenements of the East, hunch-shouldered greycoat slabs pockmarked with windows fronting the river, were sliced abruptly short by the Wall, dead-ending purposeless streets . . . The little railway bore me across to the raucous glitter of a largely American garrison town, where gaudy strip shows vied with supermarkets for hoarding space. I had taken a fifteen-minute, one-mark journey from the 1940s to the 1990s, and it was not entirely clear that the neon glitter of the West was an improvement on the stately shabbiness of the East.

The crowds went on their three-mile pilgrimage because they knew human history was being made across the breeding ground of some of the most terrible events this century. Reunification might be just a matter of Germany regaining its national identity – or was it the joining together of two elements that would ignite a critical mass of explosive proportions? The night before, which I had spent in a provincial town to the sound of firecrackers and carousing, the West German flag had been raised over the Reichstag, to make the point that Germany was not being 'reunified', but that the East was being absorbed into the West.

The most orderly and model prisoner of all had walked through the door of the cell.

One occupant of the cell, brave in his day, who had suffered terribly following acts of defiance more than thirty years before under a Stalinist regime, was one of the slowest to test whether the door had really been unlocked. Czechoslovakia under the darkly repressive Gustav Husak had been permitted only the bare bones of an opposition movement. Husak's successor, after his elevation as President, had been the brutally efficient Milos Jakes in 1987. The regime's only really positive achievement was properly organized food production; this helped to keep popular discontent to a minimum, although the industrial economy had long been stagnant. At least overseas borrowing, at some \$3–4 billion, was comparatively modest.

With all political dissent ruthlessly suppressed, a mere handful of opposition leaders stood out – Peter Uhl, a Trotstkyist, Vaclav Benda, a Catholic intellectual, and Vaclav Havel, the country's leading playwright, a chain-smoking philosopher with an apparently dismaying lack of political sense. As he famously put it:

> When a person behaves in keeping with his conscience, when he tries to speak the truth, and when he tries to behave as a citizen even under conditions where citizenship is degraded, it may not lead to anything, yet it might. But what surely will not lead to anything is when a person calculates whether it will lead to something or not.

The three men had founded Charter 77, and three years later were all jailed, Havel for four years hard labour during which he contracted pneumonia, which his smoking did nothing to improve. In 1988 opposition tentatively resurfaced, encouraged by developments in the Soviet Union. Jakes paid lip service to perestroika, but broke up the first demonstration by 4,000 people in January 1989 in honour of Jan Palach, who had burnt himself to death protesting at the 1968 Soviet invasion. One hundred people were arrested, including Havel, who was sentenced to nine months' imprisonment.

Not until 17 November, at a ceremony to commemorate the murder of a Czech student by the Nazis, did another major public demonstration take place, when the 30,000 who marched in Wenceslas Square were intercepted by the police in the time-honoured way: several were badly injured. The Berlin Wall had just fallen; Zhivkov had just been deposed in Bulgaria; Solidarity had come to power in Poland; the round-table agreement had been reached in Hungary; and perestroika and glasnost had long been under way in the Soviet Union.

Continued repression was impossible. Jakes was removed by his colleagues from power and Ladislav Adamec, a moderate communist, was appointed Prime Minister. The opposition, caught unprepared, gathered as the 'Civic Forum' in the Magic Lantern Theatre in Prague to draw up a programme. Huge demonstrations took place almost nightly. Gale Stokes, an expert on Eastern Europe, captures the scene:

> Different people have different memories of when they became convinced the regime was finished. Some thought so from the beginning, others remember when Alexander Dubcek, looking, as [Timothy] Garton Ash puts it, as if he had stepped out of an old black-and-white photograph, appeared together with Havel on the balcony of the Socialist Party publishing house in the middle of Wenceslas Square. The crowds cheered him ecstatically, honouring him as a symbol of honourable resistance to the Soviets, even if they found his idea of socialism with a human face passé. Others cite the moment when Prague Party leader Stepán tried to rally the workers of a huge local factory against the students by telling them, 'We do not intend to be dictated to by children'. 'We are not children,' the workers roared back. Then there was the moment when the People's Militia, which played a very important role in the communist seizure of power in 1948, came from the provinces into Prague and Brno but proved completely unusable, ashamed, as interviewed participants said on television, to be there. And finally there was the two-hour general strike, called for lunch hour on 27 November so as not to interfere with work. (It was a very Czech revolution – the Prague demonstrations did not start until after working hours for the same reason.)

The general strike on 27 November 1989 was a huge success. Adamec's attempts to form a government that excluded the opposition failed. Husak was deposed as President. The National Assembly, presided over by the veteran leader of the Prague Spring, Alexander Dubcek, appointed Havel Prime Minister. In June 1990 Civic Forum won nearly 60 per cent of the seats in the new Federal Assembly (the country had been renamed the Czech and Slovak Federative Republic in April), although more conservative Slovakia began to drift away from the federation, which finally resulted in the creation of two independent states. Thus even battered Czechoslovakia, emboldened by the example of the others, also walked through the door.

It was now the turn of the most backward of all communist regimes in Eastern Europe, and the one least susceptible to Soviet pressure. By the late 1980s Nicolae Ceausescu's Romania had become a byword for misgovernment even among the Eastern European leadership. He ruled through decrees from his presidential palace ordering his people to work harder – which had almost no effect. The bogus production figures his regime issued far exceeded even the mendacity of such neighbours as Zhivkov – for example, grain production was said to be 60 million tons in 1989 when the true figure was 17 million. Due to electricity shortages the people were restricted to one 40-watt light bulb in a room and heating worked for only a few hours a day. Opposition activists simply disappeared.

Ceausescu embarked on a pharoanic building programme, creating the House of the Republic in central Bucharest, demolishing eighteen churches and dozens of historic buildings in the process. Half of Romania's picture-postcard villages were to be replaced with concrete apartment blocks; many city centres were similarly scheduled for demolition, although luckily the process had only just begun by 1989. In addition Ceausescu waged war upon Romania's Hungarian minority.

In November, as the regimes around him collapsed, it was business as usual in Bucharest. At the Communist Party Congress, Ceausescu was unanimously re-elected President. In a country where opposition was non-existent and the people cowed, it was far from apparent what would shift him: it seemed he might be left in charge of one of the last hold-outs of primitive Communism in the world. When the change came, it did so unexpectedly, and with alarming suddenness.

On 17 December 1989 in Timisoara in eastern Romania, the authorities' attempts to seize a Hungarian Reformed Church minister, Laszlo Tokes, and move him to a small village were obstructed by 5,000 of his parishioners. Infuriated by this defiance, Ceausescu ordered his army commanders to mow down the protestors Tiananmen-Square style. That same night firing broke out and a hundred people were killed (a figure initially believed to be much higher). No one, it seemed, dared defy the dictator.

But after he left on an official visit to Teheran, a general strike erupted in Timisoara. The armed forces, which thought themselves demoted to second place behind the dreaded security service, the Securitate, decided to withdraw from the town. Protests began to spread to other towns. Returning from Iran Ceausescu ordered a major crackdown and summoned a loyalist rally in Belgrade for 21 December.

Usually perfectly choreographed, with entry to the square restricted to the dictator's loyal card-carrying supporters, there was general astonishment when whistling and hostile shouts broke out as Ceausescu addressed the crowd. The live television coverage was switched off. Two days later the centre of Bucharest witnessed street fighting between army units, now hostile to Ceausescu, and his loyalists, mainly from the Securitate (although many of these had now deserted to what they perceived to be the winning side).

On the evening of 2 December, the Communist Party's Central Committee building was attacked and Ceausescu barely escaped in a helicopter that landed inside the country, allowing the dictator to be seized. A firing squad executed Ceausescu and his hated wife on Christmas Day after a cursory 'trial'. Clearly, as Ceausescu's son Nicu put it, a 'coup d'état . . . took place against the background of popular revolt'.

Undoubtedly the dictator's fall was highly popular; but it was not the masses that had risen against him, except in a few towns. The army, part of the Securitate and Ceausescu's old communist colleagues now formed the National Salvation Front, headed by Ion Iliescu and Petra Roman, leader of the Communist Party's mildly reformist wing. In a country without a real opposition, and with the army and security forces supporting the new leadership, Iliescu successfully rallied the people behind anti-Hungarian Romanian nationalism, winning 85 per cent of the presidential votes and two-thirds of the seats in parliament.

The results were dubiously overwhelming. In June the regime used a large army of miners wielding clubs and iron bars to enforce its authority against student protesters, underlining the fundamentally authoritarian nature of the new government. Post-communist nationalists held power in Romania, likewise in disintegrating former Yugoslavia, a depressing departure from the general democratic spirit flowing elsewhere in Eastern Europe. Yet another brutalized prisoner, after so many decades of incarceration had tottered out of the cell only to be grabbed by a warder who had locked him into another, albeit more open, prison.

Albania quietly followed its own course, as ever. After the death of its obscurantist dictator Enver Hoxha in 1985, his successor, Ramiz Alia, survived the end of Communism until 1992, when he was voted out of power.

In just four months, six seemingly impregnable regimes, based on force and the 'popular' will, had crumbled. It was an event without precedent. There has been a tendency to emphasize the differences between East European regimes, as regards their evolution and the forms of Communism they espoused. But they fell together, less like dominoes than skittles bowled over by the same ball.

This was no coincidence, and not the result of a spontaneous upsurge of popular discontent in all these countries. The instigator was Mikhail Gorbachev. Having announced at the end of 1988 that the Soviet Union would not forcibly intervene again in Eastern Europe, no one quite believed him. When General Jaruzelski – a reluctant oppressor even in 1980 – recognized that he could no longer govern without the support of his opponents, and Solidarity decided to talk, they discovered to their amazement that Gorbachev would not intervene, even if Western pluralism and democratic elections allowed the opposition to take power.

The Hungarian opposition needed no further prompting, nor did Zhivkov's palace opponents in Bulgaria, particularly with their active Soviet backing. In East Germany, Gorbachev delivered the coup de grâce to the regime, refusing to authorize mass killing and even accepting the open borders that would inevitably lead to reunification. In Czechoslovakia the post-1968 Stalinists were abandoned without a tear, permitting the installation of the opposition.

If Gorbachev had shown even the slightest opposition to pluralism, the regimes would have fought ferociously for survival and many might not have fallen at all, particularly if underpinned by the traditional Soviet threat of military intervention. Great courage was displayed by those that had been repressed and then rose to the occasion in the 'velvet' and other revolutions of 1989. But few, if any, of these uprisings would have occurred, let alone succeeded, but for Gorbachev's deliberate decision.

Apart from the liberation of millions of people in Eastern Europe, there had been two immensely far-reaching consequences of Gorbachev's resolve to set Russia's satellites free in 1989. First, the United States and its allies, who up to now had regarded him as merely a new, much more sophisticated face on the Russian bear, suddenly realized as never before that Gorbachev was 'for real'. Second, Gorbachev had shown that he was prepared to tolerate not just political liberalisation within the context of a one-party system, but outright democracy and victories for the non-communist opposition, relegating the communist parties themselves to the 'dustbin of history'.

America's new President, George Bush, told the press: 'If the Soviets are going to let the communists fall in East Germany, they've got to be really serious – more serious than I realize.' Soon afterwards on 1 December, Bush flew to Malta for a summit meeting with Gorbachev to be held aboard ship, so as to attract the minimum of publicity.

Unhappily, a storm was raging, and the two men had trouble travelling between the vessels. But the Americans seemed at last to take Gorbachev at face value, proposing to accelerate strategic arms talks in time for an agreement in June that would also encompass reductions in conventional forces in Europe and an agreement to destroy chemical weapons.

Gorbachev was delighted that the Americans at last recognised his sincerity. He declared: 'We don't consider you our enemy any more. Things have changed.' He warned, however, against American triumphalism about 'winning the Cold War'. To be fair, Bush's reaction to events in Eastern Europe had been exceedingly low-key, to avoid embarrassing Gorbachev. It was the turning point in the two superpowers' relations. The Americans also suggested Russia should be given observer status within GATT – a further major step towards integrating the country into the world economy. At last Gorbachev was being trusted, and his peace offensive seemed likely to reap benefits that would be useful back home; the hugely expensive arms race was over.

The Return of Yeltsin

The second consequence of Russia's abandonment of Eastern Europe was just as important, however; it belied the idea that Gorbachev was basically an apparatchik dedicated to the maintenance of the Communist Party at all costs, as he had been happy to permit free elections in Eastern Europe and let opposition parties triumph. One can only speculate whether he had always intended this to happen or whether he had come to these decisions pragmatically after he had reached supreme power; if he had decided earlier, he never revealed it, because expressing such heresies would undoubtedly have tilted the balance of power in the Soviet Party against him when his priority was to consolidate his authority – as we have seen, no easy task.

In January 1989 Gorbachev had rammed his slate of contenders for what would become the new Soviet parliament through the Party's Central Committee. The following month the Soviet withdrawal from Afghanistan had been completed after nearly a decade of occupation.

Gorbachev now bore down on the agricultural sector, his old fiefdom. He insisted, in response to continuing food shortages, that peasants be given the right to farm their own land, declaring the entire Soviet collective sector had been bankrupt for a decade. Specifically, farmers would receive life-long leases on their farms – although Ligachev, his principal opponent, fought a bitter rearguard action to ensure the collective farms survived as an entity.

The ferocity of the infighting was illustrated when rumours, almost certainly true, flooded Moscow that an assassination attempt had been made against Gorbachev – the first of several. But the Soviet leader, undeterred, continued to enact reforms to make his revolution irreversible. In March 1989 the first genuinely contested elections in Soviet history to the Congress of People's Deputies went ahead as scheduled, although the Party retained its monopoly. Boris Yeltsin, now a bitter enemy of Gorbachev and viewed in the West as the leader of the opposition within the Communist Party, topped the poll to enter the congress in the Moscow region. When the congress in turn elected a new Supreme Soviet, to operate as a standing parliament, Yeltsin – initially excluded because of the Party's monopoly in the congress – joined it in May when another member stepped aside, and would later become its President. In the same month, the congress elected Gorbachev as its Chairman.

Yeltsin had called for greater internal democracy, although his public reputation had been tarnished by being dismissed by the Party for antics such as apparently falling into the river in Moscow – possibly the result of a bout of drinking or a suicide bid in the depression that he suffered after his public humiliation. Once in parliament, however, he ferociously promoted himself as the leader of the Russian opposition, advocating raising the Russian republic's living standards to match those in the other republics of the Soviet Union, and urging a new union treaty to reshape its relations with them.

He wanted even greater land rights for the peasants than Gorbachev. He proposed direct elections for the Soviet presidency, and the curtailment of the power of the KGB and the army. He urged a transition to a genuine free market economy as well as cuts in capital spending by the state. Most radical of all, Yeltsin seemed to be abandoning the very label of 'socialist':

> I think the capitalism [the Marxists] classics tell of does not exist; nor does the socialism. There have been various kinds of socialism: developed socialism (the Brezhnev slogan), national socialism or Pol Pot socialism. I myself am not just socialist for the sake of it. Judging by our standard of living, we are still only approaching it.

For Gorbachev at this stage, Yeltsin was almost certainly a help rather than a hindrance. Still believing that the threat to him came from the old guard, Gorbachev could point to Yeltsin as a dangerous extremist from whom he, the orthodox communist, was trying to save the Soviet Union. Gorbachev underestimated, however, both the danger posed by Yeltsin and the degree of hatred the latter felt for him after his public humiliation.

Significantly the new Supreme Soviet became almost immediately the focus for legislative activity, sidelining the previously more powerful Communist Party Central Committee, and rejecting motions submitted by the government for approval, previously a rubber-stamp formality. With this election process – the first time in the course of Russian history as well as the 70-year old Soviet Revolution that the entire Russian people had been free to express a choice – they had voted overwhelmingly against orthodox communists; reformist candidates triumphed everywhere.

A real turning point had been reached. From now on the democratic revolution inexorably gathered momentum. It was a subject of immense historical curiosity whether Gorbachev had in fact planned this all along; he continued to be denounced by Yeltsin and his radical opponents as, at heart, a communist loyalist. The probability must be that the Russian leader was the reverse. Gorbachev was a highly intelligent man, even a political visionary. Nobody had prodded him in a reformist direction: the Soviet people were sullen and obedient. There had been pressure for change, of course, in terms of delivering economic improvement; but apart from the usual dissident and Jewish groups, he was under no real pressure to respect human rights and certainly not to install democracy, which would have been regarded as a wildly unrealistic goal even for the dissidents – if they had ever been allowed to express such views.

The democratic revolution in Russia, in other words, was imposed from above by Gorbachev in response to the communist elite's realization that the command system was demonstrably not delivering the goods economically. This required a massive leap of imagination and courage because, as can be seen elsewhere, those at the top of the structure found it far easier to pretend that the system was working, crushing dissent and presiding over general decline camouflaged as the glorious advance of the Soviet state: there was no real challenge from outside the system, certainly not from ordinary people, to the overwhelming monopoly enjoyed by the Party and the other power structures.

Gorbachev, in providing a genuinely competitive element under the umbrella of the Party's monopoly, probably knew he was unleashing a revolution by replacing the old apparatchiks with his own supporters – a revolution which gathered momentum and drove him along with it. The only way to lock the genie back into the bottle would be at gunpoint, which would require armed confrontation, international condemnation and was now probably impossible. As that fateful spring of 1989 turned to summer, the old guard realized what had been so subtly done to them. Ligachev protested, with the sudden understanding of a man who realized he had been sentenced to execution: 'This issue is to strengthen the leading role of the Party, not just its coordinating one. Proposals to limit our Party's functions and even to deprive it completely of some of them are not new. They aim to dismiss communists from the leadership of society.'

Nikolai Ryzhkov, a competent apparatchik who had been appointed Prime Minister, was similarly alarmed: 'The entire course of current events shows that the Party has lost its authority and the possibility of exerting an influence on everything taking place in society. Meanwhile, wittingly or unwittingly, we maintain the appearance that nothing extraordinary has happened and that the levers are still in our hands.'

Gorbachev hastily tried to ease these fears by parroting some of the old slogans. 'The Party remains the main organizing and coordinating force capable of leading people towards socialist renewal. It plays an integrating and consolidating role in society.'

But events had passed the point of no return. In July 1989 a coal strike in Mezhdurechensk in Siberia triggered a wave of strikes across the Soviet Union. The following month, millions of people throughout the Baltic republics formed a wall of protest by joining hands: the authorities took no action. Then the collapse of Russia's puppet states in Eastern Europe began, promoted by Gorbachev. He was the agent of change, and he knew what he was doing, whatever he might say to guard his back against stunted and ageing conservatives. But where it all might end remained a crucial, and unanswered, question.

12

The Kill

'On a brighter note, let me sign the decree suspending the activity of the Russian Communist Party.'

Boris Yeltsin

The Soviet Union Unravels: The Fall of Gorbachev

There are, broadly, three types of political leader: those who win the greatest admiration nail their colours to the mast and, like Old Testament prophets, are unashamed and outspoken in their political opinions. This requires immense courage and conviction (of course disaster can follow if those convictions are wrong). They also set a standard against which others can be judged. In terms of political achievement, however, their impact is usually small. Vaclav Havel, until he became President of Czechoslovakia, was an example; in a sense the Russian dissidents were another (although few could be graced, or disgraced, with the title of politician).

A much more common type is those so often denigrated by Soviet historians as careerists – those who aim to reach the top of the hierarchy and enjoy the status and perks, bending with every prevailing wind to ensure they remain there. Yet however despised, they sometimes perform a useful function: conciliating, oiling the wheels, often administering well and ensuring that government caries on regardless; in a sense they are civil servants rather than politicians. Probably accounting for two-thirds of the politicians in any society, they are not there to change things but are as necessary as accountants and bricklayers; indeed, in a society where nothing is radically wrong, they – rather than the first category – may prove to be the most effective kind of political leader.

Gorbachev belonged to a third, much rarer species. In a society where much was desperately wrong, the rarest of politicians was an idealist whose ability, political skill and sense of what was possible enabled him to rise the summit of an inert and repressive system and stay there. This was a feat of remarkable strength of character and personality; while reflecting the opinions of the most clear-sighted of his own generation by publicly espousing as much reform as the system would permit, he retained his own reformist goals, which were remarkably radical in the context of the Brezhnev era.

Having decisively accumulated personal power under an authoritarian system, he was beginning to suffer the consequences, which can have come as little surprise, and was now beset by a truly violent storm in which his first goal was survival and his second staying on course.

A naval analogy comes to mind: there are captains who know where they are headed, and sail into the wind to get there: usually they do not get very far. Others simply steer according to the wind; as Seneca, the Roman statesman put it, 'If one does not know to which port one is sailing, no wind is favourable.' The third kind knows their direction, and tack and wear to follow it. Gorbachev would now display this most difficult and effective of political skills in a virtuoso performance of astonishing energy and ability which, although he became shipwrecked sooner than most expected, steered the country to freedom beyond the point of no return.

Gorbachev, it bears reasserting, had initiated Russia's first free elections in that tyrannical country's history, which would ultimately lead to a devastating defeat for the old regime. He had also permitted virtual freedom of the press, achieved the dissolution of an old collectivist governmental system and an end to the command economy, brought the troops back from the war in Afghanistan, embarked upon a radical programme of disarmament which so surprised the West that it was only just beginning to be believed and finally, and most astonishingly, had permitted, or rather encouraged, the Russian Empire in Eastern Europe to collapse almost overnight. This was not someone steeped in communist traditions, as his successors were later to allege, nor at this stage were any of these choices forced upon him – as what he said to Rakowski and Honecker made clear.

An even more difficult problem was raising its head – discontent within the former Soviet Empire. The decision to withdraw from Afghanistan, announced in July 1986 – not a Gorbachev initiative but one taken by the entire Soviet governing class, including the armed forces, the KGB and the bureaucracy, as well as the Party – had been made as Soviet casualties had swelled to 20,000 with no prospect of victory. The Afghan catastrophe was one of the prime reasons for the replacement of the old guard by the new and was a catalyst, although on a much more moderate level than feared by the old guard, for the rumblings of Islamic discontent in the southern Soviet Union.

At the same time political liberalization and the abrupt Soviet withdrawal from Eastern Europe had triggered off previously suppressed demands among Russia's colonies to the north and west – the Baltic republics of Latvia, Lithuania and Estonia and, potentially more worrying, the Ukraine. To imagine Gorbachev's ruling group were surprised by the events in these territories and the Islamic south is absurd: volumes of analysis in Russia had been devoted to these possibilities, which had been one of the main reasons advanced by Kremlin conservatives against any relaxation of central control. Gorbachev never doubted he would confront these issues – that was inevitable – but the problem was where, when, on what scale and how to handle them. He proceeded not faultlessly, but about as skilfully as possible under the circumstances.

As far as the south was concerned, some 55 million Moslems, one-sixth of the total population of the Soviet Union, were principally to be found in what are now the independent republics of Azerbaijan, Uzbekistan, Kazakhstan, Tajikistan, Turkmenistan and Kyrgyzstan. The most sophisticated of these was Azerbaijan, which had even tried to secure its independence as far back as 1918. So the explosion of national sentiment there in 1988, threatening the Armenian non-Moslem enclave of Nagorno-Karabakh, was no surprise. Meanwhile rioting had also broken out in Uzbekistan.

To the hardliners, Russia's southern empire now seemed to be fraying at the edges – although this was largely a product of the Soviet defeat in Afghanistan. However Gorbachev thought it inconceivable that any of these southern states should break away – and fortunately for him the West evinced little concern about this obscure struggle (later, another essentially Islamic uprising in Chechnya was handled with extraordinary brutality but very few Western tears).

The Baltic states, part of the old Hanseatic League, presented a more difficult problem. They regarded themselves as sophisticated and prosperous non-Russian colonies and were determined to achieve their independence. Yet even if the old guard could just about stomach Gorbachev's other reforms, a Baltic breakaway represented the beginning of the collapse of the Soviet Union itself. After the sudden fall of the regimes in Eastern Europe, it was impossible for Gorbachev not to believe that the Baltic states would be far behind.

In January 1990, with characteristic courage he grasped the nettle and went to Lithuania, where he formally offered independence, appealing for peace with an almost pathetic frankness:

> Nothing will be decided without you. We shall decide everything together. We have embarked on this path and I am the one who chose it. My personal fate is linked to this choice. If someone succeeds in bringing us into conflict, there will be a great tragedy. The main thing is not to let this happen, and then we'll find an answer to everything.

One of Gorbachev's Lithuanian hosts commented, 'We must remember that he has enemies everywhere. But we support what he has done for democracy and freedom.' He added, 'Lithuania is moving towards independence, and no one can stop it.' Within a few weeks Lithuania was declared independent. Gorbachev was meanwhile forced to declare a state of emergency in Nagorno-Karabakh.

In February in response to an astonishing march by 200,000 people demanding an end to the leading role of the Communist Party in the Soviet Union, as had already happened in Eastern Europe, Gorbachev appeared in person and advocated further reform. At Gorbachev's prodding, the Supreme Soviet now endorsed his idea for a strong presidency. This would finally relegate the older generation to subordinate status. Ryzhkov, the Prime Minister, was furious.

In early 1990, for the first time, Gorbachev began to tack as conservative outrage mounted against his reforms and concessions. The decision was made to get tough with Lithuania, which was ordered not to issue its own currency or put up customs posts – the nominal trappings of independence – and Russian troops occupied strategic buildings in Vilnius, the capital, including the radio station, where several people were injured. Russia cut its supply of natural gas to the Baltic republics by four-fifths and threatened further economic sanctions, warning Estonia and Latvia not to follow Lithuania. But both voted for independence.

The Yeltsin challenge meanwhile continued to grow. In 1990, the Soviet parliament would pass constitutional amendments to permit the secession of republics from the Soviet Union and end the Communist Party's monopoly of power. The republics had followed the election of the new Supreme Soviet by electing their own new equivalent bodies – in effect, national parliaments – and in a further round of elections held in the republics in early 1990, the communists did badly; for example, in Leningrad and Kiev, the Party's communist bosses were trounced. In the Baltic republics the Popular Fronts – nominally subordinate to the Party but as everyone knew, in opposition to it and openly advocating self-rule – won overwhelmingly. Yeltsin, already President of the Supreme Soviet, was elected leader of the Russian republic by its own parliament, hitherto a rubber-stamp body, on 29 May, and in June the Russian republic declared sovereignty. Yeltsin immediately proclaimed that its interests had been subordinated to those of the Soviet Union. Then, on 16 July, Ukraine declared sovereignty, to be followed by Armenia, Kazakhstan, Kyrgyzstan, Turkmenistan, Tajikistan, and Uzbekistan. Gorbachev wanted all the republics to be represented in a new federally-based government, but finally accepted a revised union treaty which gave them a far looser relationship with it.

Meanwhile the President proposed freedom of worship and finally, on 9 October, the creation of a multi-party system. By that time Gorbachev had held another summit with Bush at which the conditions for German reunification were resolved. He declared: 'Whether we like it or not, the time will come when united Germany will be in NATO, if that is its choice. Then, if that is its choice, to some degree and in some form, Germany can work together with the Soviet Union.'

Although little more than an acceptance of reality, this further appalled Gorbachev's hard-line critics. He was not only appeasing the legendary German enemy but also permitting its resurrection as a single state.

But if there was progress in relations with the West, Russia domestically was in dire economic straits. The West had furnished little extra aid. Two years of stalling meant that few reforms had properly worked through, while strikes had cut production. Ryzhkov now chose to introduce his own further limited reforms that in effect tripled the price of bread – a possibly deliberate attempt to sabotage Gorbachev's reforms. After panic buying, bread disappeared from the shops, as did rice, cereal and flour. Fiona Fleck in the *Guardian* described how in late 1990 these developments affected the ordinary Russian:

Soviet shopping methods have always differed from those in the West. People rarely fail to take several 'ovoiska' – carrier bags, from the Russian 'ovois' meaning 'just in case' – whenever they go out and are constantly dropping into shops when passing by in case something has arrived. Sometimes they join queues in the hope that something will eventually arrive that day. If in the past queues were a hazard, today they have become a way of life for it is almost impossible to buy anything without queuing.

Queuing has always been a life-principle for the Soviet shopper and is enshrined in what must be the most roundabout way of buying in the world. Soviet food products are rarely pre-packed. To buy a piece of cheese the shopper must queue three times: to have a piece cut and weighed; to pay for it; and to exchange the piece of cheese for a receipt that shows it has been paid for. This explains why people go shopping in teams and also why they buy in bulk. The success of a Soviet shopper depends very much on luck and personal perseverance.

Yet in the summer Gorbachev stuck unblinkingly to his reformist guns although, unprecedentedly, he was heckled during the annual May Day Parade. Then, at a Red Square speech in October 1990 to mark the seventy-third anniversary of the Russian Revolution, he was shot at – although this may have been just an isolated act and not a deliberate conspiracy. At the Twenty-Eighth Party Congress in July, during which Boris Yeltsin formally resigned his membership of the Communist Party, Gorbachev had been ferociously criticized for losing the Baltic republics and Eastern Europe and for weakening the Party. But as its chosen leader he had shamed his detractors by recalling the victims of Stalin's crimes and proposing a referendum on private land ownership.

Soon afterwards Gorbachev, after two years of frenzied reform, decided to bow to pressure from the hardliners. Why Gorbachev tacked so dramatically at this stage has never been satisfactorily explained, According to his critics, he lost his nerve; it was certainly the most controversial decision of his extraordinary career and utterly untypical of the man, but almost certainly derived from his perception that a coup attempt by the hardliners was imminent. But the consequences were that he sold his soul, engineered his own downfall, and gave Yeltsin his chance. With the apparent disintegration of the Soviet Union, the communist collapse in Eastern Europe, the concession in principle of a united Germany, and the proposed return of a large part of the economy to private hands, the bureaucracy, armed forces and KGB were united in wondering what remained of the old glories of the Soviet Union and joined with the conservatives in the Party in resolving that Gorbachev must be deposed.

But it was probably too late: such an action at that stage would have involved massive bloodshed and almost certainly triggered off civil war as there were too many independent sources of power – the Supreme Soviet, the republics with their own parliaments, the trades unions and the press. But Gorbachev felt it was his duty to try and avert a coup attempt. For a long time Yeltsin had been vigorously denouncing Gorbachev in populist terms as a would-be dictator:

> His growing power could lead to the temptation to solve our complex problems by force. Without even noticing it, we might find ourselves captives of a new dictatorship.

This was pure demagoguery: Gorbachev had concentrated power in his own hands to strip it from the hardliners and had moved quickly to establish independent and democratic sources of power, such as the Supreme Soviet. He had gathered power in order to devolve it.

For a brief moment, it was back to the bad old days. Gorbachev rejected the Russian republic's parliament's proposal for a radical transformation towards a market economy; he refused to subscribe to a UN resolution calling for condemnation of the Iraqi invasion of Kuwait; he refused to attend Stockholm to accept the Nobel Peace Prize he had just been awarded; and he announced that the power of the President and the army would be increased. The conciliatory Interior Minister, Vadim Bakatin, was replaced by a hardliner, Boris Pugo.

Gorbachev claimed darkly that sinister forces were trying to destroy the union. His most steadfast ally, Eduard Shevardnadze, resigned, claiming that dictatorship was imminent. It seemed that Gorbachev's remarkable career was finally over: the liberator of the Soviet Union and Eastern Europe was now, apparently, the prisoner of the hard men who were manoeuvring to control the country once again. Bloodshed and repression beckoned with this once dazzling figure reduced to mere mortal stature. The transformation seemed confirmed early in 1991 when another conservative, Valentin Pavlov, was appointed Prime Minister.

In the most terrible act of Gorbachev's rule, on 13 January 1991 fourteen people were killed when Soviet troops stormed the television centre and other public buildings in Vilnius; a week later four people died in Latvia as the Interior Ministry was stormed. Yeltsin promptly flew to Vilnius to urge Russian troops to disobey orders. Gorbachev threatened to clamp down on press freedom. Yeltsin urged him to resign. It was the nadir of Gorbachev's leadership: the bright energetic reformer now appeared to have sold out to the hardliners to the extent of sanctioning murderous brutality in the Baltic states; the shadow of Tiananmen Square, so narrowly averted in Leipzig, now loomed.

Gorbachev later denied that he had ordered the troops to fire, also claiming that he only found out about the order after the event. This was almost certainly true: it would have been totally against the grain for him to order the killings. But that was equally depressing: the reality seemed to be that the hardliners now believed themselves to be in control, and were acting without the President's authority. A dictatorship was being reimposed on the Soviet Union – but Gorbachev was not the dictator: the new dictatorship was built around the doleful combination of Pavlov and Pugo, supported by their ally in the KGB, Kryuchkov, the Defence Minister, Dmitri Yazov, and the new Vice-President, Gennadi Yanayev. This new collective leadership appeared to be acting as Brezhnev and Kosygin had in ousting another erratic reformer, Khrushchev, in 1964.

But this time a huge democratic constituency had been set loose – unlike 1964 – and Gorbachev himself was of an entirely different calibre. After five months of seeming to side with the hardliners, or at least being relegated to purely nominal power, he suddenly re-emerged on 2 March with a remarkable attack on those to whom he was supposed to have sold out – 'dogmatic conservative forces upholding socialism without democracy'. This astonishing speech startled the radicals as much as the hardliners: had he tacked again?

If he had, it was not immediately apparent on the streets. With the West expressing its repugnance at the crackdown in Vilnius and the Russians' equivocal attitude to Iraq in the crisis following Saddam Hussein's invasion of Kuwait in August 1990 (the result of old ties between Russian hardliners and that country; Russia's former spy chief, Yevgeni Primakov, had tried to broker a settlement) relations with the West became strained and Gorbachev's attempt to broker a 'Marshall Plan' to secure the transition to a market economy fell on deaf ears. Meanwhile strikes erupted around the country, following a coal miners' strike in the Donets Basin in the Ukraine. In April 1991 some 80,000

workers downed tools in Byelorussia. That same month a large demonstration in Moscow was held peacefully but the presence of 50,000
security forces on standby shocked the nation. Yeltsin and the radicals
now joined the hardliners in calling on Gorbachev to step down.

But the Soviet leader, increasingly confident he could prevail against
the hardliners, had decided to return to his reformist origins. In May, he
reached a surprise agreement with Yeltsin to respect the right of the
republics to join a new Union of the Soviet Republics – later to be
named the Commonwealth of Independent States – and when he
offered to resign at the Communist Party Central Committee, he was
unanimously supported both by hardliners, who now feared a possible
lapse into chaos if he departed, and by reformers apprehensive that the
hardliners would take over. He travelled to Stockholm belatedly, to
accept the Nobel Peace Prize:

> I have made a final and irrevocable decision. Nothing and no one, no
> pressure either from the Right or from the Left, will make me abandon
> the positions of perestroika. I do not intend to change my views or con-
> victions. My choice is a final one . . . if perestroika fails, the prospect of a
> new peaceful period in history will vanish.

He had made his choice: let the hardliners do their worst. If they
decided to seize power, they could not count on Gorbachev acting as a
front man. An attempt to persuade him to delegate his sweeping presidential powers to the Prime Minister, Pavlov, failed. Attending the
summit of G7 leaders in July he received few concrete pledges of
financial support for Russia's ailing economy. But when he returned on
25 July to defy the hardliners, he insisted that the Central Committee
must reform and abandon Marxism-Leninism:

> The Party will lose any right to claim a role in political life, far less to be
> the ruling party, if it departs from the path of reform. It should abandon
> claims to be the backbone of the state and adopt as its ideology all the
> riches of Soviet as well as world socialist and democratic thought.

He stood exposed at last; hitherto he had qualified his every reform
with a reference to the Marxist-Leninist sacred texts. He now admitted he
was not a Marxist-Leninist at all – tantamount to saying he was not a
communist. This was an astonishing attitude for a man who had always
publicly underlined his adherence to Leninism – a concept so broad, in
his definition, as to be almost meaningless (but Lenin had after all
attempted to abandon the market economy shortly before his own death).

Gorbachev had nailed his colours to the opposition mast and reached out towards Yeltsin, who had been elected President of the Russian Federation (the new name for the Russian republic) with an astonishing 57 per cent of the 80 million votes cast in May 1990. Yeltsin knew, as did Gorbachev, that he now had the authority to challenge Gorbachev, who had been merely been selected by the chosen few at the pinnacle of the Soviet Communist Party. An extraordinary confrontation had thus developed between three rival centres of power in Russia: Gorbachev, nominally in charge, was the weakest; having lost command of the bureaucracy to the hardliners, he now headed a divided Communist Party which now demonstrably did not represent the Soviet people. Yeltsin, by contrast, had the overwhelming mandate of the Russian people, while the hardliners now controlled the bureaucracy, the armed forces and the security apparatus – three out of the Soviet Union's four traditional centres of power. Technically, Yeltsin's power had still to be tested as his was a new authority. But the self-elected officials of the Soviet Union lacked his popular support and the institutions of the Soviet Union and the Russian Federation were now on a collision course; Yeltsin, although still theoretically a communist, was about to flex his muscles.

The hardliners – the men who controlled the guns – made the first move. At 6.30 a.m. on 20 August 1991, Russian television and radio broadcast some astonishing news: Gorbachev, on holiday in the Crimea, had fallen ill and been replaced by Vice-President Yanayev, a long-serving Party hack who had been head of the Soviet trade union movement. The pretext was disbelieved by virtually everyone.

It was soon clear that a 'State Emergency Committee' had taken power after careful preparation. The three principal leaders of the coup were the Prime Minister, Pavlov; the Defence Minister, Yazov, its chief strategist; and the Interior Minister, Pugo, who had earlier described the Communist Party as 'undermined from within by corruption, parochialism, servility and lies'. The frontman, Yanayev, declared at a press conference that the coup had been:

> forced and dictated by the vital need to save the economy from ruin, and the country from hunger, to prevent the threat of a large-scale civil conflict with unpredictable consequences.

Yanayev claimed that Gorbachev was 'on holiday and undergoing treatment in the Crimea', and that he would take over again when he recovered. In Latvia, Special Forces stormed the Riga television station. Tanks rolled onto the streets of Moscow to enforce a ban on demonstrations and strikes and to uphold the state of emergency. The capital's television and radio stations were all occupied. Only communist newspapers were allowed onto the streets.

In the Crimea, Gorbachev and his family and his bodyguards had been placed under house arrest in the luxurious holiday complex of the Soviet leader, while the coup leaders attempted to persuade him to support their seizure of power. Gorbachev heatedly refused:

> I made no deals, I maintained a firm position, demanding the immediate summoning of a session of the Congress [of People's Deputies] or the Supreme Soviet. Only they can decide the issue. Otherwise, after any other step I would have to finish myself off. There could be no other way out.

He described the tense standoff later:

> I was cut off from any communication. The sea was closed by ships. There were troops all round. It was complete and total isolation . . . Even in these conditions I acted, and got my demands out through the people here on my side, constantly, regularly during the day, and managed to do everything. My guards were given orders to open fire and defend us against anyone who tried to break in. That's how we lived in complete isolation for almost four days and nights.

Meanwhile two men quickly denounced the coup. Boris Yeltsin, the country's only leader with a clear popular mandate as President of the Russian Federation, issued a ringing declaration: 'Soldiers, officers and generals, the clouds of terror and dictatorship are gathering over the whole country. They must not be allowed to bring eternal night.' He expressed his defiance from the top of a tank outside the Russian Federation parliament building. In Lithuania, Vytautas Landsbergis, the President, appealed to his nation: 'Do not allow the tragedy of Budapest and Prague to be repeated.'

But other signs were less promising, with only a patchy response to calls for a general strike. The Azerbaijani Government supported the plotters, as apparently did Leonid Kravchuck, the old-style Party chief in the Ukraine. There was widespread condemnation in the West. Eduard Shevardnadze, the former Foreign Minister who had long predicted a coup, declared:

I must say I was expecting it. In principle I have been morally and psycho-logically prepared for it. Our democratic movement already thought during the weekend that there was a real possibility of a rightwing coup.

It seemed indeed that the worst had happened: the entire armed forces high command had concurred in the coup and the KGB appeared solidly behind it. All strategic installations had been seized. The only major centre of resistance was the Russian Federation parliament build-ing, now ringed by troops and tanks. There seemed a real possibility of civil war, if enough people heeded Yeltsin's call.

But on that dismal first day, it seemed that, as in the past, stoic Russians would hunker down and accept the reality of brute force as a fait accompli. All the plotters needed was a decisive show of strength against Yeltsin – indeed, an earlier staging of the coup would have found Yeltsin in Kazakhstan. During the day Yeltsin's supporters erected flimsy barricades around the parliament building. Few doubted that the tanks and elite forces massing on the streets of Moscow could have blasted their way in, but inexplicably they were not ordered to do so on that first day; the coup leaders were waiting for Gorbachev to give them the authority to act when he returned to Moscow. This fatal hesitation reflected the plotters' lack of self-confidence. They had ignored the first rule of coup-making, indeed of any military operation: always act de-cisively and with maximum force while your enemy is off balance. This reflected the inner contradiction of the coup: it was not a simple seizure of power by the forces of order and suppression of the opposition. The plotters were striking at the pinnacle of the Party that enshrined the whole repressive system, yet in whose name ironically they claimed to be acting. Yet their actions could have no legitimacy without Gorbachev's support, as head of the Party. Without it, they were rebel-ling against their own system as well as the Russian people.

On the second day, the crowds increased. About 50,000 people around the parliament building saw Yeltsin appear defiantly on the balcony. 'We will hold on here as long as we have to, to remove the junta from power and bring it to justice,' he declared to thunderous cries of 'Yeltsin, Yeltsin.' Later he broadcast:

Citizens of Russia, fellow countrymen, comrades-in-arms, friends! I am appealing to you in this fatal hour for our country.

On the night of 18 August a coup d'état was carried out in our country. A group of political adventurers declared themselves to be the supreme

power and entered a constitutional conspiracy, thus committing a most
serious state crime.

Deceiving the people, the fatherland and the constitution, they have
placed themselves outside the law.

Meanwhile more barricades – this time consisting of paving stones,
buses and concrete blocks – had been erected around the parliament
building. Several hundred weapons had been smuggled inside and some
300 armed men were said to have arrived to defend Yeltsin, to be followed by a dozen armoured vehicles from the usually loyal crack Soviet
airborne divisions and a couple of tanks from the Tamanskaya Guards
Motor Rifle Division. As the coup leaders moved more troops into the
capital, a showdown looked increasingly likely, in which the building's
defenders could only mount a heroic and doomed defence.

Yeltsin issued a flurry of statements: Gorbachev must be seen by a
team of international doctors, censorship must be withdrawn, troops
should disobey their commanders' orders, which were legal neither in
terms of the existing constitution nor the popular power he represented,
the coup leaders must be prosecuted, an emergency parliamentary
session had to be summoned. He seized every opportunity to emphasize
that the junta was acting illegally and rebelliously, without the authority of the leader under the communist system, Mikhail Gorbachev.

In Leningrad, over 200,000 people peacefully demonstrated in a
massive show of support for the elected Mayor, Anatoly Sobchak, who
secured a guarantee from the army that it would not enter Russia's
second city – a sign of the first cracks in the military façade. At last the
Ukraine came out against the coup, as did Kazakhstan. General strikes
were called in Estonia and Latvia. But few yet believed the putsch would
actually fail. An unpublished editorial in the *Nezavilismaya Gazeta*
caught the mood:

> Mr Yeltsin, who got back to Moscow on the evening of August 18, im-
> mediately denounced the Committee of State for calling a state of
> emergency. All democratic forces are ready to resist. But what kind of resist-
> ance can they offer? Can it be active resistance? Certainly not in Moscow
> – not without a bloodbath. Moscow certainly can, and will, offer passive
> resistance.
>
> The key question is whether they will be able to do anything to stop
> Mr Yeltsin, the man whose power comes from the people, the symbol of
> an independent perestroika. If he is arrested, the leaders of the putsch will
> be half way there.

But as the day wore on, senior Soviet operational officers objected when ordered to attack the parliament building; without the President's authority, they were not even sure such orders were legal. As night fell, thousands of protestors defied the curfew and stayed outside the building. For several hours the troops surrounding it waited.

Just past midnight there was a burst of gunfire. Soon afterwards a large column of tanks crashed through the first barricade; they were showered with petrol bombs and stones. Youngsters jumped on the tanks with tarpaulins to cover their sights while others stood in front of them, Tiananmen-style. It was a night of fearlessness and heroism on the part of a largely unarmed civilian crowd against overwhelming firepower. The casualties were surprisingly small; just three people dead, with twenty injured.

Having broken through the barricades, the tanks seemed to have been given orders to halt. The enraged crowd surged forward and pulled some of the crews out, while others fled. By 5 a.m. nine armoured personnel carriers had been captured, although the main column of tanks remained motionless as the plotters reportedly could not agree whether they should advance. There were unconfirmed reports that the Prime Minister, Pavlov, had suffered a heart attack. The standoff continued. By 2 p.m. Kryuchkov, the KGB chief, had offered to fly Yeltsin to the Crimea to see Gorbachev. Yeltsin, fearing an attempt to seize him, refused.

Shortly after, he learned that the coup plotters were seeking to flee Moscow. At 4 p.m. the Soviet Defence Ministry ordered all troops to leave the cities. Media restrictions were lifted an hour later. The nightmare was over; the coup had completely failed. It was now confirmed that the coup leaders had left Moscow, two of them, Kryuchkov and Yazov, having flown to see Gorbachev in the Crimea along with Alexander Rutskoi, Yeltsin's deputy. At just past 7 p.m. it was announced Gorbachev was flying back to Moscow, and he was welcomed as President by the Soviet parliament. Gorbachev described the allegation that he was ill as 'complete rubbish, the crudest pretext'. He added, 'I think this putsch has collapsed. It needs to be investigated by the competent organs.' Both the KGB chief and the Defence Minister were arrested on their return to Moscow.

Although tired the Soviet President seemed in good spirits, but his wife Raisa had experienced a nervous breakdown. Boris Pugo, the Interior Minister who had masterminded the plot, committed suicide as police came to arrest him. The following day Yeltsin held a triumphal rally, addressing half a million people from the parliament building, as Muscovites joyfully took to the streets. But his old rival Gorbachev was not invited to the party.

Instead he was asked the following day to address the Russian Federation parliament that would now, as the elected authority, make its own bid for power from the legitimate but unelected Gorbachev. Few could have imagined that this would be no triumphant reunion of reformist colleagues but a carefully planned public humiliation of a rescued President, Yeltsin's revenge for his Gorbachev-inspired political humiliation a couple of years before. As Gorbachev rose to demonstrate his vigour and authority, he declared:

> Once again I want to point out the outstanding role played in these events by Russian President Boris Yeltsin . . . I was always convinced that these adventurists would be defeated.
>
> They wanted to turn us into meat, they wanted to annihilate us, and for that they must bear severe responsibility. There are people who lost their heads. You could even call them traitors . . . [but] in no case must we allow ordinary people – the worker in the Party, the peasant in the Party, the intellectual – to turn into the target of persecution.
>
> In this Party there are people who indeed were involved [in the coup]. They have to bear their responsibilities, legally and politically. But I never will say we have to drive out all workers and peasants who happen to be communists.

As he began describing his detention, he was heckled and jeered from the floor: 'We've heard all this.' 'Talk about the future.' Yeltsin marched up to Gorbachev on the podium and asked him to read a list of cabinet ministers who had backed the coup that Monday morning, like a teacher instructing a rather dim pupil. Startled, Gorbachev did so.

'On a lighter note, let me sign a decree suspending the activity of the Russian Communist Party,' Yeltsin then announced, angrily.

'Boris Nikolayevich, Boris Nikolayevich,' spluttered Gorbachev, but realizing he had no choice countersigned the paper.

Yeltsin had treated the President of the Soviet Union like a flunky, humiliating a man who had just endured a terrible ordeal with great courage and dignity. But Yeltsin had grasped the essential fact – Gorbachev, like the coup plotters, lacked electoral legitimacy and Yeltsin was determined, moreover, to present the coup's defeat as a triumph for democratic forces, his own defiance and that of the crowds that supported him. In fact it was just as much Gorbachev's refusal to endorse the coup that had stripped it of legitimacy, even among the forces of order and the loyalists to the regime. But Yeltsin was too shrewd and decisive a politician to allow the President any credit.

Over the following months Yeltsin effectively elbowed Gorbachev out of office, asserting the primacy of an elected President over the last purely nominal leader of the Soviet Union. But the significance of the failure of the coup was even greater still. Alexander Yakovlev, Gorbachev's reformist ally, had asked caustically just before of the Communist Party, 'The Party has buildings and people who sit in them and draw a salary, but what else do they do?' The Party leader in Kazakhstan, Nursultan Nazarbayev, revealed that during the coup he had received instructions from Party leaders in Moscow: 'In connection with the instruction of the state of emergency, measures should be taken to ensure that communists support the State Committee for the State of Emergency.'

Many of the higher echelons of the Party had been involved in the coup up to the hilt. Now Yeltsin took revenge. Party offices and newspapers were closed down across the Soviet Union, and in some places it was even banned. Onlookers cheered when the Communist Party building in Old Square in Moscow, the historic seat of the Russian Revolution, was closed, a sign being erected on the premises by the prosecutor's department stating, 'This building is sealed.' If this were not momentous enough, Gorbachev issued the decree dissolving the Communist Party and resigning as its General Secretary:

The Secretariat and Politburo of the Central Committee of the Communist Party of the Soviet Union did not come out against the coup d'état. The Central Committee did not manage to take a firm position of condemnation and opposition and did not call on communists to fight the trampling of constitutional law. Among the conspirators were members of the Party leadership. A number of Party committees and the mass media supported the actions of the state criminals. This put millions of communists in a false position. Many members of the Party refused to collaborate with the conspirators, condemned the coup, and joined the fight against it.

No one has the right to blame wholesale all communists, and I as President consider it my duty to defend them as citizens from unfounded accusations. In this situation, the Central Committee of the CPU must make the difficult, but honest decision to disband itself.

The fate of republican communist parties and local Party organizations should be decided by themselves. I consider it no longer possible to continue to carry out my duties as General Secretary of the Central Committee of the Communist Party of the Soviet Union and I relinquish corresponding authority.

I believe that democratically minded communists, who remained faithful to constitutional law and to the course of the renewal of society, will speak up for the creation of a new basis of a party capable, together with all progressive forces, of actively joining in the continuation of fundamental democratic reforms.

Everywhere communist power and the images that defined it were fast disappearing. The statues of Dzerzhinsky, first head of the secret police, and others were toppled. Yeltsin recognized the independence of Estonia and Ukraine. The Russian flag replaced the Red Flag over the Central Committee building in the Kremlin. The Communist Party and KGB archives were seized. Communism was out, in the land in which it had first taken root.

Conclusion

Yeltsin was shortly to proclaim that Communism in Russia was, indeed, dead. This most powerful of extremist political and ideological forces had lasted just seventy-four years, sweeping like a *tsunami*, a tidal wave, across the globe, affecting every continent except North America, radically changing the lives of hundreds of million of people and bringing about the imprisonment or death of tens of millions more and then collapsing in on itself with astonishing rapidity.

The twentieth century has been labelled 'the American century', because of the emergence of the USA as the dominant power in the latter half of it. But it could equally be labelled 'the Communist century', because it was decades before American free-market theories triumphed. Now, at a stroke, Communism had become relic of history, a creed seemingly so crude that the world could marvel at its phenomenal appeal.

Communism's patent absurdity was already a truism just a few days after the failed August coup attempt. Only three people had died in the Party's last struggle to survive – a toll reminiscent of the handful of casualties during the Bolshevik seizure of power – which proved the communist regime was as rotten as the Tsarist one in 1917. The real tragedy lay in the fate of Mikhail Gorbachev. Only eight men had been General Secretary of this most powerful and absolutist of political parties and only five for any appreciable length of time (Malenkov, Andropov and Chernenko had ruled only briefly), each a symbol of the different eras of Communism – Lenin the ruthless revolutionary founder of the system, Stalin the psychopathic institutionalizer, Khrushchev the insensitive chief executive, Brezhnev the corrupt machine politician and Gorbachev, a genuinely warm-hearted man and, at last, the dismantler. The five were perhaps the most powerful rulers the world has ever seen, eclipsing the Tsars both in territory and means of repression, controlling greater resources than the Chinese communist leaders, disposing of an absolute power no American President, shackled by Congress and the States, could ever aspire to.

This seems to negate the theory that history is the interplay of the masses, not the individual. The whole experience had been ended not by inevitable historical forces or some relentless and unseen economic deus ex machina, but by a single individual, now left beached as the tidal wave receded.

In just six years Mikhail Gorbachev, given the powers of an earthly god over a superpower of 300 million people wielding the world's second greatest military force, had, sometimes methodically, sometimes under pressure of events, sought to transform the lives of those under him for the better. He recognized the blind alley of remorseless decline and failure down which the Soviet system was headed, and began the transition to sanity that inevitably disrupted the lives of millions of ordinary people, holding out the promise of a decent life for all of them and proposing to confer upon them the dignity of democracy. He was not afraid to brave intense unpopularity, the main cause of his downfall, to do this.

In foreign policy, he presided with verve and even theatrical ability over virtual surrender in the Cold War, hustling his people, if not the sour handful of military leaders, into an abandonment of virtually every entrenched Soviet position on nuclear arms, the Third World, the irreversibility of revolution, conventional arms and the threat from the West. He aimed to lift the colossal burden of defence expenditure from the Soviet economy – perhaps half its GDP was defence-orientated. There could also be little doubt about Gorbachev's desire to end the primitive eyeball-to-eyeball confrontation that had so long dominated the post-Second World War world, thereby making the Reagan and Bush administrations look like old-fashioned Cold War warriors.

In Eastern Europe he liberated 100 million people from the neo-colonial, quisling regimes that had blighted those countries for two generations; his vigorous pursuit of this agenda and the speed with which it happened means that he can fairly be considered the sole author of the remarkable autumn of 1989. That this change was achieved virtually without bloodshed is a tribute to Gorbachev's decisiveness and political skills.

He accepted that political liberalization within Russia's grimly oppressive political system was a prerequisite for economic reform and, despite being heavily criticized at the end for being essentially a communist, a creature of the Party, it is simply impossible for this author at least to believe that he was unaware of the consequences of creating multi-party systems in Eastern Europe which overwhelmingly repudiated Communism, or of permitting free elections within the Soviet Party structure, freedom of the press and the development of indigenous political systems in the Soviet republics.

No Russian leader who contemptuously rejected the right of the Polish and East German communists to a monopoly of power could have believed in anything less for the Russian people. His lip-service to the need to preserve the one-party system must be seen in the context of someone trying to protect his colossal totalitarian society from the ever-present danger of a seizure of power by the old guard – and the longer he was successful, the more genies he set free from the bottle and the harder it would be to return them.

So it proved. Can he really have been surprised by the August 1991 coup attempt? Only because it had taken so long to materialize. Whether he tried to compromise with his kidnappers remains unresolved. Yakovlev later bitterly complained that he never tried to return to Moscow and that if he had, he could not have been stopped. If this is correct, did it just show Gorbachev's human weakness in a desperate situation, or a lack of fundamental principle? It is possibly the biggest question mark against his claim to greatness.

He certainly was surprised and embittered by Yeltsin's subsequent seizure of power – but in retrospect he had achieved his objective as his country's almost single-handed liberator. History must reserve a special place for a man whom absolute power did not corrupt; unlike Lenin, who used his decisiveness and extraordinary strength of personality to brutally concentrate power into the hands of a tiny clique, Gorbachev absolutely divested himself of it by dismantling the most authoritarian and feudalistic system on earth almost without bloodshed and returning authority to the people.

This was a more impressive revolutionary achievement than the Russian Revolution and arguably makes Gorbachev not only more significant historically than either Lenin or Stalin but also Russia's most enlightened leader; even Peter the Great and Catherine the Great were essentially authoritarian, however enlightened, and neither possessed the absolute power Gorbachev enjoyed.

Parts of Gorbachev's subsequent hatred towards Yeltsin stemmed from the certainty that he, as a man of high intelligence, global vision and superb administrative ability, would have guided liberated Russia through the post-communist years far more skilfully than the seemingly crude buffoon who succeeded him. Yet the two rivals were, in a way, complementary: Gorbachev, the quintessential representative of the newly prosperous meritocratic Soviet middle class and Yeltsin, appealing to the much larger Soviet working class dominant under a one-man-one-vote system and essentially a political boss of a kind long familiar in American politics, although beginning to date.

By ushering in democracy, Gorbachev had inaugurated the era of men like Yeltsin, who would consolidate his achievement. The crude new democratic inheritors of power, sometimes playing to a populist gallery, were at least committed democrats, not extremists of the Left or Right. Yeltsin himself would display a crudeness and a brutality – for example in suppressing the coup soon afterwards mounted against him – that the fastidious Gorbachev lacked. But his saving grace was that however corrupt, second-rate and even sometimes vicious his rule, he never departed from his commitment to democracy because he understood that his power derived from it.

As the great wave subsided as quickly as it had arisen, it left not only devastation and new hope in its wake but also pockets and pools of stagnant water. How could these survive? Did their existence suggest that the communist ideal still flickered? The most unrepentant were North Korea, Vietnam, Cambodia (no longer bogusly called Kampuchea after 1989) and Cuba. In Africa, following the fall of Colonel Mengistu's regime in Ethiopia, a number of one-man or one-party regimes still brandished Marxist-Leninist credentials, including those in Mozambique and

Zimbabwe; but for the most part the systematic organization of a communist society was missing and their economies were anything but centralized. Cambodia itself half-slipped out of its horrendous communist past under the leadership of the former Vietnamese puppet, Hun Sen. He, however, remained an authoritarian, staging a coup to assert his own authority over the non-communists following a power-sharing arrangement brokered by the United Nations after the Vietnamese withdrawal.

But the three other red dwarves underlined the lack of a future for the whole creed. North Korea's nuclear programme in the 1990s unsettled its neighbours, and further fuelled international anxiety when medium-range missiles were tested in the proximity of Japan – adding to the latter's drive for rearmament. Isolated from the rest of the world and viewed with distaste even by its ally China, the country became a key American foreign policy concern. In 1994 the 'Great Leader' Kim il-Sung died and his son, Kim Jong-il, appeared to be sidelined for a while, so unpromising did this dynastic heir apparent appear to be for the backward mountain country. After the new 'Dear Leader' took office, intense pressure on the regime forced it to accept that its nuclear capability should supposedly be diverted to peaceful purposes and at least partly monitored by outsiders. In 2002, the North Koreans announced they had been secretly developing a nuclear capability, presumably to exert leverage on an unsympathetic Bush administration.

These belligerent rumblings had been accompanied by the continuation of the most totalitarian aspects of command Communism and the collapse of the agricultural sector together with a serious drought. This resulted in a nationwide famine that inflicted appalling suffering on the people and led to North Korea's relegation to the very poorest of nations. South Korea, by contrast, had risen to the forefront of the Asian 'tiger economies', a model of booming capitalist prosperity.

By late 1996 North Korea had become almost a living grave; peasants were reduced to eating just two meals every three days with a daily grain intake of just 200 grams; many had resorted to consuming leaves and tree bark. Young children stole food from the elderly, leaving them to die; thousands were simply fading away. More than a third of boys between the ages of 12 and 24 months and a quarter of girls were regarded by the World Food Programme as 'wasted' – suffering so severely from disease and malnutrition as to be in danger of death without urgent medical attention. The June 2000 Summit between the leaders of North and South may have been no more than a sham, but it did raise the intriguing possibility that the young Kim was a closet reformer who had finally asserted himself against the hardliners.

While Vietnam, by no means as brutal, belligerent or economically desperate as North Korea, had even opened its doors to international tourism, it remained steeped in the sterile communist academic debates that had so absorbed Eastern Europeans in the 1960s. At the Party Congress in 1998, the three Party chiefs – President Le Duc Anh, 75, Party Secretary Do Muoi, 79, and Prime Minister Vo Van Viet, 73, were confirmed in power. Anh represented the conservative military wing, and was cautiously supported by the more centrist Muoi, a northerner; Viet, from the more enterprising south, favoured greater pragmatism and privatization.

The economy had dramatically benefited from the previous five-year reform programme: inflation had fallen from around 600 per cent a year to 12 per cent, with growth averaging 8 per cent a year after starting from a low base. In two years some $18 billion in foreign investment had poured in. In 1990 Vietnam had just 100,000 telephones, and by 1998 around 800,000. Hanoi had no taxis in 1996 and a year later, 1,000. Vietnam had become the world's third biggest rice exporter from being a net importer in just two years and had established diplomatic relations with the United States, signed a trade agreement with the European Community and had joined ASEAN.

Yet the pace of economic reform strained the nerves of some of the elderly cadres at the top, and in particular the country's still colossal and pivotal army, 600,000 strong and with reserves of around 32 million. The fear was that political change would follow economic change. At a Party Congress 'hostile forces' were denounced for seeking to introduce 'political instability' and 'rebellion'. Retired Party Secretary Nguyen Van Linh denounced 'peaceful evolution' – a euphemism for reform – and alleged that young American backpackers swarming the country were working for the CIA.

Le Kha Phieu, the shadowy 64-year-old 'younger generation' general tipped to replace Do Muoi in the long run, who also enjoyed the backing of the powerful Defence Minister, Doan Khue, had steadfastly argued that 'since the opportunists and sceptics have changed their attack methods – holding economics and politics as the keys – there is a combination of forces and armed interference aiming to eradicate the remaining socialist countries in a short time'. The Central Committee's chief spokesman reinforced the new cautious approach: 'We don't have stable, steady targets that we can fulfil. We are not extremists. We will see the reality in the future, and on the way forward if we see measures that are better, we will try and take them.' After a few years of accelerated economic reform it seemed the generals and Party conservatives were applying the brakes.

In Cuba, the world's longest-serving absolute ruler continued to radiate his own mixture of political jurassicism and personal charm. Like almost no other dictator, before or since, Fidel Castro dazzled a host of Western intellectuals, while simultaneously being treated, particularly by his sworn enemy, US Senator Jesse Helms, as a serious security risk to the United States, a combination doubly improbable after the fall of Communism in the Soviet Union. With Cuba's Soviet subsidies cut off by Gorbachev, in particular the purchase of sugar at four times the market price (sugar still being produced in private plots), the country's ever deeper economic decline was only marginally relieved by welcoming foreign tourists, who could swim in protected beach hotel enclaves while visiting picturesque, crumbling Havana and its impoverished but eager-to-please people.

Castro's army, his huge network of informers and his grip on all aspects of Cuban political life ensured the country remained loyal. Castro's revolutionary ambitions for Latin America had been dashed when ordinary Nicaraguans abandoned Sandinism, while Africa, with Mengistu fallen and Angola's regime still locked in civil war, seemed more unpromising than ever. The Caudillo of Cuba, after forty years in office, appears immovable until driven out by his own mortality – with no guarantee that the ageing Party figures around him will follow Gorbachev's lead in Russia and Eastern Europe.

Cuba lacks a middle class, a new generation of communists, or even any real internal debate. The question is whether Castro's demise will deprive the regime of the charisma and personality that has so long sustained it, or whether bureaucratic repression will allow it to continue in office unreformed. The speed with which once the once giant figure of Castro has become a museum-piece anachronism in Latin America suggests that Cuba has become the relic of a distant past rather than a pointer towards the future.

All three of these mastodons survived not only by using central control and repression, but also by beating the battered old nationalist drum. This is no coincidence. One of the themes of this book is that a driving force of Communism has always been nationalism. North Korea with its paranoid tub-thumping against powerful neighbours, Vietnam, with its ageing revolutionary leadership reared on colonial wars against the French and the Americans, and Cuba, based on a perpetual David and Goliath struggle with America, possessed nationalism in lashings.

The most obvious demonstration of how Communism has fallen back on its crude nationalist origins is perhaps Serbia, the central part of the post-Tito Yugoslav Federation that collapsed so dramatically at the beginning of the 1990s. There Slobodan Milosevic, a narrow-minded, intense Party functionary and protégé of Party boss Ivan Stambolik suddenly emerged in 1987 preaching racial superiority to the majority of fellow Serbs who believed that Kosovo, with its Albanian majority, should always remain part of Serbia.

> I want to tell you that you should stay here. Here is your land, here are your houses, your fields and gardens, your memories . . . [By leaving] you would betray your ancestors and continue to endure a situation with which you are not satisfied. On the contrary, we have to change it . . . Don't tell me that you can't do it alone. Of course you can't do it alone. We will change it together, we in Serbia and everyone in Yugoslavia . . .

This message propelled him to power as the virulent protagonist of Serbian nationalism. This led to war with Croatia, Bosnia and finally Kosovo, drawing in the major powers and ending after thousands of casualties in a still more truncated Serbian state. Milosevic was subsequently toppled after the elections in Serbia in September 2000, and eventually arrested and put on trial in The Hague in February 2002, although he remains defiant and retains a significant nationalist popular following. In that the regimes above were almost entirely nationalist-based, it is possible to argue that Communism has been eclipsed even in these last holdouts.

So back to the question posed at the very beginning, which the narrative has attempted to answer: what is, or was, Communism? As Robert Conquest and others have argued, on a superficial level it was simply an idea, and not a very good one at that. Marx developed a pseudo-science, based on the philosophy of the German tradition of the Enlightenment and his own highly competent economic analysis, to create a heady, if not particularly profound, ideological brew that appealed to intellectuals everywhere. Lenin created a Machiavellian-style of political activism – how to seize power, and what to do with it – that used Marxism as its intellectual rationale.

The Bolshevik Revolution was, as most are, a reaction: against the suffering caused by the First World War, the corruption of the Tsar's court held responsible for both and the dislocation of society created by Russia's pre-war industrial revolution. Up to the beginning of the war, Bolshevism, better defined as Marxism-Leninism and perpetuated as Communism, was simply a formula used by a tough and determined minority to seize and hold power. It was Lenin's inspired political leadership, preaching an end to the war and combining this with the vacillations of others, which permitted Communism to triumph. Confounding both Right and Left, he then ruthlessly consolidated power, which enabled him to win a major civil war, although with the transparent failure of Marxist economics Lenin quickly showed every intention of dumping the ideological baggage he had acquired.

Leninism's justification of direct action, violence and the harsh imposition of minority rule were perfectly adapted not just to Russia after the First World War but to those future occasions when traditionalist societies, suddenly confronted with the immense challenges of the twentieth century, more or less fell apart, their legitimacy questioned because while traditional institutions were discredited, new ones had yet to gain legitimacy and power structures were collapsing.

Yet because the seizure of power in Russia, as elsewhere, had taken place in a traditional society, the key feature of Communism was that it was neo-feudal authoritarian, namely a rigidly structured society, tightly controlled at the top, with the assertion that individuals were mere specks of sand on the tides of history, to be disposed of as their masters saw fit.

The landowners and noblemen who still clung to their privileges in the early years of the twentieth century may have considered the communists revolutionary, but for most ordinary Russians they simply proposed restoring order and national pride as strong Tsars had done. The country's two historic preoccupations had been containing the periodic anarchy that raged through much of that huge land and the foreign intervention that threatened it; the Leninist regime proposed to fight both, which made it entirely traditional and nationalistic as well as very Russian. One can argue, half plausibly, that Leninism was little more than the substitution of historically strong central rule for the weakness of Nicholas II's final years – weakness at the top being the real aberration in Russian history.

Authoritarianism, nationalism, feudalism – these were the roots of Marxism-Leninism. Authoritarianism – an insistence through the doctrine of democratic centralism that those at the top order those at the bottom with an iron rigidity of the kind exercised by the harshest Tsar; nationalism – the assertion of Russia's national interests at every opportunity; and feudalism, as already defined.

As already observed, one man had to stand at the apex of this tripod, as the Tsars had. The system would be no mere abstract; Lenin, Stalin, Khrushchev and Brezhnev embodied it – until Gorbachev, another demigod, used his power to dissolve the heavenly pantheon and return it to man.

Three elements, however, appeared to differentiate Marxism-Leninism from traditional feudal rule. The first was ideology, the second modern methods of mass mobilization and control, and the third twentieth-century progress and social change. The ideology as crafted by Marx was, as has been observed, enormously powerful in a religious sense. It pandered to the human yearnings for equality, security, prosperity, and the brotherhood of man and created its own vast scripture of barely comprehensible intellectual mysteries. It featured a priesthood, an episcopate, prophets and even a deity in the white-haired figure of Karl Marx himself (Marx's resemblance to traditional religious representations of the Creator has rarely been commented upon). One middle-aged Russian remarked to the great documentary filmmaker, Yuris Podnieks, that Christ was a communist, adding that, after all, 'the Ten Commandments are communist commandments'.

So extensive was the liturgy that many highly intelligent people subscribed to it, although not the cynics at the pinnacle of power who merely used it as an instrument. Men like the Politburo ideology chief Mikhail Suslov in the Soviet Union and indeed Erick Honecker in East Germany were, for all their faults, absolute believers and high priests. Its appeal to millions meant that it could not be dismissed as simply the cynical verbiage of a brutal and corrupt power elite, and gave its priesthood an authority they would not have enjoyed if they just been the tools of despotism. Again, the comparison is religious. Both Christianity and Islam were at times the instruments of temporal powers, some of them self-serving and brutal; but the two faiths also existed independently of their temporary masters and survived them.

Not much more need be said about mass mobilization and control; both were products of late nineteenth century advances in technology (although the mass mobilization of earlier ages should not be under-estimated – for example the construction of the Egyptian pyramids, the Great Wall of China or the terraces of Inca Peru. As the orientalist Karl Wittfoegel has pointed out in *Oriental Despotism*, these largely occurred in societies that required a huge communal effort just to survive; and they would have been available to despots of any hue – as occurred in Hitler's Germany, for example – whether feudal, militaristic or communist).

Although Soviet technology permitted the movement of peoples, raw materials, finished goods and the dissemination of propaganda, the advent of radio and television gave those in charge an opportunity for increasing social control that medieval kings or the Tsars' officials could only have dreamed of. Unfortunately this coincided with a period when only a very few countries had a traditional respect for the rights of man, the legal framework to defend them and the concept of constitutional government to neutralize these methods of central control. Communism did not create mass mobilization or the totalitarian society – if anything the First World War did – but it seized them with such gusto that they became its trademarks (as they did of Nazism).

The Marxist-Leninist adaptation of twentieth-century instruments of social control as they became available was not unique; even democratic societies attempted to do the same – most notably Britain with its mass mobilization in the Second World War. As Ivan the Terrible, for example, would have used them were he able to, identifying totalitarian communist methods of control specifically with Marxism-Leninism, or indeed with Marxism, is a mistake: they happened to be the instruments of tyranny around at the time, although subsequently developments such as global television, mobile phones, the Internet and mass travel have seriously undermined them. The speed of technological change, powered by innovative economies and one of the great drivers of social change is, ultimately, bad news for tyrannies.

Communism finally was shaped by the dramatic economic and social transformations of the twentieth century. But did this neo-nationalist-feudalist-authoritarian system, combining its crudely appealing ideol-ogy with twentieth-century methods of control, justify itself by dramatically transforming the lives of millions in a manner that was not possible in any other way? To this day it is argued that, despite the ter-rible consequences of Stalinism or Maoism, there was no alternative method of wrenching impoverished peasant societies into the urban organization and sophistication of the twentieth century. In late 1987 even Gorbachev contended that Stalin was right in his collectivization and crash industrialization programmes.

Yet the jury can no longer stay out on this question. As observed at the beginning of this book, both Russian and Chinese industrialization were well under way before Communism took control – indeed the dislocations caused by such industrialization were principal founts of communist support. Modernization was happening and would have happened regardless. Indeed, even under Russian tsars or Chinese warlords, it might have happened faster than as a result of the enormous upheavals wrought by Communism. Or did Communism accelerate the process? For Russia, it has long been suggested that, despite the disruption of the decade after 1917 largely due to the Revolution itself, only enforced industrialization could have enabled Russia to catch up with its neighbours in time for the Second World War, and that the country then required a further burst of coercion to allow it to catch up with the Western democracies in the 1950s.

This, politely put, is bunkum. Western countries industrialized both in the nineteenth and twentieth centuries. The transition was far from painless, but neither were millions killed nor tens of millions forcibly resettled in the process. In the second half of the twentieth century, many developing societies have undergone a near complete transformation from rural-based feudalism to urban prosperity at least as dramatic as Russia's transformation in the 1930s and 1940s, and again, without mass murder and deportation.

As for China, not only were the huge economic changes of the 1920s cut short by civil war in the 1930s and then the war with Japan, but also successive murderous Maoist experiments destroyed each step forwards until the Gang of Four were finally routed in the 1970s, after which economic development surged forward. It is impossible to argue (and only the most diehard Maoist would) that economic development was not shackled to the slowest possible pace between 1950 and 1975, or that under virtually any other system it would not have progressed more quickly. When the dragon's energies were released, the transformation was astonishing, socially wrenching and proved – as in any other Asian economy – that free-market transformation was much faster than enforced Soviet and Maoist economic experiments and could be achieved without expending millions of lives.

The defenders of Communism will immediately hit back: Russia and China were different from the rest of the world; they occupied vast continents and China was hugely overpopulated. Not so; compared to Western countries communist ones did far worse economically, the only exception being East Germany, efficient Communism's shop window, which was anyway only less than half as developed as West Germany by the time of unification. The United States is a country of vast distances and comparable natural resources to the Soviet Union, and the disparity between them became all too apparent during the Gorbachev years. India, the only country comparable to China in population terms was, with its democratic institutions and lack of central political repression, well ahead in almost every area before 1975; but China, because of its partial espousal of the market, has caught up and overtaken it. Communism not only inflicted unbelievable suffering on the countries it governed; it massively retarded their economic development.

Was this just a failure of the Idea, of misplaced idealism, of a flawed nineteenth-century economic theory pursued for the best of motives that had simply been mistaken, or overtaken by events? The answer, as suggested in these pages, is simpler and more fundamental that that. What was labelled Communism was, in my view, nothing more than a nationalistic form of feudalism using twentieth-century methods, indeed an attempt to impose traditional methods of control against the bubbling pressure for political, economic and social change rushing in from the world outside. The near-impossibility of the task – maintaining absolute authority against a newly diverse society – explains the need for so many millions to be slaughtered.

Communism was a reaction against the breathtaking changes imposed by the twentieth century: it was a reassertion of feudal values – absolute obedience to the system, loyalty to the Marxist creed and the Party Tsar and his privileged elite, because the traditional church and court of the medieval Tsar had been overthrown. Collectivization was no more than a more comprehensive reassertion of the large estate system, because the massacre of the kulaks in Russia destroyed the class of independent farmers who had enjoyed prosperity under the Tsars.

Both Stalin and Mao ran absolute empires that sought to preserve their power by persecuting the very middle classes responsible for powering the industrialization of other nations. Yet Stalin failed to understand that even the large centralized bureaucracy he set up would one day father a middle class, and in China, Deng Xiaoping, a leader bent upon economic development, permitted the system to change overnight to quasi-capitalism, which is now breeding a large middle class that will one day sweep away the remaining cobwebs of Communism.

Because Communism projected feudalism into the twentieth century, nationalism was its natural accompaniment – not, it must be said, the stridently aggressive variety, but rather the defensive nationalism of countries threatened by systems richer and more efficient than their own – in some ways nationalism in its most acceptable form, particularly when fighting for colonial freedom. Russia's revolution, born of defeat in war, reflected the injured, dogged patriotism that represents all that is best about the Russian people, which reasserted itself in the Second World War.

China's flagging revolution was re-ignited by Mao's assuming the leadership of the nationalist struggle against Japan from Chiang Kai-shek's corrupt and incompetent war effort, and it is one of history's great tragedies that the new communist leader, instead of confining himself to this great patriotic achievement, interpreted his victory as a mandate to carry out of one of the purest Marxist revolutionary programmes in history and turned himself into an authoritarian monster. Cuba's revolution was essentially a nationalist one against its over-mighty northern neighbour; so was Vietnam's and the few that succeeded in the anti-colonial struggles of the developing world.

A nationalistic form of feudalism, wrapped in a quasi-religious creed that enthralled millions and still retains the residual loyalties of many: that was the essence of the communist phenomenon which dominated so much of the last century, whose collapse makes analysis and understanding so much easier. The price paid in severely retarded and lopsided economic development was terrible. At least 40 million people were killed as a direct result of communist methods, and more than 30 million went through re-education, labour or prison camps, while around 10 million fled their countries and maybe as many as 50 million their homes in the name of scientific socialism to achieve a standard of living anywhere between a fifth or half those in the West or in comparable developing countries.

Ignoring external wars, adding up the casualties of revolution indicates a conservative figure for Russia of 11 million, comprising 6 million during the Revolution and civil war, 4.5 million during the first Stalinist purges and collectivization drive, and 0.5 million during the wave of purges before the Second World War. Others put the toll as high as 15 or even 30 million. During the whole period, some 18 million were imprisoned or hounded into labour camps. Such figures cannot begin to describe the suffering of hundreds of millions of Russians who faced almost continual disruption to their lives during the enforced upheavals of collectivization and industrialization and extreme hardship between 1917 and 1922, 1929 and 1932, and 1940 and 1945. Khrushchev's experimentation in the late 1950s provided further disruption, before Brezhnev settled for a quiet life, economic stagnation and decline.

In China the death toll from slaughter and famine was at least a horrendous 30 million, even if it was proportionally lower as a percentage of the population, with some 15 million passing through re-education camps. The disruption, though, was even greater from 1946 and 1952, recurring again in 1964 and continuing for a decade. In Vietnam the war was largely a nationalist, not a communist one, but cost 2 million lives. Tens of thousands died in the purges after the reunification of Vietnam, in addition to the thousands that fled the country in small boats and drowned. Maybe 500,000 passed through 're-education' camps. In Cambodia, the horror probably took as many as 2 million lives and reduced the lives of the 4 million people that remained to one of hardship and civil war. In Cuba the murder count was lower, although the number of political prisoners was initially in tens of thousands. In Eastern Europe there were few deaths but high numbers of detentions during the Stalinist period. More recently in Afghanistan probably 200,000 people, mostly civilians, were killed as a result of the Soviet occupation.

Mass refugee exoduses have usually accompanied Marxist-Leninist victories: from Russia maybe 2 million, from China maybe 1.5 million people from the country's few outlets, from Eastern Europe – in particular East Germany and Czechoslovakia – maybe 1 million, from Vietnam some 300,000 boat people, from Cambodia approximately 500,000, from Afghanistan around 4 million, from Cuba 500,000. In all, perhaps 10 million left their countries as a result of Communism.

The untold cost of Communism in Russia was also huge. The Chernobyl disaster in April 1986 was a horrific reminder of the environmental impact of poor technology – a tab later picked up by the West, which provided some $20 billion to destroy nuclear material. The Aral Sea is ruined beyond repair by agricultural pollution. The huge economic costs of Communism have taken a decade to begin to rectify, while corruption and maladministration have surfaced in their appalling reality, as has organized crime that flourished in the previously illegal economy.

So to the question put at the beginning. Could it happen again? The answer is moderately reassuring, if the analysis of this book is correct. The laboratory conditions that created the explosion have all but vanished. There are fewer traditional agrarian societies making a rapid transition to industrialization. Europe, West and East, has already made the leap, South America's economic development is probably past danger point, while eastern Asia, although staggeringly transformed over the past two decades, probably now has too large a class of people with a stake in the new prosperity.

China, whose breakneck industrialization is generating enormous tensions among its large rural population, could yet experience another revolution within the revolution, as has happened three times since 1949 (the Great Leap Forward, the Cultural Revolution and the Gang of Four's attempt to seize power). In Russia the prospect of a new revolution succeeding are small: the middle class is too big, the old order too discredited and collectivism and central planning are detested by the mass of farm workers and probably by the urban masses as well.

What remains is a commitment to state spending, social security and the guarantee of a job, to which the Soviet Communist Party under Gennady Zhuganov appeals. This retains a considerable constituency; but these are the ideals of a social democratic party, not an authoritarian communist one (the same fate has befallen the communist parties of Eastern Europe). The much greater danger in Russia, where nationalism runs deep, is a reaction against the economic uncertainty, unemployment and gangsterism of the post-Gorbachev period, coupled with a thoroughgoing disillusionment towards the ideals of the West and its comparative lack of economic help, which could yet bring a more assertive and uncooperative nationalist regime to power – although I believe it is no longer possible for this to rule as a dictatorship. Stalin remains the most popular of all Russia's communist leaders precisely because he was a nationalist hero. Arguably, with Vladimir Putin's assumption of power that resulted in Boris Yeltsin's resignation in 1999, there has been a shift towards nationalism.

There will be no return to nuclear confrontation or Cold War – Russia cannot afford either. But Russia always has the potential to become an alternative focus of power to the United States, pursuing its own policies in the Balkans or the Middle East or towards Asia in a way that thoroughly discomfits the West.

The two areas of the world where the laboratory conditions still exist for a communist seizure of power are Africa (outside South Africa, whose economic and social development is probably past danger point) and parts of the Middle East. The former contains more nominally quasi-Marxist regimes than anywhere else – but their lack of international clout means that the misery and retarded development usually brought by such regimes only affects the people of the region themselves. Fortunately, as Africans progress to a new generation of post-independence leaders, many of them less egocentric, steeped in old anti-colonialist creeds or educated in Eastern European training schools, there is every sign that on that continent command socialism is withering.

The Middle East is more complex. While the region retains a strong authoritarian socialist tradition, particularly in its most developed societies (Egypt, Algeria, Lebanon, Palestine, Iraq and Syria), only in the last two are they still in control and there are signs that even there their appeal may have peaked. Saudi Arabia and most of the Gulf states are rich fields for extremist movements – the conditions are almost laboratory perfect (feudal rule, raging corruption, a repressed opposition, rapid industrialization and, in some, America's military presence) except for two factors: large oil revenues have been used to buy off discontent among their populations; and most workers are foreign labourers who can be expelled at the first sign of trouble. But militant Islam remains a much more serious contender for power there than militant socialism. However it seems that militant Islam is on the wane in Iran and Afghanistan. In the former people are wrestling with the privations imposed by fundamentalist feudal rule, and in the latter the Taliban regime has been overthrown and replaced – in Kabul at least – by the more pluralist regime of Hamid Karzai.

So Communism, which bestrode the world with such fearsome power barely a decade and a half ago, seems likely to continue dwindling as an international force. It leaves three significant traces. The first, already alluded to, is the anachronistic red dwarves, which will surely one day collapse or be transformed. North Korea, Vietnam, Cambodia, Cuba and the quasi-Marxist African states demonstrate how Communism and nationalism have become almost indistinguishable – and, as this book has argued, nationalism is a much older, more potent and more enduring force.

Because most of the communist states were in fact nationalist-feudal ones legitimized by communist thought – only Russia was not, initially, but became so, while China and Cambodia were at various stages hijacked from nationalism by genuinely revolutionary elements – it is not inconceivable that some countries could witness a nationalist-communist renaissance. In a sense the remaining Stalinist holdouts are examples of this – North Korea, Vietnam, Cuba and Cambodia emphasizing the nationalist aspects of their regimes much more than the communist ones. The prime example of such a country was, of course, Serbia, where nationalism was the entire underpinning of Slobodan Milosevic's rigidly Stalinist regime; but for that identification he would surely have gone the way of Ceausescu much earlier (Iraq and Syria also to some extent fit into this category).

There is a particular reason for fearing that such a phenomenon could one day become more widespread. With the collapse of Communism, American free-market doctrines have proliferated across the developing world, as has Western culture – pop music, television, jeans and so on. For an entire generation accustomed to the bleakness of poverty, the drabness of communist rule or the stultifying inertia of their parents' societies, these values have provided a liberating beacon of light. But there could easily be a reaction one day, as people seek to preserve disappearing values, as disparities of income strain once flattened social structures and as the power and economic dominance of the United States begins to create resentment.

The sensation that countries are increasingly prey to large and uncontrollable market forces and the disruption of financial flows inexplicably moving in and out of economies is another spur to indignation and self-assertion. This is more likely to take a nationalist and cultural form than any other – such as the resurgence of Islam. But, skilfully orchestrated as an essentially anti-American, anti-free market reaction, communist parties in some parts of the world could benefit from such sentiments – which even so would be more nationalist than communist. The days of a global communist 'threat' are probably past; the days of assertive and dangerous nationalism, which may masquerade under the traditional tyranny of the Red Flag, are not. What is left? The religion, principally, consisting of thousands of huddled devotees with fists raised across the world, their intellectual priests still poring over turgid Marxist tomes delivering their interpretations of the scriptures, the old congregation of workers and peasants still chanting their hymns. There are still millions of the faithful, although congregations are dwindling. Other religions have endured long periods of neglect and persecution, and re-emerged to massive new followings; the communist faithful have no reason to think anything will be different for them. One day, they believe, humanity will realise the justice of their cause. The call for economic equality, after all, will always be hugely potent in a world of such inequality and widespread poverty.

Yet this author, for one, is sceptical. Behind the remarkable similarities that the communist creed enjoys with religious movements, there exist huge differences: Communism promises redemption in this life and nothing beyond, while the others promise paradise in the next. Communism has palpably failed to provide paradise in this life, and unless another generation can be persuaded that it is likelier to do so than Western free-market capitalism – which although improbable is not impossible among those left behind in the latest capitalist surge around the world – the communists offer nothing. Their promise of a better life for the great mass of ordinary people can only be fulfilled in this world, and most ordinary people today probably believe that their chances of a better life are greater under capitalism, which is delivering goods and jobs.

Religion everywhere has to a great extent prospered at a time and in places of material deprivation, where the hope of betterment in the next life compensates for the misery in this one. In a more prosperous world for many – although by no means all – the appeal of religion can be expected to decline except among those approaching the next world; but as long as people think about the next world and look for greater fulfilment, and indeed begin to rise above the immediate satisfaction of their material appetites in this one, most religions probably have a future. Communism has no future once people realize – and many may take a lifetime to do so – that it delivers neither equality nor prosperity in this world, and even worse, only extinction in the next.

One of the most famous images of the Russian Revolution was that of black, stick-like, Lowryesque figures silhouetted against the snow. But many of the figures are prone and most of the others are running, in one of the frequent violent clashes that preceded the Revolution. The most famous episode of the October Revolution was, of course, the taking of the Winter Palace, shelled both by the frigate *Aurora* and the cannon of the Peter and Paul Fortress from across the River Neva, and captured by the Bolsheviks with overwhelming strength. Trotsky has a fine passage describing the occasion. The fall of the Winter Palace, the beginning of the whole epic and terrible history of Communism, was accomplished with the loss of a handful of lives in those autumn snows, more like a palace coup or a changing of the guard than a full-bodied revolution.

The end of Communism, in a beautifully exact historical circle, an irony of dialectical symmetry, was accomplished in almost exactly the same way, with very few casualties. This time the defenders of the palace won: the Russian parliament was not taken by the overwhelming show of armed force outside. Again there were stick-like crowds, although no snow: but they were demonstrating in solidarity with the elected president and parliament against the armed forces and their guns outside. Three quarters of a century of tyranny and bloodshed thus ended, as it had begun, on a note of anti-climax, with very little blood spilt. The old order simply crumbled away, as it had in 1917.

Appendix

Sunday Times
28 July 1985

Russia's March to Capitalism

By a member of the House of
Commons Foreign Affairs
Committee, which recently
visited Moscow

Hold on to your hats: Russia, for the first time in two decades, is being ruled by a youngish dictator, not a doddering committee of elderly gentlemen.

Mr Mikhail Gorbachev's grasping of the reins of power in the short five months he has been in office has been astonishing. With four of his placemen installed on the Politburo in April, with the Foreign Minister Mr Andrei Gromyko, kicked upstairs to the presidency, and armed forces influence at a new low – there is no military representative on the Politburo – Mr Gorbachev has a nearly free hand in economic and foreign policy.

A purge of dead wood throughout the bureaucracy is now taking place in advance of a major economic shake-up away from centralized economic planning to more capitalist methods. In turn, Mr Gorbachev's ambition of raising his people's standard of living provides the best hope yet of a stop in the arms race.

As Russia's farm supremo in the early 1980s, Mr Gorbachev introduced autonomous work teams with the power to make three-year contracts, organize their own work, and distribute the profit according to results. When I asked Mr Gorbachev on his visit to Britain last December whether he wanted to extend such reforms, he told me flatly: 'Of course. We want decentralization and market forces in industry, and the kind of technical innovation that exists in your ICI.'

The appropriate ideological flimflam overlies the changes. Mr Gorbachev says that 'change must be within a Marxist-Leninist context.' The deputy head of a major Soviet planning institute says: 'Our economy does not reject the limited use of forces of the market. Through price-fixing at the individual enterprise level there are quite active market forces even today. Everyone spends their money according to price and quality.' The private housing and dachas increasingly fashionable among the Soviet middle class are not private, insists this official: 'They're individual.'

Individuality is to be extended. The main economic reforms now being considered in the 12th Soviet Five-Year Plan which is likely to be ready early next year (Mr Gorbachev tore up the first draft on taking office) are:

- Giving individual plants greater independence. They will have freedom to fix their own prices and wages and to re-invest profits.
- Breaking the big ministries up into 'regional planning units', which can coordinate industrial activities at a lower level.
- Easing up on the rigidities of the five-year plan system: plan targets are to be set on a one-year basis, with the five-year objective as a much hazier goal.
- Increasing consumer goods production by buying Western assembly lines. The availability of consumer goods, the planners hope, will further increase the incentive to work and will undermine the black economy.
- A big agricultural investment programme.
- A crash programme of automation and new technology. Already some 77,000 teachers are being trained to teach computer use in schools.

The economic shake-up is likely to precede any major foreign policy change. The Russians say there is no hope of progress in the Geneva arms talks unless the Americans are prepared to put their Star Wars programme on the agenda. The Russians claim that Star Wars is doubly destabilizing, because it would not only give the Americans a first-strike capability without fear of retaliation, but because the long-term purpose of the programme is to develop space-based nuclear weapons targeted at Russia.

Soviet leaders quietly overlook their own space research programme when they say that Russia is against the militarization of space 'in whatever form'. The Russians make no distinction between research, testing and deployment of space weapons. But if the Americans stop Star Wars in its tracks, they promise 'a radical and dramatic reduction in both strategic and medium-range weapons'. The Russians have yet to spell out what they mean. But the two sides are not irreconcilably apart.

From the Soviet point of view, it is the cost of a Star Wars race that is persuasive, though they add: 'If we have to, we'll make the sacrifice.' Mr Gorbachev has bluntly spelt out the connection between foreign and economic policy: 'The foreign policy of a nation,' he told our committee, 'is inseparable from developments on its domestic scene, its socio-economic goals and requirements . . . the chief aim of our policy is to raise the prosperity of the nation by boosting the living and cultural standards of our people . . . The Soviet Union needs peace to implement its huge development programme.'

Mr Gorbachev represents the coming to power of the new, educated, American-envying Soviet middle-class, unscarred by memories of wars and privations. Mrs Gorbachev's appearance, so gushed about in the Western press, says less about her personality than about the fact that it is now acceptable to look smart, not frumpy, in the Soviet Union. Russia no longer pretends to be about equality; it is about material self-advancement. On that sea-change lies the main hope that the country will move away from military competition with the United States towards economic competition.

The danger lies in Mr Gorbachev's very power. The last real dictator of Russia, Nikita Khrushchev, embarked on a violently disruptive series of economic experiments which failed, while also bringing the world to the brink of nuclear war through foreign policy experimentation. Mr Gorbachev's economic reforms are much more carefully crafted, but frustration may boil over if he finds his attempts at change blocked by the world's stodgiest bureaucracy.

In foreign policy, failure to reach agreement on Star Wars would set the world moving into a very unpredictable new round in the arms race;

and if Mr Gorbachev were tempted to bring experimentation and brink-manship back to Soviet foreign policy, the world would become a much more dangerous place. The hope of the West should be tempered with much caution.

Index